Barcode in Back

MW01121993

Innovation Policies and International Trade Rules

Innovation Policies and International Trade Rules

The Textiles and Clothing Industry in Developing Countries

Edited by

Kaushalesh Lal
Senior Researcher at UNU-MERIT, Netherlands

Pierre A. Mohnen
Professorial Fellow at UNU-MERIT and Professor, University of Maastricht, Netherlands

palgrave
macmillan

First published 2009 by
PALGRAVE MACMILLAN

Palgrave Macmillan in the UK is an imprint of Macmillan Publishers Limited,
registered in England, company number 785998, of Houndmills, Basingstoke,
Hampshire RG21 6XS.

Palgrave Macmillan in the US is a division of St Martin's Press LLC,
175 Fifth Avenue, New York, NY 10010.

Palgrave Macmillan is the global academic imprint of the above companies
and has companies and representatives throughout the world.

Palgrave® and Macmillan® are registered trademarks in the United States,
the United Kingdom, Europe and other countries.

ISBN-13: 978–0–230–57743–5   hardback

This book is printed on paper suitable for recycling and made from fully
managed and sustained forest sources. Logging, pulping and manufacturing
processes are expected to conform to the environmental regulations of the
country of origin.

A catalogue record for this book is available from the British Library.

A catalog record for this book is available from the Library of Congress.

10   9   8   7   6   5   4   3   2   1
18   17   16   15   14   13   12   11   10   09

Printed and bound in Great Britain by
CPI Antony Rowe, Chippenham and Eastbourne

Contents

List of Figures

List of Tables

Notes on the Contributors

Donatus Kosi Ayitey is currently a PhD Researcher at the United Nations University, UNU-MERIT, Maastricht. He holds BA and MPhil. degrees in Economics with specializations in Econometrics and Public Economics from the University of Ghana and has worked with the Department of Economics as a teaching and research assistant. He is currently working on technical change, competitiveness and poverty research.

Fang Chen graduated from Renmin University and is now at the National Academy of Sciences.

Danbo Guo is a PhD student at Renmin University, China.

Kaushalesh Lal is Senior Researcher at UNU-MERIT. Prior to joining UNU, he was associate professor at the Institute of Economic Growth, Delhi University. His research interests are ICTs and associated aspects, the economics of technological change, open source initiatives, innovation and growth, micro-level technological change, and globalization.

Enjing Li is an undergraduate at Renmin University, China.

Haodi Li is an undergraduate at Renmin University, China.

Zhi Li is a postgraduate student at Renmin University, China.

Pierre A. Mohnen is Professor in the Faculty of Economics and Business Administration, Maastricht University, Professorial Fellow at UNU-MERIT, Associate Fellow at CIRANO (Montreal) and METEOR Fellow. His main research interests are applied econometrics, R&D, innovation and technological change, but he has also published in the areas of international trade, regulation and development.

K. Narayanan graduated from the Delhi School of Economics, India, and carried out Post-doctoral research at the Institute of Advanced Studies United Nations University, Japan. His research interests include industrial economics, international business, and the economics of technological change and innovation. He has published in the fields of industrial competitiveness, technology transfer, and trade. He is currently a professor of Economics in the Department of Humanities and Social Sciences at the Indian Institute of Technology, Bombay, India.

Aveeraj S. Peedoly is a researcher at the Centre for Applied Social Research, University of Mauritius. He is a graduate in sociology and social policy from Warwick University, UK, and is currently studying for his PhD on the impact of changing global flows of labour by assessing the linkages between globalization, export-oriented employment and social exclusion. His other research interests include gender and ethnic inequalities.

Adriana Peluffo has a teaching position at the Scientific Research Council and at the School of Economics at the University of the Republic, Uruguay. She holds a Masters degree in International Economics and is a PhD candidate at the University of Antwerp, Belgium. Her research interests are trade and economic development, innovation and manufacturing performance.

Qingping Zhang is an undergraduate at Renmin University, China.

Yanyun Zhao is director of the Research Centre for Applied Statistics, a key national research institute accredited by the Chinese Ministry of Education. His current research activity is the development of national and industrial competitiveness.

Feng Zhen graduated from Renmin University and is now studying at the School of Statistics, Central University of Finance and Economics, Beijing.

Acknowledgements

This book is an outcome of a UNU-MERIT project 'Textiles and Clothing Sector and Technological Capacity Building Initiatives in Developing World'. The motivation to work on this project came from Professors Luc Soete, Lynn Mytelka, and Banji Oyeylaran-Oyeyinka. Prof. Luc Soete, the present Director of UNU-MERIT (formerly UNU-INTECH), encouraged us to include in the project some of the largest players in the global textiles and clothing (T&C) industry. His advice has proved to be extremely useful in analysing the T&C industry in a global context. Prof. Mytelka, the former Director of UNU-INTECH, took a keen interest in the project because of her concern with job losses and the consequences thereafter in many developing countries resulting from the abolition of the Multi-Fibre Arrangement quota system on 1 January 2005. Prof. Banji Oyeylaran-Oyeyinka, Director, Monitoring & Research Division (MRD), UN-HABITAT, Nairobi and former colleague at UNU-MERIT, contributed to the project to a great extent by sharing his experience and knowledge about innovation and capacity-building initiatives in general and on the African continent in particular. We sincerely acknowledge their contributions.

The discussions with Shampa Paul, a former colleague and friend, have noticeably improved data analysis and the presentation of results. The other colleagues who contributed to the project are: Marc Vleugels, Wilma Coenegrachts, Ad Notten, Eveline in de Braek and Monique Raedts. While perfect administrative support was provided by Marc Vleugels and Wilma Coenegrachts, the secretarial support of Ms Eveline in de Braek and Ms Monique Raedts has been incomparable. It would have been virtually impossible to complete the project without the help of Ad Notten who very willingly provided library support and access to the various databases used in the study. The contributions of Sandeep Kumar are also acknowledged. Finally, we would like to thank all of the country coordinators and the representatives of firms who participated in the project.

Kaushalesh Lal
Pierre A. Mohnen
May 2008

1
Introduction

Kaushalesh Lal and Pierre A. Mohnen

This volume addresses the very critical question of the role of international trade rules and capacity-building initiatives in the growth of the textiles and clothing (T&C) industry in developing countries. This issue has taken a pivotal place in the development literature as a result of the complete abolition of the quota system of the Multi-Fibre Arrangement (MFA) in the T&C industry since 1 January 2005. In several countries there are visible effects of the abolition of the WTO quota provisions. Countries such as China and India have benefited from it while some African countries, such as Kenya and Ghana, have lost substantial international markets that had been protected for them under the previous WTO quota system. On the other hand, many developing countries, such as Vietnam and Mexico, were almost unaffected by the abolition of WTO provisions. Is the abolition of the quota system the real cause of the difficulties encountered by the T&C industry in many developing countries over the last ten years?

This book considers several aspects that could explain the differential evolution of export performance in the T&C industry of several developing countries. The explanation could lie in the trade liberalization in the T&C industry, changes in the cost of production, the level of development, national policies in favour of T&C industry, and their association in the present scenario of the international trade in T&C products.

Chapter 2 provides a foundation for the analysis offered in the subsequent chapters. It investigates the role of wage rates and the level of economic development in the international trade of textiles and clothing. Data for 51 developing countries for the period 1975–2004 are used in the analysis presented in this chapter. The selection of countries is constrained by the availability of data.

The countries in the sample have been grouped into three categories according to their performance in international markets. Several countries, such as China, India, Indonesia, and Singapore, which ventured into the export market of clothing during the 1960s and 1970s still continue to maintain their share of international trade. In fact, countries such as China and India have increased their share of the global trade in clothing, particularly since the early 1980s. Trends in textiles exports have, by and large, followed similar patterns in several developing countries with few exceptions, such as Singapore, where textiles exports have been declining since the mid-1990s while there is no sign of decline in the level of garment exports. All such countries where garment exports have not declined have been categorized as 'first tier' countries. There is another category of countries, such as Korea, the Dominican Republic, and Uruguay, that experienced decline in their T&C industry during the late 1980s. Such countries have been grouped together as 'second tier' countries. Most of the second tier countries emerged into international markets either in the late 1970s or the early 1980s. The decline of T&C exports in the second tier countries may be attributed to a lack of innovation policies (Mytelka and Ernst, 1998). A third group of countries began to experience a decline in garments exports during the late 1990s and almost exited in the next few years. Labelled as 'third tier' countries, their presence in international markets was short lived. The average sustainability period of their presence in the global market has been around 7–9 years, albeit with a few exceptions, such as Argentina, Brazil, Costa Rica, Israel, Malaysia, Mexico, and Thailand, that entered the international market in the 1970s.

The findings of the chapter suggest that the level of income, technological policies at the national level, rising wages, and the shifting of the manufacturing base from labour-intensive sectors to high profit and capital-intensive sectors can have influenced the production and exports of T&C, in addition to protectionism and changes in WTO rules.

It seems that the rise in per capita GDP has been one reason for the downfall of the T&C industry in most developing countries. However, there are some exceptions – such as Macao (SAR China), Hong Kong (SAR China) and Singapore. Despite a very high GDP per capita, T&C exports from these countries show no sign of decline. The most reasonable factor in Macao and Hong Kong seems to be the business model adopted by these countries. Garment manufacturing firms in these countries shifted their manufacturing base to mainland China, where average wage levels are much lower. Singapore might be following the same business model by subcontracting to Indonesia. Alternatively, Singapore might still be competitive in the global markets as the result of technological capacity-building initiatives.

The association between the rise in wages and the export performance of the T&C industry is not uniform across the sampled countries. With the exception of Hong Kong and Singapore, clothing exports continue to increase in first tier countries, even though they have reached average wage levels of US$12,000. In other countries, with the exception of third tier African countries, the decline has been experienced at a wage rate ranging from US$4,000 to US$10,000. T&C exports in African countries declined at a wage rate of around US$2,000. We can infer from the export performance of third tier African countries that the main reason for their exit from export markets was the result of a lack of technological capabilities rather than wage pressures. This shows that they came under competitive pressure sooner, and may not have had the chance to build capacity, upgrade or become increasingly innovative. In most of these countries, however, there was no big shift, just a decline in exports and this was premature – that is, it took place before there were internal wage pressures to do so.

The statistical analysis presented in Chapter 2 is complemented in the remaining five chapters by in-depth case studies of five countries: two first-tier countries (China and India), one second-tier country (Uruguay) and two third-tier countries (Mauritius and Ghana). The case studies of China and India are important in that these two countries were among the earliest entrants in international markets in T&C and still continue to increase their market share. It is expected to reveal factors other than wages and shifting to other sectors that have enabled these countries to increase their T&C exports, despite successfully developing high-tech sectors such as software in India and electronic hardware in China. This set of countries also enables us to examine these hypotheses in the context of four different sorts of international trading environments: those of the MFA under GATT (1974–1994) and the Agreement on Textiles and Clothing (ATC) in WTO (1995–2004), the Lomé IV (1990–2000) and Cotonou (2000–2020) agreements between the Africa, Caribbean, and Pacific (ACP) countries and the EU, the Caribbean Basin Initiative (CBI: 2000–2008) between the US and Caribbean region, and the Africa Growth and Opportunity Act (AGOA: 2000–2015) between the USA and Africa.

The researchers in Chapter 3 analyse the performance of the T&C industry in China. The chapter examines the efficacy of the Chinese textiles and clothing policies and its relationship with the growth trajectories followed by the T&C industry over the course of the past two decades. While assessing the relevance of T&C policies it was considered vital to take into consideration all of the stakeholders in the industry. Hence in addition to analysing the policy initiatives the authors have interviewed several large firms to understand the role of policies in technological capacity building. Consequently, the chapter is divided into three parts. The first part discusses T&C policies and their impact on the performance of the industry. The other two parts present case studies of firms in the clothing sector and the textiles sector respectively.

The analysis of foreign trade, the trade competitive index, and the revealed comparative advantage index indicate two important features. First, China's foreign trade has been increasing significantly and the international market share has seen a continuous improvement over the past few decades. The primary exports have changed completely from textiles products to clothing. On the one hand, a favourable economic environment is provided by the high rates of economic growth and the promotional policies of the government.

On the other hand, entry into WTO and the abolition of the textiles and clothing quota system appear to have provided further opportunities for China.

Secondly, China's T&C industry as a whole has become more competitive on the world stage, and the competitive advantage of the textiles sector is stronger than that of the clothing sector. China's competitiveness is based on the advantage offered by its abundant labour resource and the extensive use of traditional techniques. However, because of the increase of labour costs and the transformation of the T&C industry from labour-intensive to technology-intensive, the trade competitiveness of China's T&C at the aggregate level has been weakening over the period between 1980 and 2005. Therefore, China, on the one hand, needs to improve the labour productivity of its T&C industry. On the other hand, it should optimize the trade patterns, form powerful brands and increase the exports of high added-value, high-quality T&C products, in order to improve its international competitiveness in the trade of the textiles and clothing industry.

The case studies suggest that, in addition to taking advantage of international trade rules and government policies, T&C firms have also invested huge amounts in capacity-building programmes. The case studies of two clothing sector firms – Youngor and Hongdou – reveal many similarities in the processes of internationalization within these corporations, albeit with different emphases. They both began as small enterprises operating a single production unit. Learning from international experience and independent innovation activities they succeeded in generating new business ideas, improved their technological levels and operational patterns, experienced independent development processes and internationalization, paid attention to reform and the development of brand strategy, created self-determination and brand culture, and built up a huge sales network. At the same time, they paid attention to digitized projects and information technology and made use of high technology to enhance competitiveness. In their brand strategy, Youngor paid attention to the use of others' experience. By contrast, Hongdou focussed on independent innovation strategies and relied on the traditional culture of China to create its brand culture.

From the case studies of leaders in the Chinese textiles sector – the Changshan Group and the Weiqiao Group – it is clear that several characteristics in their development trajectory were common to every one of these firms. Their growth processes were based mainly on expansions in scale. In switching from a controlled economy to a market economy, the Changshan Group and the Weiqiao Group grasped the opportunities of markets and benefited from policies to increase the scale of the operations. In the course of their expansion, they improved their management systems and upgraded their equipment and technology in order to remain competitive. These groups faced the new challenges of the WTO positively by making efforts to enlarge markets and achieve the status of international enterprises.

The Indian T&C industry is analysed in Chapter 4. The analysis suggests that the structure of the T&C industry in India is to some extent a limitation. India's T&C industry has been dominated by fragmented small producers, and there is little vertical integration in the apparel sector (USITC 2004). Even given all of these lacunae the Indian textiles sector is still the second-largest employer in the nation. In order to grow and compete in the new post-MFA era the Indian textiles sector has to overcome structural difficulties. Similarly, new strategies will be required to meet the competition from firms around the world in a post-MFA era. The industry has made efforts to upgrade technology, but only to a limited extent.

In recent decades, the Indian domestic textiles sector has been quite competitive and has been subjected to many upheavals. Domestic and foreign firms need to be encouraged to invest in export production in order to produce more output. There is a need to bring about technological improvement, structural changes, and liberalization from controls and regulations, increased labour and machine productivity and reliable quality assurance systems for the betterment of the industry. The textiles sector has gone through significant changes in the expectation of increased levels of international competition. For the overall development of the economy, the textiles sector should be treated more favourably than any other sector, within the larger framework of India's industrial policy. Despite the insufficient initiatives taken towards capacity-building initiatives, India's T&C industry has benefited from the abolition of the quota regime of WTO.

The performance of the T&C industry in Mauritius is examined in Chapter 5. The findings suggest that having been one of the main engines of growth of the Mauritian economy, in recent years the local T&C industry has suffered an important downturn over the past few years. Inherent weaknesses such as rising costs of labour, unfavourable terms of trade and declining productivity, notwithstanding the liberalization of trade and the dismantling of the MFA, have forced the industry to restructure itself.

Until very recently, in a context where thousands of workers were being laid off as long-standing companies relocated to greener pastures, many observers had nearly written off the industry and the mood was downbeat. There is now some evidence, as shown in the cases studied, that the sector has been successfully making an important transition to the manufacture of upper-range commodities where it can compete more successfully with emerging low-cost producers. What remains of the sector is predominantly a core group of large enterprises which account for the lion's share of the stakes in terms of exports as well as employment. However, the experience and high standards of quality and reliability which Mauritian T&C producers have acquired and their constant endeavour to innovate and focus on the needs of the customers have enabled them to secure niche markets.

Moreover, together with the challenges of globalization, there have also been some important opportunities presented to the sector, particularly in the form of the African Growth and Opportunity Act (AGOA). The considerable investment in new spinning mills and the establishment of strategic partnerships and production sites in India (in the case of FKL) and China (in the case of CMT) reveal the attempts of the industry to make the most of preferential access to the US market.

Nonetheless, there is a need for further research to find out how far the smaller firms are able to cope with a context that is becoming increasingly difficult. As Hurreeram and Little (2002) note, many companies have almost deliberately ignored the implications of competing against low-cost producers on a level playing field (without any protectionist policies including duty- and quota-free access to the markets) given the pressures of increasing demand from the market. These firms have been worst hit by the liberalization of trade. A series of policies and measures taken by the government to redress a number of important weaknesses in the industry, particularly concerning the need to restructure their operations, upgrade technology, upgrade quality and design, innovate, produce high value-added products for niche markets are expected to assist the industry and provide positive signals to the players in the industry.

Time will tell if the objective of the government to position the local T&C industry as a 'textile hub' in the region will materialize itself. Certainly the employment of more than 50,000 workers and the Mauritian economy itself will depend on this.

The findings of the study of the Ghanaian T&C industry, presented in Chapter 6, suggest that the industry registered its greatest output in the mid-1970s and that it has been in continuous decline since that time. Trade liberalization, which was initiated in 1983, could be seen as a new condition to which the industry needed to adjust. Prior to liberalization, the inefficiencies of the sub-sector were not as evident because competition was just among the local manufacturers who must now also cope with external firms. For the textiles industry, historically the larger firms such as GTP, ATL and GTMC had been producing to the satisfaction of the local demand and taste and were not essentially big exporters. This implies that since the entire production processes were not automated, the cost of production is much higher than it would normally be with full automation without incorporating the local designs and tradition.

Even given the high costs of production the firms were still doing relatively well until the pirating of designs and logos by external firms that tended to flood the local markets with fake products. Buyers consider these products to be authentic ones and go for them at their relatively lower price levels compared to the authentic ones. What makes the difference between the price competitiveness of the local and foreign companies is that, whereas the foreign companies use fully automated processes to produce their products at relatively cheaper cost and market them to unsuspecting customers using pirated local logos and designs, the local companies employ a more cost-inefficient but higher-quality combination of traditional and automated techniques. This is essentially the problem associated with the Ghanaian textiles companies.

In recent years, the Ghanaian garments sector has exhibited some positive trends, particularly by firms located in export processing zones. The bottom line is that the upstart apparel companies in the sample appear to be performing relatively well compared to their textiles counterparts which have survived both internal and external shocks for many decades. Such internal shocks comprised of changes in policy resulting in change of governments and external factors such as international trade policies. The recent AGOA between the USA and Ghana has somehow provided ready markets for Ghanaian textiles and apparel products, but it appears that the garments companies located in the export processing zones have been the greatest beneficiaries. The incentives and tax holidays, together with the available pool of trained labour, has given them the edge over those textiles companies that are not located within the Free Zone. In fact, the taxes on finished products instead of the incentives have made matters worse.

The VAT/NHIL levy alone is currently 15 per cent on finished products. Some experts tend to favour the extension of the favourable conditions enjoyed by the companies located within the Free Zone to those that are outside the Zone. Furthermore, textiles companies must find ways of fully automating their production processes whilst simultaneously accounting for local taste in order to survive. Government must help to curb the influx of pirated goods into the market and minimize, if not eliminate, the smuggling of fake and other products into the country. To help especially the exporters meet their delivery times, measures should be put in place at the nation's ports to facilitate administration procedures. As it stands now, it takes a Ghanaian exporter an average of 40 days for the products to be delivered to a US partner compared to only 20 days for their Asian counterparts.

The findings of the study of the Ghanaian T&C industry suggest that although international trade rules such as AGOA and the Lomé Convention have contributed to some extent to the improvement in the performance of the garments sector, governance has been a major problem for the expected growth of both textiles and garments sectors. For the garments sector government has to help exporters by providing better and more efficient shipment facilities. One of the possible ways could be to provide single window services to exporters for shipment and delivery in international markets. For the textiles sector, which is predominantly domestically oriented, government can help local producers by enforcing existing piracy laws, and, if needed, it could enact suitable new legislation to curb the menace of smuggling and other illegal trading activities. Firms in textiles need to be encouraged to adopt automated production technologies. We conclude that good governance, coupled with international trade rules, could change the present levels of performance of the textiles and clothing industry in Ghana.

Chapter 7 investigates the development trajectory of the Uruguayan T&C industry. The author concludes that over the course of the past twenty years, the two firms interviewed in the textiles sector changed their product mix, moving from wool only to mixtures of wool and other fibres. This has required changes in machinery and in the retraining of workers. The two firms interviewed that are still in business are involved in joint research projects with the University of the Republic in Uruguay, but neither of them has made use of the DINACYT programme to promote innovation. The two textiles firms are vertically integrated, and more than 90 per cent of their production is exported. In every case, the company representative said that the firm has learned from its participation in foreign markets. In all the cases training is considered to be essential for the firm to perform well. They all participate in global networks as fabrics suppliers.

The best-performing textiles firm (Paylana) has made a strong commitment to improving quality and design in order to gain access to high-quality segments of the market. It is also the firm with the largest number of links to Uruguayan networks and institutions, and to foreign enterprises. Paylana has a good level of technology. Keeping up to date with the international technology standards and continuous workers' training are cornerstones of the company's culture. The plant is completely automated and information and computer technologies are used intensively. This is the only firm they interviewed that actually has a marketing department. It engages in ongoing market and technology research and it has a very close working relationship with its customers. Hisud is geared to middle-high market segments, where competition from Asia and Eastern European countries is more intense, and their most important lines are menswear.

In the clothing sector, the three firms interviewed are clearly export-oriented and they have all introduced changes in response to fashion market trends. Pelsa is a relatively small firm that has managed to survive and grow in recent years. Its strong points are that it is flexible, it specializes in accessories, and its markets are diversified. It invests in training and technology, and computers and information technologies are in operation in some of the firm's activities.

Over the course of the interviews, these firms did not dwell particularly on high costs or the need for some form of state assistance, but they did state that it is necessary to have clear long-term rules and that trade agreements were essential in order to allow the sector to progress and grow. Of the firms interviewed, Sirfil has shown the worst performance over the past few years. Its level of profitability has declined, and its technology is ten years old because it has not been unable to make the necessary investments to keep up to date in this area. Thus, it seems that the main factors that enable firms to compete successfully in foreign markets are continuous investment in training and technology, the existence of trade agreements, that sales are targeted to high-quality segments of the market, and that the firm has a clearly defined marketing strategy.

It is crystal clear from the findings of the Uruguayan T&C industry case studies that those firms that have failed to invest in innovation and technology have experienced a decline in performance whereas technology and quality-conscious firms have survived in the quota-free trading environment of the T&C industry. Over the past few years the declining trend in T&C exports at the national level is attributed mainly to the lack of technological promotional policies and export promotion policies at the government level.

In conclusion, we may argue that liberalization and the ensuing market expansion have been beneficial to the export performance in those countries that had developed and continued to develop the capacity to innovate in various ways: through new products, especially in the high value-added segment, the adoption of new technologies, in particular computer and automation technologies, successful marketing and brand name development, and training activities. Firms are also assisted in getting on the right track through the provision of government assistance in the form of export processing zones, technology promotion policies, capacity building, development of infrastructure and market monitoring.

2
The Textiles and Clothing Industry and Economic Development: A Global Perspective

Kaushalesh Lal

2.1 Introduction

In recent decades, the major changes in the pattern of production and in the nature of competition have altered the competitive environment for firms and farms in both developed and developing countries. These have particular significance for competitiveness in traditional industries with a potential for export. Since the 1970s, production has become increasingly more knowledge-intensive as investments in intangibles such as knowledge of soils and farming techniques, research and development including the production of software and the application of biotechnology, design capabilities, engineering skills, training, monitoring, marketing and management have come to play a greater role in the production of goods and services. Much of this involves tacit rather than codified knowledge and mastery requires a conscious effort at learning by doing, by using, and by interacting.

Gradually the knowledge intensity of production extended beyond the so-called high-technology sectors to reshape a broad spectrum of traditional industries from the shrimp and salmon fisheries in the Philippines, Norway and Chile, and the forestry and flower enterprises in Kenya and Colombia, to the textiles and clothing firms of Italy, Taiwan and Thailand. Indeed, where linkages were established to a wider set of knowledge inputs and the local knowledge base was deepened, these traditional industries have shown a remarkable robustness in the growth of output and exports. Most developing countries have not kept up in building these knowledge-based capabilities.

Within the context of increasing levels of knowledge-intensive production, firms began to compete not only in terms of price but also on the basis of their ability to innovate. The entrenchment of an innovation-based mode of competition has increased the speed with which new products are developed and moved to markets across the manufacturing sector. This, coupled with rising levels of productivity and quality improvements in traditional industries and the entry of large numbers of newcomers, has given rise to the need for a continuous process of innovation that introduces product variety, adds value to products, enhances productivity and meets environmental, labour and quality standards as well as delivery schedules. Competitiveness can no longer be based on static comparative advantage. Nor can tariffs protect inefficient local industries. The liberalization and deregulation of domestic markets have accelerated the pace at which innovation-based competition has diffused worldwide, drawing further attention to the need for learning and innovation in traditional industries. New types of policies will be required to meet these challenges. It is in this context that conventional views on innovation in developing countries must be rethought and new concepts that embody dynamic change, such as the notion of an 'innovation system' must be introduced into policy making.

Among the more common beliefs still encountered in discussions of innovation systems, however, is the notion that innovation is something that only takes place in countries like Japan or the USA, in large multinational corporations or in what are regarded as the high-tech industries. Indeed, much of the conventional literature continues to associate innovation with the kind of activity by firms that takes place at the technological frontier or what Schumpeter has termed invention. A narrow definition that equates innovation with invention of this sort, however, denies the importance of:

- building upon indigenous knowledge,
- exercising creativity in the development of new products, processes, management routines or organizational structures that correspond to local conditions and needs,
- creating the local linkages that support the modification of production processes to bring costs down, increase efficiency and ensure environmental sustainability,
- mastering imported technology in order to transform it in new ways and
- developing policies that stimulate and support a continuous process of learning and innovation.

In this study, innovation is understood to be the process by which firms master and implement the design and production of goods and services that are new to them, irrespective of whether or not they are new to their competitors – either domestic or foreign. This definition acknowledges a role for developing countries as producers and not only as users of technology. The study aims at identifying the role of innovation initiatives taken at the firm level, innovation and technology policies, and international trade rules in influencing the export performance of the textiles and clothing industry in developing countries.

Historically, textile and clothing (T&C) production has played an important role in securing economic growth and development. It sparked the first industrial revolution, and relatively less capital intensive and reasonably stable, mature and widely accessible characteristics, coupled with the availability of cotton, a key raw material input, made it the leading sector in early processes of industrialization. Along with garment production where labour intensity of production remains high, the textiles and clothing[1] industry has played an important role in development strategies designed to meet basic human needs as well as generate revenue through exports.

From the 1960s onwards, textiles exports from a number of developing countries began to rise dramatically. China, India, Korea, Hong Kong, Indonesia and Singapore were in the forefront of this development and their export successes, coupled with increased international subcontracting in the garments industry, soon sparked the entry of newcomers from Asia and a few new entrants from Latin America in the 1980s. Throughout this period and despite the existence of incentives provided by the general system of preferences for poorer countries and the special provisions of the Lomé and Cotonou Conventions governing imports from the African, Caribbean and Pacific (ACP) countries associated with the European Economic Community, Mauritius and, to a lesser extent, Jamaica, were the only notable few exporters among the ACP countries.

For early exporters, technological capabilities became increasingly important in sustaining an export success that was based initially on labour cost advantages. Through a process of technological capability building firms were able to adjust, on the one hand, to trade restrictions contained in the Multi-Fibre Arrangement (MFA) (in the GATT regime 1974–94) and the Agreement on Textiles and Clothing (ATC) (in the WTO regime 1995–2004) and, on the other hand, to new cheap labour competitors by moving to more sophisticated products and by diversifying markets. Over time they 'learned to learn' through their textiles and clothing exports, transforming themselves from subcontractors into partners with their northern collaborators as they contributed not only labour skills, but design, full-scale manufacturing including input sourcing and new management techniques. These innovative capabilities would later be transferred to other higher-skilled manufacturing activities in which they came to dominate as original exporters. Soon, these developing countries also began to delocalize production to countries with lower wages.

During the 1990s, the increased delocalization of textiles and clothing production to poorer developing countries coupled with a variety of new trade initiatives stimulated the emergence of a set of new exporters – for example, Bangladesh and, more recently, Kenya. Over the same period, however, exports from a number of entrants during the 1980s, such as Kuwait, Barbados, and Uruguay, had already begun to decline. However, some early exporters of textiles and clothing, such as China, India, Indonesia and Singapore, have been able to expand exports. Having a similar share of textiles exports to that of China in the world trade in the early 1980s, India has managed to increase its share marginally from 2.07 per cent in 1985 to 3.48 per cent in 2004 while the share of the Chinese textiles industry has increased drastically – from 5.38 per cent to 16.63 per cent during the same period.[2] The success of Indian T&C exports may be attributed to the innovation activities and the adoption of new technologies whereas it may be attributed to the aggressive marketing strategies, innovative activities, and institutional support in case of China.

The importance of the role of international trade rules in T&C exports, however, cannot be ignored. Quota restrictions of ATC in the WTO regime were removed completely on 31 December 2004. A study by Park (2005) investigated the impact of quota elimination on T&C exports by few Asian countries during the period January to September 2005. The study reports that China's exports of T&C to the American market increased by 61.3 per cent over the same period in 2004. It resulted in a huge increase in China's share of US trade. The share of Chinese T&C exports in the US market increased from 17.5 per cent during the first nine months of 2004 to 26.0 per cent during the same period in 2005. Other Asian economies have also gained due to the removal of quota restrictions, albeit to a lesser extent. For instance, India's T&C exports to the US market increased by 25.6 per cent in January to September 2005 compared with the same period in 2004 whereas Bangladesh increased their T&C exports by 18.9 per cent during the same period. While China, India and Bangladesh have been able to increase their share in the US market, T&C exports in several countries have declined since the elimination of quotas. For instance, Korea's T&C exports to the US market declined by 26.7 per cent during the first nine months of 2005. The study further reports that the decline in Korea's T&C exports was the highest among all of major exporters to the US market.

The complex pattern of changes in the emergence and decline of developing country exporters of textiles and garments creates new challenges for policy makers and trade negotiators. This is all the more so, as the factors that account for this variability in export performance are not clear and the lessons to be learned from these changes for newer entrants are thus not evident. The objectives of this study therefore are:

- To develop a theoretical framework that is useful in identifying the turning points of growth in the textile and garment industry in developing countries;
- To examine the impact of technology and innovation policies pursued by these countries on the performance of the two sectors;
- To investigate the effects of trade policies on the changing spectrum of opportunities and constraints on the growth of textile and clothing exports and their impact on incentives for innovation in these sectors;
- To identify factors that have been impediments in using the textile and garments industry as a platform for growth and development by late entrants in international markets.

The remainder of the chapter is organized as follows. The sample of developing countries included in the analysis and methodology are discussed

in section 2.2 and the data analysis is presented in section 2.3. The results
are discussed in section 2.4 and the findings are summarized in section 2.5.

2.2   Sample and methodology

We have tried to include all of the developing countries in our analysis.
However, the selection of countries is constrained by the availability of data.
The study uses data series for 1975 to 2004. Three sources of data, namely
COMTRADE, WDI, and UNIDO, have been used in the study. Data related
to export performance of the T&C industry have been taken from United
Nations COMTRADE database while GDP and wage rates have been compiled from WDI and UNIDO respectively. Finally we could get usable data
for 51 countries. The list of countries included in the analysis and their
continental affiliation is presented in Appendix Table 2.1.

As discussed in the previous section, several countries, such as China,
India, Indonesia and Singapore, which had ventured into the clothing
exports market during the 1960s and 1970s still continue to maintain their
share of international trade. In fact, since the early 1980s several countries,
such as China and India, have increased their share of global trade in clothing. Trends in textiles exports have, by and large, followed a similar pattern
in several developing countries with a few exceptions, such as Singapore,
where there has been a decline of textiles since the mid-1990s, while there
is no sign of a decline in garment exports. We have categorized all such
countries where garment exports have not declined as first tier countries.

There is another category, including countries such as Korea, the Dominican Republic and Uruguay, that experienced a decline of their T&C industry
during the late 1980s. Such countries have been grouped as second tier countries, most of which emerged into international markets in either the late
1970s or the early 1980s. The decline of T&C exports in second tier countries may be attributed to the lack of innovation policies (Mytelka and Ernst,
1998). We have identified another group of countries that started to experience decline in garments exports during the late 1990s and almost exited in
the next few years. Labelled as third tier countries, their presence in international markets was short lived. The average sustainability period of their
presence in the global market has been around 7–9 years – with a few exceptions such as Argentina, Brazil, Costa Rica, Israel, Malaysia, Mexico, and
Thailand that entered the international market in the 1970s.

A number of explanations might be offered for the rather short-lived period
of export success for second and third tier developing country entrants, especially when compared to the longer period of steady growth in textiles and
clothing production and exports from first tier exporters. One hypothesis
derives from the literature on learning and upgrading in traditional industries. This would argue that 'premature' decline among second and third

tier countries, as evidenced by a decline in exports in a context characterized by relatively low wages and an absence of movement into higher value-added products, was the result of a failure to build domestic capabilities. But this, alone, does not explain why that failure took place. A second hypothesis draws its inspiration from the literature on international trade and focuses on the international trading environment as a stimulus to growth and development. What, however, explains which countries have seized these opportunities or whether such opportunities have changed over time? A third hypothesis would embed the problem of capability building within a broader international and policy context. Applying an innovation system framework, it would suggest that today's trading environment provides fewer opportunities for learning and innovation, while the spaces for policies that drove the process of capability building forward in the past have also narrowed.

This chapter will analyse the first hypothesis by relating the export performance of our sample of 51 developing countries to the evolution of their wage rates and national income. We intend to use polynomial curve fitting to examine the trend lines of exports in textiles and garments (T&G[3]) and their correlations with the wage rate and national income.

2.3   Statistical analysis

For each of the three categories of countries we shall plot the exports of textiles and garments over time and then separately their relationship to changes in wage rates and national income.

2.3.1   First tier

As mentioned earlier, the exports of textiles and garments in first tier countries are still increasing. The phenomenon is substantiated in Figure 2.1. Subsequently, we have tried to relate the increasing trend in the T&C industry with wage rates and GDP in this set of countries. The results are presented in Figures 2.2 and 2.3.

It can be seen from Figure 2.2 that slope of trend[4] lines of textiles and garments sectors are positive. However, the pace of growth of the clothing sector is higher. This could be because of the presence of stronger entry barriers in the textiles sector. The emergence of the garments sector in first tier countries might be attributed partly to the increased capability of domestic firms to compete in global markets and partly to an increase in the consumption of ready-made garments.

Figure 2.3 presents the relationship between the wage rates and export performance of first tier countries. The trends observed here are very similar to those found in relation to GDP. As mentioned earlier, the trends are significantly influenced by high-wage economies such as Hong Kong (SAR China), Macao (SAR China) and Singapore. Maximum wage rates in the first tier countries excluding these three countries were US$12,757, while trends

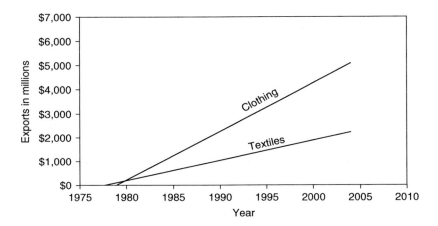

Figure 2.1   Trends in T&C exports in first tier countries
Source: COMTRADE; SITC Rev. 1 code 65 excluding 651 and 654 for textiles and code 841 excluding 8413 and 8416 for clothing.

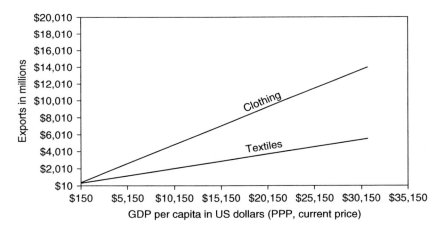

Figure 2.2   GDP and export performance of T&C in first tier countries

show that even after attaining wages greater than US$20,000 T&C exports are still on the increase.

We can infer from Figure 2.3 that one of the reasons why first tier countries did not 'prematurely' lose their ability to compete in export markets as wages rose was because there was a shift across textiles garments in order to reduce the more labour-intensive clothing exports and increase the more capital-intensive textiles. The shift from garments to textiles exports in the case of

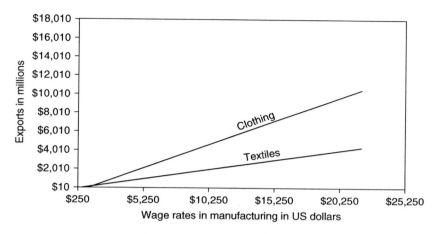

Figure 2.3 Wage rates and export performance of T&C in first tier countries

Singapore is a case in point. Underlying these changes, case study material (from Ernst, Ganiatsos and Mytelka, 1998; Gereffi, Spener, and Bair, 2002) shows that there was a conscious effort at technological capacity building, upgrading, and innovation in this group of countries.

2.3.2 Second tier

Figure 2.4 presents the trend in T&C exports in second tier countries. It can be seen from the figure that clothing exports in these countries began to decline in the mid-1980s while the exports of textiles reached their peak in the early 1990s and then declined. In value terms the pattern is very different from first tier countries where textiles exports have always been lower than clothing. In most of the second tier countries textiles exports were higher than garments during the infancy days of the apparel industry. However, within a span of five to ten years clothing exports superseded the other sector. The widening of this gap continued until the mid-1980s when second tier countries experienced a downward trend in the level of apparel exports while their textiles exports continued to rise until the early 1990s. Consequently, the gap between textiles and apparel exports narrowed down during the period from the mid-1980s to the early 1990s. Although the presence of second tier countries in international markets in both the textiles and clothing sectors is beginning to wane, the decline has been steeper in the clothing sector. Consequently, the value of textiles exports superseded the clothing sector in the later period. Another distinguishing aspect between first and second tier countries is the value of T&C exports. It ranges between US$10,000–12,000 million in first tier countries to between US$5–25 million in second tier countries, with the exception of the Republic of Korea.

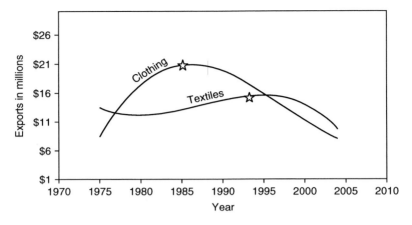

Figure 2.4   Trends in T&C exports in second tier countries

We have tried to explain the performance of the T&C industry in second tier countries in terms of their economic development. The impact of economic development on the T&C industry could be felt in two ways: first, the availability of opportunities to entrepreneurs in other sectors; and, secondly, the non-availability of competent workers at globally competitive wage rates. By and large, firms in the T&C industry are family owned rather than professionally managed firms. The first generation that began business in the late 1970s continued as long as the founder of the firm could do so. The next generation might not wish to continue in the same business because of the better opportunities available in other sectors. This could be because of the opening of new sectors in the economy. Consequently, more options are available to the second generation – which is likely to be more professional and qualified. Another reason for the new generation to be switching over to newer industries could be higher profit margins compared to traditional sectors such as T&C where profit margins are volatile due to low entry barriers, particularly in the manufacture of garments. Opportunities in other sectors are also expected to lead to the non-availability of workers at internationally competitive wage levels. Hence higher GDP per capita, which could be the result of the emergence and the growth of other sectors in the economy, are expected to result in an exit of T&C firms from the sector.

It can be seen from Figure 2.5 that exports of both the textiles and clothing sectors began to decline when GDP per capita reached a threshold level of more than US$10,000 in this group of countries. The interesting aspect is that sector-specificity seems to have played no role in the exit of this industry from the global market. Although T&C belong to the same industry, there are some sector-specific factors – for example, the textiles sector is more capital intensive and has higher entry barriers. This suggests that firms in both

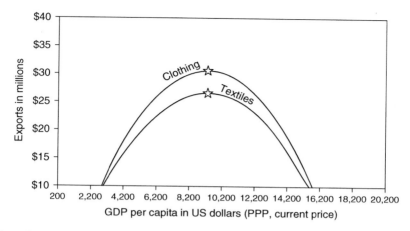

Figure 2.5   GDP and export performance of T&C in second tier countries

the sectors were surviving on abundant labour and that as soon as the labour markets became flexible, the sustainability of T&C firms became untenable.

The T&C industry, being labour-intensive and traditional, provides jobs for millions of unskilled workers. Of course, we are not claiming that there is no high-tech component in this industry. In fact, there are stages in the manu-facturing processes of the apparel sector – for instance, design – that are highly knowledge intensive. But employment at these stages forms only a very small percentage of the total workforce (Lal, 2001). We are trying to test the hypoth-esis that if there is a rise in the wage levels in other manufacturing sectors, the possibility of getting cheap labour into the T&C industry vanishes. Con-sequently, entrepreneurs may find that the continuance of business in the T&C industry may not be economically viable. This might result in the exit of vulnerable firms.

Polynomials representing the export performance of the T&C industry and wage rates in manufacturing are shown in Figure 2.6. It can be seen from Figure 2.6 that exports of T&C declined when wages in manufacturing sec-tors reached a threshold level of more than US$6,500. The decline of both sectors at the same threshold of wages suggests that firms were surviving only on a supply of cheap labour. They did not keep pace with worldwide technological development and relied on old production technologies. Tech-nological improvement could have enabled them to have exclusively trained rather than unskilled workers to use new technologies efficiently. Conse-quently, firms might have survived in global markets for a longer period. Comments may be true for most of the firms in the second tier countries.

Although the Republic of Korea, subsequently Korea, falls into the category of second tier countries, its volume of T&C exports is much higher than other

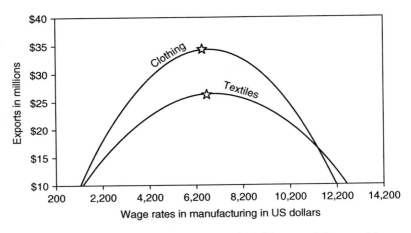

Figure 2.6   Wage rates and export performance of T&C in second tier countries

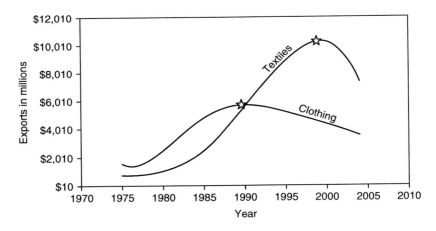

Figure 2.7   Trends in T&C exports in Korea

countries in the group. Hence it became necessary to analyse the Korean data separately. The polynomial presented in Figure 2.7 suggests that the exports of garments began to decline in the late 1980s, whereas the exports of textiles continued to increase until the late 1990s. The decline of Korean T&G exports may be attributed to a lack of innovation policies (Mytelka and Ernst, 1998). Like other second tier countries the value of apparel exports was higher than textiles until the former experienced some reversal. Figure 2.7 shows that, in contrast to other second tier countries where the exports of textiles did not rise much before they began to decline, Korean textiles exports rose

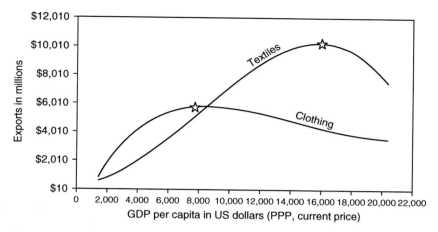

Figure 2.8   GDP and the export performance of T&C in Korea

rapidly before its decline in 1997. This could possibly be attributed to the technological capacity-building efforts of textiles firms in Korea.

Figure 2.8 depicts the relationship between the rise of GDP per capita and the decline in Korean T&C exports. In common with other second tier countries Korea experienced a negative growth rate in clothing when GDP per capita reached the magical figure of around US$8,000. However, textiles exports followed a different pattern than other countries in the group. In contrast to other second tier countries, the exports of textiles and garments did not decline at the same time. In fact, exports in textiles continued to rise until GDP per capita attained a threshold level of more than US$16,000. The major reason behind the rise in textiles exports between 1989 and 1997 could be the technological capability-building initiatives of Korean textiles firms. Apparently, firms have been upgrading technologies in line with developments in the world market. Consequently, they remain competitive in international markets even after the explosive growth of other sectors which led to the dramatic increase in per capita GDP. Korean firms might have found it economically unviable to remain in this sector due to the emergence of newcomers such as Bangladesh who could exploit the advantage of low production costs.

The relationship between T&C exports and wages is presented in Figure 2.9. It can be seen from this figure that the trend of GDP per capita and wage rates vis-à-vis export performance of T&C followed a similar pattern in the case of Korea. The trend exhibited is very different than that observed for other second tier countries in the sample. Like GDP per capita and T&C export relationship, the clothing exports began to decline at a much lower level of wages compared to textiles. The former sector experienced decline at a

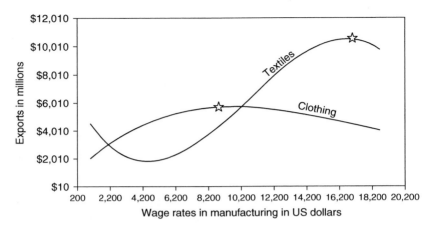

Figure 2.9   Wage rates and export performance of T&C in Korea

wage threshold of more than US$8,200, whereas the textiles sector began to lose ground in global markets when wages in manufacturing attained a level of US$18,200. As argued earlier, textiles manufacturing firms might be using efficient production technologies which require a highly skilled workforce. The firms might have remained competitive in international markets despite being paid wages that were on a par with manufacturing firms in other sectors. Raising wages beyond a certain point might not be economically viable in export markets. The low-wage advantages of new exporting countries might have eroded the efficiency gains of the advanced technologies used by Korean firms. Hence they might also have opted to exit from the textiles sector.

A comparison of T&C exports of Korea and other second tier countries suggests that the adoption of new technologies by Korean firms enabled firms to remain competitive in global markets for a longer period of time than those that did not keep pace with global technological developments. The garments manufacturing sector in all of the second tier countries experienced a decline when GDP per capita reached approximately US$9,000. Clothing sector firms were also affected by a rise in wages in manufacturing and could not sustain their business in exports markets when wages rose beyond US$8,500. However, the pattern is dissimilar for the textiles sector in Korea and other second tier countries.

2.3.3   Third tier

It was not possible to conduct a single analysis of all the third tier countries. This was for two main reasons: First, the magnitude of the T&C exports from various third tier countries and second due to missing data problem. Hence a

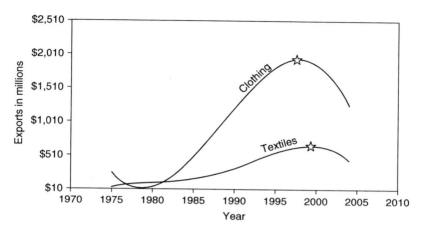

Figure 2.10   Trends in T&C exports in Asia and the Middle East

regional dimension has been added to the analysis of this group of countries. We will deal with: (i) Asia and the Middle East; (ii) Africa; and (iii) Latin America and the Caribbean.

2.3.3.1   Asia and the Middle East

The export performance of third tier countries in Asia and the Middle East region is presented in Figure 2.10, which shows that the exports of textiles and clothing sectors of these countries declined at around the same time in the late 1990s. The pattern observed is very different from second tier countries where the decline of clothing exports was followed by the textiles sector. Another contrasting aspect is that the third countries of this region could remain in the global market for a shorter period than the second tier countries. This is illustrated by the fact that almost all of the second tier countries in this region entered into the exports markets in the early or late 1980s while the second tier countries had been present in the exports markets since the mid-1970s.

The association between economic growth and export performance of T&C is shown in Figure 2.11. The pattern is very similar to that observed amongst second tier countries (with the exception of Korea). It can be seen that the exports of both textiles and garments started to decline when GDP per capita reached a figure of around US$12,000. The major dissimilarity is in terms of the differences in the value of textiles and clothing exports. The level of garments exports is several times higher than that of textiles. This phenomenon might be related to the high entry barriers in the textiles sector, because garments manufacturing is less capital intensive than its twin. Hence latecomer firms in Asia and the Middle East region might have started

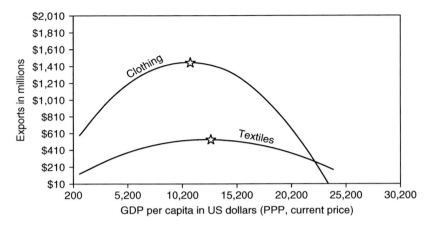

Figure 2.11   GDP and export performance of T&C in Asia and the Middle East

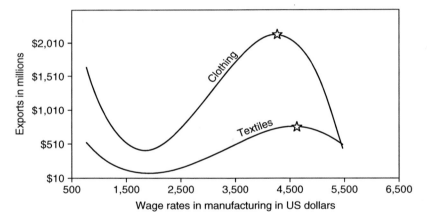

Figure 2.12   Wage rates and export performance of T&C in Asia

a garments-exporting business to exploit the availability of an abundant unskilled workforce in these countries whereas the capital intensiveness of the twin sector might have prevented them from entering into global markets.

Figure 2.12 depicts the trend of T&C exports from third tier Asian countries. (Israel has been dropped from the analysis as the data on wages were fluctuating and were considered unreliable.) Figure 2.12 may be viewed in two parts: First the trend up to a wage level of US$2,000 and second beyond that. The first part of the graph is influenced by the export performance of

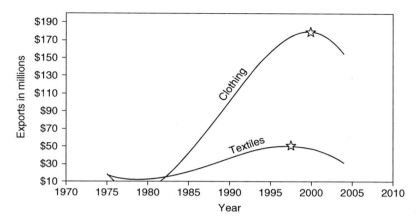

Figure 2.13 Trends in T&C exports in Africa

Thailand which exited the market in the early 1990s. The steep decline in exports in the first part of the graph shows the declining trend of Thailand. Apparently, Asian latecomers ventured into T&C exports in order to compete in global markets on the basis of the advantages of cheap labour. They exited from the business when that advantage disappeared as a result of the rise in wages. This might have happened as the result of the increasing integration of these economies within the global economy. Given the fact that firms in the textiles sector exited at the same level of wages as garments, the textile firms seem did not make efforts in innovation and technological capacity development and consequently died when low-wage advantage eroded.

2.3.3.2 Africa

Third tier African countries ventured into international markets during the 1980s. As is also the case for Asian and Middle East late entrants, African third tier countries initially focussed on garments as well as textiles sectors. But the growth of garments exports has been much higher than textiles. In fact, textiles exports grew only nominally during the mid-1980s before declining in the late 1990s. As is evident from Figure 2.13 third tier African countries and their counterparts in Asia and the Middle East differ substantially in terms of the magnitude of their T&C exports. Another noticeable fact is that this is the only group of countries where exports of textiles experienced earlier exit than the garments sector. Several explanations could be offered to explain the phenomenon. One, due to change in cropping pattern in agriculture, farmers might have shifted to other cash crops. Consequently, the production of cotton, which is the main input of the textiles sector, might have declined drastically, leading to an exit from the textiles sector.

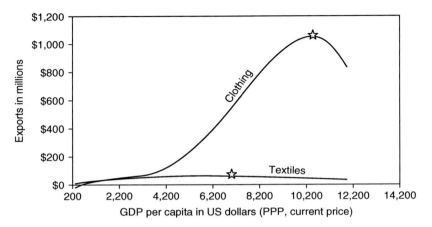

Figure 2.14   GDP and export performance of T&C in Africa

Second, textiles-exporting firms may not be local firms. They could be Asian firms that were unable to export textiles from their own countries because of quota restrictions such as MFA. Since 1995 these restrictions have been removed in a phased manner. Consequently, foreign firms might have preferred to relocate to home countries, leading to a decline in textiles exports from third tier African countries. In either case local firms did not seem to develop enough capacity to remain competitive in international markets.

Figure 2.14 presents the trend followed by T&C exports vis-à-vis the economic growth of third tier African countries. It can be seen from Figure 2.14 that the decline in garments exports was experienced at more or less the same level of GDP per capita as in the case of their counterpart in Asia and, to some extent, similar to that of second tier countries. However, there is a noticeable difference in terms of the exit from the textiles sector at a lower level of GDP than latecomers in other parts of the world. As explained earlier, this could be due either to international trade rules such as the ATC during the WTO regime or because textiles exports were attributable to foreign firms which began to disappear after 1995. The decline in the garments exports could be explained by three factors: greater integration of African economies with the world economy; garments manufacturing firms becoming uncompetitive in global markets; and the disappearance of foreign firms from African countries.[5]

Polynomials depicting the export performance of the T&C industry and wage rates in third tier African countries are presented in Figure 2.15. Unlike Figure 2.14, which showed that the textiles and apparel exports declined at different levels of GDP, in this case both sectors experienced decline at the same level of wages in manufacturing. This is similar to the experience of their Asian counterparts. In value terms the exports of T&C started declining

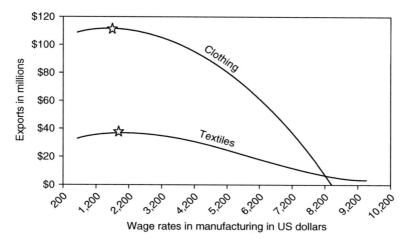

Figure 2.15 Wage rates and export performance of T&C in Africa

at a much lower level (around US$2,000) than was the case for third tier Asian countries. For that matter third tier African countries began to lose ground in international markets at lower levels of wages than in countries in other regions. The exit of African latecomers from global markets at these lower levels of wages suggests that they could not even exploit low wage advantages. This finding also reflects the fact that these countries made no effort to develop technological capabilities in order to remain competitive in international markets. The pace of decline of apparel exports has been higher than in the textiles sector, suggesting an exit of foreign firms from African countries. A lack of capacity building in these countries in T&C exports substantiates the findings of other studies that argue for the less visible spillover effects of FDI.

2.3.3.3 Latin America and the Caribbean

The results of Latin America and the Caribbean region third tier countries' analysis is presented in Figure 2.16. It can be seen from the figure that the T&C exports of this group of countries began to recover in the early 1990s. Although both of the sectors began at a similar level of exports, apparel exports achieved a phenomenal growth rate while the growth rate of the textiles sector has only been moderate. Figure 2.16 shows clearly that the exports of garments began to decline in early 2000 whereas there is no such clear-cut turning point in textiles exports. This is because of the case of Brazil – where garments exports reached a turning point in 1993, but the level of textiles exports is continuing to rise. Given the magnitude of their exports, the polynomials are influenced by Brazilian data. In every third tier country in

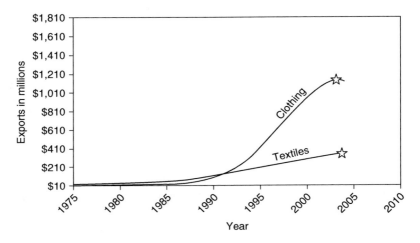

Figure 2.16   Trends in T&C exports in Latin America and the Caribbean

this region, with the exception of Brazil, there has been a decline in both the garments and the textiles sectors. Like their counterparts in Asia and Africa, textiles and garments sectors experienced a reversal in exports markets at more or less the same time – although the exports of Asian and African third tier countries started declining earlier than Latin American and Caribbean region countries.

Figure 2.17 depicts the pattern of T&C exports in relation to a rise in GDP per capita. In contrast to their African counterparts, exports of both textiles and clothing started to decline at the same level of GDP. However, the level of GDP at which third tier Latin American and Caribbean region countries have experienced negative growth rates in garments exports is similar to the third tier countries of other regions as well as second tier countries. Textiles exports tell a different story. The exports from third tier African countries began to decline at a much lower level of GDP than third tier countries in this region, whereas Korean textile exports declined at a much higher level of GDP.

The declining trend of the T&C industry in this region could be attributed to the emergence of other dominant sectors. For instance, although the share of the software industry of Brazil in the global market is not very high, the country has developed a very strong base in software technology in its domestic market. Similarly, there are now well-developed tourism industries in both Jamaica and Costa Rica. The emergence of new sectors in many of the countries in the region has boosted economic growth which might have raised the production costs in both the textiles and the clothing sectors. Consequently, T&C firms in these countries might have become economically unviable in international markets, resulting in the decline of T&C exports.

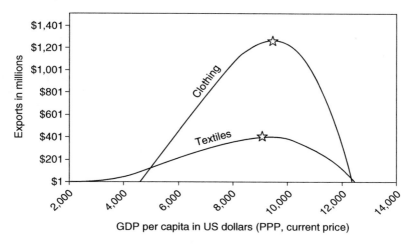

Figure 2.17 GDP and export performance of T&C in Latin America and the Caribbean

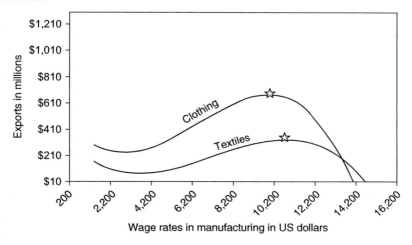

Figure 2.18 Wage rates and export performance of T&C in Latin America and the Caribbean

Figure 2.18 presents the decline in T&C exports as the wages in manufacturing sector rose. Both of the sectors experienced negative growth in international markets at the same level of wage rates. This trend is uniform across all the countries in different regions of the world, with the exception of Korea. However, the level of wage rates at which T&C exports declined varies from one region to another. For instance, second tier countries experienced a decline when the wage rates in the manufacturing sector were at a level of around US$7,000, whereas in third tier Asian countries the level was US$5,000. It was lowest in third tier African countries (US$2,500), whereas it was US$10,000 in Latin American and Caribbean region third tier countries.

Apparently, T&C firms in these countries survived in international markets due to capacity-building efforts and the adoption of new technologies. However, beyond a certain point the efficiency gains due to technological progress are eroded by price competition in international markets. The third tier countries of this region might be facing stiff price competition from their Asian counterparts. These countries might have lost their competitive edges due to low wage advantages prevalent in Asian countries. Consequently they preferred to exit from export markets in this industry.

We could have included some technological capacity-building indicators such as the Index of Technological Progress (ITP) in the analysis. However, the lack of data on such indicators in many sample countries led us to exclude such indicators. Having presented the performance of the T&C industry of several developing countries in global markets and its association with GDP per capita and wage rates, we discuss the findings of the econometric analysis in the next section.

2.4   Discussion

The central hypotheses in investigating the role of the T&C industry in the economic growth and development of latecomer exporting countries was that changes in economic structure and high production costs have led to an exit of countries in this industry from international markets. To some extent this has been found to be true. For instance, almost all of the second and third tier countries' T&C exports declined when they attained a threshold level of GDP of around US$12,000. The only exception is Korea when exports of textiles continued to rise until Korean GDP per capita reached around US$17,000. On the other hand, T&C exports from first tier countries are still rising – even after some countries have reached a per capita income level of US$30,000. This is somewhat misleading because if we exclude Macao, Hong Kong and Singapore, the maximum GDP per capita in first tier countries is US$7,709. But the question that remains is: how do these rich Asian economies deal with price competition in global markets? The rising T&C exports of Macao and Hong Kong are not difficult to explain. They are exploiting the low production cost advantages available in mainland China. This is being done by shifting their manufacturing base to mainland China. It may be worth mentioning that China's GDP per capita in 2004 was US$5,495, which is well below the turning point.

Although the levels of textiles exports of Singapore have been declining since 1995, the level of garments exports is still increasing – even though GDP per capita in 2004 was US$27,273. The rate of technological progress in the country can also be a factor in sustaining competitiveness in global markets.

Alternatively, the country might be taking advantage of the availability of cheap labour in neighbouring countries such as Indonesia. In 2004 per capita income in Indonesia was US$3,584. Given this circumstance, Singaporean garments manufacturing firms might have shifted their manufacturing base to Indonesia. It is clear from the discussion that the T&C exports performance of developing countries cannot be explained solely in terms of their income levels.

There is another interesting dimension to income turning points – i.e. the value of income. For example second tier countries faced reversals in the garments exports sector during the late 1980s, with the income turning point being around US$10,000. The decline in clothing exports in third tier countries was realized in the late 1990s, and the income turning point more or less remained same. For instance, the turning point was US$11,000 in Asia & the Middle East and African countries, while it was slightly less than US$10,000 in countries in Latin America and the Caribbean. The value of US$10,000 for second tier countries in the late 1980s is not the same as a value of US$10,000 (the average of all third tier countries) in the late 1990s. Hence, we can conclude that the effective income turning point of third tier countries was much less than that for second tier countries, suggesting that the income levels of countries cannot wholly explain the phenomena. This is where the role of technological capacity building and international trade rules comes in.

The second main hypothesis was that increases in wage rates in other manufacturing sectors could lead to exit from the T&C sector. The analysis of first tier countries suggests that having reached average wage rates of more than US$20,000 there is no sign of decline of T&C exports in this group of nations. Again, this finding has to be interpreted with care because the analysis is significantly biased towards Hong Kong and Singapore. In 2002 the wage rates in the manufacturing sectors in Singapore in 2002 were US$20,275, while in Hong Kong they stood at US$19,533. Maximum wage rates in first tier countries excluding Hong Kong and Singapore were US$12,757.

The wage rate turning points in other second tier countries were around US$7,000 while Korean textiles and apparel sectors declined at a different level of wages. For instance, the wage turning point for clothing was US$9,000 whereas the textiles exports declined at a much higher level of wages, i.e. US$17,000, in Korea. The wage turning points in third tier countries varied considerably. For instance, Asian third tier countries experienced a decline in T&C at wage rates of around US$4,600, while the average level was as low as US$2,000 in African nations. Countries in the Latin American and Caribbean region could sustain their T&C exports at a wage rate level of US$10,000. These variations in wage turning points are a real puzzle.

The wage rate turning point in second tier countries and third tier Latin American and Caribbean region countries are, to some extent, comparable. But the puzzle deepens when we compare the wage rates of first tier countries (excluding Hong Kong and Singapore) with second tier and Latin

American countries. First tier countries' export is still increasing while second tier countries exited from global markets at a lower level of wages. This is true for countries in Latin America and the Caribbean region. A more surprising scenario is that the wage rate turning point for third tier Asian countries is US$4,600 whereas first tier countries in the same region still surviving even after the wages have risen to US$12,000.

Apparently, the rise in wage rates has not played a critical role in the export performance of T&C sectors in Africa. Otherwise, African third tier countries would have remained competitive in international markets. It did not happen – rather they exited from the global market at a very low level of wages (US$2,000). In no way are we concluding that wage rates have no role to play in influencing the export performance of this industry. We believe firmly that if wage rates in other manufacturing sectors are significantly higher than they are in the textiles and garments manufacturing sectors, the latter is expected to experience reversals. The exit of African and Asian second and third tier countries may not be due to wage increases in other manufacturing sectors. They might have exited because of factors that cannot be captured by econometric analysis. One needs to examine the role of other factors such as the role of institutional environment and international trade rules in explaining the premature exit of second and third countries from global business in the textiles and clothing sectors.

2.5   Summary and conclusions

This chapter has examined the export performance of the textiles and clothing (T&C) industry in a large number of developing countries. While several developing countries continue to be competitive in global markets, others could not remain in export markets and exited in the late 1980s. There is another category of nations, regarded as latecomers, who entered into international markets during the late 1980s or early 1990s and had to exit prematurely after a short period in the global markets. The main objective of the study is to identify and analyse the factors that have resulted in this scenario. It has been argued in the literature that technological capacity-building initiatives by nations played an important role is sustaining export performance while others argue that international trade rules such as the Lomé Convention between the EU and Africa, the Africa Growth and Opportunity Act (AGOA) between selected African countries and the USA, the Caribbean Basin Initiative between the USA and Caribbean region countries, and the ATC in the WTO regime have also influenced T&C exports in international markets.

While not disputing the findings of other studies (World Bank, 2002; Gibbon, 2003; Mortimore, 2002), we argue that technological policies at the national level, increases in wages, and a shifting of the manufacturing base from labour-intensive sector to a high profit- and capital-intensive sector can also influence the production and exports of T&C. National policies include tax incentives and technological policies that enable firms to import new technologies without following archaic procedures and also exemption of customs duties on imported machinery and equipment. It has not been possible to analyse the role of national policies due to a lack of information relating to such policies.

In the recent past, several countries, including Malaysia and Taiwan, have moved from T&C manufacturing to more high-tech sectors such as electronics. The shift has resulted in realizing higher GDP per capita than those who have been unable to do so. Hence GDP per capita has been assumed as a factor behind structural change that might have resulted in the downturn of T&C exports in several developing countries. We have analysed the roles of economic wealth, i.e., GDP per capita and wage rates in manufacturing in influencing export performance of developing countries. The data for the study come from three sources – namely COMTRADE, UNIDO, and WDI. We tried to include as many countries as possible in the analysis. However, we could get complete data for only 51 countries. In order to go into much deeper analysis, we grouped sample countries into three categories. The first group of countries, labelled first tier countries, are those that have maintained their competitiveness. Most of these countries entered into world market in the late 1960s or early 1970s and maintained their share of the world market. The second group of countries, labelled second tier countries, began to see a decline of their garments exports in the late 1980s. Almost all such countries ventured into exports markets in the late 1970s or early 1980s. The third tier countries are those that experienced a reversal in clothing exports in the late 1990s. Such countries are regarded as latecomers as they largely entered into T&C export business in the early 1990s.

The findings of this study suggest that the rise in GDP per capita has been one of the reasons for the downfall of the T&C industry in most developing countries. However, there are exceptions, such as Macao, Hong Kong, and Singapore. Despite having very high GDP per capita, T&C exports from these countries currently show no signs of decline. The most reasonable factor in Macao and Hong Kong seems to be the business model adopted by these countries. Apparel manufacturing firms in these countries might have shifted their manufacturing base to mainland China where wages are much lower than in the countries in question. Singapore might be following the same business model by subcontracting to Indonesia where wages are much lower. Alternatively, Singapore might still be competitive in the global markets due to technological capacity-building initiatives.

The association between the rise in wages and the export performance of the T&C industry is not uniform across all sample countries. Like the GDP–export performance relationship, despite having reached average wages of US$12,000 in first tier countries, excluding Hong Kong and Singapore, clothing exports still continue to increase. In other groups of countries, the decline has been experienced at a wage rate of around US$4,000–10,000 – except for third tier African countries. T&C exports in African countries declined at a wage rate of US$2,000. We can infer from the export performance of third tier African countries that they have exited from export markets principally as the result of the lack of technological capabilities rather than wage pressures. This shows that they came under competitive pressures sooner, and may not have built capacity, upgraded or become more innovative but exited the industry and/or shifted to a different industry. However, in most of these countries there was no big shift, just a decline in exports and this was premature – it took place before there were internal wage pressures to do so.

Several studies (Gibbon, 2003; Mattoo et al., 2002; Mortimore, 2003) investigated the impact of international trade rules on the export performance of the T&C sector in developing countries. The findings of Gibbon (2003) suggest that the response of AGOA has been significant for African countries. However, this has been largely confined to enterprises that followed a particular business model. Mattoo et al. (2002) found the mid-term benefit of AGOA to be an 8–11 per cent addition to current non-oil exports. They also estimated that the benefit could have been five times greater if no restrictive conditions had been imposed. Mortimore's (2003) study examined the role of tax incentives and low wages in the Caribbean basin. The study did not find sufficient evidence to suggest that preferential access to the North American markets designed to assist US apparel firms compete better against Asian imports in their own market. He concluded that it was primarily because the business model was based on illusory competitiveness rather than on the transfer of modern technologies. We have been unable to capture the role of international trade rules and the business model on the T&C export performance of developing countries. The case studies of a few representative countries could reveal the role played by factors that are not quantifiable.

Appendix Table 2.1   Sample countries

Country Classification Continent	First Tier	Second Tier	Third Tier	Total
Asia	Bangladesh, China, Hong Kong (China), Macao (China), Fiji, India, Indonesia, Pakistan, Singapore, Sri Lanka, Turkey	Republic of Korea	Malaysia, Philippines, Thailand	15
Middle East	Jordan	Kuwait	Israel	3

(Continued)

Appendix Table 2.1   (Continued)

Country Classification Continent	First Tier	Second Tier	Third Tier	Total
Africa	Malawi, Morocco, Tunisia	Ethiopia	Algeria, Benin, Egypt, Ghana, Kenya, Mauritius, Togo, Zimbabwe	12
Latin America and Caribbean	Bolivia, Colombia, Ecuador, El Salvador, Guatemala, Peru	Nicaragua, Uruguay, Venezuela, Barbados, Dominica, Grenada	Argentina, Brazil, Chile, Costa Rica, Honduras, Mexico, Panama, Jamaica, Trinidad and Tobago	21
Total	21	9	21	51

Notes

1. In the text the words 'clothing', 'apparel' and 'garments' have been used interchangeably.
2. Data sources: COMTRADE, SITC Rev. 1 code 65 excluding 651 and 654; http://unstat.un.org.
3. T&G stands for Textiles and Garments. T&G and T&C have been used interchangeably.
4. Trends in Figure 2.2 are significantly influenced by three countries, namely; Hong Kong (SAR China), Macao (SAR China), and Singapore. Although T&C exports from these countries are large, the actual manufacturing is done in main land China where wages are much lower compared to these countries. Maximum GDP in first tier countries excluding these three countries is GDP US$7,709. Hence the conclusion that despite attaining a very high GDP per capita (more than US$30,000) by first tier countries, there is no sign of declining T&C exports will have to interpreted with care. The same comments are applicable for wage rates.
5. It was found during a field survey that several Asian garments manufacturing firms were operating from African countries such as Kenya and Madagascar to exploit the benefits of low-production cost and provisions of ATC. Most of such firms started shifting their business to home countries after 1995 due to relaxation of quota restrictions.

References

Ernst, Dieter, Ganiatsos, Tom and Mytelka, Lynn (eds) (1998) *Technological Capabilities and Export Success in Asia*, London and New York: Routledge.

Gereffi, Gary, Spener, David and Bair, Jennifer (eds) (2002) *Free Trade and Uneven Development: The North American Apparel Industry after NAFTA*, Philadelphia: Temple University Press.

Gee, San and Kuo, Wen-Jeng (1998) 'Export Success and Technological Capability: Textiles and Electronics in Taiwan Province of China', in Ernst, Dieter, Ganiatsos, Tom and Mytelka, Lynn (eds), *Technological Capabilities and Export Success in Asia*, London and New York: Routledge, pp. 46–86.

Gibbon, Peter (2003) 'The African Growth and Opportunity Act and the Global Commodity Chain for Clothing', *World Development*, 31(11): 1809–27.

Lal, K. (2001) 'Information Technology and Global Competitiveness: A Case Study of Indian Garment Industry', in Pohjola, Matti (ed.), *Information Technology, Productivity, and Economic Growth: International Evidence and Implications for Economic Development*, New York: Oxford University Press, pp. 149–72.

Mattoo, Aditya, Roy, Devesh, and Subramanian, Arvind (2002) *The African Growth and Opportunity Act and its Rules of Origin: Generosity Undermined?* Development Research Group World Bank, Policy Research Working Paper no. 2908.

Mortimore, Michael (2003) *Illusory Competitiveness: The Apparel Assembly Model of the Caribbean Basin*, UNU-INTECH Discussion Paper No. 2003–11.

Mytelka, Lynn and Ernst, Dieter (1998) 'Catching Up, Keeping Up and Getting Ahead: the Korean Model Under Pressure', in Ernst, Dieter, Ganiatsos, Tom and Mytelka, Lynn (eds), *Technological Capabilities and Export Success in Asia*, London and New York: Routledge, pp. 87–156.

Park, Hoon (2005) 'Impact of the Changing US Trade Environment on Korea's Textiles & Clothing Industry and Suggestions', *KIET Industrial Economic Review*, 10(6): 27–34. Published by Korea Institute for Industrial Economics and Trade (KIET).

3

The Institutional Environment and the Textiles and Clothing Industry in China

Yanyun Zhao, Danbo Guo, Fang Chen, Feng Zhen, Zhi Li,
Enjing Li, Haodi Li and Qingping Zhang

Introduction

This chapter examines the efficacy of Chinese textiles and clothing policies and their relationship with the growth trajectories followed by the T&C industry over the course of the past two decades. While assessing the relevance of T&C policies it was considered vital to take into consideration all of the stakeholders in the industry. Hence in addition to analysing the policy initiatives we have conducted surveys of several large firms to understand the role played by state policies in technological capacity building. Consequently, the chapter is divided into three parts. The first part of this chapter discusses T&C policies and their impact on the performance of the sector. In Part II we present case studies of clothing sector firms while Part III presents case studies of textiles firms.

PART I: DEVELOPMENT OF CHINA'S TEXTILES AND CLOTHING SECTORS AND RELEVANT POLICIES

3.1.1 The development of China's T&C industry

Since the policies of reform and the opening up of the economy, China's T&C industry has transformed into a mature industrial system in which the upper, middle and lower streams of the T&C industry have been interconnected – cotton, fabric, poplin, clothing, and related machinery are mutually matched. Until 2003, China was ranked as the world's largest producer in terms of the output of major T&C products such as cotton yarn, cotton fabric, woollen yarn, woollen fabric, silk, clothing, chemical fibres, and so on, and the country also became the world's largest clothing producer and exporter. The performance of the T&C sectors since 1980 is presented in Table 3.1.

From Table 3.1, it can be seen that the actual scale of the textiles industry has been increasing continuously throughout this period, but that its share in terms of overall industrial output is decreasing. Regarding both imports

Table 3.1   Gross output, import, and export value of the T&C industry

Year	The output value of the textiles industry		Export value of textiles and clothing		Import value of textiles and clothing	
	US$ bill.	Share of total output (%)	US$ mill.	Share of total exports %	US$ mill.	Share of total imports (%)
1980	87.1	17.4	4,409	24.1	856	4.4
1981	100.3	19.4	4,544	20.7	1,398	6.3
1982	100.9	18.1	4,445	19.9	859	4.5
1983	110.9	18.0	4,966	22.3	567	2.7
1984	126.2	17.9	6,345	17.6	960	3.5
1985	145.7	17.6	6,440	23.5	1,622	3.8
1986	156.1	17.4	8,570	27.7	1,634	3.8
1987	175.5	17.0	11,338	28.8	1,856	4.3
1988	199.2	16.4	13,085	27.5	2,416	4.4
1989	213.8	16.5	15,138	28.8	2,883	4.9
1990	332.5	16.1	16,786	27.0	2,796	5.2
1991	365.9	15.6	20,153	28.0	3,750	5.9
1992	439.9	15.6	25,335	29.8	7,097	8.8
1993	551.6	15.6	27,132	29.6	7,297	7.0
1994	665.9	15.6	35,548	29.4	9,116	7.9
1995	703.5	13.3	37,967	25.5	11,883	9.0
1996	660.6	12.9	37,095	24.6	13,020	9.4
1997	696.7	12.2	45,577	24.9	13,328	9.4
1998	684.4	11.9	42,889	23.3	12,078	8.6
1999	742.5	11.5	43,062	22.1	12,088	7.3
2000	819.6	9.6	52,078	20.9	13,887	6.2
2001	921.1	10.0	53,280	20.0	13,720	5.6
2002	1,019.5	10.0	61,769	19.0	14,362	4.9
2003	1,287.8	9.0	80,484	18.4	15,586	3.8
2004	1,632.6	7.3	97,385	16.4	16,804	3.0

Note: The output values of 1978–1989 and 1990–2000 are based on constant prices at 1980 and 1990 respectively; the figures for 2003 and 2004 are based on current prices; the value for 2004 comes from the 1st Economic Census.
Source: National Bureau of Statistics of China, annual data of industrial enterprise statistical report.

and exports, both shares in the national value experienced a trend of 'rising then falling', and the turning points began in the mid-1990s.

By 2003, the total amount of fibre processed had reached 20 million tons (the amount of fibre actually manufactured in China was 17.2 million tons), which constituted 30 per cent of total global volume and was almost six times the figure achieved in 1980. In terms of the output of major T&C products, such as cotton yarn, cotton fabric, woollen yarn, woollen fabric, silk, chemical fibres and clothing, China was ranked number one in the world. The output in volume of T&C products is shown in Table 3.2.

Table 3.2 Output volume changes of the main T&C products

Products	Unit	Output		Growth rate (%)
		1980	2003	
Chemical fibre	10,000 tons	45.0	1181.1	26.2
Yarn	10,000 tons	292.6	983.7	3.4
Cloth	100 mill. m.	134.8	374.6	2.8
Printed and dyed fabric	100 mill. m.	80.7	319.0	4.0
Knitting wool	10,000 tons	5.7	65.7	11.5
Woollen piece goods	100 mill. m.	1.0	4.4	4.4
Ramie cloth & linen Cloth	100 mill. m.	0.4	3.7	9.0
Silk	10,000 tons	3.5	11.1	3.1
Silk products	100 mill. m.	7.6	63.3	8.3
Loom clothing	100 mill. piece	9.4	136.7	14.5
Knitrted fabric clothing	100 mill. piece	35.0	225.0	6.4
Technical textiles	10,000 tons	53.0 (1988)	261.8	4.9

Source: China National Textile and Apparel Council, China Textile Industry Development Report 2003/2004.

The domestic market share of T&C sectors is presented in Table 3.3, which shows that the market share of the textiles industry has been decreasing from year to year – from 12.20 per cent in 1985 to 4.98 per cent in 1995 – with a slight increase between 1994 and 2000. In the period from 1985 to 1995, the average annual growth rate of sales income is 16.02 per cent, and that of the period between 1995 and 2005 is 11.26 per cent, indicating that over the past decade the T&C industry has experienced a slower rate of increase.

When examining the Chinese clothing sector, the annual growth rate of sales income between 1985 and 1995 is shown to be 23.65 per cent, while between 1995 and 2005 it was at the much lower rate of 13.51 per cent. On the other hand, Table 3.3 shows that between 1985 and 2000, the scale of the T&C industry actually expanded continuously. Therefore, the declining market share of the textiles industry and an almost unchanged share of the clothing industry demonstrate a faster growth of total industrial sales income.

Labour productivity and value added in the sector are presented in Table 3.4. As is shown in the table, labour productivity in the textiles and clothing sectors and of the whole nation has been increasing during the period 1993 to 2005. The figures for these two sectors are close to each other, but consistently below the national value, indicating that the textiles and clothing sectors have similar – but relatively low – levels of productivity.

The value added in both sectors follows a similar trend as that seen in respect of labour productivity. Between 1993 and 2005, the annual growth rate of value added in the textiles sector was 10.77 per cent, lower than the rate observed in the clothing sector (13.07 per cent). But during the period

Table 3.3   Domestic market share of T&C sectors, 1985–2005

Year	Textiles		Clothing	
	Sales income (Y100 mill.)	Market share (%)	Sales income (Y100 mill.)	Market share (%)
1985	963.48	12.20	161.11	2.04
1986	1,060.70	11.83	171.06	1.91
1987	1,258.19	11.55	203.60	1.87
1988	1,587.03	11.33	255.79	1.83
1989	1,790.53	11.30	307.29	1.94
1990	1,936.42	11.53	344.23	2.05
1991	2,199.67	10.68	438.13	2.13
1992	2,424.92	9.37	560.93	2.17
1993	3,101.00	8.14	818.00	2.15
1994	3,654.00	8.62	1,101.00	2.6
1995	4,257.00	8.04	1,346.00	2.54
1996	4,118.00	7.10	1,491.00	2.57
1997	4,160.00	6.56	1,600.00	2.52
1998	3,863.00	6.02	1,779.00	2.77
1999	4,148.00	5.94	1,847.00	2.64
2000	4,810.45	5.72	2,133.01	2.53
2001	5,209.10	5.56	2,415.97	2.58
2002	6,038.59	5.52	2,725.50	2.49
2003	7,495.51	5.24	3,239.42	2.26
2004	10,021.11	5.04	3,802.17	1.91
2005	12,374.53	4.98	4,780.00	1.92

Source: Compilation of 50 Years Statistics Data of China Industry, Traffic and Energy (1949–1999); 2000–2005 Industrial Annual Report.

between 2002 and 2005, the former developed faster than the latter, with an annual growth rate of 27.34 per cent compared to 23.92 per cent.

Table 3.5 presents the assets, profitability, and employment opportunities in the textiles sector. It shows an increasing trend of the total assets of China's textiles sector under current prices. Note that during the past 20 years, product prices have not experienced substantial fluctuations, rather they have been the subject of a smooth increase. Thus, it is reasonable to assume that the actual assets value of the textiles sector is increasing continuously. The average annual growth rate (current prices) has been 14.86 per cent.

Table 3.5 illustrates an upward trend in the share of the Chinese textiles industry's total assets in the nation's total assets up to the year 1992 – from 8.1 per cent in 1985 to 9.5 per cent in 1992. However, after that year, this figure began to decrease, falling to just 4.2 per cent in 2005. Several factors could be seen as contributing to this trend. In the 1980s, the textiles industry achieved a significant development and an increasing share of its assets.

Table 3.4 Value added and labour productivity, 1993–2005

Year	Textile		Clothing & other fibre products		National total	
	Value added (Y100 mill)	Labour productivity (Yuan/ person)	Value added (Y100 mill)	Labour productivity (Yuan/ person)	Value added (Y100 mill)	Labour productivity (Yuan/ person)
1993	950.86	10523.25	325.23	12670.64	12842.63	15473.31
1994	1117.31	12229.08	355.12	13032.40	14700.06	17270.09
1995	898.45	10350.45	347.29	12959.55	15446.13	18476.85
1996	1046.37	12910.82	449.52	17224.31	18208.79	22240.99
1997	1116.67	15291.82	463.79	19019.48	19835.18	25194.73
1998	1017.30	17600.04	481.93	22762.61	19421.93	31346.88
1999	1117.12	21867.01	505.97	24963.98	21564.74	37148.24
2000	1272.84	26359.34	592.02	27455.36	25394.80	45679.36
2001	1387.52	29057.40	688.12	29026.03	28329.37	52062.36
2002	1569.10	32747.57	746.08	28074.51	32994.75	59765.95
2003	1906.70	38198.17	916.54	31693.35	41990.23	73044.65
2004	2647.95	45039.23	1086.36	32730.54	54805.10	82761.03
2005	3240.19	54829.26	1419.86	41029.30	72186.99	104680.12

Note: 1. The value added of Textile & Clothing industries in 2004 is estimated under the same value added rate of 2005.
2. Data of value added have been published since 1993.
Source: Compilation of 50 Years Statistics Data of China Industry, Traffic and Energy (1949–1999): labour productivity = value added/average number of employed persons.

But since 1990, the contradiction between the overproduction in the former years and the unreasonable structure became increasingly apparent. Moreover, the rapid development of China's industry resulted in a considerable increase in the total level of total assets, meaning that the share of the textiles sector has declined year by year.

With respect to sales profits, in the 1980s the textiles sector was enjoying a net, but unstable earning, which was fluctuating at around 10 billion RMB Yuan. The proportion to the total profit of industry reached its peak at 17.51 per cent in 1981 – and remained above 10 per cent in the following years. However, at the beginning of the 1990s, the profits of the textiles industry began to decrease. In some years, it even recorded a loss. However, in 1997, in order to relieve state-owned enterprises, the government adopted a series of measures to deepen the reforms in the textiles sector, and to accelerate the process of structure adjustment. After several years' efforts, the proportion of textiles profit declined in the year 2000, with a value of 10.99 per cent. In the following few years, although the proportion decreased to a certain extent, the overall profit is increasing.

Table 3.5 Productive elements of the textiles sector

Year	Total assets (Y100 mill.)	Total profits (Y100 mill.)	Number of enterprises (units)	Employment (10,000 persons)	Proportion of assets to total industry (%)	Proportion of profits to total industry (%)
1980	–	100.90	14,066	340.10	–	14.64
1981	–	118.80	15,656	389.00	–	17.51
1982	–	87.90	16,633	412.10	–	12.57
1983	–	74.40	16,878	423.50	–	9.72
1984	–	72.20	18,088	411.50	–	8.55
1985	564.96	75.75	18,846	721.32	8.1	8.15
1986	662.30	74.31	21,181	–	8.1	8.47
1987	799.73	99.98	23,026	852.86	8.4	9.95
1988	971.23	120.72	24,017	896.32	8.7	10.15
1989	1,213.29	94.45	24,760	913.64	9.0	9.44
1990	1,465.86	29.85	24,584	928.43	9.2	5.33
1991	1,757.46	−0.43	24,596	958.35	9.3	−0.07
1992	2,688.54	13.06	23,831	934.78	9.5	1.34
1993	3,524.51	−4.73	24,613	903.58	7.6	−0.30
1994	4,565.60	33.97	24,774	913.65	7.3	1.89
1995	5,505.27	−41.30	25,686	868.03	6.9	−2.53
1996	5,783.35	−71.30	24,297	810.46	6.4	−4.79
1997	6,098.88	−26.52	21,844	730.24	5.9	−1.56
1998	5,891.74	−32.33	11,276	578.01	5.4	−2.22
1999	5,872.50	38.58	10,981	510.87	5.0	1.69
2000	5,917.01	482.88	10,968	158.41	4.7	10.99
2001	6,196.26	477.51	12,065	164.33	4.6	10.09
2002	6,680.47	479.15	13,248	170.23	4.6	8.28
2003	7,801.29	499.16	14,863	195.55	4.6	5.99
2004	9,352.12	587.92	24,192	247.48	4.3	4.93
2005	10,357.97	590.96	22,569	316.51	4.2	3.99

Source: Compilation of 50 Years Statistics Data of China Industry, Traffic and Energy (1949–1999); 2000–2005 Industrial Annual Report.

Table 3.5 shows parallel changes in the number of textiles firms and the level of employment. Over the course of the past two decades or so, the general trend followed by these two indicators is 'rising and then falling, before rising again after 2001'. The textiles sector was at its greatest extent in 1992, before experiencing a long period of decline. This was partly because some enterprises were closed as the result of heavy losses. From 1997 to 1999, with the support of government reforms, the total scale of textiles enterprises reached its lowest point. Until 2001, enterprises' economic condition began to improve so that the scale expanded accordingly.

Table 3.6 Productive elements of the clothing sector

Year	Total assets (Y100 mill.)	Total profits (Y100 mill.)	Number of enterprises (units)	Employment (10,000 persons)	Proportion of assets to total industry (%)	Proportion of profits to total industry (%)
1980	–	9.60	19,852	–	–	1.39
1981	–	10.10	21,079	–	–	1.49
1982	–	8.40	21,257	–	–	1.20
1983	–	9.40	20,580	–	–	1.23
1984	–	10.60	21,694	–	–	1.26
1985	79.87	13.30	18,196	207.29	1.15	1.43
1986	96.65	10.24	20,590	–	1.19	1.17
1987	114.67	11.96	18,965	217.58	1.21	1.19
1988	138.86	15.43	18,017	216.72	1.25	1.30
1989	165.87	15.45	17,301	216.96	1.22	1.54
1990	195.28	12.51	17,241	227.75	1.22	2.23
1991	252.28	13.90	17,499	242.89	1.34	2.16
1992	444.66	20.27	16,706	246.83	1.57	2.08
1993	724.92	28.94	17,921	256.68	1.56	1.81
1994	1,009.12	32.55	18,439	272.49	1.61	1.81
1995	1,260.49	24.39	20007	267.98	1.59	1.49
1996	1,397.26	33.13	19,502	260.98	1.55	2.22
1997	1,526.76	38.14	17,224	243.85	1.48	2.24
1998	1,581.18	41.76	6,768	211.72	1.45	2.86
1999	1,633.74	61.76	6,611	202.68	1.40	2.70
2000	1,758.77	86.44	7,064	215.63	1.39	1.97
2001	1,905.82	100.68	8,037	237.07	1.41	2.13
2002	2,078.57	111.19	9,061	265.75	1.42	1.92
2003	2,377.25	132.57	9,717	289.19	1.41	1.59
2004	2,805.13	154.60	12,029	331.91	1.30	1.30
2005	3,188.77	206.16	11,865	346.06	1.30	1.39

Source: Compilation of 50 Years Statistics Data of China Industry, Traffic and Energy (1949–1999); 2000–2005 Industrial Annual Report.

The productive elements of the clothing sector are presented in Table 3.6. Similar to the condition of the textiles sector, the total assets of the clothing sector also show an increasing trend (whether or not the influence of price fluctuation is excluded). The share in the national assets increased smoothly during the period 1986–92, and remained almost stable after 1992 (albeit with a slight decrease). The profit element has experienced some fluctuations, but, in general, the value of profits increased continuously and no losses occurred. The share of total profits in the national value was relatively stable in the 1980s – at between 1 per cent and 1.5 per cent – but it fluctuated substantially in the 1990s, with peaks in 1990 and 1998. After 1998, the downward trend became apparent.

Table 3.6 shows that the overall scale of clothing sector enterprises had experienced similar changes to those seen in the textiles sector. Before the reforms in 1997, the total number of enterprises had decreased slowly, with a slight increase in the number of employed persons. When enterprises adopted the policy of reducing the level of personnel to increasing benefit, the scale of the industry began to decrease sharply. After the year 2000, as a result of further reform, the economic condition of enterprises improved significantly; therefore, the total scale increased year on year.

3.1.2 Analysis of the development of the T&C industry

Since the introduction of economic reform and the opening up of its economy, China has experienced four phases of T&C development: 1980–1989 (Steady Development Phase), 1990–1995 (Rapid Development Phase), 1996–1999 (Adjustment Phase), and 2000–2003 (Recovering Development Phase). During the period 1980–2005, the T&C industry expanded rapidly and played a major role in accumulating construction funds for the nation. The total value of T&C industry output in 2002 was 13.9 times greater than that in 1980 and the amount of tax revenue reached 490 billion Yuan. In the same year, China's T&C product exports accounted for 17.53 per cent of total global exports, jumping from being only the 9th largest exporter to being the world's largest exporter. Today, China undoubtedly plays the pivotal rule in the world T&C raw materials, processing, and trade markets.

3.1.2.1 Development of the T&C industry in the 1980s

The 1980s was a period of rapid development for the T&C industry. Given the impetus of China's reform and its opening up to the outside world, the huge domestic demand, and the background of structural adjustments in the world's textiles industry, the T&C sector grasped the rare opportunity provided by both the internal and external environment. Its total output value, beginning at 87.1 billion Yuan in 1980, reached 332.5 billion Yuan in 1990, with an annual growth rate of 14.33 per cent.

The abolition of cloth tickets[1] in 1983 indicated that China had met the domestic needs for basic living. After this time, the T&C industry fixed its sights on both the international and domestic markets, a change from its original concentration on meeting domestic consumers' needs. Over the course of the following years, China gradually cancelled the monopoly on the purchase and marketing of T&C products, and adopted liberalized operation/management for raw materials in the T&C market (with the exception of cotton and silkworm cocoons). With these measures, the character of market competition in the T&C industry became evident.

In the mid-1980s, China proposed an export-oriented development strategy for the textiles sector. As a result, the degree of dependence on foreign trade increased gradually. In the meantime, when the power for the examination and approval of investment projects began to be granted to the authorities at lower levels, the investment resources became diversified. Township enterprises and three types of foreign-invested enterprises[2] accordingly expanded and shared a significant part in the T&C market together with state-owned enterprises.

During this period, China became the world's largest T&C producer. The amount of total processed fibre rose from 3.41 million tons in 1980 to 6.3 million tons in 1990, with an average annual growth of 6.33 per cent, which was higher than the average world level. The global share of China's processed fibre also increased to 16.6 per cent from 11.4 per cent (1980).

3.1.2.2   Development of the T&C industry in the 1990s

In the 1990s China's T&C industry experienced one of its fastest periods of development. In the period between 1991 and 2000, total output value reached 819.6 billion Yuan compared with a figure of 365.9 billion in 1991 – an annual growth rate of around 15 per cent. Paid tax increased to 273.1 billion, with an annual average of 27.3 billion. The production capacity of the industry also improved dramatically. The total volume of processed fibre exceeded 10 million tons in 1999, accounting at that time for 20 per cent of world production. Since 1995, China has been the world's largest producer of cotton yarn, cotton fabric, clothing, chemical fibre and knitted fabrics and is also ranked second in the output of wool yarn. China also became the world's largest producer of chemical fibres in 1997 (46.09 million tons), after overtaking both the USA and Japan.

Between 1990 and 1995, the export of China's T&C products increased rapidly, rising from $16.79 billion to $37.97 billion – an average annual growth of 27.3 per cent. Its contribution to the value of global exports also increased – from 7.48 per cent in 1990 to 13.2 per cent in 1995. At this time, clothing became the T&C's industry's major export, with a share of exports growing from 40.9 per cent in 1990 to 69.7 per cent in 1995.

However, because of the over-expanded low-level processing capacity in the 1980s, at the beginning of the 1990s, contradictions began to emerge between the overproduction and unreasonable product structure (Xu, 1996). At the same time, raw material prices rose significantly due to the lag in the development of T&C materials. This resulted in an unfavourable financial condition for T&C firms, especially for the state-owned enterprises, many of which began to experience net losses after 1993. In 1996, the loss reached its peak at 8.3 billion Yuan, before falling to 4.5 billion in 1997 and 2 billion in 1998. Since 1999, T&C firms started to become profitable.

In response to this situation, China's T&C industry adopted a series of reforms and adjustments in order to control the overall output volume, optimize the stock, promote labour productivity, and transform the enterprises' management structures. In 1997, the Chinese government issued a slew of supporting policies to accelerate the pace of T&C reform and adjustment. In the following three years, the T&C sector experienced a major adjustment of productive capacity. Particularly noticeable is the decrease in silk reeling machines – from 4.1 million spindles in 1995 to 3.2 million in 1998. In the year 1998–99, the total eliminated backwards productive capacity were 9.06 million spindles, 86.5 per cent of which were supplied by the state-owned large and medium-sized enterprises. In the meantime, these enterprises accordingly laid off and made appropriate arrangements for around 1.16 million workers. From 1999, after three years of decreasing the number of spindles and reducing personnel, most of China's state-owned T&C enterprises emerged from their financial plight and began to make profits, entering a period of industrial upgrading.

Great strides were also made in the area of product structure upgrading. The chemical fibres and clothing industry developed rapidly due to the effects, respectively, of market competition and state support. As a result, the share of cotton textiles, woollen textiles, and plant fibre textiles experienced a gradual decline. The proportion of chemical fibre to the total amount of processed textile fibre increased from 35 per cent (in 1995) to 60 per cent (in 2000) while differential polyester fibre proportion reached 20 per cent at the same time. Furthermore, the capacity of print-dyeing and finishing had also improved substantially since 1995. The pattern, brand, and quality of T&C products were also promoted widely. Another structural change comes from the proportion of clothing, home textile and technical textile industry – which adjusted from 80:13:7 in 1995 to a ratio of 67:20:13 in 2000. Focus of export products has also shifted from its original emphasis on the primary product (gauze, etc.) to clothing and other final products – the export proportion of clothing rose from 20 per cent in 1978 to 69.5 per cent in 2000.

In terms of fixed asset investment, there has been a continuous decreasing trend since the 1980s. The main factor contributing to this phenomenon was the reform of the financing system (Hong 2000), and the increasingly diversified investment sources for the competitive T&C industry. From 1999 onwards, the Chinese government has almost entirely ceased making investments in its T&C infrastructure.

The exports of China's T&C industry in this period continued to grow rapidly. Following the adoption of an open-door policy and an export-oriented development strategy, China's share of the global market increased rapidly and remained in first place for the seven years from 1994. The exports of T&C products reached US$52 billion in 2000, constituting 21 per cent of China's total exports and 13 per cent of global exports, growing at an annual rate of 16.2 per cent since 1991. In 2000 the export of textiles products and clothing were US$20.58 billion and US$41.19 billion, accounting respectively for 9 per cent and 18 per cent of the global T&C trade value.

Table 3.7 Import–export of China's T&C product in 1999–2004 ($100 mill.)

Year	Item	Total value of export & imports	Exports	Imports	Balance
1999	National value	3,606.5	1,949.3	1,657.2	292.1
1999	T&C industry	551.5	430.6	120.9	309.7
1999	Share of T&C industry	15.3	22.1	7.3	106.0
2000	National value	4,743.1	2,492.1	2,251	241.2
2000	T&C industry	659.7	520.8	138.9	381.9
2000	Share of T&C industry	13.9	20.9	6.2	158.4
2001	National value	5,097.7	2,661.6	2,436.2	225.4
2001	T&C industry	670.0	532.8	137.2	395.6
2001	Share of T&C industry	13.1	20.0	5.6	175.5
2002	National value	6,207.9	3,255.7	2,952.2	303.5
2002	T&C industry	761.3	617.7	143.6	474.1
2002	Share of T&C industry	12.3	19.0	4.9	156.2
2003	National value	8,512.1	4,383.7	4,128.4	255.3
2003	T&C industry	960.7	804.8	155.9	649.0
2003	Share of T&C industry	11.3	18.4	3.8	254.2
2004	National value	11,547.4	5,933.6	5,613.8	319.8
2004	T&C industry	1,141.9	973.9	168.0	805.8
2004	Share of T&C industry	9.9	16.4	3.0	252.0

3.1.2.3 The development of the T&C industry in the twenty-first century

In the twenty-first century, with the improvement of people's living standards and the gradual elimination of quotas, China's T&C industry began to face huge demand from both domestic and international customers. Over the course of the first four years of this century, the total value of trade soared to US$114.2 billion in 2004 – exceeding US$100 billion for the first time. Exports reached US$97.385 billion, with a year-on-year growth rate of 21.01 per cent. This meant that the T&C trade surplus was $80.581 billion – 2.52 times that of the country's overall trade balance. Trade balance data for the period from 1999 to 2004 are presented in Table 3.7.

3.1.2.4 The share of China's T&C industry in the global market

In 1986 the global market share of China's T&C sector was only 5.35 per cent, a figure that increased rapidly to 15.4 per cent in 2002 – an annual growth rate of 64 per cent. The share in 1995 and 1996 decreased by a certain amount because the export tax rebate (ETR) rate was reduced three times between 1 July 1995 and 1 July 1996 – from 17 per cent to 19 per cent – which had a negative effect on exports. Generally speaking, over time China's T&C industry assumed a greater share in the global market, which indicated that China

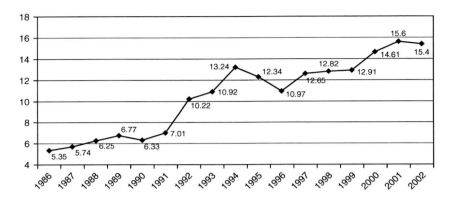

Figure 3.1   Global market share of China's T&C exports, 1986–2002
Source: GATT & WTO Annual Report. Online at www.wto.org/english/nes_e/_booksp_e/anrep_e/.

has enormous competitive strength in this sector (Wang & Li 2005). The global share of Chinese T&C exports is presented in Figure 3.1.

3.1.3   The competitiveness of China's textiles and clothing sectors

3.1.3.1   Trade Competitiveness Index in China's T&C sectors

The global competitiveness of a country's industries is based on the revealed advantages of a particular industry in one country when compared to industries in other countries. Overall, there are various factors that affect the competitiveness of the T&C industry in China: the workforce, the techniques, the level of business administration and the international economic environment. At present, several revealed indexes are used regularly to reflect the changes of the world competitiveness in an industry, including the Trade Competitiveness Index (TC), the Revealed Comparative Advantage Index (RCA), the Net Export Index, the Labour Compression Index (LCI). Of these, the TC and the RCA are based on the theory of international trade to measure the relative advantage of exports and the intensity of world competitiveness. In this section, the empirical analysis of TC index in China's T&C industry is presented.

The TC, also called the Trade Specialty Competitiveness Index, can be indicated as the balance of one country's exports and imports divided by the level of total trade. Formally, the index can be presented as:

$$TC = (\text{exports} - \text{imports})/(\text{exports} + \text{imports})$$

This index reflects the relative scale of the net exports or net imports. The numerical value of the index is between -1 and $+1$. If the value of the TC

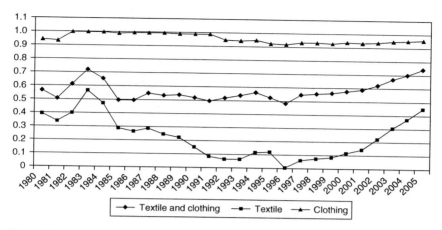

Figure 3.2 Trade competitiveness index of textiles and clothing, 1980–2005

index is positive, it indicates that this country's productivity is higher than international standards and the world competitiveness is stronger, while the opposite is true if the value of the TC index is < 0. If it equals to 0, it indicates that the productivity is completely the same as the international standards and the foreign trade just exchanges different kinds of products with the world. In addition, in order to conduct a profound analysis of China's T&C industry, this section uses the general standard of the TC index. If TC > 0.8, it suggests that the industry/product have the strongest competitiveness. Similarly, a TC value of 0.5–0.8, 0–0.5, 0, −1 to −0.8, −0.8 to −0.5 and −0.5 to 0 indicates stronger, strong, intermediate, weakest, weaker and weak industry/product competitiveness, respectively. As a monomial index, the TC index cannot accurately reflect the actual superior or inferior situation of the industry/product competitiveness, because the policies encouraging the exports and discouraging the imports are ubiquitous in China. As a static analysis, however, it can be used to examine the competitiveness or the relative advantage at special time and special protection. The TC index of China's textiles and clothing sectors calculated for aggregate and disaggregated levels are displayed in Figure 3.2.

As is evident from Figure 3.2, both the textiles and the clothing sectors enjoy comparative advantages. The TC value of textiles is between 0 and 0.6, with significant fluctuations. In the 1980s, the TC index of textiles showed a declining trend, with the exception of 1981–83, with an average value of 0.348. In the 1990s, the value of TC was relatively low, at around 0.8. It had been increasing steadily over the period between 2000 and 2005, and the average annual growth rate exceed 100 per cent. This is related to a significant increase in the level of exports. Compared with textiles, the TC value of

Table 3.8 Trade competitiveness index of T&C industry in selected countries

Year	1980	1985	1990	1995	2000	2002	2005
China	0.568	0.498	0.519	0.523	0.576	0.622	0.741
	stronger	stronger	stronger	stronger	stronger	stronger	stronger
India	0.930	0.882	0.903	0.920	0.906	0.857	0.763
	stronger	strongest	strongest	strongest	strongest	strongest	stronger
Indonesia	−0.209	0.637	0.566	0.64	0.729	0.763	0.824
	weak	stronger	stronger	stronger	stronger	stronger	stronger
Japan	0.273	0.182	−0.334	−0.525	−0.531	−0.546	−0.586
	strong	strong	weak	weaker	weaker	weaker	weaker
Thailand	0.542	0.619	0.603	0.622	0.529	0.529	0.514
	stronger	stronger	stronger	stronger	stronger	stronger	stronger
Turkey	0.712	0.878	0.782	0.646	0.621	0.595	0.567
	stronger	strongest	stronger	stronger	stronger	stronger	stronger
Hong Kong	0.296	0.242	0.160	0.09	0.118	0.113	0.121
	strong	strong	strong	strong	strong	strong	strong
Pakistan	0.658	0.823	0.933	0.959	0.961	0.945	0.911
	stronger	stronger	strongest	strongest	strongest	strongest	strongest
United States	−0.308	−0.729	−0.632	−0.574	−0.619	−0.667	−0.710
	weaker	weakest	weakest	weakest	weakest	weakest	weakest

Source: http://www.wto.org.

clothing is higher, at about 0.96. It implies that the global competitiveness of clothing is stronger than textiles and that it depends to a larger degree on the low cost of the labour force. In general, the TC value of textiles and clothing as a whole is relatively high. The average value is 0.57. Its fluctuating trend is almost the same as the TC index of textiles. Since 1998, the T&C industry has experienced a developing period which has had the effect of improving the structure of the industry. Therefore, the competitiveness of the T&C industry improved over this period.

The TC indexes of the textiles and clothing industry at both aggregated and disaggregated levels in the primary T&C trade countries are reported in Tables 3.8, 3.9 and 3.9A. It can be seen that the TC values of T&C as a whole in China, India, Thailand, Turkey and Pakistan are all greater than 0.5, indicating that all of these countries have stronger comparative advantages. Indonesia also has comparative advantage – with the exception of 1980. The value of TC in Hong Kong ranges from 0.1 to 0.3, while United States and Japan change from high competitiveness to low competitiveness. Regarding the trade competitiveness aspect of textiles, it can be divided into three groups: the first group includes India and Pakistan, which have stronger competitiveness, with TC value > 0.5. The second group includes China, Indonesia, Japan, Thailand and Turkey, which have strong competitiveness and TC

Table 3.9 Trade competitiveness index of the textiles sector in selected countries

Year	1980	1985	1990	1995	2000	2002	2005
China	0.396	0.286	0.154	0.121	0.114	0.223	0.452
	strong	strong	strong	strong	strong	strong	strong
India	0.895	0.788	0.802	0.853	0.825	0.741	0.577
	stronger	stronger	strongest	strongest	strongest	stronger	stronger
Indonesia	−0.651	0.312	0.225	0.349	0.474	0.535	0.640
	stronger	strong	strong	strong	strong	stronger	stronger
Japan	0.509	0.447	0.174	0.091	0.175	0.142	0.086
	stronger	strong	strong	strong	strong	strong	strong
Thailand	0.309	0.291	0.016	0.116	0.092	0.122	0.164
	strong	strong	strong	strong	strong	strong	strong
Turkey	0.623	0.757	0.435	0.165	0.267	0.198	0.229
	stronger	stronger	strong	strong	strong	strong	strong
Hong Kong	−0.253	−0.17	−0.107	−0.09	−0.01	0.015	0.001
	weak	weak	weak	weak	weak	strong	strong
Pakistan	0.626	0.784	0.909	0.944	0.944	0.923	0.876
	stronger	stronger	strongest	strongest	strongest	strongest	strongest
United States	0.193	−0.324	−0.144	−0.172	−0.187	−0.228	−0.291
	strong	weaker	weaker	weaker	weaker	weaker	weaker

Source: http://www.wto.org.

Table 3.9A Trade competitiveness index of the clothing sector in selected countries

Year	1980	1985	1990	1995	2000	2002	2005
China	0.944	0.988	0.990	0.923	0.936	0.936	0.957
	strongest	strongest	strongest	strongest	strongest	strongest	strongest
India	0.999	0.999	0.998	0.997	0.992	0.990	0.984
	strongest	strongest	strongest	strongest	strongest	strongest	strongest
Indonesia	0.939	0.984	0.981	0.984	0.984	0.979	0.972
	strongest	strongest	strongest	strongest	strongest	strongest	strongest
Japan	−0.518	−0.478	−0.878	−0.945	−0.947	−0.948	−0.957
	weaker	weaker	weakest	weakest	weakest	weakest	weakest
Thailand	0.978	0.985	0.979	0.967	0.933	0.920	0.901
	strongest	strongest	strongest	strongest	strongest	strongest	strongest
Turkey	0.999	0.997	0.990	0.984	0.922	0.932	0.875
	strongest	strongest	strongest	strongest	strongest	strongest	strongest
Hong Kong	0.755	0.602	0.381	0.255	0.204	0.177	0.194
	stronger	stronger	strong	strong	strong	strong	strong
Pakistan	0.995	0.989	0.999	0.998	0.996	0.993	0.985
	strongest	strongest	strongest	strongest	strongest	strongest	strongest
United States	−0.692	−0.908	−0.826	−0.723	−0.772	−0.834	−0.882
	weakest	Weakest	weakest	weakest	weakest	weakest	weakest

Source: http://www.wto.org.

values > 0.1. The third group includes Hong Kong and USA, which have weak competitiveness and lower TC values of −0.3 − 0.015 and −0.6 − 0.9, respectively. Regarding trade competitiveness in the clothing industry, most of the countries – with the exception of Japan and the United States – have comparative advantages.

Based on the results of the foregoing analysis, it is clear that China's T&C industry is still the world leader in terms of trade competitiveness, although it is now being confronted by a relatively complex trade environment. Each year, China exports large amounts of T&C products to Japan, accounting, for example, for 73.4 per cent of Japan's T&C imports market. In the middle- and low-end product fields, Japan cannot compete against China. But it takes a vital position in the top-grade field which is full of further processing and high-quality T&C products (Fu, 2006). In the same way, the United States also gains a large amount of monopoly profits in the international trade of T&C products tied to labour productivity advantages. Otherwise developing countries, such as China, India, Pakistan and Thailand, benefit from the advantages of labour force, land and nature resources. All of these countries also have comparative advantages, becoming major competitors to China in low-end markets.

3.1.3.2 *Revealed Comparative Advantage Index in China's T&C sectors*

The Revealed Comparative Advantage Index (RCA), also called the Relative Export Performance Index, is an indicator of the trade of a particular product/industry by the share of that product/industry in the country's total exports relative to the product or industry's share of total world exports and was derived by Balassa (1965). The index can be presented as:

$$RCA_{ij} = \left(X_{ij}/\Sigma_j X_{ij}\right) / \left(\Sigma_i X_i / \Sigma_i \Sigma_j X_i\right)$$

Where RCA_{ij} represents the revealed comparative advantage index for industry j of country i, X_{ij} is exports of industry j of country i, $\Sigma_j X_{ij}$ is the world total exports of industry i, $\Sigma_i X_i$ the total exports of country i, $\Sigma_i \Sigma_j X_i$ is the total world exports. According to the standard of the Japan External Trade Organization (JETRO), the values of RCA > 2.5, 1.25 < RCA < 2.5, 0.8 < RCA < 1.25 and RCA < 0.8 denote strongest, stronger, middle, and weak competitiveness. It utilizes the trade structure and trade dependence relation to interpret the realization of the international competitiveness in trade, which accords with the theory of comparative advantage.

This section calculates the RCA of T&C industries in the aggregate and for each industry in 1980 and 1989–2005. On the condition of using individual index, we also compare the RCA index of different countries for the sake of conducting a sufficient analysis of China's world competitiveness. The RCA index of China's textiles and clothing at aggregate and disaggregated levels are displayed in Figure 3.3.

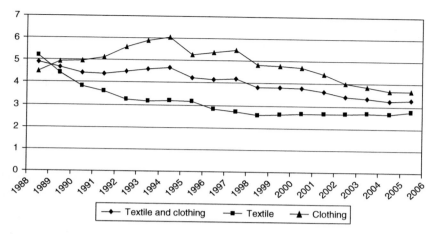

Figure 3.3 Revealed comparative advantage index of T&C sectors

The figure illustrates that the international trade competitiveness of T&C industries at aggregate or disaggregated levels are all powerful, with all of them having values of RCA > 2.5. However, the competitive advantage of clothing is stronger than that of textiles, and their values are 4.8 and 3.1, respectively. It can be seen that the results of RCA analysis is almost the same as in the case of TC. China has competitive advantages in labour-intensive industries due to the abundant labour resources (26.3 per cent of the world's labour resources) and economic restructuring. However, unlike the results produced by the TC analysis, the RCA of textiles and clothing industries and the industry as a whole assume a declining trend over the period between 1980 and 2005, accounting for 46 per cent, 18 per cent and 32 per cent in 1980. Although the share of T&C exports in the total world exports increases, it is still below the world average level, presenting it with various challenges in international competition. It is evident that there is some limitation to the analysis of comparative advantages by just using exports because exports can be affected by imports especially in the context of vast imports of raw materials (Li et al., 2006). In addition, the trade policies also have an influence on it.

The RCA index of the textiles and clothing industries as an aggregate and for each industry in the primary T&C trade countries are reported in Table 3.10.

China, India, Hong Kong, Turkey and Pakistan have the strongest compet-itive advantages – all having values of RCA > 2.5. By contrast, Indonesia, Thailand and Italy have stronger competitive advantages, with values of RCA > 1.25, while the competitive advantages of Japan, USA and Germany are weak. Regarding the variation trend of RCA, most of the countries'

Table 3.10   RCA index of the T&C industry in selected countries

Year	1980	1990	1995	2000	2002	2005
China	4.891	4.415	4.242	3.809	3.424	3.296
	strongest	strongest	strongest	strongest	strongest	strongest
India	4.906	4.254	4.595	5.224	4.414	3.699
	strongest	strongest	strongest	strongest	strongest	strongest
Indonesia	0.139	1.826	2.229	2.291	2.083	2.162
	weaker	stronger	stronger	stronger	stronger	stronger
Japan	0.914	0.363	0.289	0.287	0.281	0.271
	middle	weaker	weaker	weaker	weaker	weaker
Thailand	1.952	2.635	2.046	1.505	1.485	1.356
	stronger	stronger	stronger	stronger	stronger	stronger
Turkey	3.463	5.976	6.642	6.681	6.147	5.607
	strongest	strongest	strongest	strongest	strongest	strongest
Hong Kong	7.065	4.653	3.357	3.378	3.109	3.068
	strongest	strongest	strongest	strongest	strongest	strongest
Pakistan	7.963	10.627	12.146	13.446	12.757	14.639
	strongest	strongest	strongest	strongest	strongest	strongest
United States	0.474	0.314	0.399	0.455	0.434	0.419
	weaker	weaker	weaker	weaker	weaker	weaker
Italy	2.382	2.033	1.941	1.922	1.896	1.968
	stronger	stronger	stronger	stronger	stronger	stronger
Germany	1.013	0.845	0.696	0.599	0.562	0.544
	middle	middle	weaker	weaker	weaker	weaker

Source: http://www.wto.org.

RCA has declined moderately – with the exception of Pakistan, which has increased by 83.8 per cent over the last 25 years.

The RCA indexes of the textiles and clothing sectors at disaggregated levels in the main T&C trade countries are reported in Tables 3.11 and 3.12.

The results for T&C as a whole are entirely consistent with those of T&C as a disaggregated industry. With the exception of India, Pakistan, USA, Japan and Germany, other countries' competitive advantages of exports in clothing are stronger than that of textiles. In this respect, India and Pakistan have stronger competitive advantages in the price, scale and quality of textiles (cotton yarn), and USA, Japan and Germany in the high-end textiles field. In the trade competitiveness aspect of clothing, Italy, being extremely developed in this field, has a stronger competitive advantage. Although China has been trying to improve its competitive advantage in the high-end field, most of its exports are low-end. China can only earn meagre profits in the processing trade, and cannot form powerful brands in the world. Overall, the competitiveness of China's T&C industries mean that it is still a world leader.

Table 3.11 RCA index of the textiles sector

Year	1980	1990	1995	2000	2002	2005
China	5.185	3.843	3.172	2.66	2.652	2.769
	strongest	strongest	strongest	strongest	strongest	strongest
India	5.627	4.009	4.823	5.814	5.141	4.243
	strongest	strongest	strongest	strongest	strongest	strongest
Indonesia	0.077	1.598	2.025	2.202	2.056	2.054
	weaker	stronger	stronger	stronger	stronger	stronger
Japan	1.451	0.674	0.549	0.602	0.607	0.597
	stronger	weaker	weaker	weaker	weaker	weaker
Thailand	1.876	1.329	1.164	1.166	1.246	1.29
	stronger	stronger	middle	middle	middle	stronger
Turkey	4.354	3.674	3.959	5.431	4.943	4.948
	strongest	strongest	strongest	strongest	strongest	strongest
Hong Kong	3.222	3.295	2.694	2.724	2.584	2.433
	strongest	strongest	strongest	strongest	strongest	strongest
Pakistan	12.383	15.672	17.971	20.622	20.296	22.885
	strongest	strongest	strongest	strongest	strongest	strongest
United States	0.616	0.423	0.427	0.575	0.646	0.703
	weaker	weaker	weaker	weaker	weaker	weaker
Italy	1.969	1.842	1.867	2.056	2.003	2.059
	stronger	stronger	stronger	stronger	stronger	stronger
Germany	1.207	1.101	0.932	0.808	0.742	0.661
	middle	middle	middle	middle	weaker	weaker

Source: http://www.wto.org.

3.1.4 The role of government in T&C industry development

Since reform and the introduction of the 'open door' policy, the Chinese government has taken a series of measures to support and encourage the development of the T&C industry. It includes the following measures:

3.1.4.1 T&C industrial policies

The T&C industry has been a development priority in several respects: First, as a labour-intensive industry, China's T&C sector has a strong competitive advantage in term of its abundant cheap labour resources, enabling it to succeed in the increasing inflow of foreign products. Secondly, the T&C industry is – and will continue to be – the pillar industry of China. It has a long history of a solid material base which serves as the foundation for economic development. The clothing industry, although it started comparatively late, is developing rapidly. Thirdly, another competitive advantage of China comes from its rich resources for the agriculture industry, whose by-products constitute the major part of textiles processing materials.

Table 3.12   RCA index of the clothing sector

Year	1980	1990	1995	2000	2002	2005
China	4.494	4.967	5.271	4.722	4.003	3.683
	strongest	strongest	strongest	strongest	strongest	strongest
India	3.929	4.491	4.376	4.756	3.868	3.299
	strongest	strongest	strongest	strongest	strongest	strongest
Indonesia	0.225	2.046	2.424	2.361	2.104	2.241
	weaker	stronger	stronger	stronger	stronger	stronger
Japan	0.187	0.063	0.039	0.037	0.037	0.031
	weaker	weaker	weaker	weaker	weaker	weaker
Thailand	2.054	3.895	2.894	1.775	1.666	1.404
	stronger	stronger	stronger	stronger	stronger	stronger
Turkey	2.256	8.198	9.222	7.673	7.051	6.092
	stronger	strongest	strongest	strongest	strongest	strongest
Hong Kong	12.27	5.965	3.994	3.897	3.505	3.536
	strongest	strongest	strongest	strongest	strongest	strongest
Pakistan	1.977	5.757	6.543	7.748	7.094	8.568
	stronger	strongest	strongest	strongest	strongest	strongest
United States	0.281	0.208	0.371	0.36	0.275	0.209
	weaker	weaker	weaker	weaker	weaker	weaker
Italy	2.941	2.217	2.012	1.815	1.816	1.900
	strongest	stronger	stronger	stronger	stronger	stronger
Germany	0.749	0.597	0.469	0.433	0.427	0.459
	weaker	weaker	weaker	weaker	weaker	weaker

Source: http://www.wto.org.

Therefore, the development of the T&C industry is conducive to the transfer of a redundant rural labour force, the process of rural industrialization and urbanization, and to increasing the peasants' income. Fourthly, as a developing country, China has a favourable environment for the clothing industry which could absorb a large amount of high tech, but also has a relatively low technical and capital threshold.

The government's industrial policy focuses on two aspects. On the one hand, it coordinates the relationship between the T&C industry and other industries, such as transportation, business, trade and maritime transportation, thereby encouraging common development. On the other hand, it coordinates the relationship between T&C internal enterprises. Specifically, the government lends its support to the development of the T&C industry by adopting policies of both direct and indirect interference, first to increase the input of the productive elements, then to optimize the industrial structure through T&C development, and finally to obtain a dynamic comparative advantage in the textiles industry. Since the reform and 'open door' policy, the government has made a slew of adjustments in supporting the T&C industry. These are:

3.1.4.1.1 Policy in the 1980s. In 1983, the Chinese government announced its objective of doubling GDP by the year 1990, and quadrupling GDP by the year 2000, in order to realize its goal of building a prosperous society. In accordance with this objective, important strategic adjustments were made to the T&C industry.

China aimed to speed up the development of the chemical fibre industry. From 1980 to 1983, the investment in the chemical fibre industry reached 5.1 billion Yuan. Through the end of the 1970s and the 1980s, four major chemical fibre plants were built, and several key projects – such as Yizheng, Jinshan and Pindingshan lianzibu – were expanded or reconstructed, laying a solid foundation for the development of the chemical fibre industry.

From 1981 to 1985, the total fixed asset investment in the T&C industry increased to 28.7 billion Yuan, of which 17 billion were used for innovation (note that the annual total for fixed asset investment in China was only 40 billion). In the following years, efforts were made to solve the problem of the shortage of T&C products. At the end of 1983, cloth tickets were eliminated, ending the era of planned supply and hardship.

In 1984, the Ministry of Textiles adopted a development strategy which aimed to develop the clothing, home textiles and technical textiles industry, with a particular emphasis on the clothing industry. In 1986, the State Council transferred the ownership of the clothing sector to the Ministry of Textiles, thereby connecting the production of raw T&C materials to the final product. A complete system of T&C production was consequently formed. Under the guidance of the 'Ready-made clothes industrialization' policy, modern garment enterprises spread rapidly, not only greatly changing people's way of living, but also creating a brand new industry with an annual sales income of 387.9 billion Yuan (according to the T&C Enterprises Above Designated Size in 2004) and total products sales value of more than 1 trillion Yuan. Meanwhile, the home textiles and technical textiles industry, as independent industries, accelerated the pace of development.

In the same year, in accordance with the spirit of the policy to 'accelerate the development of the export-oriented economy' the Ministry of Textile Industry adopted the development strategy: 'With the objective of increasing export as breakthrough point, revitalize the textile industry in a all-round way'. During the period of the 7th Five-year Plan, this theory served as guidance for the whole of the T&C industry. In realizing the goal of 'By utilizing both domestic and international resources and markets, integrating into the world trade system', China's T&C industry and export-oriented economy progressed rapidly. In 1990, the exports of T&C products increased to $13.8 million from only $5.5 million in 1985 and, for the first time, accounted for half of the total export value. The strategy of developing an export-oriented economy also accelerated the technical advances and improved the enterprises' management level, thus providing a solid base for the further expansion of exports. During this period (1986–1990), the fixed asset investment of T&C industry reached 71.2 million Yuan, including 48 million Yuan of technical innovation. This figure was 2.5 times as large as during the period of the 6th Five-year Plan, apparently at a faster development speed.

3.1.4.1.2 Policy in the 1990s. At the beginning of the 1990s, China began the process of quadrupling its GDP by 2000 and constructing a prosperous society after realizing its first objective of doubling GDP by 1990. In 1994, the Fourth Plenary Session of the Fourteenth Central Committee of the Communist Party of China (CPC) proposed two fundamental transformations – (i) the economic system is transformed from a planned economy to a socialist market economy; and (ii) the economic growth mode changes from an extensive mode to an intensive mode. Under the guidance of these reform policies, China's T&C sector pursued four historical changes in rapid succession: (i) the market gradually became the foundation for the allocation of T&C resources; (ii) private enterprises increased and developed substantially; (iii) the three different types of foreign enterprises adopted the track of rapid development; and (iv) China began its reform of the state-owned enterprises.

In the 1990s, the condition of production and marketing of T&C industry took on great changes. Some common products (such as gauze) turned to a buyer's market from a seller's market. Other problems, such as unreasonable product structure, overstocked T&C products, a shortage of raw materials, increasingly fierce market competition, and the enterprises' (especially the state-owned enterprises') inability to improve their management system and equipment, were becoming increasingly serious. Facing this situation, the Central Committee and the State Council implemented several reform policies in structural adjustment and made great efforts to promote the science and technology of the textile industry.

In 1997, the State Council proposed the policy of 'Decreasing spindles for reorganization, reducing personnel to increase benefit'. Through two years' effort, 40 billion Yuan was used to merge the bankrupts' capital. About 10 million spindles were eliminated and 12 million workers were laid off and received appropriate arrangements. These procedures greatly assisted the development of the T&C industry, in the following ways: (1) They reversed the backward management concept of T&C enterprises (esp. state-owned enterprises), encouraging them to actively participate in the market instead of resorting to the government; (2) A certain amount of state-owned enterprises emerged from of the difficulty and got on the right track of development, thus further advancing the pace of T&C reform; Some old T&C industrial bases (e.g. bases in Shanghai, Qingdao, Tianjin, etc.) adopted relevant adjustments. Enterprises in Nanjing, Hangzhou, Jinan etc., accelerated their development through reform and adjustment. An example is Ningbo Veken Lo, Ltd, which played a leading role in the home textiles industry and in the year 2004, merged with ZhenJiang Textile Lo., Ltd. (3) A large amount of outmoded equipment was eliminated, providing a favourable environment for the technical advancement.

In 1998, the government continued to carry out the policy of merging the bankrupt companies and the re-deployment of laid-off workers from the T&C industry, indicating its preferential support. During the time of planned adjustment between October and November, particular attention was paid to spindle reduction, emphasizing that the reduced scales should still be applied to origin projects. Therefore, after adjustment, the total scale of China's T&C industry was approximately the same as originally planned, 170 million of which are added into the Spindle Reduction Project.

3.1.4.1.3 Policy in the twenty-first century. The structural adjustment policy of the T&C industry in 2000 focused on two aspects: first, it effectively eliminated outmoded industrial production capacity; and secondly, substantial achievements have been made in the strategic restructuring of the economy.

With the improvement of China's socialist market economy and the favourable environment for entering the WTO, the government took another round of adjustment in the T&C industry; namely: (i) it reduced the work of administrative examining and approving, bringing the market forces into full play; (ii) it continued the work of eliminating the outmoded equipment and total volume regulation; (iii) it adopted the administration of tariff quotas instead of the Import Quotas License, and revised the 'Measures on the Administration of Import of T&C Products'. The development objective of the Chinese government set forth in the twenty-first century is centred on the cotton textiles, woollen textiles printing & dyeing, and chemical fibres, through capital reconstruction and technology upgrading, to improve the design level and product quality (National Development & Reform Commission, 2005).

3.1.4.2 The financial policies for the T&C industry

In the mid-1990s, China implemented finance and investment reforms, making it difficult for traditional T&C sectors, which had a high asset/liability ratio, to secure commercial loans. It was determined largely by their economic conditions and development prospects, thus making ROI (return on investment) an important factor to be taken into consideration. In addition, policies were implemented in the following areas: (i) unifying the income tax system and abolishing the system of turning over funds to the state. This benefited enterprises' development in that, when the income tax of 17 per cent was adopted, the actual tax increased nearly 0.5 per cent, thus greatly reducing tax exemption under the tax distribution system;

(ii) the focus of foreign exchange regime reform was the merger of exchange. Specifically, the aim was to apply the unified exchange settlement to private and foreign trade export enterprises instead of using the dual rate.

Given that the level of import duty remained constant, the actual tax burden would increase, which could help to stimulate exports and restrict the level of imports, but, on the other hand, would also restrain the introduction of equipment by using loans (Guo, 2005). Generally speaking, these macro-reform policies reduced the level of government interference and strengthened the force of economy and legislation, creating an environment of fair competition among the T&C enterprises and an opportunity for the structural readjustment of the T&C industry under the conditions of a market economy. In addition, they provided an inner motivation for the enterprises to participate actively in the reform and adjustment by ending the era of supporting them through tax reductions. From 1997 to 1999, in order to ease the difficulties of state-owned enterprises, the government adopted several measures in the T&C industry.

3.1.4.2.1   The policy of spindle reduction subsidies and discount loans.   Under this policy, state-owned T&C enterprises eliminated outmoded production capacity of 10,000 spindles annually, with the aid of a government subsidy of 1.5 million and a local subsidy of 1.5 million. In addition, the local public finance provided a 2 million discount loan, whose repayment period ranged between 5 and 7 years. Over the course of three years, 100 million spindles were removed, paid for by 1.5 billion of both central and local financial subsidies. In 1998, 720 million Yuan were allocated for the elimination of 4.8 million spindles. In order to guarantee that the central financial subsidies should be allocated in a timely and proper fashion, the Ministry of Finance and former China Textile Association implemented the 'Policy of State Financial Subsidies to Reduce the Spindles of Textile Industry' which specified the prerequisites and procedures for the allocation of subsidies, indicating that the subsidies should be used principally in arranging for the redeployment of laid-off workers.

3.1.4.2.2   Asset restructuring.   As a result of the scattered distribution of firms, many of China's small-scale enterprises were affected by poor management. Therefore, under the Ninth Five-year Plan, a policy of asset restructuring was adopted to readjust the structure of enterprises through capital flow, and further to optimize the capital allocation. The main target was to build 50 large companies and enterprises, and to accelerate the development of collective and private enterprises. These measures in asset restructuring yielded substantial results. Some powerful enterprises were transformed into limited companies and were listed on stock exchanges. In 1996, 58 T&C enterprises were listed, attracting foreign capital of 8 billion. In 1998, five listed T&C companies successfully extended their scope of business into new areas, such as home and technical textiles industries. The trend among state-owned enterprises is for them to be transformed into joint stock companies, in which non-governmental capital assumed the main role, while governmental capital was gradually withdrawn from the T&C industry.

3.1.4.2.3 Bad debts written-off and debt–equity exchange. In 1997, China put 9.72 million Yuan into cancelling the bad accounts of state-owned T&C enterprises. In 1998, 12.6 million was allocated to the over-indebted enterprises, reducing their loss by 2.6 billion. As a result, the asset/liability ratio decreased from 77 per cent to 73 per cent. The writing-off of bad debts was a new measure taken from the year 2000; its aim was to put 15 billion into a debt-for-equity swap for 50 T&C industries, with the aim of decreasing their asset/liability ratio by 3 per cent. Moreover, several relevant measures were implemented in order to reduce the ratio by another 3 per cent, including merger, bankruptcy and clearing 15 billion of bad debts.

At the beginning of the twenty-first century, the T&C industry made full use of the government's policy of national bonds and discount loans. In response to the overimportation of textile materials, the industry made efforts to renovate such fields as woollen textiles, cotton textiles, plant fibre, silk, chemical fibre materials, and differential fibres, in order to realize the goal of import substitution and export promotion.

In 2000, the wool and cotton industry became the key field for structural readjustment. With the support of a central financial subsidy of 150 million, 280,000 spindles were removed. The economical condition of enterprises began to recover. State-owned enterprises also eliminated losses and began to make profits. At the same time, the reduction of spindles in the silk industry achieved substantial results: 520,000 were eliminated as a result of bankruptcies, 410,000 as the result of a central financial subsidy, and 270,000 through administrative and market measures. As a result of these developments, the task of reducing capacity by one million spindles had been achieved.

3.1.4.3 Technological development policies

3.1.4.3.1 The policies of accelerating the T&C technological development. With the rapid pace of marketization, and increasingly fair and fierce competition, enterprises became fully aware of the importance of technological developments. Between 1993 and 2004, the total value of imports of advanced equipment reached US$19.63 billion. In the meantime, China-made equipment, which had a value equal to the amount of imports, had been applied to T&C production. These advanced technologies and equipment greatly sped up the progress of the T&C industry. The chemical fibre industry was also substantially developed by adopting some key technologies such as high-capacity polyester, HOY (high oriented yarn), elasticity-adding machinery, and so on. A notable advance came in the area of high-capacity fibre polyesters, which had become world leaders, but only required one-eighth of the investment on imported ones, thus successfully accelerating progress in this field. In 2004, chemical fibres accounted for 45 per cent of the total volume of domestic fibre, becoming the chief material resources for the textiles industry.

Developments in cotton textiles are demonstrated by the proportion of knotless yarn, which increased from 2.25 per cent in 1980 to 50 per cent in 2003, and the share of non-shuttle cloth, which increased to 45 per cent in 2003 from 3.5 per cent in 1980. Moreover, the yarn count reached 32^S ('s' is the unit of yarn count which means 1 kilogram cotton can be spun into yarn of 32 kilometres long) in 2003 from 25^S in 1980. The clothing industry adopted such advanced technology as CAD/CAM and moved production lines (Wang, 2000). By attracting overseas investment, the Chinese T&C industry had not only greatly improved its technological base, but also spread modern management techniques. Until 2003, the share of foreign capital and capital from Hong Kong, Macao and Taiwan in the total paid-in capital of T&C enterprises above the designated size had reached 33.61 per cent.

At the beginning of the 1990s, the State Council implemented a policy of technological renovation, whose target was knotless yarn and non-shuttle cloth. Some key textiles machinery enterprises introduced advanced technologies and equipments, in order to achieve the localization (Zhao and Ning, 2000). The government also invested 1.6 billion Yuan and US$160 million. The combined efforts of enterprises and government meant that the pace of technological progress in cotton textiles machinery was accelerated dramatically. During this time, the main problem facing the Chinese clothing industry was the over-importation of clothing materials, which accounted for 70 per cent of clothing exports. After 1994, the scheme of promoting the technology in clothing materials as a breakthrough was implemented. Some print & dying enterprises were listed into the discount policy for technological innovation project, and significantly improved their production machinery.

Another important measure taken from the 1990s was the elimination of outmoded equipment. During the period of the Ninth Five-year Plan, 10 million spindles of outdated machinery were eliminated by state-owned enterprises. Concurrently, efforts were made in terms of upgrading and innovation. The share of equipment made in and after 1990 rose from a quarter to a third.

3.1.4.3.2   The development of fibre material technologies.   The introduction of world advanced fibre production technology and independent development increased China's fibre output from 450,000 tons in 1980 to 11.81 million tons in 2003. With a share of one-third of total global output, China has now become the world's largest producer of chemical fibres. Since 1998, the home research & development (R&D) for textiles machinery and textile

Table 3.13 Comparison of chemical technology between 1983 and 2003

Techniques	Target of production capability	Throughput of single line	
		Before 20 years	In 2003
Polymerization	Continuous condensation polymerization (t/d)	100	600
Filament	Winding speed (m/min)	3,000	7,000
Staple	Production line (t/a)	7,500	40,000
Added elasticity	Textured (m/min)	600	1,500

Source: China National Textile and Apparel Council, *China Textile Industry Development Report 2003/2004.*

processing technology has been successfully developed, greatly reducing the investment on the big projects of polyester spinning and the construction cycle. By 2004, the proportion of chemical fibre to total fibre raw materials had increased to 65 per cent from 15 per cent in the late 1970s, and the export of chemical fibre products accounted for 35.55 per cent of total fibre exports. A comparison of chemical technological improvements is presented in Table 3.13.

By 2004 the differential ratio of chemical fibre had reached 25 per cent. Great progress was made in fields such as higher fibre technology used in hygienic protection, and the aerospace industry. In addition, China developed soybean fibrin, bamboo fibrin, PBT fibrin, profiled fibre and other new fibres, and has made great strides in the areas of new materials and application fields.

3.1.4.3.3 Progress in fibre processing technology. Progress in fibre processing technology has greatly enhanced the production quality and the ability of design innovation. The continuous automation and high efficiency of the spinning process kept pace of the trend of 'Non-shuttle Cloth, Knotless Yarn and Combed Yarn' in the foreign market (see Table 3.14).

The overall development, from fibre materials to the technique of spinning, weaving, and dyeing, facilitated a substantial improvement in the production of domestic cotton, wool, linen, silk, chemical fibre and computer-based knitting machines, flat knitting machines, circular looms and new dyeing and finishing technologies. An improvement in materials enabled the export share to increase from 37.5 per cent in 1996 to 65.93 per cent in the early years of the twenty-first century. In general, the knitting industry adopted efficient blending materials. Moreover, the clothing industry generally adopted advanced technologies such as CAD/CAM, and the assembly line. Some enterprises used

Table 3.14   Share of combed yarn, non-shuttle cloth, and knotless yarn

Year		In 1980	In 2003
Ratio non-lap (%)		With no blowing-carding unit	36.8
Ratio of combed yarn (%)		8.6	23.8
Ratio of knotless yarn (%)		2.25	50
Ratio of shuttle-less fabric (%)		3.5	45
Yarn count variety	Cotton spinning	25^S	32^S
	Worsted spinning	52^N	70^N

Note: 'S' is the Yarn count number of UK Standard. 'N' is the Yarn count density number of UK Standard.
Source: China National Textile and Apparel Council, China Textile Industry Development Report 2003/2004.

CIMS skills and 3-D body measurements, developing a number of famous brands.

Technical textiles also absorbed these advanced technologies and applied them into such fields as soil engineering, construction, transportation, fishery, medical treatment and sanitation, agriculture, and other light industrial sectors. The non-woven cloth assembled advanced techniques from all over the world, with an annual output volume of over 830,000 tons, ranking it third in the world after North American and Europe. As a result of this progress, the total output of technical textiles products had grown significantly from 530,000 tons in 1988 to 2.61 million tons in 2003, and it became the driving force in the development of the textiles industry.

3.1.4.3.4   Application of ICTs in the T&C sector.   The application of ICTs in the T&C sector promoted technological progress and scientific management. Improvements in information technology stimulated the development of the T&C industry, and labour productivity increased significantly – from 34,412 per capita to 44,600 per capita. Great advances could also be seen in the development of CAD/CAM and special management. In the field of textiles machinery production, China established several CIMS model enterprises. Based on the intensive application of ICTs in managerial functions (personnel, finance, supply-marketing-inventory, and so on), a number of model enterprises developed integrated application software systems such as enterprise resource planning (ERP). The development of an electronic commerce system also began in the year 2004.

3.1.4.3.5   The implementation of international standards.   During this period China actively implemented international standards and gradually constructed a fully-fledged T&C standard management system. By August 2003, the T&C industry had established 1,359 standards, and built relatively fully-fledged T&C management and product technical standard systems. In 1978, the China Textile Industry Standard Organization was formally accepted as a member of the ISO (International Standard Organization). In 2004, the adoption rate of international standards in TC83 product reached 80 per cent (Tao, 2005).

3.1.4.4 Policies of increasing T&C exports

Since the 1980s, great changes have taken place in government policy, which shifted its priority from an inward-oriented economy to an outward-oriented economy, from central planning to a focus on market regulation, and from single ownership of the state-owned enterprises to the coexistence of various ownership forms. With respect to the T&C industry, government support has played a fundamental role in its future development. The policy of increasing exports is an important part and is discussed below:

3.1.4.4.1 Subsidy policies in the T&C industry.
As a developing country, China is a T&C producer of mostly labour-intensive products. The management and technological level of Chinese enterprises is relatively low. Thus, for the Chinese T&C industry, competition in world markets requires subsidization. Most notable is the ETR (Export Tax Rebate) policy which has served as a great impetus in stimulating T&C exports.

Since 1979, great efforts have been made by the Ministry of Finance, the State Administration of Taxation and other departments to build a mature import and export tax system. In 1985, China implemented the ETR policy as a driving force for promoting exports. It was also a reasonable measure that could be accepted by the WTO members, as long as the rebate rate did not exceed the effective tax rate. The main purpose of this policy was to avoid double taxation and guarantee fair competition in global markets. In its extensive application, it has been the most powerful impetus for China's T&C exports. The average rebate rate had several different levels – for example, 6 per cent, 15 per cent and 12 per cent.

In 1994, China fixed the ETR rate at a high level, 17 per cent and 13 per cent. As a consequence, the exports in that year achieved a significant increase, with a growth rate of 32.9 per cent compared to that in 1993. Over the course of the following years, due to the inadequate quota of ETR, the rebate rate was reduced.

In late 1997, the Asian financial crisis occurred. The world economy experienced a period of low development, shrinking markets, and fierce competition. Under the promise of a stable exchange rate of RMB, in 1998, the Chinese government raised its ETR rate of some products by 2 per cent in order to maintain the level of exports. For T&C raw materials and products, the rate was adjusted to 11 per cent and then to 13 per cent (on 1 January

1999). In addition, in order to further promote the export of T&C machinery, the government adopted a policy of export credits and zero tax rate policies.

In recent years, some T&C enterprises in provinces such as Guangdong, Zhejiang, and Fujian were faced by many problems. These included the increasing export competition resulting from overproduction, the appreciation in the value of the RMB, anti-dumping investigations and other non-trade barriers, the increasing cost of raw materials and decreasing export profits. Each of these developments rendered them unprofitable by only adopting price differentials. Thus, a large number of enterprises chose the ETR as the only way to make profit (Zhao, 2005). Normally, a profit rate of 3 per cent to 5 per cent required an ETR rate of 10 per cent or higher.

Admittedly, raising the ETR rate undoubtedly promoted exports and greatly strengthened the international competitiveness of products. On the other hand, China implemented various subsidy policies (especially preferential tax policy), many of which would be influenced and regulated by SCA (an article to oppose subsidy in WTO files). Therefore, improvement and adjustment should be made in order to build a subsidy and tax preferential system that will meet the WTO requirements. The first step is to regulate the 'special' export and import substitution subsidy polices. Some T&C export enterprises, especially those who possess advanced technology and famous brands, are obtaining increasing benefits from these policies, such as cost and expense subsidies, income tax and drawback of circulation tax, reduction or exemption, withdrawal depreciation and science expense, preferential loans and land purchases, all of which are prohibited under the WTO framework. Thus, the right of local government to introduce these policies should be ended, and corresponding adjustments should be made by the central government – for example, cancelling those prohibited subsidies, and finding other forms of subsidies in order to achieve export and import substitution. Secondly, the government should adjust or abandon the tax preferential policies, such as preferential policy for science and technology, and for enterprise development.

3.1.4.4.2   Export quota system and reform.   Importing countries can use export quotas to limit their exports. In the past, China export products followed the 'Principle of quota allocation according to performance'. In other words, the allocation of the quota should be based on a certain year's export volumes. This method to some extent guaranteed the export order of T&C product, but also exposed problems. Some enterprises had a low utilization rate, or even solely relied on the transfer of quota.

The reform of the quota allocation system is one way to end the enterprises' life tenure in this system. Quotas were allocated according to the market mechanism through three methods: namely, public auction, application, and allocation according to performance. The first approach was implemented in 1998, with the emphasis on 21 best-selling T&C products.

Enterprises obtained the quota through bid submission. 10 per cent of the successful ones should pay the bid security, the share of which increased from 30 per cent to 80 per cent. The second approach focused mainly on quotas with a low utilization rate. (In 1998, they covered 98 categories.) Enterprises obtained the quota through public application, with early applicants receiving their quota first. For the rest of the quotas, the third approach was adopted, that is, enterprises got the quota according to their export performance. In 2000, 30 per cent of these quotas were allocated to the enterprises that had the self-support import and export rights, increased by 10 per cent from the year 1999. At the same time, the MOFTEC (Ministry of Foreign Trade and Economic Cooperation of China) committed CIECNET (China International Electronic Commerce Network) to the development of the feedback system in order to better evaluate the utilization rate of these quotas. Enterprises with a rate lower than 30 per cent in the current year would be deprived of the future right of bid submission. For those with a rate lower than 70 per cent, they would not be able to attend the following year's bid submission.

In the period between 1997 and 1999, the export quota allocation was focused largely on the T&C self-support export enterprises. In 1998, more than 15 per cent of the total planned quota for textiles from Europe and America were allocated directly to the T&C self-support export enterprises. After 1999, a certain increase was made according to the specific condition. These enterprises were given the right of bid submission for both planned and active quota. It was an important step to allocate export planned quota directly to T&C enterprises, indicating the start of the reform of China's foreign trade system and providing important foundation for enterprises' participation in the world competition and market exploration. On the way to meet government's requirement of fully utilizing the quota, T&C enterprises made great efforts in improving the economic condition and utilization rate, thus substantially increasing the export benefit.

Following the development of the market economy, the current export quota management system no longer benefited the entry of the T&C industry into the global market and a growing level of exports. As a result, China increased its power to undertake reforms (Wang Hui, 2005). Measures were made in the following areas, including quota supervision and management, enhancing the utilization rate, increasing the quantity and variety of the quota public bidding, improving the transparency, and increasing the quota allocated to the major self-support export enterprises. Under these measures, T&C exports achieved a sustained period of growth.

As part of China's protocol of accession to the WTO, according to the Agreement on Textiles and Clothing, the quota system, which had been in place for 40 years, was ended at the end of 2004. Prior to this time, the annual export growth rates through China's third three-year phase of quota elimination process were 51 per cent, 49 per cent, 26 per cent – a declining trend.

Therefore, in the post-quota era, China will be faced with both opportunities and challenges.

3.1.4.4.3 Other export promotion policies.   In the mid-1980s, major efforts were made to promote horizontal economic links in order to increase the level of T&C exports. The forms and contents of the horizontal economy were very flexible. Among the characteristics of the policies are: (1) the flourishing of the combinations which were represented by the famous brands and centred on the key enterprises greatly enhanced the export share and the share of the domestic market; (2) departmental and trans-trade integration increased the proportion of final product; (3) taking full advantage of the 'radiation effect' of central cities, developing a sound environment in which urban and rural enterprises complemented each other; (4) the combination of scientific research and production activity provided a new way of realizing the goal of 'Technology and Economy integrated into a united whole'; (5) targeting resource exploration, enterprises and material producing areas formed a combination with supply and marketing; and (6) in order to further develop the international market, industry and trade were linked together, and exerted a profound influence on export promotion. All of these combinations greatly helped the T&C enterprises to develop their final products and improve their economic conditions. Meanwhile, efforts were made in developing new products and strengthening management, serving as a solid base for increasing export and earning exchange.

In 1986, the Ministry of the Textile Industry adopted a development strategy which could be described as follows: 'With the objective of increasing exports as breakthroughs, revitalize the textile industry in an all-round way'. During the period of the Seventh Five-year Plan, this strategy provided the direction for the development of the T&C industry, and made significant contributions to export promotion and the progress of establishing an export-oriented economy.

During the 1980s other incentive measures for increasing export included the policy of foreign exchange retention for industrial enterprises, and the policy of allowing enterprises to control the quota based on the difference of exchange rate. These measures enabled industrial and foreign trade enterprises to estimate their export benefits according to the actual swap exchange rate. That is, if the cost of export products was lower than this rate, there would be profits, and vice versa.

Between 1997 and 1999, export policy focused on areas such as the following: reduced personnel, allocating export quota directly to producing enterprises, increasing the ETR, and further deepening cotton circulation system reform. At the same time, the government devoted great efforts to carrying out anti-dumping activities and cracking down on smuggling, thus preventing the dumping of some foreign products and guaranteeing both fair competition among enterprises and also an orderly market.

3.1.5 The role of institutions in the development of the T&C industry

3.1.5.1 Personnel education and training

In the mid and late 1980s, the T&C industry experienced transformations both at the level of the overall economic system and at the level of individual enterprises. Every aspect of the T&C system achieved rapid development during this period – particularly in terms of the education and training of personnel. The political, cultural, technological, and professional qualities were improved and a large number of specialities were cultivated. All of these achievements significantly propelled the organizational transformation of the T&C industry.

In order to strengthen leadership training and enhance managerial qualities, in 1984 the State Council adopted the policy of making managers of large and medium-sized enterprises take the national examination. Grading training classes were held, helping managers to master the fundamental managerial knowledge and economic development policies since the Third Plenary Session of the Eleventh Central Committee.

In the mean time, several short training courses for S&T personnel and specialities were also held in order to meet the requirements of industrial transformation. These dealt with areas such as: modern management, quality control, product design, industrial foreign trade, counselling, discipline supervision, accounting and computer software. In accordance with the reforms of price and finance, the Ministry of the Textile Industry organized price research seminars and finance director courses, participants of which were from the local Textile Industry Bureaus, and from other institutions engaged in planning, finance, materials, economic research, etc. Other programmes, such as engineering training classes, were also held in order to expand their knowledge and broaden their horizons.

In addition, the cultural and technological training of workers made rapid progress. Since 1985, intermediate-level training classes, which aimed to improve the professional skills and capability of dealing with technical problems, have helped workers to refine their skills and arouse their initiative.

3.1.5.2 The reform of T&C institutions

In March 1998, the first plenary session of the 9th CPC Central Committee approved the 'State Council's Institutional Restructuring Plan' and the 'Circular of the State Council Concerning the Organizational Structure of State Bureaus (Administrations) under the Management of Ministries and Commissions'. According to this plan, the State Administration of the Textile Industry was formally established as a replacement for the China Textile Association (CTA) and was placed under the management of the State Economy and Trade Committee. Along with the final measures of establishing the CTA and closing the Ministry of the Textile Industry, this was another vital reform in the T&C development history, a reform that adapted the market economy and institution transformation.

Acting wholly on the principle of the separation of government functions from enterprise management, delegating power to the lowest levels, and bringing about the unity of rights and obligations, the State Administration of Textile Industry made several adjustments in the allocation of functions, including: (1) the government was separated from the enterprise management. They could not assume the functions of investment project approval and implementation, nor could they issue plans relating to production and allocation; (2) powers were delegated to the authorities and to strengthen the functions of local governments and social intermediary organizations. They were authorized to take over responsibilities such as the construction and management of the T&C market, an examination of the qualifications, quality testing, personnel training, and verification of achievements, and so on; and (3) the rights and obligations were united. Related responsibilities were assumed by the same department – for example, functions in these fields such as industry policies, economic regulation, production operation, investment and finance guidance, technology advancement, safe production, etc, were arranged by the State Economic and Trade Committee. Higher education institutions were under the management of the Ministry of Education. The function of quality supervision was assigned to the General Administration of Quality Supervision.

During the period of institutional reform, the textiles industry accelerated the process of forming trade associations. With the development of the market economy, these associations played an irreplaceable role in connecting the government and enterprises. Great efforts were made by the State Administration of Textile Industry in readjusting the current T&C trade association system and in building a new system centring on China National Textile & Apparel Council (CNTAC). On 30 September 1998, the CNTAC was formally listed.

3.1.5.3   *The development of S&T enterprises*

Some state-owned key institutions, such as the China Textile Academy, the China Textile Industrial Engineering Institute, the Shanghai Textile Academy, and so on, have changed their system into S&T enterprises, and achieved significant technological progress. In addition, several national-level and province-level key laboratories and a large number of non-state-owned S&T enterprises also played increasingly important roles in the technological development of the T&C sector.

3.1.6   **The influence of government policies and international trade rules**

3.1.6.1   *China's accession to the WTO*

Since the year 2001, when China became a member of the WTO, the internationalization and economic condition of the T&C industry have been promoted (Ianchovichina and Martin, 2001). Structural readjustment and industrial upgrading also achieved substantial results. But the most notable change came from the increasing T&C exports due to China's accession to WTO.

To begin with, the phasing out of nearly a hundred quotas provided a new way to expand exports, and also eliminated the restraint on export volumes. In addition, the cancellation of access fees also alleviated the financial burden on enterprises. In 2002, the export of T&C products to the countries of restriction reached $14.9 billion, with a growth rate of 19.8 per cent. This is above the average increase level and 5 per cent higher than the growth rate of exports to countries who had no restrictions.

Secondly, the accession to WTO resulted in a considerable reduction in China's import tariffs. The Import Quotas Licenses of 42 HS code categories such as cotton and chemical fibres were eliminated. At the same time, import tariff quota on cotton was adopted instead of the export subsidy policy. China also made efforts to deepen the cotton circulation system reforms and to integrate its domestic cotton price with the global market. All of these measures helped to increase the exports of China's cotton textiles products by 31.8 per cent in 2002 – higher than for any other raw materials (Liu, 2006). Meanwhile, with the rapid pace of the further opening of the T&C material market, production costs were accordingly reduced, thus improving the international competitiveness of products.

3.1.6.2 Multi-Fibre Arrangement (MFA)

The basic objective of the MFA is to promote world trade, by removing the barriers to its liberalization. At the same time, it guarantees an orderly and balanced development, and protects the markets of both import and export countries from disaster. However, the MFA is in contrast with the principle of 'general elimination of quantitative' and 'Most-Favoured-Nation Treatment', which were stipulated by GATT (the General Agreement on Tariffs and Trade). The restraints were only imposed on the developing countries, but did not exist among the developed countries. It is, to some extent, T&C trade protectionism in some developed countries that has resulted in this departure. Particularly significant is the definition of 'Market Disruption', which refers to neither dumping nor subsidies, and differs from the protective measure in the 19th article of GATT. In fact, it is a word that has been intentionally created by developed countries in order to protect their domestic T&C market from the entry of other foreign products (especially China), which normally have much lower production costs. Thus, the MFA provided a theoretical basis for the developed counties to carry out trade protectionism, and gave them excuses for adopting discriminatory quantitative restrictions.

The MFA has governed the T&C industry for nearly 30 years, and has been extended on five occasions. In general, it has helped to stabilize world trade, but in some ways, it actually discouraged the development of T&C trade. It was often used by developed counties to act against protectionism.

In addition, they implemented high tariffs and Voluntary Export Restraints (VER) in order to protect their domestic markets. MFA also permitted them to adopt a special quota system when the so-called 'market disruption' occurs (Kathuria et al., 2001). All of these measures taken by the developed countries had huge negative effects on the T&C industry of developing countries. In respect of its violation of the principle of 'trade liberalization and full employment', it is an irreversible trend for MFA to withdraw from the global T&C industry.

3.1.6.3   The Agreement on Textiles and Clothing

The Agreement on Textiles and Clothing (ATC) is one of the most significant outcomes of the Uruguay Round trade talks in 1986, as the ATC was designed to facilitate 'the integration of the textiles and clothing sector into GATT 1994'. Under the ATC, bilateral quotas under the MFA were to be enlarged in three stages and fully integrated by 1 January 2005. That is, from the year 2005, the T&C industry had entered a post-quota era.

As the world's largest T&C exporter, China has undoubtedly benefited greatly from the ATC since its accession into the WTO (Yao et al., 2005). These advantages have been felt in two specific aspects: (1) the liberalization and opening of the global market provide invaluable opportunities for China to expand its market share. With the increasing competitiveness of China's T&C products, China will have the chance to compete in the market that has already been integrated. Moreover, the benefit obtained from the supplemental growth rate during the process of integration will also help to promote T&C product exports; (2) the integrated products could enjoy the GATT (1994) 'Most-Favoured-Nation Treatment'. Under this condition, China's T&C products will have more competitive advantages and also the opportunities to reverse the passive situation under discriminatory quantitative restrictions.

3.1.6.4   Green Trade Barrier

With China's accession into WTO and the elimination of quotas, the 'Green Trade Barrier', a form of non-tariff barrier imposed by developed countries, has become the major obstacle to China's T&C exports. It links environmental requirements to world trade (Ruo, 2006). That is, under the claim of protecting international environmentally related agreements and the laws in importing countries, it restrains or refuses imported products which violate those laws or agreements.

3.1.6.4.1   Positive effects on China's T&C industry.   Since the 'Green Trade Barrier' calls for environment protection and healthy living, it has led to a decrease in the share of T&C primary products, which have negative impacts upon the environment. As a result, China has made great efforts in terms of the structural adjustment of products and in developing green, deep-processing products, all of which are becoming the new export growing points. Moreover, these measures will help to overcome the trade barrier and increase the market share of China's T&C products.

In addition to the export challenges brought about by the 'Green Trade Barrier', motivation is also generated to accelerate the process of T&C technological development. There have also been further improvements to the construction of T&C standard legislation system (Nie, 2005), which has provided favourable condition for fair competition and for customers to choose satisfying products.

3.1.6.4.2 Negative effects on China's T&C industry. As a developing country, China should conform to the 'green' trend in order to overcome the barrier. This process will undoubtedly involve every link, from production to marketing, or even to disposal. Expenses will consequently rise, rendering enterprises less competitive in the international market. Thus, enterprises' financial condition will be affected adversely.

'Green' trade and newly erected barriers will gradually end the production of some unhealthy products. Given China's current environmental technology level, it is difficult for China to meet the requirements set by some developed countries and newly industrialized countries in a short time. Therefore, the export of China's T&C products may decrease, and so does the growth rate.

PART II: CASE STUDIES OF SPINNING AND WEAVING CLOTHING SECTOR LEADERS

3.1.7 Youngor Group Co., Ltd.

3.1.7.1 *The basic situation of the corporation*

Youngor Group (http://www.youngor.com) was founded in 1979. Over the course of more than 20 years, Youngor has developed an operational pattern of multiplicative growth and professional development, based on fabric, garment production, real estate and foreign trade. Today Youngor has grown into a leading corporation in the Chinese garment sector with 5 billion RMB net assets and 2,500 employees. The comprehensive strength of Youngor ranks it as no. 144 of the top 500 Group Corporations of China, and in the early twenty-first century Youngor maintained the first place of the top 100 largest sales and profits in Chinese garment sector for four consecutive years. The main products – Youngor brand shirts and suits – have maintained the largest market share in the Chinese market for 11 years and 6 years respectively, leading in terms of the production of suits, shirts, trousers, jackets and neckties. Youngor Group Co., Ltd, the subsidiary of the group, is a public corporation.

Table 3.15 Basic data of the Youngor group

Year	Operation revenue (million RMB)	Overall assets (million RMB)	Employed persons
2005	16,766	15,025	28,640
2004	13,971	13,496	24,596
2003	10,140	10,187	19,304
2002	6,923	7,133	17,068
2001	5,661	5,105	14,639
2000	4,889	3,536	19,231

Source: National Bureau of Statistics of China, Large Corporations of China, China Statistics of China, 2001, 2002, 2003, 2004, 2005, 2006.

3.1.7.2 *Basic data of the corporation*

During 'the first five years' development strategy of the company, the sales of Youngor rose by an average rate of more than 50 per cent every year, and the profits rose at an annual rate of more than 30 per cent. Having been China's leading sellers of shirts for several years, in 1999 Youngor gained the first place in the sales of both suits and shirts. By 2000 (at the end of 'the first five years'), the operating income of Youngor had reached 4.885 billion RMB, the overall profits were 350 million RMB, the fixed assets had reached 1.107 billion RMB, and the overall level of fixed assets reached 3.536 billion RMB. In 2003 the group realized net sales of RMB10.12 billion Yuan, 46.17 per cent more than in the previous year; the realized profits were RMB658 million Yuan, 12.3 per cent more than in the previous year; the exports reached US$520 million, 41 per cent more than in the previous year; and the realized tax was RMB348 million Yuan, 25.31 per cent more than in the previous year.

In 2004, the group realized net sales of RMB13.935 billion Yuan, profits of RMB899 million Yuan, and exports of US$650 million, ranking it as no. 49 of the Top 500 Chinese enterprises. In 2005, the group realized net sales of RMB16.717 billion Yuan – an increase of 19.88 per cent; profits of RMB1.018 billion Yuan – an increase of 13.18 per cent; and exports of US$950 million. Furthermore, in three successive yeas the Youngor corporation achieved record exports: 10.86 million pairs (2003), 14.15 million pairs (2004) and 18.22 million pairs (2005).

3.1.7.3 *History and orientation of the corporation*

The Youngor Group was initially called the Youth Garment Factory, a small collectively owned enterprise in Duantang town in Ningbo City with a fund of only RMB20,000. In August 1990, Ningbo Youngor Garment Co., Ltd was founded jointly by Ningbo Youth Garment Factory, Ningbo Shiqi Township Industrial Corporation and Macao Namkwang International Trade Co., Ltd.

This new corporation began to manufacture 'Youngor' brand shirts. Through attracting foreign capital, and acquiring advanced technology and management, the business ideas, the technological level and operational pattern of Youngor made significant progress.

In 1993, Youngor Group Co., Ltd, a joint venture, was established through the issuing of stocks to the Ningbo Youth Garment Factory, the Ningbo Shiqi Township Industrial Corporation and the Ningbo Shengda Development Corporation. From 1993 to 1997, the sales of Youngor increased by a rate of 88 per cent every year, while the profits grew by 95 per cent, and the net assets increased tenfold. In 1993, it also began to move into the field of suits by importing advanced large amounts of suit manufacturing equipment. As a result of these developments, the Youngor Group advanced to become one of China's top eight garment sector companies. In 1997, the Youngor Group was listed among the Top 1,000 Chinese Large and Medium-sized Industrial Enterprises, and began to establish its retailing sales network. The overall tax paid by the group ranked it no. 2 among firms in the Chinese garments sector, which was published by the Garment Association of China.

In November 1998, Youngor Group Co., Ltd issued 55 million A shares on the Shanghai Stock Exchange. This IPO was a considerable success. This brought Youngor Group to a new development phase of connecting to the world (Li, 2006).

3.1.7.3.1 *Sales network of the corporation.*

To date, Youngor has established 140 subsidiary companies in China (excluding Taiwan and Tibet), a network of more than 5,000 commercial points of sales, and 600 exclusive agencies. The enterprise is cooperating with global management and consultant companies in order to construct a marketing network system which has the Chinese characteristics and features of Youngor. Meanwhile, as subsidiary companies in Hong Kong and Japan were established, Youngor tried to establish more markets gradually in Europe, America, Russia, Southeast Asia and so on. At the same time, the corporation launched the Youngor brand on the international market, with the aim of establishing it as a world-famous brand. The aim of the corporation is to become an internationally renowned multinational corporation.

3.1.7.3.2 *Exponential growth strategies.*

Youngor carried out a continuous process of implementing its operating strategies of exponential growth and professional development. In doing so, it achieved good results in the areas of real estate, world trade, investment and public facilities. As a result, the corporation became a world-famous garment group. Real estate, as one part of its operating area, developed quickly and became a very important part of Ningbo real estate. In addition, the increase in world trade has also provided considerable impetus to the development of the group – several subsidiary groups manufacturing shirts, suits and leisure wear had established departments dedicated to global trade, and the exports of ready-made clothes increased rapidly.

3.1.7.4   Digitized project and information technology

Since the 1990s, Youngor has achieved great success through a strategy of creating the Youngor brand. For many years, the core products – shirts and suits – have maintained the largest share of the Chinese market (Youngor, 2006b). In the twenty-first century the international and domestic clothing markets are experiencing substantial transformations. Increasingly, sellers' markets are becoming buyers' markets. There is a reduction in the life cycle of products and the competition between the low-grade and medium-grade clothing sector is becoming increasingly intense. Especially following China's accession to the WTO, the process of ranking again in the Chinese garment sector has already started. The companies are embarking upon a new stage of development. Increasing numbers of foreign brands are being brought into China. Furthermore, some domestic clothing enterprises carry out new strategies of production and sales, making use of foreign brands. These companies have made more rapid progress in a short period of time.

In the background, the leaders of the Youngor Group have proposed a digitization project, making use of informationization to bring about the development of industrialization. Since 2001, in cooperation with the Chinese Academy of Sciences, the Youngor Group has begun to implement the 'Youngor digitization project'. The purpose of the project is to establish the leading operational pattern of the national clothing sector, enhancing operating efficiency, realizing the effective information management of the entire enterprise, helping the enterprise unceasingly to expand the new market with the aid of an information system, the ability of nimble inquiry, improving the support system of the policy-making, satisfying the demand for unceasing development and changes, providing the ability of continual improvement. At the same time, Youngor has made further plans for the overall needs of the group, optimizes the service, set up the standard of the management, and established a supply chain management system, including the product flow, the information flow and the capital flow. The system can also enhance communication between the headquarters and the subsidiary companies, both inside and outside the group. In this manner the image of Youngor, the efficiency, and the comprehensive competitive ability of the corporation could all be enhanced considerably.

In 2003, the digitized project of Youngor was ranked 18th in the list of the top 500 informationization projects of Chinese enterprises and also gained the honour of being recognised as the 'Best strategy' of informationization. Youngor became one of the top 10 companies in the informationization of China. Furthermore, in 2004 the supply system of the Youngor Group gained the prize for the achievement in the informationization of China.

3.1.7.5   Technological innovation

Youngor has already planned to pursue a new method of earning more profits as the result of technological improvements. It has promoted the development of shirts which use HP (High-temperature Phase technology) cotton materials that are unnecessary to iron. The method was used widely in other companies in the domestic market. Youngor later promoted the VP (Vapour Phase technology) method, which also eliminates the need for ironing. Those shirts using the VP method won the title of 'important new product of China'. In addition, Youngor shirts developed the DP (Delicate Phase) technology in shirt production. These new shirts used advanced new materials and initiated a technological revolution in shirt manufacture.

Another main product of Youngor – western-style clothes – has similarly embraced technical developments. In 1993, Youngor introduced an advanced production line and technologies which are used to design and produce an excellent clothing model. In 1994, the company introduced automatic shrinking and advanced finalization equipment was introduced. In 1996, the most advanced western-style clothes model centre and the French CAD system were built. These developments meant that production – run from four workstations – could be measured to an accuracy of a few millimetres. In 2000, the system of automatic hanging and advanced clothing machines were both introduced. In 2005 Youngor introduced other advanced machines from countries such as Japan, Germany, Italy and the USA, which had further promoted the market competition strength and the quality of products.

In the development plan of the textiles sector of '11th Five-Year' plan, there are 10 complete sets of essential equipment and 28 items of new fibrous material and new craft technology. This is not only the key point behind technological innovation in the Chinese spinning and weaving profession, but is also central to Youngor's technological innovation.

In recent years, Youngor has invested more than 2 billion RMB in the technological transformations of textile city and clothing city plants. It has also implemented eight significant technological transformation projects, introducing advanced equipment and the technology of spinning and weaving clothing in the world in order to achieve its four key goals: 'high beginning, high tech, high investment, high production'. Up to the end of 2004, Youngor has finished the research of 27 new products, new technologies and new craft. Because of the increased rate of product research, the new product enterprise standard has more than 30 items and nearly 50 per cent of product enterprise standards are equated with international standards.

3.1.7.6   World trade and the WTO

From the beginning of the negotiations to enter the WTO, Youngor has begun the step-by-step expansion of its production base. The international reputation of Youngor improved remarkably after the investment of 900 million

RMB for the clothing city plant. In the export section of Youngor the US share is very small. This is mainly because of the previous quota limit which has made Youngor mainly centralize in those countries where there was no quota limit such as Japan. 60 per cent of the products were sold in Japan, 20 per cent in the Europe, and very little in the USA.

The cancellation of the quota limit presents an outstanding opportunity for Youngor. In recent years Youngor has turned its focus from Japan to the USA, the world's largest textiles market. In February 2004, Youngor made an appointment with Kellwood, a leading company in the American garments sector, and made a decision to establish a shirt corporation. In December 2004, the US subsidiary corporation of Youngor was launched. It has developed a four-stage strategy to break into the US market over the course of the one or two years: (i) to establish a retail shop in the locality; (ii) to cooperate with the American local retail merchant; (iii) to set up special boutiques within the shop and also to consider cooperation with the overseas brand; (iv) to capture the market and obtain a marketing channel in the USA through the purchasing and sharing of stock.

Meanwhile, internationalization not only includes the establishment of overseas branches, but also involves the adoption of a series of operational systems and the transformation of their business philosophy. This is a long process. During the process of transformation, Youngor has paid great attention to the selection of personnel, recruiting not only people with skills in international marketing, but also specialists in technology and research and development who have a familiarity with global markets. On the other hand, Youngor positively adjusts the management system of the enterprise, and promotes the production management method of ERP (Youngor, 2006a).

3.1.8   Hongdou Group Co., Ltd

3.1.8.1   The enterprise

The Hongdou Group (http://www.hongdou.com) is located in the Gangxia town of Wuxi, Jiangsu province. It is an important company in Jiangsu. The Hongdou Group has nine branches, one of which is a listed corporation, 85 third-class companies and two subsidiary companies – in New York and Los Angeles. There are 20,000 employees in the enterprise. The products of the corporation include clothing, rubber, machine and real estate. In 2004, the sales of Hongdou reached 7.808 billion RMB, and the profits were 689 million RMB.

In 1983, the Hongdou Group was established to produce knitted underwear. From 1992, the group has formed the clothing product series. One after another, shirts, western-style clothes, jackets, woollen sweaters, T-shirts, leatherwear, women's clothes, and children's clothes were released onto the market. In 1995, Hongdou completed the successful purchase of the Shanghai Shenda Motor Corporation. This promoted two brands of motorcycles and the electrically operated bicycles, 'the Chitu horse' and 'the European leopard', and led to industrial diversification.

In 1998, Hongdou began a collaboration with the famous fashion design institute ESMOD in France. They established the 'Hongdou–ESMOD International Training Centre' to cultivate their own designers, and to establish the global leisure brand 'Yidify'. In January 2001, Hongdou was listed on the Shanghai Stock Exchange. In 2003, Hongdou began to operate the real estate and it gained some initial successes. On 8 September 2004, in the uncertain conditions of the Chinese stock exchange, Hongdou stock successfully increased 35.8 million stock by 8.2 Yuan per stock, thereby raising a fund of nearly 300 million RMB. The stated development plan of the group is: 'The 10 billion Hongdou is the result of setting up the independence brand for 23 years. To establish the centennial enterprise, the 10 billion Hongdou must choose the way of producing the independence brand' (Hongdou Group, 2006).

3.1.8.1.1 The corporation in recent years. In 1983, the corporation sold 630,000 items. From 1984, the corporation moved into profit for the first time and the sales quantity in that year rose to one million items. By 1987, the quantity of sales had reached 10 million and just four years later sales had reached 1.985 billion. Following the listing of Hongdou stocks in 2001, the sales quantity in 2002 was more than 5 billion. In 1998, sales of Hongdou shirts, western-style clothes, neckties, fashionable dress, children's clothing and underwear produced by the corporation topped 10 million, the sales were 1.71 billion RMB, and the profits reached 151 million RMB. The corporation's products were sold to more than 20 countries, and the capital earned by exports stood at more than 13 million RMB. At present, the overall assets of the company stood at 809 million RMB and the number of the employees was 7,000. In 2005, the sales of Hongdou products achieved more than 10 billion RMB, reaching 11.73 billion RMB – an increase of 47.8 per cent. In addition, the profits reached 809 million RMB – an increase of 17.4 per cent. Additional data for the company are presented in Table 3.16.

3.1.8.2 The philosophy of the management

The Hongdou Group emphasizes the virtues of hard work. The philosophy of the corporation is expressed in the following statement: 'Let the idleness go home, let the talentless employees out of work, let the talentless leaders be the employees, pay the talent general managers 1 million a year, break out of the intrinsic thinking model, step forward in the consciousness of crisis' (Hongdou Group, 2004).

The innovation tenets of the company are that: (i) continuous innovation and great success can only be achieved through self-denial and self-improvement; (ii) advanced management can make up for the lag in

Table 3.16   Basic data of the Hongdou Corporation

Year	Sales (million RMB)	Overall assets (million RMB)	Number of employees
2005	11,730	6,480	16,594
2004	7,912	4,400	13,329
2003	6,078	4,058	13,400
2002	5,042	2,618	10,466
2001	2,838	1,861	5,324
2000	2,260	1,205	5,415

Source: National Bureau of Statistics of China, Large Corporations of China, China Statistics of China, 2001, 2002, 2003, 2004, 2005, 2006.

technologies, but advanced technologies cannot compensate for inadequate management; and (iii) great innovation leads to great development, little innovation results in little development and no innovation contributes to no development.

3.1.8.2.1 Innovation.   The development history of Hongdou is the history of establishing the brand name. Innovation is the main part of the history. The Hongdou Group gained great achievements through the innovations of property rights, technology, management and marketing. The Hongdou Group has never loosened its recognition of the importance of innovation. By 2005, Hongdou has already had more than 110 registered patents. The planting and cultivation of yew gained the title of the national invent patents; it was listed in the items of technology star in Jiangsu province. The innovation project of Hongdou is not only the innovation of the technology, but also the innovation in terms of management and marketing. In the words of the director.

> The increase of innovation strength of the corporation is not just a slogan; it can't leave the introduction and the cultivation of the talents. The sensible enterprise should understand how to encourage the innovation passion of every employee and provide them with the condition of cultivating their innovation strength.

After entering into WTO, China has merged to an increasing extent with the global economy. Chinese enterprises are also increasingly faced by intense competition in the world economy. It is no longer enough to depend on its inexpensive labour force to participate in the competition for the international low-end market. They need to adjust and promote the industrial structure. On the other hand, in this environment of economic globalization, following the lowering of the tariff barrier, the developed countries should adopt the new method of intellectual property (Fang, 2006; Tian, 2003), the trade barrier and so on, to seize and control the market. We must pay great attention to the enhancement of independent innovation ability, and regard it as an important work.

3.1.8.2.2 Quality management. The quality of the products is the guarantee for the brand name. In several recent years, Hongdou has not only introduced advanced clothing machines to make sure that hardware remains state of the art; it has also cooperated with the ESMOD clothes design college (a famous International Fashion School in France). It trains its designers to improve the fashionable content and the brand image of the Hongdou products. The corporation increased the skills and quality consciousness of their employees by holding training courses and competitions, in order to drive up their product standards. In 1997, the company achieved the ISO9002 standard and Hongdou's western-style clothes, shirts and jackets have been labelled as the 'the Chinese brand name' and they became the first series of the 'famous brand of China'.

3.1.8.2.3 Wages performance link. In 1986, the system of wage benefits at the end of the year was revised. From this date, the wages of the workers are linked to the quantity and quality of the products, the wages of leaders are determined by the achievements of the corporation, the wages of the supply and marketing agents are determined by the profits of the corporation, the wages of skilled personnel are determined by the efficiency of the corporation. In sum, the interest of every member of the corporation is linked with the benefits of the corporation.

3.1.8.3 Brand strategy and culture of the group

In 1983, the Hongdou Group began to develop its own brand. The chairman of Hongdou Group Zhou Yaoting named the product 'Hongdou'. In 1987, Hongdou promoted its strategy of brand development and paid a large amount of money for an advertisement on CCTV. The company succeeded in achieving its objective. Consequently 'Hongdou' is very popular in the domestic market and it is also creating a good impact in global markets.

Half of the name brand is the culture. The corporation chose the name 'Hongdou' which carries with it an abundance of national affection. From the time of its inception, 'Hongdou' has not only 'affection' as the foundation of its corporate culture, but also makes the corporation culture the core strength of the corporation. In order to secure a more stable foundation for its culture, the Hongdou Group banded together the corporation culture and the national culture. Since 2001, Hongdou has held a 'lovers' festival' on 7 July. This has involved many activities: for example, collecting ancient poetry and love stories. This way of promoting the corporation culture through an embrace of national culture has been very successful, and has been supported by cultural celebrities, such as He Jingzhi, Yu Guangzhong and Feng Jicai.

3.1.8.4   *WTO and the application of information technology*

After entering WTO, every textile and clothing enterprise faces direct participation in, and competition with, the world market. Therefore, it became essential for the enterprises to promote the ability of quick reaction and to speed up the assembly of information. The core of the ability of quick reaction is informationization. This brings together the production process, the marketing process and the management process; it forms the service flow which has high efficiency and the ability to react quickly in order to create more customer value and enterprise value. The informationization of the corporations' processes marks a change in traditional competition. This kind of situation forces the enterprise to increase the level of IT investment, to establish modern logistics, and to quickly satisfy customers' demand.

In 1992 Hongdou Group Co, Ltd. made its first use of computers. Since then, it has made great strides in terms of establishing the informationization of the corporation. By 2004, the network contained 250 computers, across every major branch of the corporation. Computer management was used in every domain of the corporation through connections to the Internet, which allowed data to be transferred rapidly. It effectively enhanced the enterprise's competitive abilities. At present, the emphasis of the group is on breaking away from its old methods, adding the traditional ideas of computers and automatization, fundamentally redesigning the service flow, and realizing improvements in quality, cost, service and speed through the use of information technology.

COMPARISON OF THE STRATEGIES OF THE TWO ENTERPRISES

3.1.9   Youngor Group

The Youngor Group was founded in 1979. Over the course of more than 20 years, Youngor has developed an operational pattern of exponential growth and professional development, based upon fabric and garment production, real estate and foreign trade. In order to save capital, Youngor pays considerable attention to learning from others: in creating its Youngor brand, many successful strategies, including brand extensions, marketing strategies and so on, have been acquired from the study of other companies.

In August 1990, Ningbo Youngor Garment Co., Ltd was founded jointly, Youngor transformed from a collectively owned enterprise to joint-venture enterprise, the business ideas, the technological level and operational pattern of Youngor had made significant progress. In 1993, Youngor Group Co., Ltd was established. In November 1998, Youngor Group Co., Ltd issued 55 million A shares on the Shanghai Stock Exchange.

In the middle of the 1980s, Youngor introduced the constant advanced technology of manufacture and management methods, and thereby gained a relative industrial advantage in the quality of machines, the scale of production and management methods. It also tried hard to focus on the domestic clothing market, leading to the rapid growth of the corporation. Since 1995, it has established an extensive country-wide network of distribution. In 2003, it established itself as the top-ranking fabric producer. Youngor carried out the operating strategies of exponential growth and professional development all the time, conceived the development of digitized project and the use of information technology, made use of informationization to bring about the development of industrialization. They tried to find a new way industrialize. Youngor introduced advanced equipment and techniques, paid attention to the innovation of technology, and developed many new products and new technologies.

After entering WTO, Youngor has a chance to internationalize. During the process of internationalization, Youngor pays great attention to the selection of talented personnel. On the other hand, Youngor positively adjusts the management system of the enterprise, promotes the production management method of ERP.

3.1.10 Hongdou Group

In 1983, the Hongdou Group was founded on knitting underwear. From 1992, the group has focused on the production of other clothing. In January 2001, Hongdou stock was listed on the stock market in Shanghai. The development plan of the group is: 'The 10 billion Hongdou is the result of setting up the independence brand for 23 years. To establish the centennial enterprise, the 10 billion Hongdou must choose the way of producing the independence brand.'

The culture of Hongdou emphasizes hard work. It has successfully introduced the initial market system and the interior stock cooperation system. Hongdou emphasized the construction of the corporation culture from the beginning, bringing together the corporation culture with the national culture. It also emphasized independent innovation. Innovation is the main rhythm of the history of Hongdou. The innovation project of Hongdou is reflected not only in terms of technology, but also in respect of management and marketing. It encourages the innovation passion of every employee and provides them with the conditions to cultivate their innovation strength. It used the computers first in 1992, from then on, it has gained great achievements in the informationization of the corporation, realizing improvements in quality, cost, service and speed through the use of information technology.

3.1.11 Contrast and conclusions

There are many similarities in the process of internationalization followed by the two corporations, albeit they have different emphases. Both corporations have developed from small enterprises employing a single production unit. Learning from international experience and independent innovation, they have achieved a move away from traditional business ideas, technological levels and operational patterns. They have also experienced independent development and internationalization, paying attention to the reform and development of a brand strategy, creating a brand name and brand culture, and building up an extensive sales network. At the same time, they paid attention to digitized project and information technology, and made use of high-tech equipment to enhance competitiveness. Regarding the brand strategy, Youngor pays attention to the use of others' experience. By contrast, Hongdou pays attention to the independent innovation and relies on China's traditions in order to create brand culture.

PART III: CASE STUDIES OF CHINESE TEXTILES SECTOR FIRMS

3.1.12   Shijiazhuang Changshan Textile Group Co., Ltd

3.1.12.1   The enterprise

Changshan Textile Group Co. Ltd. (http://www.changshantex.com), located in Shijiazhuang City, Hebei Province, China, consists of 25 exclusively invested enterprises, 13 textiles production enterprises, two trading companies (including international trading), six service firms and several firms with design institute, research institute of textile, school of technology and cadre. In addition, there are two share companies controlled by the Changshan Textile Group Co., Ltd – the Changshan Share Corporation and the Shenzhen Changshan Textile Trade Corporation. Changshan Textile Group Co., an example of reform of a Chinese state-owned enterprise, is successful, in which the successful experiences for management development indicate a created development outlet with new and high-tech driving the process of corporation reformation. The basic information of the firm is presented in Table 3.17.

3.1.12.2   The development and growth of the company

Changshan Textile Group Co., Ltd. is a large synthetic textiles corporation based on the Shijiazhuang Textile Corporation and engaged in cotton spinning & weaving, printing & dyeing, knitting, clothing, and spinning machines. It trades on both the Chinese domestic market and the export trade. In 1996 it was reorganized as a state-owned company. It was listed in the first group of 520 national key enterprises and was one of the 50 national key textiles groups. It was one of the 30 large mainstay groups in Hebei Province and one of the 10 flagship companies in Shijiazhuang City. In 2000, it was placed 9th of the top 100 enterprises in Hebei; in 2001, it was ranked third in terms of sales revenue in the textiles sector in China; in 2002, it ranked 441st of the top 500 enterprises in China, 14th of the textiles

Table 3.17 The basic statistical data of the Changshan Textile Group

Year	Operation revenue (million RMB)	Overall assets (million RMB)	Employed persons
2005	3,240.17	6,428.95	30,390
2004	3,232.15	6,506.74	31,845
2003	2,657.59	5,879.97	38,711
2002	2,502.16	5,292.13	39,619
2001	2,338.93	5,405.81	40,243
2000	2,605.59	4,898.60	41,990

Source: National Bureau of Statistics of China, Large Corporations of China, China Statistics of China, 2001, 2002, 2003, 2004, 2005, 2006.

enterprises in the top 500 enterprises, and 12th in terms of Hebei Province's enterprises. In July 2000, Changshan Textile made its initial public offering (IPO) of 'A' shares on the Shenzhen Stock Exchange. The initial financing of 0.6 billion RMB established a stable base for the development of the corporation.

3.1.12.2.1 Product profile.

The company's main products are cotton yarn, cotton, printed and dyed fabric, chemical fibre and clothing. Eighty per cent of products are sold in more than 60 countries and regions across the world. The main equipment of throughput is 510,000 spindles, 14,000 weaving machines, and the annual dyeing capacity is 0.38 billion metres.

3.1.12.2.2 Performance.

In 2000, Changshan Textile Co. Ltd, one of the corporations of Changshan Textile Group Co., Ltd, achieved a sales income of 1.832 billion RMB; the pre-tax profit was 0.286 billion RMB and the net profits were 0.133 billion RMB. In 2000, the Changshan Textile Group Co. Ltd produced 111,200 tons of cotton yarn, 0.438 billion metres of cotton, and 0.151 billion metres of printed and dyed fabric, sector enterprises realized yearly sales income of 3.025 billion RMB, the pre-tax profits were 0.392 billion RMB, and the profits were 0.184 billion RMB.

In 2002, Changshan Textile Group Co., Ltd achieved an industrial added-value of 0.74 billion RMB, 4.51 per cent higher than in the previous year; in the same year the yearly sales income was 2.478 billion RMB – an increase of 7.65 per cent; the pre-tax profit amount totalled 0.24 million RMB up 34.66 per cent; finally, profits were 78.08 million RMB – an increase of 128.37 per cent. At the end of 2002, the corporation enjoyed total assets of 5.259 billion RMB with net assets reaching as high as 2.3 billion RMB and total liabilities of 2.544 billion RMB, employing just under 40,000 staff and workers.

3.1.12.3   *Management strategies and skill advancement*

At the end of 1996, the Changshan Textile Group Co., Ltd. had 650,000 spindles. The group promoted the essential principles of 'decrease spindles & regroup, reduce quantity & add value, reduce staff & increase efficiency, keep stabilization, promote development', based on the status quo of firm equipment. In respect of the operation to decrease the number of spindles, it stuck to the principles 'first concentrate reduction, second disperse reduction', and dealt well with the 'Four Combinations': combining the reduction of spindles with asset regrouping; making good use of the policy on optimizing capital profile/structure; with changes in profile for making up the deficits and achieving surpluses; with technology advancement for sector upgrading, with reduction of staff, increase efficiency and re-employment project. It actively finished the assigned task in the overall policy of the adjustment of Hebei province to the textiles sector, as well as to keep advantages of Shijiazhuang's textiles sector.

In 1998, in order to boost the level of skills and to optimize the operation of major corporations, it invested 0.13 billion RMB, by adjusting the product profile, improving quality, upgrading and rebuilding key procedures, key equipments and key parts, increasing the use of advanced technology, and increasing its competitive capacity in the home and overseas markets.

In its efforts to strengthen management the Changshan Group Co. Ltd focused on streamlining the organization and increasing its efficiency. In 1998, it reduced 7,700 workers from various resources; this measure alone cut almost 50 million RMB when compared to the same period in the previous year. In order to achieve this, it adopted measures including naturally reducing workers and not renewing contracts that had run out.

Since 1998, it has successively taken 'Five Groups' measures to redirect laid-off workers. The so-called 'Five Groups' are as follows: priority enterprises purchasing the available resources of bankrupt enterprises to add 5,400 new job opportunities; providing training to 1,800 workers who could be redeployed in other sectors; retaining 1,600 workers without pay; advancing the retirement of 6,200 workers based on relative policy; and establishing service sectors to take on 2,100 workers. With these measures 80 per cent of the laid-off workers are covered. Since 1998, it has successively provided 25.1479 million RMB (of which self-financing accounts for 1.7757 million RMB) for basic living standards and the re-employment of laid-off workers, guaranteed the basic needs of 7,000 laid-off workers, and maintained the basic stability of textiles employees.

3.1.12.4   *The effect of China's entry into WTO and global trade*

In 2000, in the face of the challenges posed and the opportunities provided by China's entry into WTO, the corporation outlined a three-year innovation and reform plan. In order to increase the level of competition both within and outside the nation, the company also laid an emphasis on exploring new products with high tech which can substitute for imports and increase exports.

At present, the stiff competition caused by the price reduction of textiles export corporations inside China is becoming increasingly severe. The only result of this 'civil war' is to drive down the profits of the corporations themselves. It is essential to adding the export tax, in order to prevent the trade friction that may be caused by the country's textiles rushing into the international market after the abolition of the global quota system. Adding an export tax causes great pressure on low-quality, low-price products, but less pressure on high-quality, high-price products. So this policy can achieve the purpose that the export tax duty of products with high annex is low and the export tax duty of products with low annex is relatively high, thereby encouraging the export of products with high annex and carry out the goal that optimizes the structure of the exportation of domestic textiles.

Shijiazhuang Changshan Textile Group Co., Ltd has tried to address the challenges of globalization by extending the domestic sales network, and establishing branches in Europe, Japan, Korea, and the USA. It also developed joint venture corporations with the large corporations abroad, searching for ways to set up factories abroad, achieve multinational management and meet with international market standards and tradition.

Combined with this technical transformation, Changshan Textile Group Co. Ltd has introduced an advanced recruit and use mechanism at home and abroad, clearly defining posts and recruiting personnel rationally and scientifically, sparing no effort in promoting the two-way selection of the workers, and improving efficiency, on the premise that the improvement of productivity levels increases the income of workers and staff. At the same time other measures such as selecting and dispatching excellent technicians to master up-to-date technology in a planned and systematic way, to take in the best talent, and to pay attention to train workers who are on the production line, improve the workers' manipulative skill to make sure that the advanced equipment runs properly and efficiently were also taken. Moreover, Changshan Group Co. Ltd actively promotes the systems of salary, shares and options to managers and workers.

3.1.13 Shandong Weiqiao Pioneering Group Co., Ltd

3.1.13.1 *History of the corporation*

Shandong Weiqiao Pioneering Group Co., Ltd. (http://www.weiqiaocy.com), has a registered address of No. 1 Weifang Road, Weiqiao Town, Zouping County, Shandong province. Under the group heading there are six subsidiary companies: Weiqiao Textile Shares Co., Ltd, Binzhou Weiqiao Thermoelectricity Co., Ltd, Binzhou Weiqiao Aluminum Co., Ltd, Shandong Weilian Printing and Dyeing Co., Ltd, Shandon Weiqiao Hongyuan

Home Textile Co. Ltd, and Shandong Weiqiao Apparel Co., Ltd. With a clear market orientation, and focusing on the economic benefits, cotton weaving production as a basis and 'weaving-dyeing and finishing-apparel' and 'thermoelectricity – smelting and pressing of metals' as wings, the corporation advocates scaled production and diversification into a number of different businesses. Weiqiao Textile Shares Co., Ltd is the largest holding subsidiary corporation of the Weiqiao Pioneering Group Co., Ltd. In September 2003, it was offered publicly on the stock exchanges in Hong Kong.

The chairman of the Shandong Weiqiao Pioneering Group Co., Ltd stated that 'in the case of production, we don't have any rivals and there is no such corporations that has the same scale as us' (WeiQiao, 2005). In this sector, the superiority in scale is of the utmost importance. In addition, China has an abundance of cheap labour, which can be seen as providing the corporation with a competitive advantage.

3.1.13.2   Production and business

Located in the south end of North Shandong Plains, close to the Jiaozhou–Jinan Railway and the Qingdao–Jinan Railway, Shandong Weiqiao Pioneering Group Co., Ltd is an enormous synthetic textiles corporation engaged in cotton spinning, weaving, dyeing and finishing and thermoelectricity products. Occupying an area of 1,000 hectares, with gross capital of RMB 13.5 billion, the corporation has first-class technical equipment. With the production scale and economic benefits occupying the No. 1 position in the cotton spinning lines all over the country, the corporation is one of top 100 industrial enterprises, the top 100 export companies and the top 100 import companies in China and 26 super large enterprises of Shandong Province. It has the world's greatest production capacity of textiles. World Brand Lab published China's 500 most influential brands on 28 June 2004. Weiqiao Pioneering Group Co., Ltd. is listed in the 120th position with 4.6 billion RMB.

3.1.13.2.1   Product profile.   Shandong Weiqiao Pioneering Group Co., Ltd has strong technical resources and has the ability to produce the products with high technology content and value added. The proportion of cloth products with high technology content reaches 60 per cent, of shuttleless fabrics 50 per cent, of knotless yarn 100 per cent and of combed yarn 85 per cent. The corporation is engaged mainly in the production of various cotton yarn, cotton fabrics, polyester cotton yarn, polyester cotton fabrics, high-count and high-density fabrics, elastic fabrics, jean fabrics (normal series and elastic series), corduroy, chemical fibre fabrics, dyed yarn, dyed fabrics (high-class cotton series, double elastic series) with 10 varieties (more than 2,000 kinds) and an annual output of 300,000 tons of cotton yarn and 800 million metres of fabrics. As an internationally famous product of Shandong Province, Weiqiao brand products cover more than 20 countries and regions, including the USA, Japan and Europe for their high class, good quality and

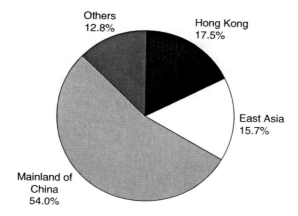

Figure 3.4   Regional market of Shandong Weiqiao Pioneering

complete specifications. The sales distribution of the countries and regions in 2005 is presented in Figure 3.4.

3.1.13.2.2 Performance. In 2002, the corporation realized sales revenue of RMB 6 billion, tax of RMB 800 million, profits of RMB 500 million, and sales of export of US$260 million, respectively increasing by 48 per cent, 36 per cent, 36 per cent and 73 per cent compared to the previous year. The sales revenue, tax and self-run export profits of foreign currency all place the corporation as no. 1 in terms of China's cotton spinning enterprises.

In 2003, the corporation realized a sales revenue as high as 11.43 billion RMB, an 88 per cent increase over the previous year; paid income tax of 1.51 billion RMB, an 84 per cent increase over the previous year; total profits of 0.856 billion RMB, a 75 per cent increase over the previous year; and the total amount of foreign currency earned through exportation reaching 0.439 billion RMB, a 66 per cent increase over the previous year.

In 2004, the corporation realized a sales revenue as high as 23.12 billion RMB, a 102.34 per cent increase over the previous year; paid income tax of 2.53 billion RMB, a 67.57 per cent increase over the previous year; a total profit of 1.51 billion RMB, a 76.68 per cent increase over the previous year; and the total amount of foreign currency earned through exports reached 0.583 billion RMB, a 32.85 per cent increase over the previous year.

In 2005, the corporation realized a sales revenue as high as 35.51 billion RMB, a 53.57 per cent increase over the previous year; paid income tax of 4.05 billion RMB, a 60.16 per cent increase over the previous year; achieved total profits of 2.11 billion RMB, a 39.2 per cent increase over the previous year; and the total amount of foreign currency earned through exportation reached 0.762 billion RMB, a 30.51 per cent increase over the previous year.

Table 3.18   Employment and asset data of the Shandong Weiqiao Pioneering Group

Year	Operation revenue (million RMB)	Overall assets (million RMB)	Employed persons
2005	35,669.27	25,690.88	110,257
2004	23,233.53	22,296.53	83,588
2003	11,466.73	15,041.44	55,753
2002	5,214.92	6,975.62	40,621
2001	3,382.38	4,791.94	20,307
2000	2,612.86	2,384.55	11,645

Source: National Bureau of Statistics of China, Large Corporations of China, China Statistics of China, 2001, 2002, 2003, 2004, 2005, 2006.

In the year 2006, from January to March, the corporation achieved sales revenues of 0.99 billion RMB, a 32.71 per cent increase over the previous year; it paid income tax of 0.78 billion RMB, a 15.04 per cent increase over the previous year; total profit of 0.39 billion RMB, a 15.62 per cent increase over the previous year; and the total amount of foreign currency earned through exportation reaching 0.18 billion RMB, a 4.32 per cent decrease over the previous year. Employment and assets data are presented in Table 3.18.

3.1.13.3   Development trajectory

The Shandong Weiqiao Pioneering Group Co., Ltd. expanded to its existing size by relying on local resources and innovation. The development can be divided into four stages:

3.1.13.3.1   The First Stage, 1951–1980: increase with stagnation.   Under the bondage of the planned economy, the corporation engaged in simplex cotton machining, and there were, broadly speaking, no changes in 30 years. In 1980, the total capital was less than 1 million, and the total amount of tax paid was 0.5 million.

3.1.13.3.2   The Second Stage, 1981–1988: increase with change.   Under the economic system's transformation from the planned to the market economy, the corporation began to expand its business domain, and entered into the areas of oil plant machining and washcloth machining. The economic benefits improved obviously due to the transformation of the system and the expansion of the business. The total paid tax increased from 0.93 million in 1981 to 8.6 million in 1988. With an average annual increase of 37.4 per cent, the corporation was undergoing a high growth development.

3.1.13.3.3   The Third Stage, 1989–1998: increase with persistence.   In this period, while expanding the business in existence and making sure that it achieved the leading position in terms of textile production, the market economy was kept on to boost, the level of marketization of the business having been improved step by step. The total amount of tax paid increased from 1.085 million in 1989 to 18.11 million in 1988 – an average annual increase of 36.7 per cent.

3.1.13.3.4 The Fourth Stage: 1999–now: increase with leap. The market economy system was set up step by step, the level of marketization of the business was improved remarkably, the business domain expanded to printing and dyeing, home cotton, thermoelectricity and so on. The total amount of tax paid increased from 0.24 billion in 1999 to 2.53 billion in 2004, with an average annual increase of more than 0.4 billion. This development meant that the corporation entered the stage that can be labelled 'increase with leap'.

3.1.13.4 Strength of corporation and effect

3.1.13.4.1 Economic strength. Centred on the principle of 'while expanding oneself, bring along the corroborative corporations', Shandong Weiqiao Pioneering Group Co., Ltd. initially formed a sector system mainly including textile, printing and dyeing, clothes, food, medicine, machining, smelt, paper making, chemical and so on, provided support to a set of key enterprises, pillar enterprises and famous-brand enterprises. Consequently the level of regional industrialization improved remarkably. Up to 2004, Shandong Weiqiao Pioneering Group Co., Ltd contributed to the local finance with 0.235 billion, made up 40 per cent of the local finance, handed in tax to the nation for 2 billion in total from 1995 to 2004, and earned foreign exchange through exports of more than 2 billion dollars.

3.1.13.4.2 Influence of the corporation in regional economic development In Weiqiao town, where Shandong Weiqiao Pioneering Group Co., Ltd. is located, the number of individual catering enterprises which rely on the group is more than 300, private enterprise more than 200. The tax paid by the catering sector alone is roughly 20 per cent of the town's financial income. The move also promotes employment and re-employment. Preliminary statistics shows that since 2001 Weiqiao sector garden has run more than 70 new programmes, promoted 3,500 individual business operators who entered the garden, provided more than 90,000 jobs, and absorbed 80,000 of the rural labour force.

3.1.13.4.3 External orientation activities. Shandong Weiqiao Pioneering Group Co., Ltd has business relations with many countries and regions such as Japan, the USA and Hong Kong in the area of top-grade textiles, printing and dyeing, bleaching and dyeing, knitting, colour weave, costume and home spin. On 24 September 2003, it was successfully offered for public sale on stock exchanges in Hong Kong, collecting HK$2.441 billion. On 28 May 2004, the group collected HK$3 billion in total.

3.1.14   Innovation initiatives

In the middle of the 1980s, at a time when the country's entire textiles sector was stagnant, Weiqiao Pioneering Group Co., Ltd. began to swim against the stream and confirmed that it would move from oil cotton machining to spin machining. Through these efforts the cost of cotton move from declined. For 10,000 spindles it used 110 workers, for 100 looms used 87 workers. Affected by the Southeast Asian financial crisis and a substantial drop in domestic demand, the Chinese textiles sector after 1997 faced a harsh situation, export being obstructed and the economic efficiency of the sector declining. Weiqiao Pioneering Group Co., Ltd started with strengthening management and rapid technological transformation, deepened the innovation, and established a modern enterprise system. Over the course of nearly ten years, they invested 0.8 billion RMB for technological transformation and finished 45 programmes. There were continuous quality and technological improvements, thereby demonstrating the overall improvement in performance. It exported to South-east Asia and the West in large quantities and the economic benefits keep increasing. By means of capital expansion, in the situation where the whole sector was in difficulty, it grasped chances, purchased and efficiently ran a set of hard corporations, lead to the situation where the extension and competition force of the corporation kept enhancing.

One thing that is worth mentioning in particular is that, in 1999, the self-prepared steam supply and power generating plant that invested 0.12 million and an annual power generation of 0.2 billion kilowatts was put into use. In 2000, the second phases – 0.45 million kilowatts – was put into use. The self-built power-generating plant guaranteed the demand and the development of the corporation. This point, in face of the fact that there was a national shortage of electric power, is rather praiseworthy. After the construction of the power-generating plant, the electricity used for the sector was 0.2RMB/ kilowatt-hour, the electricity used for living was 0.35 RMB/ kilowatt-hour, and the price of other corporations in Zouping was more than 0.4 RMB/ kilowatt-hour. This saves a large amount of cost for the corporation. The installed power-generating capacity of the self-prepared steam supply and power-generating plant is 0.45 million kilowatts. By 2007, the installed power generating capacity was projected to be 3 million kilowatts.

3.1.14.1   *The influence of global trade*

Benefiting from the free commercial environment since China entered the WTO, the global textiles trade should be more open; and China's textiles sector would enjoy unprecedented market superiority. Weiqiao Pioneering

Group Co., Ltd has grasped this chance, put the eye on the world with full confidence (Ding, 2005); and pledged to become the largest textiles corporation in the world. The corporation is relying entirely on its own efforts, trying to exploit international markets, extending into intermediate or high quality markets. It is yet to be seen whether the company can achieve its ambitions.

The culture of the enterprise can be summarized as *Spirits*: Striving, Enterprising, Practical, Innovating, Rapid, Efficient, Pursuing First Class; *Developing Strategy*: With market as orientation, economic benefits as focus, cotton weaving production as basis and 'weaving-dyeing and finishing-apparel' and 'thermoelectricity – Smelting and Pressing of Metals' as wings, the corporation advocates scaled production, multi-business; *Business Guideline*: selling based on market, production based on sales, supply based on production and plan based on profits; *Management Guideline*: strict management, tight production, good quality, activating business, caring for staffs' life; *Quality*: Guideline based on human resources, practical, innovating, delicate spinning and weaving, customers' satisfaction; *Technical Revolution Strategy*: do according to our abilities, rolling development, leaping increase, benign development; *Guideline of Technical Revolution Management*: five 'synchronous' and five 'early', i.e., synchronous progress of land construction, equipment installation, training, product development and market exploitation, early construction, early installation, early putting into production, early mass production and early reward; *Guideline of Quality Management*: Not pass even there is only one denial, two 'forbids', three 'never let pass'.

3.1.15 Summary and conclusions

3.1.15.1 Changshan Textile Group Co., Ltd

Changshan Textile Group Co., Ltd is a large synthetic textiles corporation based on the Shijiazhuang Textile Corporation and engaging in cotton spinning & weaving, printing & dyeing since 1991. In 1996, having been reorganized as a state-owned limited company, it was one of 50 national key textile groups. In July 2000, Changshan Textile made its initial public offering (IPO). 'A' shares issued on the Shenzhen Stock Exchange provided a stable base for corporation development. Changshan Textile Group Co., Ltd experienced a steady expansion in scale. Meanwhile, Changshan Textile Group Co., Ltd actively boosted the enterprise's technical renovations and managerial improvements, washed out backward spindles, and optimized major business. It also reduced staff and increased efficiency, promoted capital optimization and regrouped, promoted structure adjustment and adjusted variety, exploited market.

The corporation renovated and reconstructed its printing and dyeing equipment, emphasizing an increase in the amount of advanced equipment to improve the ability of technology innovation and the exploitation of new products. The company enlarged its marketing net, establishing sales offices in Japan, Korea, the West, Africa and so on, and also increased its market share. In the face of the new challenges of WTO, the corporation improved its management strategies. The measures enabled the optimization of the staff, capital and product, and effectively improved the economic benefits of the group.

3.1.15.2   Shandong Weiqiao Pioneering Group Co., Ltd

Incorporated in 1951, the transformation of the Shandong Weiqiao Pioneering Group Co., Ltd from a small cotton machining plant to its present scale depended upon its ability to seize opportunities and to undertake timely reformation. When the economic system transformed to a market economy, the corporation took advantage of new policies and introduced variety in products – it quickly reaped economic benefits. While the market economy continued to grow, the corporation ensured the leading position in textiles production. The level of marketization of the business has been improved remarkably, the business domain has been expanded to printing and dyeing, home cotton and so on that has resulted in a further expansion of scale.

In the process of scale expansion and raising economic benefits, constantly improving management techniques and emancipating the minds of those in the business. The economic system of enterprises constantly increased the level of technological innovation. Following China's accession to WTO, the corporation began to establish new goals and to constantly improve a multilevel management concept in order to further bring into play manufacturing preponderance itself, and to crystallize the idea of the Weiqiao Pioneering Group Co., Ltd. brand.

3.1.15.3   Contrast and conclusions

From the case studies of Chinese textiles sector leaders, namely the Changshan Group and the Weiqiao Group, it is clear that there have been several common characteristics in their development trajectories, although there have also been a number of significant differences. Their growth processes saw expansions in scale as the main objective. In the transformation to the market economy the Changshan Group and the Weiqiao Group utilized the prospects of new environments, and grasped the opportunities of markets and policies to expand their corporations. In order to remain competitive, they improved the quality and levels of management and upgraded the manufacturing equipment and technology. In the era of new challenges of WTO, these groups faced them positively, made efforts to enlarge their markets, and achieved the status of international enterprises.

Notes

1. In China people used to hold a special ticket to buy a certain amount of clothes.
2. The three types are: Sino-foreign joint ventures, enterprises with Sino-foreign cooperation, and wholly foreign-owned enterprises.

Bibliography

Balassa, Bela (1965) 'Trade Liberalization and Revealed Comparative Advantage', *Manchester School of Economic and Social Studies*, 33: 99–123.

Ding Haitang (2005) 'The Experiences and Notices from the Grow of Wei Qiao Pioneer Group', *Shandong Economic Strategy Research*, 6: 24–6.

Fang Chunquan (2006) 'The Reform of Textile Export Tariff Rebate and its Influence', *World of Entrepreneurs*, 5: 87–110.

Fu Dahai (2006) 'The Research of Competitiveness and Potential of Textile and Clothing Industry in China', *Journal of University of Zhong Nan Economic & Law*, 3: 15–22.

Guo Weixing (2005) 'The Development and Financial Support of Textile Industry under the Restraint of Government Policies and Markets', *Ji Nan Finance*, 9: 132–44.

Hongdou Group (2004) 'Striving For the First Speed', *Manufacturing Information Engineering of China*, 12: 37–9.

HuaFang Group (2005) 'Speed up the Technological Innovation to Obtain the Sustained Development', *JuangSu Textile*, 102–22.

Hongdou Group (2006) 'Constructing the Enterprise's Culture and Building the Long-history Enterprise', *Zeng Gong Yan Jiu Dong Tai*, 19: 211–18.

Hong, Qingjun, Feng, Jianqi and Zhao, Huatao (2000) 'Present Status and Development of China Textile Industry', *Journal of Zhen Zhou Textile Institute*, 11(2): 55–60.

Ianchovichina E. and Martin, W. (2001) 'Implications of China's Accession to the WTO for China and the WTO', *World Economy*, 24: 23–7.

Kathuria, S., Martin, W., and Bhardwaj, A. (2001) 'Implication for South Asian Countries of Abolishing the Multi-fiber Arrangement', World Bank Policy Research Working Paper No. 2721, Washington, DC, November.

Liu, Yingyuan (2006) 'The Tariff Policy and its Influence', *Northern Economy*, 2: 17–22.

Li, Chuang, Wang, Liping (2006) 'Empirical Study on the Competitiveness of China's T&C Industry' (3), *Progress in Textile Science & Technology*, 4: 179–90.

Li Rucheng (2006) 'Search for an Innovative Way for the Development of Private Enterprise – Interview with Li Rucheng, CEO of Youngor Group', *China Non-Governmental Science, Technology and Economy*, 7: 88–97.

National Development & Reform Commission (2005) *Development Outline of The 11th-Five-Year Planning in Textile Industry*, National Development & Reform Commission, Beijing, 2005: 355–61.

Nie Zilu (2005) 'On WTO Rule's Influence in the Law-making and Practices of China's Textiles Industry and the Countermeasures of China', *Herbei Law Science*, 6: 113–18.

Ruo, Shui (2006) 'Prospect of Textile Exports', *World Market*, 4: 42–9.

Tao Haimei (2005) 'Present Situation and Development of Textiles and Garment Standards in China', *Shang Hai Textile Science & Technology*, 5(3): 12–21.

Tian Shuhua (2003) 'The Effects of Reduction of Tariff on Textile Industry', *Journal of Dandong Teachers College*, 1: 79–90.

Wang Cheng (2000) 'The Trend of Clothing Technology in Respect of Technological Development', *Tian Jin Textile Science & Technology*, 39(4): 23–35.

Wang Hui, Guangixi (2005) 'Current Status and Development Trend of China's Textile Industry after the Elimination of Quota', *Textile Science & Technology*, 34(3): 233–51.

Wang, Liping, Li, Chuang, (2005) 'An Overview of the International Competitiveness of the Chinese Textile Industry', *Chemical Fiber & Textile Technology*, 4(2): 42–9.

Wei Qiao (2005) 'Made in Shan Dong', *First Chinese Business Daily*, 5: 12–13.

Xu, Hui (1996) 'The Development Trend and Countermeasures of China's Textile Trade', *International Economic and Trade Research*, 2: 37–41.

Yao, Zhiwei, Luo, Xian, Feng, Gao, Yanli (2005) 'Influence of Complete Practice of ATC on The Competing Power of Chinese Textile Industry', *Northern Economy and Trade*, 6:175–82.

Youngor (2006a) 'The Special Characters of Youngor', *Manufacturing Information Engineering of China*, 9: 53–66.

Youngor (2006b) 'The E-strategy of Youngor – Interview with CIO of Youngor Group', *Manufacturing Information Engineering of China*, 9: 167–79.

Zhao Hongshan, Ning Jun (2000) 'The Phase of Textile Economy and China's Textile Product Trade', *China Textile & Apparel*, 1: 49–50.

Zhao, Lei (2005) 'Overview and Prospects on China's Textile Economy (2004–2005)', *China Textile Leader*, 4: 13–17.

4
The Indian Textiles and Clothing Industry and Innovation Policies

K. Narayanan

4.1 Introduction

The Indian textiles and clothing (T&C) industry is one of the largest and oldest sectors in the country. It is an important sector of the economy in terms of output and investment and employs nearly 35 million people, making it the second-highest employer in the country behind agriculture. It accounts for around 4 per cent of gross domestic product, 14 per cent of industrial production, 9 per cent of excise collection, 18 per cent of employment in the industrial sector and 16 per cent of the country's total exports earnings. It has a direct link with the rural economy and the agricultural sector. The salient features of the Indian textiles industry are that it has a strong raw materials production base, a vast pool of skilled and unskilled labour, freely available cheap labour, export potential and a low level of dependency upon imports. This is a traditional, well-established industry which is enjoying considerable demand in both the domestic and the global markets.

The T&C industry is one of the important industries in the Indian economy. During the 1990s textiles and clothing items have been significant in India's export basket, accounting for around 20 per cent of total exports. By 2003, T&C exports were the largest export group, accounting for 23 per cent of Indian exports. In addition, this industry is the second-largest generator of employment (35 million – or around 10 per cent of the workforce). This is one of the significant earners of foreign exchange, and it contributes 4 per cent to GDP and 14 per cent value added in manufacturing (Ministry of Textiles, Annual Report 2003–04).

India has a competitive advantage stemming from its large and relatively low-cost labour force, a large domestic supply of fabrics, and the industry's ability to manufacture a wide range of products (USITC 2004). India has a very strong and diverse raw material base for manufacturing natural and artificial fibres. Furthermore, India also has capacity-based advantage in textiles and spinning, and India's textiles industry covers the entire supply chain.

In this context this study has made an attempt to understand the Indian textiles industry from a variety of aspects. The study begins with a brief history of Indian textiles and presents the present scenario. The production of different textile products, employment, and the structure of the industry is briefly narrated in this study. Furthermore the trend of import, export and growth of the industry are analysed and there is also a brief discussion of the policy measures undertaken by the government. To understand the Multi-Fibre Arrangement (MFA) period and its impact on world textiles trade in general, and Indian textiles in particular, the study presents a review of literature, and analyses firm-level performance, in selected firms in this sector, during the most recent years. The impact of MFA on the Indian textiles industry and the challenges ahead are also taken into account in the study.

The study used data from secondary sources to analyse the performance of the Indian textiles industry. Most of the data are collected from the website of the Ministry of Textiles. We have also made use of the Economic Surveys of Government of India from different periods. In addition, various five-year plan periods are carefully studied to gather the relevant data. Data have also been gathered from the *Foreign Trade Statistics of India (Principal Commodities & Countries)*, DGCIS (Directorate General of Commercial Intelligence and Statistics), Kolkata. Export/Import data from DGCIS, Kolkata, *Compendium of Textile Statistics, 2004* was also used in order to sketch the Export and Import scenario of Indian textiles. The production data of cotton for different countries are collected from the *US Cotton Market Monthly Economic letter* published in October 2006. The data for the firm-level analysis are collected from Capitaline Databases, and from the homepages of the respective firms. The study uses simple statistical techniques for the analysis of data.

4.2   Review of literature

A large body of literature attempts to analyse the impact of the post-MFA situation and also the impact of the removal of quantitative restrictions. Some of this literature is cited below. The literature is collected form various sources (printed documents and also web searches).

Whalley (2006) has pointed that in India, export growth in both clothing and textiles exports to both the USA and the EU provides a positive post-MFA employment picture. Prior to January 2005 there had also been considerable speculation as to what the impacts of MFA termination would be on the dynamic and more rapidly growing Asian exporters, especially in the area of clothing. Much of this focused on China as the largest shipper, and India as the second largest; but they also included Pakistan, the Philippines, Korea, Hong Kong, Indonesia, Bangladesh, Sri Lanka, Nepal, Cambodia, Vietnam and other countries.

In their study Prasad and Jain-Chandra (2005) raised some issues and opportunities for India. They narrate that the dismantling of the quota presents an opportunity for India to increase its share of the global export market. They analyze the impact of the quota elimination on India using GTAP 6, a global network of researchers. In addition to examining the impact of the full removal of the quotas as is standard, they also analyze the impact of the removal in the presence of safeguards on China. The results of the simulations do not present an optimistic scenario for India in terms of the export growth of T&C in a quota-free world (Scenario I). They also show that Indian exports of T&C will continue to expand in the presence of the safeguards on China, but will be adversely affected once these are lifted (Scenario II), essentially providing India's T&C industry some respite until 2008, when all safeguards on China will be lifted. It appears that in the face of falling prices, Indian industry needs to become more competitive. Most of the domestic reforms in India's T&C sector took place after 2000, with substantial policy initiatives in 2004. The impact of these policy changes of the past few years in the T&C sector would produce results after a lag. India could emerge much stronger and expand its trade in textiles and apparel at a much faster pace if the some of the key weaknesses are overcome.

With regard to environmental standards, Uimonen and Whalley (1997) observe that the argument of 'unfair trade advantage' for those countries that have low environmental standards neglects the likelihood that the environmental standards may reflect different approaches to attain similar levels of environmental protection and different priorities with respect to such protection. Efficient differences in standards in abatement costs argue against the harmonization of such measures. However, in the absence of standards, there would be no incentive to undertake environmental policy interventions, which necessitates the importance of effective policy instruments. A study by ICICI (1996) based on interviews with Indian garment exporters and US buyers throws light on the fact that the buyers are keen that Indian exporters adopt global standards in environment and labour.

Parikh et al. (1995) conducted a questionnaire-based survey of Indian exporters to understand the awareness of environmental standards, costs of compliance and impacts of eco-labelling on trade. Their results show a good level of awareness among the large-scale exporters, an increase of 3–5 per cent in product costs on compliance with environmental standards and a prominent notion among the garments exporters that environmental factors come only after fashion and feel, even in Germany. Almost all of the exporters to the EU have complied with packaging standards.

4.3 History of Indian textiles

The Indian textiles industry has a great legacy, which is perhaps unmatched in the history of the country's industrial development. The origin of Indian textiles can be traced to the Indus valley civilization, who used homespun cotton to weave their garments. The first literary evidence about textiles in India can be found in the Rigveda, which refers to weaving. Ample evidence on the ancient textiles of India can also be obtained from the various sculptures belonging to the Mauryan and Gupta eras as well as from ancient Buddhist scripts and murals (Ajanta caves). India had numerous trade links with the outside world and Indian textiles were popular in the ancient world. Indian silk was popular in Rome in the early centuries of the Christian era. Many fragments of cotton material originating from Gujarat have been found in the Egyptian tombs at Fostat, which date from the 5th century AD. The antiquity of Indian textiles exports can be established from the records of the Greek geographer 'Strabo' and from the first-century Greek source 'Periplus', which mentions the Gujarati port of Barygaza as exporting a variety of textiles. Archaeological evidence from Mohenjodaro establishes that the complex technology of mordant dyeing had been known in the subcontinent from at least the second millennium BC. The use of printing blocks in India may date as far back as 3000 BC, and some historians are of the view that India may have been the original home of textiles printing. The Portuguese were the first to arrive, having discovered a sea route from Europe to the East that allowed them to avoid the heavy taxes on goods sent overland through the Middle East. Soon Indian textiles were exported directly to Europe, where they became highly fashionable. Silk fabrics from south India were exported to Indonesia during the thirteenth century. India also exported printed cotton fabrics or chintz, to European countries and the Far East before the coming of the Europeans to India.

The colonization period put an end to India's textiles inheritance. At this time India was forced to become a net importer and by 1880 the domestic market was being serviced by British manufacturers. From the post-independence era until about the late 1980s, the government introduced numerous policies and regulations and thus labour-intensive textiles were produced in India. Large-scale production was discouraged by restrictions on the total capacity and mechanization of mills. The high production cost was due to the labour regulations which did not allow capital investment in the sector. The imposition of price restrictions, along with decreased productivity, resulted in a lower level of competitiveness on the global market.

4.4   The present scenario of Indian textiles

The 1985 Textile Policy marked a new beginning in the history of the Indian textiles industry. It addressed the issues of raw materials supply at reasonable and stable prices, the progressive reduction of duties on synthetic raw materials, the removal of entry and exit barriers along with an emphasis on technology modernization and an increase in the international competitiveness of Indian textiles. The policy illustrated the government's attempt to relax the regulatory burden on the composite mill sector through the elimination of compartmentalization in the industry, the lifting of restrictions on composite mill loom capacity expansion and the equalization of taxation among composite mills, power looms and independent processing units.

The reforms in the 1990s provided another boost to the Indian textiles industry. The textiles industry was de-licensed as per the Statement of Industrial Policy of 1991 and the Textile Development and Regulation Order of 1992. The textiles policy of 1985 and the economic policy of 1991 accelerated the economic growth during the 1990s. The number of cotton/man-made fibre textiles mills rose from 1,035 in 1987–88 to 1,741 in December 1997. Similarly, the number of spinning mills rose from 752 in 1987–88 to 1,461 in December 1997. Currently, India has the second highest spindleage in the world after China. Aggregate production of cloth in 1996–97 was 34,265 million sq. metres, an increase of 9 per cent over the figure for 1995–96. India's contribution to the world production of cotton textiles was about 12 per cent a decade ago, while currently it contributes about 15 per cent of world cotton textiles. The production of silk has increased from 9,498 tonnes in 1987–88 to 14,093 tonnes in 1996–97. The growth rate in the exports of textiles/clothing during 1996–97 was 11 per cent. The apparel industry accounts for nearly 16 per cent of the country's total exports. In 1996 Indian textile exports amounted to approximately Rs 35,000 crores[1] (INR 350 billion), of which apparel accounted for Rs 14,000 crores (INR 140 billion) (Ministry of Textiles, GoI).

With an installed capacity of 40 million spindles, India accounts for about 22 per cent of the world's spindle capacity. In 2003–04, India's spinning sector consisted of about 1,135 small-scale independent firms and 1,564 larger-scale independent units. Independent spinning mills account for around 75 per cent of capacity and 92 per cent of production. The woven fabric production industry can be divided into three sectors: the power-loom, handloom and mill sectors. In 2003–04 it consisted of about 3.9 million handlooms, 1.8 million power-looms, and 0.1 million looms in the organized sector. The decentralized power-loom sector accounts for 95 per cent of the total cloth production. Knitted fabrics account for 18 per cent of total fabric production. The processing industry is largely decentralized and marked by hand processing units and independent processing units. Composite mill sectors are very few, falling into the organized category. Overall, about 2,300 processors are operating in the sector, including about 2,100 independent units and 200 units that are integrated with spinning, weaving or knitting units (Ministry of Textiles, GoI).

4.4.1 The structure of the Indian textiles industry

The Indian textiles industry occupies an important place in the economy of the country because of its contribution to industrial output, employment generation and foreign exchange earnings. The industry extends from fibre to fabric to garments. This is a highly fragmented sector, and comprises small-scale, non-integrated spinning, weaving, finishing, and apparel-making enterprises. The unorganized sector constitutes the majority of the industry, comprising handlooms, power-looms, hosiery and knitting, and also ready-made garments, khadi, and carpet manufacturing units. The organized mill sector are made up of spinning mills (spinning activities) and composite mills where spinning, weaving and processing activities are carried out under a single umbrella.

In 2006 there were 1,779 cotton/man-made fibre textile mills in the organized sector, which has an installed capacity of 40 million spindles and 395,000 rotors. Of these, 218 were composite mills, accounting for just 3 per cent of total fabric production, with 97 per cent of fabric production occurring in the unorganized segment. According to the Ministry of Textiles, there are 1.923 million power-looms in the country distributed over 430,000 units. The sector accounts for 63 per cent of the total cloth production in the country (Ministry of Textiles, GoI). India had about 6,000 knitting units registered as producers or exporters and most of these units were registered as small-scale units (2000). Cotton is the predominant fabric used in the Indian textiles industry. Nearly 60 per cent of the overall consumption in textiles and more than 75 per cent production in spinning mills is cotton (Ministry of Textiles, GoI).

India's wool industry located in Punjab, Haryana, and Rajasthan alone account for more than 75 per cent of the production capacity, with both licensed and decentralized players. There are more than 700 registered units in the sector and more than 7,000 power-looms and other unorganized units. The woollen industry provides employment to approximately 1.2 million people (Ministry of Textiles, GOI).

The fibre and yarn-specific configuration of the textiles industry includes almost every type of textile fibre: natural fibres, such as cotton, jute, silk and wool; synthetic/man-made fibres, such as polyester, viscose, nylon, acrylic and polypropylene (PP); and also multiple blends of such fibres and filament yarns such as partially oriented yarn (POY). The type of yarn used is dictated by the end product being manufactured. The man-made textiles industry comprises fibre and filament yarn manufacturing units of cellulosic and non-cellulosic origin. The cellulosic fibre/yarn industry is under the administrative control of the Ministry of Textiles, while the non-cellulosic industry is under the administrative control of the Ministry of Chemicals and Fertilisers (Ministry of Textiles, GoI).

The jute industry occupies an important place in India's economy, being one of the major industries in the eastern region, concentrated in particular in West Bengal. It supports nearly four million farming families and, in addition to providing direct employment to 260,000 industrial workers, it also provides livelihoods for another 140,000 people in the tertiary sector and

Table 4.1   Employment in the textiles industry, 2004–05

Sector	Employment (millions)
Organized textile mills	1.0
Power-loom	4.8
Handloom	6.5
Jute	4.4
Handicrafts	6.4
Sericulture	6.0

Source: Ministry of Textiles, GoI.

allied activities (MoT, GOI). The structure of the Indian textiles industry is presented in Appendix 4.1. The direct employment in textile sector can be viewed from Table 4.1.

From Table 4.1 it can be noted that handloom, handicrafts and sericulture are the most important sub-sectors in the textiles sector, accounting for higher levels of employment. These are followed by the power-loom and jute sectors. By contrast, the organized textile mills account for only one million of the population, which is less than any of the other sub-sectors cited above.

4.5   Policy measures for textiles and clothing

In India the policy of full-fledged liberalization began in 1991. However, in the industrial sector, the Seventh Plan witnessed the commencement of liberalization of policy measures in 1985. The major policies were: de-licensing of non-MRTP (Monopolies and Restrictive Trade Practices), non-FERA companies for 31 industry groups and MRTP/FERA companies in backward areas for 72 industry groups; raising the assets limit for exemption of companies from the purview of the MRTP Act; exempting 83 industries under the MRTP Act for entry of dominant industries, and so on. Some other changes were also made in areas such as licensing and procedures, the import of technology, the import of capital goods, and the permitting of the broad banding of products in a number of industries. The Sick Industrial Companies Act (SICA) was extended to public enterprises in 1993 enabling sick public sector enterprises to be referred to the Board for Industrial & Financial Reconstruction (BIFR). Partial disinvestment was introduced in order to encourage wider public participation and a greater public accountability (Ministry of Textiles, GoI).

With the reforms, the Indian economy in general, and industry in particular, was at liberty from controls and opened to international competition for the integration of the Indian economy into the world economy. The policy reforms continued through the Eighth Plan period and even subsequently. A number of policy initiatives were undertaken during the Eighth Plan.

The focus of the new industrial policy was on the following measures: (i) a substantial reduction in the scope of industrial licensing; (ii) a simplification of procedures, rules and regulations; (iii) reforms of the MRTP Act; (iv) a reduction of the areas reserved exclusively for the public sector; (v) a disinvestment of equity of selected public sector enterprises (PSEs); (vi) the increase of the limits on foreign equity participation in domestic industrial undertakings; (vii) the liberalization of trade and exchange rate policies; and, finally, (viii) the rationalization and reduction of customs and excise duties and personal and corporate income taxes, extension of the scope of MODVAT and so on. The basic objectives of the plans are to promote growth, increase efficiency and international competitiveness.

A Textile Modernisation Fund scheme was implemented during the period 1986–91 with a fund of Rs 750 crore (INR 7.5 billion) with the Industrial Development Bank of India (IDBI) as the Nodal Agency. Subsequently, an open-ended Technology Upgradation Fund Scheme with no cap on funding has been launched for five years with effect from 1 April 1999. Restrictions on the imports of textiles machinery have been relaxed or removed and incentives provided for the import of capital goods for modernization and exports. In fact, the slow growth recorded in the domestic textile machinery industry in the 1990s is attributable largely to its being exposed to global competition, and there has been a substantial outflow of foreign exchange due to rising imports of textiles machinery in recent years. In 1997–98 the imports of textiles machinery as a percentage of their domestic production stood at 115.41.

To enable struggling private sector mills to close down, a Textile Workers' Rehabilitation Fund Scheme has been in operation since 15 September 1986. It provides interim relief to workers rendered jobless as the result of the permanent closure of private mills. A National Renewal Fund has also been created in the Ministry of Industry for providing funds for the rationalization of labour through voluntary retirement schemes (VRS) in the public sector mills, including textile mills. Setting up a Nodal Agency to prepare rehabilitation packages for potentially viable sick textile mills in consultation with all concerned agencies and subsequently enacting the Sick Industrial Companies (Special Provisions) Act, 1985 and establishing the Board for Industrial and Financial Reconstruction (BIFR) were other measures designed to revive and revitalize the entire mill sector. The National Textile Corporation was incorporated as a public sector company in April 1968 for managing loss-making textile mills taken over by the government to rehabilitate/modernize/expand them to make them economically viable and thereby preserve the employment of workers in such mills. The NTC was also made to implement the controlled cloth scheme, and the losses incurred in the process covered by subsidy. Over the period 1988–89 to 1996–97, the NTC was given a controlled cloth subsidy of Rs 120.25 crore (INR 1.2025 billion). The observation that government 'blocked the routes to modernisation and rationalisation' is thus factually incorrect (Ministry of Textiles, GoI).

The Cotton Corporation of India has been functioning as the government agency for Minimum Support Price (MSP) operations and the stabilization of cotton prices in the domestic market to safeguard the interests of both cotton growers and the cotton textiles industry. The government's role in the textiles industry has become increasingly reformist in nature. Initially, policies were drawn to provide employment with a clear focus on promoting the small-scale industry. The scenario changed after 1995, with policies being designed to encourage investments in installing modern weaving machinery as well as gradually eliminating the pro-decentralized sector policy focus. The removal of the SSI reservation for woven apparel in 2000 and knitted apparel in 2005 were significant decisions in promoting setting up of large-scale firms. Government schemes such as Apparel Parks for Exports (APE) and the Textile Centres Infrastructure Development Scheme (TCIDS) now provide incentives for establishing manufacturing units in apparel export zones.

The Textile Policy of 2000 set the ball rolling for policy reforms in the textiles sector, dealing with the removal of raw materials price distortions, cluster approach for power-looms, pragmatic exit of idle mills, the modernization of outdated technology and so on. The year 2000 was also marked by initiatives involving the setting up of apparel parks; 2002 and 2003 saw a gradual reduction in the excise duties for most types of fabrics while 2004 offered the CENVAT system on an optional basis. The Union Budget of 2005–06 announced competitive progressive policies, whose salient features included:

- A major boost to the 1999-established Technology Upgradation Fund Scheme for its longevity through a INR 4.35 billion allocation with 10 per cent capital subsidies for the textiles processing sector.
- The initiation of cluster development for the handloom sector.
- The availability of a health insurance package to 0.2 million weavers, from an initial figure of only 0.02 million.
- A reduction in customs duty from 20 per cent to 15 per cent for fibres, yarns, intermediates, fabrics and garments; from 20 per cent to 10 per cent on textile machinery; and from 24 per cent to 16 per cent in excise duty for polyester oriented yarn/polyester yarn.
- A reduction in corporate tax rate from 35 per cent to 30 per cent with a 10 per cent surcharge.
- A reduction in the depreciation rate on plant and machinery from 25 per cent to 15 per cent.
- The inclusion of polyester texturizers under the optimal CENVAT rate of 8 per cent.

To meet the challenges of the post-MFA setup, the Government of India initiated a reform process which aimed to promote large capital investments, through measures such as pruning cumbersome procedures associated with the tax regime. The Textile Vision 2010 was born as a result of interaction between the government and the industry which envisages around 12 per cent annual growth in the textiles industry – from US$36 billion now to US$85 billion by 2010. Additionally, Vision 2010 also proposes the creation of an additional 12 million jobs through this initiative (Ministry of Textiles, GoI).

The phasing out of the international quota system is a major turning point for the Indian textiles industry which will present both an opportunity and a threat. The textiles industry is among the most SME-intensive sectors in India, largely an outcome of government policies during the early years of Independence. Focusing on promoting domestic employment, large-scale production in the textiles industry was curtailed through restrictions on total capacity and level of mechanisation. Several textile items were reserved for the small-scale segment. These policies promoted the extensive growth of small-scale textiles enterprises that were highly labour intensive, although it eroded the competitiveness of the industry and acted as a disincentive for capital investment.

These policies, pursued from the 1950s to the 1970s, resulted in the dominance of the decentralized power-loom and handloom sectors in the textiles industry, which are mainly small and medium-sized enterprises. In fact, many of the large textiles companies are also conglomerates of medium-sized mills. Statistics released by the Ministry of Textiles show a highly fragmented industry, except in the spinning sub-segment. The organized sector contributes over 95 per cent of spinning, but hardly 5 per cent of weaving fabric. Small-scale industries (SSIs) perform the bulk of the weaving and processing operations.

Since 1997 the dereservation of textiles products has been a priority area for the government, because it was believed to be the most effective way to foster productivity and efficiency within the sector. By 2005 all textiles items had been removed from the reservation list. These measures were a prerequisite to competing globally in the post-MFA regime. As trade barriers come down and capital mobility increases, large, organized and integrated firms will gain importance in establishing a presence in the global market and to tap opportunities.

In the new scenario of a quota-free world, the ready-made garments sector will play a crucial role in the Indian economy, in terms of contributing to exports as well as employment generation, considering its inherently labour-intensive nature. In the cloth production segment, the hosiery and mill sectors are likely to be among the gainers. Between 1988 and 1993, the financial institutions operated a near-defunct scheme for textile modernization. After a gap until 1999, the government launched a Technology Upgradation Fund Scheme, which is now being administered by the financial institutions. There has been some progress.

4.5.1 Industrial policy reforms and major initiatives

Among the major policy instruments that have been initiated are the following:

- Foreign direct investment policy liberalized.
- Disinvestment Commission constituted for preparing an overall long-term disinvestment programme for PSEs referred to it and the modalities for disinvestment.
- Sick Industrial Companies Act (SICA), 1985 amended to bring PSEs within the ambit of SICA, 1985 and BIFR.
- National Renewal Fund set up to protect the interest of workers likely to be affected due to restructuring or closure of industrial units.
- Growth Centres Scheme taken up to develop infrastructure in backward areas to promote industrialization.
- To promote development of specific hilly, remote and inaccessible areas, Transport subsidy scheme extended until March 2000.
- Technology Development Board set up to facilitate development of new technologies and assimilation of imported technologies.

4.5.2 Export promotion measures

In order to encourage the upgrading of the textiles sector and to give a fillip to the exports of textiles products, some of the important initiatives were taken as follows:

4.5.2.1 Announcements of the New Foreign Trade Policy

The features which are particularly beneficial to the textiles industry are:

- The handicrafts and handloom sectors, among others, have been identified as Special Focus Initiatives.
- Duty-free imports of trimmings and embellishments for the handloom and handicraft sectors increased from 3 per cent to 5 per cent of FOB value of exports.
- Import of trimmings and embellishments and samples shall be exempt from CVD.
- The Handicraft Export Promotion Council authorized to import trimmings, embellishments and samples for small manufacturers.
- A new Handicraft Special Economic Zone shall be established.
- Leftover materials and fabrics of the 100 per cent EOUs up to 2 per cent of CIF value or quantity of imports shall be allowed to be disposed of on payment of duty on transaction value only.

4.5.2.2 Announcement of the New Textile Policy

One of the main objectives of the New Textile Policy (NTxP-2000) announced in November 2000 was to facilitate the textiles industry to attain and sustain a pre-eminent global standing in the manufacture and export of clothing. Subsequent to the announcement of NTxP-2000, the woven segment of the ready-made garment sector has been dereserved from the ambit of SSI and it has also been announced that knitwear will also be dereserved.

4.5.2.3   Technology Up-gradation Fund Scheme

In view of the need to accelerate the process of modernization and to secure the technological upgrading of the textiles industry in India, the Ministry of Textiles launched a Technology Up-gradation Fund Scheme (TUFS) for the Textile and Jute Industry with effect from 1 April 1999, providing for 5 per cent interest reimbursement in respect of loans availed there under from the concerned financial institutions (FIs) for investments in benchmarked technology for the sectors of the Indian textiles industries specified there under. An additional option has been given to power-loom units for 20 per cent capital subsidy under Credit Linked Capital Subsidy (CLCS-TUFS) up to a cost of Rs 1 crore in eligible machinery with facility to obtain credit from a credit network that includes all co-operative banks and other genuine non-banking financial companies (NBFC) recognized by the Reserve Bank of India.

4.5.2.4   Export Promotion Capital Goods Scheme (EPCG)

Import duty in respect of 387 textiles machinery classed under lists 30, 31, 32, 45 and 46 of Customs Tariff has been reduced to 5 per cent BCD. This will help the Indian textiles industry to import advanced machinery which will enhance the quality and cost competitiveness of the industry in both the domestic and the export markets.

4.5.2.5   Advanced Licensing Scheme

With a view to facilitate exporters' access to duty-free inputs under the scheme, Standard Input–Output Norms (SION) for about 300 textiles and clothing export products have been prescribed. SION for a number of apparel items have been revised upwards, based on large garment sizes. Additional items – such as zip fasteners, inlay cards, cyclets, revets, eyes, toggles, velcro tape, cord and cord stoppers – are included in input–output norms for garment exports under the Advance Licensing Scheme.

4.5.2.6   Duty Drawback Scheme

The objective of the system is to reduce the burden of indirect taxes on exports and, therefore, the exporters are allowed a refund of the excise and import duty suffered on raw materials and so on under the scheme so as to make them more competitive in the international market.

4.5.2.7   Construction of an international apparel market

The Apparel Export Promotion Council has constructed an Apparel International Mart (AIM) at Gurgaon with assistance from the Indian government.

The mart will house centrally air-conditioned showrooms, which will be given on a lease and license basis to the established garments exporters in India. This will provide a world-class facility for the apparel exporters to showcase their products and will serve as a one-stop shop for reputed international buyers.

4.5.2.8 Setting up of modern laboratories

The Ministry of Textiles has assisted the Textile Committee in the establishment of modern textiles laboratories to ensure that the textiles exported from the country meet all of the international environmental standards.

4.5.2.9 Human resources development

Attention has also been paid to human resources development in the textiles sector. The National Institute of Fashion Technology (NIFT) is imparting training to fashion designers and fashion technologists in order to cater for the human resources requirements of the garments industry. Furthermore, the Apparel Export Promotion Council has been running Apparel Training and Design Centres (ATDCs) at important apparel centres located at Chennai, Delhi, Kolkata, Hyderabad, Jaipur, and Bangalore in order to impart training at the shopfloor level to meet the growing needs of the industry.

4.5.2.10 FDI policy

The number of FDI projects approved between 1991 and 2004 was 641, with a value of more than US$1.02 billion. At the time of writing, foreign investors can invest up to 100 per cent through the Foreign Investment Promotion Board (FIPB). The Foreign Direct Investment (FDI) limit of 24 per cent is removed and the foreign investors will be able to invest up to 100 per cent through the Foreign Investment Promotion Board (FIPB). The existing obligation of those firms who have received foreign investment to export 50 per cent of their production has also been removed. In line with the present policy of the Government of India, 100 per cent FDI is freely allowed in the spinning, weaving, processing, garments and knitting sector under the automatic route for both new ventures and existing companies, except in those cases where an industrial license is required because a unit is based in a locationally restricted area.

4.5.2.11 Export zones and technology parks

Two government schemes, Apparel Parks for Exports (APE) and the Textile Centers Infrastructure Development Scheme (TCIDS), now provide firms with incentives to establish themselves in apparel export zones. To encourage the development of export parks, the government exempts firms from some labour regulations and provides them with concessions on land purchases, credit and taxes. In a related move in 2002, the government also removed a regulation that restricted clothing exports to firms that exported at least half of their output, opening exports to all apparel firms. These reforms allow the formation of larger-scale firms and permit investment in the more capital-intensive production systems used to produce some apparel items.

4.5.2.12   *The elimination of export quotas*

India used annual cotton export quotas to limit exports and to ensure low and stable raw material prices for the domestic textiles industry until 2002. The quotas tended to suppress domestic cotton prices by restricting exports, and uncertainty regarding annual quota levels, were sources of price risk for growers and traders. Removal of the quotas will strengthen links between domestic and world prices, likely boosting grower returns and eliminating a source of price risk.

4.5.3   Excise tax reform

In recent years the government has made limited progress in reducing the high level of excise taxation in the textiles sector – levels that discourage the formation of larger, organized sector firms and in reducing the tax bias against the use of synthetic fibres. In 2003, the government equalized excise taxes for large and small-scale yarn producers. The government has also revived the Central Value Added Tax (CENVAT) scheme. In the 2004–05 budget, the government reduced the CENVAT rates for products made of pure cotton to 4 per cent and the rate for products made of blended fibers to 8 per cent.

4.5.4   Technology Mission on Cotton

A slowdown in the growth in cotton production during the late 1990s, together with the opportunity created by the termination of the MFA, raised the priority for addressing factors that constrain cotton production and quality in India. In 2001, the government established the high-level Technology Mission on Cotton (TMC) in order to direct, coordinate, and fund initiatives to raise the productivity and quality of Indian cotton and strengthen returns to growers. TMC activities focus on four programme areas: (1) research and technology generation; (2) the transfer of technology to farmers; (3) the improvement of the marketing infrastructure; and (4) the modernization of gins. Although it is too early to evaluate the impact of TMC on research and extension, progress in improving market facilities and, particularly, cotton gins is evident in the cotton-producing areas.

4.5.5   Import policy

Cotton imports were liberalized in 1991, when the import monopoly of the Cotton Corporation of India was terminated and imports were placed on Open General License, allowing unrestricted imports by private traders. The import duty was originally set at zero, but little import trade occurred until the late 1990s, when world prices declined and India faced domestic supply shortfalls. The import duty was raised to 5.5 per cent in 2000 and to 10 per cent in 2002, but remains low relative to tariffs imposed on most other agricultural products.

4.5.6 Modernization

In the Union Budget 2005–06, the Government of India announced a credit-linked capital support of 10 per cent, in addition to the existing 5 per cent interest reimbursement for modernizing the processing sector. This measure has been widely acclaimed by the industry and trade circles and is expected to secure between US$330 million and US$440 million investment over the course of two years. The government also provides 20 per cent capital subsidy for the procurement of modern machinery in the power-loom sector.

4.5.7 Quality improvement

The Textile Commission, under the control of the Ministry of Textiles, allows firms in the industry to improve their quality levels and also acquire recognised quality certifications. Of the 250 textiles companies that have been taken up by the Commission, 136 are certified ISO 9001. The other two certifications that have been targeted by the Textile Commission are ISO 14000 Environmental Management Standards and SA 8000 Code of Conduct Management Standards.

4.5.8 Recent fiscal duty reforms

- Far-reaching decisions have been taken to remove the discriminatory excise duty structure, which placed the organized industry at a disadvantaged position and throttled investment in modern mills.
- In the Union Budget 2004–05, the duty structure of textiles was completely revised. The excise duty for textiles was made optional with mandatory duty only on man-made fibres/yarns.
- Except for mandatory duty on man-made fibres/yarns, all other textile goods were fully exempt from excise duty.
- For those opting to pay the duty and thereby avail themselves of duty credit, the duty was reduced to a nominal rate of 4 per cent for cotton textile items (that is, yarns, fabrics, garments and made-ups) and 8 per cent for other textile items including yarn, fabrics, garments, and made-ups.
- Additional Excise Duty was abolished; Customs duty on a number of textile items was also reduced.

In conclusion, these are the major steps taken by the government at the policy level for the growth of the textiles industry in India:

1. The Technology Upgradation Fund Scheme (TUFS) makes funds available to the domestic textiles industry for the upgrading of the technology in existing units and also the establishment of new units with advanced technology. It has a budget of Rs 535 crores (INR 5.35 billion).

2. The Textile Workers' Rehabilitation Fund Scheme (TWRFS) for providing interim relief to textile workers rendered unemployed due to the closure of any textile unit or any part of it.
3. Government support in the form of grants or equity to project cost limited to 40 per cent and subject to a ceiling of Rs 40 crores under the Scheme for Integrated Textile Parks (SITP).
4. Excise duty on man-made fibres and filament yarns reduced from 16 per cent to 8 per cent.
5. Import duty on man-made fibres and filament yarns reduced from 15 per cent to 10 per cent.
6. Concessional customs duty of 5 per cent without countervailing duty.
7. Health insurance scheme for handloom weavers launched in 2005.
8. Import of trimmings, embellishments and samples shall be exempt from countervailing duty.
9. With certain exceptions the government has allowed 100 per cent foreign equity participation through automatic route in the textiles sector.
10. Exporters can refund the excise and import duty incurred on raw materials.
11. Apparel Park for Exports Scheme sanctioned in Kanpur, Surat, Thiruvananthapuram, Vishakapatnam, Ludhiana, Bangalore, Tirpur, Indore, Mahal and Nagpur.
12. The Textile Centres Infrastructure Development Scheme (TCIDS) launched to upgrade infrastructure facilities at important textile centres. At the time of writing 18 projects have been approved.
13. Encouraging and supporting common effluent treatment plants for the firms.

4.6 Production and performance of textiles and clothing

4.6.1 Trends in textiles production

India is one of the world's largest producers of cotton (Table 4.2), with nearly nine million hectares under cultivation and an annual crop of around three million tonnes. In the year 2003–04, India produced nearly 13.8 million bales of cotton.

India is the third-largest producer of raw cotton, behind China and the United States. Its share of cotton production has been increasing almost throughout the period from 1999–2000 to 2005–06 – a time when it maintained its position in the world hierarchy. However, it is clear from Table 4.2 that the percentage share fell slightly in the years 2000–01 and 2002–03. In addition, India is currently the world's second-largest producer of cellulosic fibre/yarn, one of the largest producers of jute, the second-largest producer of silk and the fifth-largest producer of synthetic fibre/yarn in the world textiles economy.

Table 4.2   World cotton production (millions of 480 lb bales)

Country	1999/ 2000	2000/01	2001/02	2002/03	2003/04	2004/05	2005/06
China	17.6	20.3	24.4	22.6	22.3	29.0	26.2
United States	17.0	17.2	20.3	17.2	18.3	23.3	23.9
India	12.2	10.9	12.3	10.6	13.8	19.0	19.2
Pakistan	8.6	8.2	8.3	7.8	7.8	11.1	9.9
Others	5.9	6.2	5.4	5.1	6.2	7.0	7.0
World total	87.6	88.8	98.8	88.3	95.1	120.3	114.2

Source: US Cotton Market Monthly Economic letter, October 2006.

Since 2000, the production of yarn and fabric production have been growing at annual averages of 1.9 per cent and 2.7 per cent respectively. Yarn production increased from 3,940 million kg in 1999–2000 to 4,326 million kg in 2004–05. Much of this has been driven by the production of man-made yarn, which was growing at an annual average growth rate of 4.3 per cent over this period. Spun yarn production and the cotton yarn sector also grew during this period, albeit less impressively, recording annual average growth rate of 2.4 per cent and 0.6 per cent respectively.

Fabric production has been growing at an average annual rate of 2.7 per cent between 2000 and 2005, driven primarily by the small-scale, independent power-loom sector. Growth in the 100 per cent non-cotton segment touched 5 per cent, followed by cotton fabrics at 1.5 per cent and blended fabrics at 0.3 per cent. Fabric production reached a peak of 45,378 million square metres in 2004–05, and in November 2006, production recorded a robust 9 per cent growth compared to the corresponding period in the previous year. The per capita cloth availability in the country has increased from 22.87 square metres in 1991–92 to 33.51 square metres in 2004–05 (Table 4.3).

4.6.2   Export performance

4.6.2.1   Ready-made garments

The provisional data for 2005–06 show that ready-made garments account for approximately 45 per cent of India's total textile exports. Ready-made garment exports recorded a growth of 26.80 per cent in 2005–06 [P] as compared to the previous year 2004–05. The major importing countries of ready-made garments are the European Union, the USA, Canada, Japan, the UAE and Switzerland. In terms of textile exports, the quantities of ready-made garments are even higher than cotton textiles. The performance of this sector was quite satisfactory in the period from 1992 to 2006. It has maintained a relatively steady growth path since 1992, although there have been fluctuations from year to year. Again, such growth can be visible in most of the years up to 2000.

Table 4.3 Per capita availability of cloth (sq. metres)

Year	Cotton	Blended/mixed fabrics	100% non-cotton fabrics	Total
1991–92	13.71	2.90	6.26	22.87
1992–93	15.57	2.57	6.36	24.50
1993–94	15.92	3.58	6.72	26.22
1994–95	15.24	3.27	7.47	25.98
1995–96	16.32	3.48	8.19	27.99
1996–97	16.24	3.98	9.08	29.30
1997–98	15.94	4.57	10.41	30.92
1998–99	13.07	4.13	10.99	28.19
1999–2000	14.16	4.48	11.91	30.55
2000–01	14.22	4.50	11.96	30.68
2001–02	14.82	4.69	12.46	31.97
2002–03	14.40	4.38	12.59	31.37
2003–04	13.41	4.51	13.09	31.01
2004–05	14.08	4.11	15.32	33.51

Source: Ministry of Textiles, GoI.

The year 2000–01 recorded the decade's highest increase in exports, but the following year saw a fall in exports. From 2002–03 to 2004–05 this sector again began to expand and the latest data (2005–06 [P]) relating to exports of ready-made garments shows a gap of Rs 7,255.24 crore (INR 72.5524 billion) than 2004–05. Ready-made garments play an important role in the export of Indian textiles, which accounts for the highest share of exports. The ready-made garments sector recorded the highest share of exports in 2005–06 as per the provisional data. Its lowest percentage share was recorded in 1996–97, when it accounted for only 37.56 per cent. However, the trend of the ready-made garment shows a more or less consistent pattern from 1992 to date. But between 1996 and 1998 we can notice that the share of the ready-made garments was recorded a lower share in the last decade (Table 4.4).

4.6.2.2 Textiles

Textiles account for 14 per cent of India's industrial production and around 17 per cent of its export earnings. From growing its own raw materials (cotton, jute, silk and wool) to providing value-added products to consumers (fabrics and garments), the textiles industry covers a wide range of economic activities, including employment generation in both the organized and unorganized sectors. The trend in Indian exports of textiles and garments is presented in Table 4.4.

India accounts for 22 per cent of the world's installed capacity of spindles and is also one of the world's largest exporters of yarn. The industry contributes about 25 per cent of the world's trade of cotton yarn. The Indian textiles industry contributes about 22 per cent to the world spindleage and

Table 4.4   Textiles and garments exports at a glance from 1992–93 to 2005–06 (values in RS crores)

Item → Year	Cotton textiles	Man-made textiles	Silk	Wool	Ready-made garments	Total textiles	Grand total textiles exports
1992–93	4,093.07	1,141.43	681.29	258.77	6,505.67	12,680.22	15,483.62
1993–94	5,474.85	1373.6	658.63	341.51	7,668.07	15,516.67	18,816.71
1994–95	7,153.47	2,008.03	792.14	475.66	9,655.23	20,084.53	23,701.32
1995–96	8,822.16	2,581.93	793.16	483.53	11,672.29	24,353.07	28,520.39
1996–97	12,656.63	2,561.34	732.35	676.04	12,740.9	29,367.25	33,920.23
1997–98	12,953.51	3,057.91	1,006.43	741.31	13,721.57	31,480.74	36,412.05
1998–99	11,868.41	3,027.62	999.45	671.31	17,756.37	34,323.15	40,171.57
1999–2000	13,465.31	3,705.27	1,601.57	982.18	19,344.58	39,098.92	45,536.21
2000–01	16,031.02	5,003.06	2,292.52	1642.2	23,239.82	48,208.63	54,799.84
2001–02	14,697.99	5,191.24	2,083.88	1378.8	22,027.52	45,379.38	51,337.34
2002–03	16,267.77	6,859.97	2,184.13	1303.5	25,815.4	52,430.79	60,071.7
2003–04	16,542.24	8,368.83	2,505.31	1553.1	26,589.13	55,558.58	62,017.29
2004–05	15,924.43	9,214.25	2,671.46	1874.1	27,069.07	56,753.27	63,024.18
2005–06 [P]	19,893.85	8,855.46	3,063.13	2098.3	34,324.31	68,235.00	75,620.67

Source: Foreign Trade Statistics of India (Principal Commodities & Countries) DGCIS, Kolkata; P – Provisional.

about 6 per cent to the world's installed rotor capacity. Indian textiles also have the highest loomage in the world – contributing around 61 per cent of the world total. The sector contributes about 12 per cent to the world production of textile fibres and yarns (including jute). It is the largest producer of jute, the second-largest producer of silk, the third-largest producer of cotton and cellulosic fibre/yarn and the fifth-largest producer of synthetic fibres/yarns. The exports of textiles (including handicrafts, jute and coir) formed 24.6 per cent of total exports in 2001–2002; however, this percentage decreased to 16.24 per cent in 2004–05. The textiles exports recorded growth of 15.3 per cent in 2002–03 and 8.7 per cent in 2003–04. During 2004–05, textile exports were US$13,039 million, recording a decline of 3.4 per cent as compared to the corresponding period of previous year.

At present, (2005–06 [P]) the exports of textiles (including handicrafts, jute and coir) account for about 16.63 per cent of India's total exports and are the largest net foreign exchange earner for the country as the import content in textiles goods is very small compared to its other major export products. Further, the export basket consists of a wide range of items containing cotton yarn and fabrics, man-made yarn and fabrics, wool and silk fabrics, made-ups and variety of garments.

4.6.2.3   Cotton textiles, including handlooms
Cotton textiles, that is, yarn, fabrics, and made-ups (mill-made/power-loom/handloom), constitute more than one-quarter of India's exports of all

Table 4.5   Share of textiles items exported to total textiles exported

	% share of cotton textiles	% share of man-made textiles	% share of silk	% share of wool	% share of ready-made garments
1992–93	26.43	7.37	4.4	1.67	42.02
1993–94	29.1	7.3	3.5	1.81	40.75
1994–95	30.18	8.47	3.34	2.01	40.74
1995–96	30.93	9.05	2.78	1.70	40.93
1996–97	37.31	7.55	2.16	1.99	37.56
1997–98	35.57	8.4	2.76	2.04	37.68
1998–99	29.54	7.54	2.49	1.67	44.2
1999–2000	29.57	8.14	3.52	2.16	42.48
2000–01	29.25	9.13	4.18	3.00	42.41
2001–02	28.63	10.11	4.06	2.69	42.91
2002–03	27.08	11.42	3.64	2.17	42.97
2003–04	26.67	13.49	4.04	2.50	42.87
2004–05	25.27	14.62	4.24	2.97	42.95
2005–06 [P]	26.31	11.71	4.05	2.77	45.39

Source: Foreign Trade Statistics of India (Principal Commodities & Countries) DGCIS, Kolkata.

fibres/yarns/made-ups. The exports of cotton textiles recorded a growth of 22.62 per cent (including raw cotton) in 2005–06 as compared to the previous year 2004–05. During this period cotton textiles exports, including hand-looms/raw cotton, were US$3,077.68 million – an increase of 22.62 per cent over the corresponding period in 2004–05. As an export item, cotton textiles have been following an increasing trend between 1992 and 2006. However, from 1992 to 1997–98 the export of cotton products was rising at a faster and a steady growth rate and reached Rs. 12,953.51 crores (INR 129.5351 billion) in 1997–98. In 1999–2000 the exports of cotton decreased, before rising in the following year. However, in spite of all these fluctuations while summing up we find an increasing trend in the export of cotton textiles in the past decade. Cotton textiles are one of the major items exported in the total textiles exports after ready-made garments. The share of cotton textiles is presented in Table 4.5, which details the changing share of the item between 1992 and 2005. We can observe from the data that the minimum share of cotton textiles is 25.27 per cent recorded in 2004–05. Its highest share was recorded in 1996–97 when it accounted for 37.31 per cent of the total textiles exports. Between 1992 and 1997 the percentage share of this item was increasing, growing from 26.43 per cent and reaching a highest share of 37.31 per cent, but thereafter the share of cotton textiles began to decline and it recorded its lowest share in 2004–05. However, the most recent data show an increasing share in 2005–06[P], which accounts for 26.31 per cent compared to the previous year.

4.6.2.4 Man-made textiles

The export of man-made textiles recorded a decline of 3.89 per cent in 2005–06. Despite this, man-made textiles remains the second-largest contributor to Indian exports – behind cotton textiles. Data from 1992–93 to 2005–06 show that there has been a steady growth in the export of man-made textiles during this period. However, there was an increasing trend in exports between 1992 and 1998 and the export of man-made textiles reached Rs 2,581.93 crores (INR 25.8193 billion) in 1995–96. The provisional figure for 2005–06 shows a decrease in the export of the man-made textiles and recorded Rs 8,855.46 crores (INR 88.5646) less than in the financial year 2004–05. The share of man-made textiles achieved its highest share in 2004–05, when it accounted for 14.62 per cent. In 1992 the share fell to only 7.3 per cent. It can be seen from the above figures that over the course of one decade the share of man-made textiles exports has almost doubled. The share of man-made textiles has, however, displayed an increasing trend between 1992 and 2004–05. But the recent provisional data for 2005–06 shows that the share of the same has decreased in comparison to the previous year and registered a percentage share of 11.71 – even lower than the share recorded in 2002–03 (Table 4.5). The annual growth rate of the export of man-made textiles is given in Table 4.6.

4.6.2.5 Silk

Silk and silk products from the Indian textiles industry enjoy a unique place in terms of exports. The data from 1992 show the trend of silk exports from the penultimate decade has taken a different course in the past decade. In the years 1996–97, 1998–99 and 2001–02 the level of silk exports fell. The percentage share of silk in total textiles exports is lower than that for either cotton textiles or man-made textiles. It accounted for 4.05 per cent of the total textiles exported in 2005–06. The sector registered its highest share in 1992–93, when it accounted for 4.4 per cent of India's total textiles exports. In 1996–97 the share of silk items recorded its lowest-ever level (2.16 per cent). The share decreased between 1992 and 1996–97 before increasing thereafter (Table 4.5). The annual growth rate of silk exports is given in Table 4.6.

4.6.2.6 Woollen textiles

The export of wool has its own identity in the Indian textiles market. Since 1992 it has shown itself to be one of the most successful export-oriented sectors. Even in the period under consideration there have been many fluctuations in the sector, although overall the trend in terms of the export of wool has been upward. The best performance was recorded in 2000–01, when the value of exports was Rs 1,642.2 crores (INR 16.422 billion), which was higher than the previous year's exports. However, after 2001, there has been a marked decrease in the level of exports. Indian wool does not have a large share of total textiles exports to the international market. In 2000–01 woollen

Table 4.6 Annual growth rate of exports of textiles

Year	Cotton textiles	Man-made textiles	Silk	Wool	Ready-made garments	Total textiles	Handicrafts	Jute	Coir and coir manufactures	Grand total textiles exports
1993	33.76	20.34	−3.33	31.97	17.87	22.37	17.96	9.52	43.50	21.53
1994	30.66	46.19	20.27	39.28	25.91	29.44	6.83	21.59	33.03	25.96
1995	23.33	28.58	0.13	1.65	20.89	21.25	12.28	31.35	21.73	20.33
1996	43.46	−0.80	−7.67	39.81	9.16	20.59	13.46	−11.20	2.95	18.93
1997	2.35	19.39	37.42	9.65	7.70	7.20	5.21	25.90	17.71	7.35
1998	−8.38	−0.99	−0.69	−9.44	29.40	9.03	24.31	−16.24	24.22	10.32
1999	13.46	22.38	60.25	46.31	8.94	13.91	15.00	−6.36	−36.83	13.35
2000	19.05	35.03	43.14	67.20	20.14	23.30	−0.23	26.87	10.44	20.34
2001	−8.32	3.76	−9.10	−16.04	−5.22	−5.87	−11.06	−11.43	33.41	−6.32
2002	10.68	32.15	4.81	−5.46	17.20	15.54	26.26	48.35	20.49	17.01
2003	1.69	22.00	14.71	19.14	3.00	5.97	−21.81	22.72	0.67	3.24
2004	−3.73	10.10	6.63	20.67	1.81	2.15	−8.66	11.42	32.72	1.62
2005[P]	24.93	−3.89	14.66	11.96	26.80	20.23	20.45	5.08	25.33	19.99

Source: Computed from Foreign Trade Statistics of India (Principal Commodities & Countries) DGCIS, Kolkata.

Table 4.7 Performance of the share of items in textiles exports

Items	Highest % share	Lowest % share
Cotton textiles	1996–97	2004–05
Man-made textiles	2004–05	1993–94
Silk	1992–93	1996–97
Wool	2000–01	1992–93, 1998–99
Ready-made garments	2005–06	1996–97

textiles exports were 3 per cent of total textile exports – its highest-ever share. By contrast, in 1992–93 the share of wool was only 1.67 per cent, suggesting that the share has increased in recent years (Table 4.5). The annual growth rate in wool exports is shown in Table 4.6.

4.6.2.7 *Handicrafts, including carpets*

Handicrafts are among the sub-sectors to make a substantial contribution to overall exports of textiles. In dollar terms, the sector recorded an annual export growth of 23.28 per cent in 2005–06. During this period handicrafts, including carpet exports, were US$910.69 million, showing a growth of 23.28 per cent as compared to the corresponding period of 2004–05.

4.6.2.8 *Coir*

In 2005–06 coir exports recorded a growth rate of 32.49 per cent. During the period April–December 2005–2006, coir exports were US$99.71 million – a growth of 32.49 per cent as compared to the corresponding period of 2004–05.

4.6.2.9 *Jute*

In 2005–06 jute exports were US$223.37 million, recording a growth of 12.62 per cent as compared to the corresponding period in 2004–05.

4.6.2.10 *The export performance of the T&C industry*

The fluctuations of exports in the T&C industry are presented in Table 4.7. The table shows the shares of the different textile items and their export performances between 1992 and 2005. The change in the share of exports can be easily understood from the table.

Table 4.8 shows the share of textiles exports in the country's total exports. From Table 4.8 we can observe that in the period 1992–93 the share of the sector was 28.84 per cent, which was the highest recorded. However, the current provisional data on the share of textiles exports to total exports from India gives a figure of only 16.63 per cent. Data from 1992 to date show a declining trend in the share of textiles exports to total exports from India.

Table 4.8   Share of textiles exports to total exports

Year	% Textiles exports to total exports
1992–93	28.84
1993–94	26.98
1994–95	28.67
1995–96	26.82
1996–97	28.55
1997–98	27.99
1998–99	28.74
1999–2000	28.62
2000–01	27.22
2001–02	24.56
2002–03	23.54
2003–04	21.14
2004–05	16.79
2005–06 [P]	16.63

Source: Foreign Trade Statistics of India (Principal Commodities & Countries) DGCIS, Kolkata.

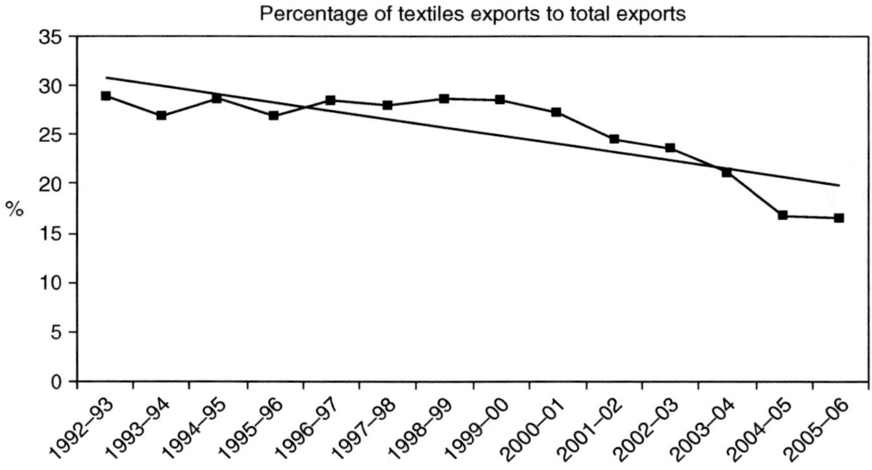

Figure 4.1   Share of textiles exports

From this figure we can observe the decreasing share of textiles exports to India's total exports in recent years. However, between 1997 and 2000 the share of textiles to total exports was increasing; thereafter the share fell suddenly, a trend that has continued to date. Graphically, the share of textiles exports to total exports is presented in Figure 4.1.

Table 4.9 Compound growth rate of the export of textiles

Exports	CGR
Cotton textiles	10.55
Man-made textiles	17.27
Silk	14.24
Wool	16.59
Ready-made garments	12.74
Total textiles exports	12.66
Handicraft	6.41
Jute	9.31
Coir	11.51
Grand total textiles exports	11.91
Total exports	16.14

Note: Period 1992 to 2005–06[P].
Source: Computed from Foreign Trade Statistics of India (Principal Commodities & Countries) DGCIS, Kolkata.

The compound growth rate of textiles exports from 1992 to 2005[P] is presented in Table 4.9. From the table we can observe that man-made textiles have registered the highest growth during the last 14 years, whereas the compound growth of handicraft exports is only 6.41 percentage points.

Total textiles exports, excluding handicraft, jute and coir, exhibit a growth rate of 12.66 per cent – compared to a growth rate of 11.91 per cent for the sector as a whole. While the total export has registered a growth rate of 16.14 per cent the growth in textile exports is slightly less over the same time period.

4.6.3 India in comparison with global textiles

In 2003 the Indian textiles trade accounted for 3.17 per cent of the world market, with a compound growth rate of 11.91 per cent (1992–2005–06[P]), making it the third-largest exporter to the EU and the fourth-largest exporter to the USA. The textiles industry also accounted for 4 per cent of GDP, 17 per cent of total exports, 12 per cent of invested capital, 13 per cent of gross output produced, and 21 per cent of employees. The installed capacity of the Indian textiles sector is 40 million spindles, 0.5 million OE rotors, 30,000 shuttle-less looms and 1.99 million shuttle looms. The Indian textiles industry is valued at US$36 billion, with exports totalling US$ 17 billion in 2005–06. At the global level, India's textiles exports account for just 4.72 per cent of global textiles and clothing exports. The export basket includes a wide range of items, including cotton yarn and fabrics, man-made yarn and fabrics, wool and silk fabrics, made-ups and a variety of garments. India's presence in the international market is significant in the areas of fabrics and yarn.

4.6.3.1 *India's position in the world textiles market*

- India is the largest exporter of yarn in the international market and has a 25 per cent share of world cotton yarn exports.
- India accounts for 12 per cent of the world's production of textile fibres and yarn.
- In terms of spindleage, the Indian textiles industry is ranked second, behind China, and accounts for 23 per cent of the world's spindle capacity.
- Around 6 per cent of global rotor capacity is in India.
- The country has the highest loom capacity, including handlooms, with a share of 61 per cent of total world loomage.

According to the provisional DGCI&S data, textile exports during the fiscal year 2005–06 stood at around US$17 billion, recording a year-on-year growth of around 22 per cent. With the exception of man-made textiles, all of the segments in the textiles industry, including handicraft carpets, wool and silk, have recorded a growth in exports during 2005–06 – the first year since the phasing out of the quota system in the global market. The largest export segment is ready-made garments (RMG), accounting for as much as 45 per cent of total textile exports. This segment has benefited significantly from the termination of the Multi-Fibre Arrangement (MFA) in January 2005. In 2005–06, total RMG exports grew by 26.8 per cent.

Exports of cotton textiles, which include yarn, fabric and made-ups, constitute more than two-thirds of total textiles exports (excluding ready-made garments). Overall, this segment accounts for 26 per cent of total textiles exports. According to the Ministry of Textiles, in 2005–06 total cotton textiles exports were worth US$4.5 billion, implying a growth of 27 per cent over the exports in 2004–05, which were worth US$3.5 billion (Ministry of Textiles, GoI). The major export destinations for India's textiles and apparel products are the USA and the EU, which together accounted for over 75 per cent of demand. Exports to the USA have increased further since 2005, following the termination of the MFA. The analysis of trade figures by the US Census Bureau shows that post-MFA, imports from India into the USA have been nearly 27 per cent higher than in the corresponding period in 2004–05. Table 4.10 presents India's textile exportsto the major countries of the world.

It can be seen from the table that in 2001–02 India had a share of 22.86 per cent of the US market – a proportion which rose during 2002–03. A fall to 21.69 per cent was recorded in 2003–04, but the very next year the share of Indian exports of all textiles rose to 23.90 per cent. However, the share of exports to the UK shows a different picture. In 2001–02 it stood at 7.16 per cent; thereafter, it followed a decreasing trend until 2003–04 (6.83 per cent), before rising to 7.36 per cent in 2004–05. However, exports to the United Arab Emirates have been increasing since 2001–02. In the same year the share of the exports was 6.65 per cent and in 2004–05 it rose to

Table 4.10   Export of all textile items in percentage terms – major countries

Sl. No.	Country	2001–2002	2002–2003	2003–2004	2004–2005
1	USA	22.86	24.46	21.69	23.90
2	UK	7.16	7.01	6.83	7.36
3	United Arab Emirates (UAE)	6.65	6.77	8.29	7.98
4	Germany	5.99	6.27	6.14	5.73
5	France	4.43	4.37	4.36	4.57
6	Other Countries	52.91	51.11	52.69	50.46
	Grand Total	100.00	100.00	100.00	100.00

Source: Monthly Statistics of the Foreign Trade of India. DGCIS, Kolkata.

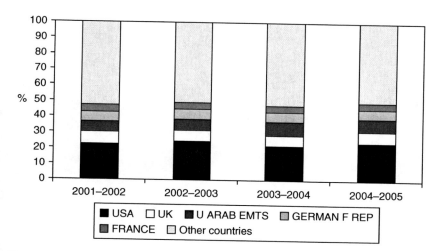

Figure 4.2   Textiles exports to major destinations

7.98 per cent. The share of exports to other country accounts for more than 50 per cent of total exports. There has also been a variation in the share of exports to other countries. In 2001–02 the share was 52.91 per cent; this fell to 51.11 per cent in the following year before rising again in 2003–04 to 52.69 per cent. But in 2004–05 the share of textile exports was only 50.46 per cent – which is lower than the previous year. The changing share of export to major countries can be viewed from Figure 4.2.

4.6.4   Textiles imports

The trend of textiles imports in India is shown in Table 4.11. From 1992–93 to 1998–99 the import of raw materials for the industry showed a steady rate

Table 4.11 Total textiles imports at a glance from 1992–93 to 2005–06 (values in Rs crores)

Item	Raw materials	Semi-raw materials	Yarn & fabrics	Ready-made garments	Made-ups	Total textiles imports	Overall imports
1992–93	8,408.40	710.2	4,307.1	0	0	13,425.7	633,745.1
1993–94	7,740.40	1261	7,166.3	0	0	16,167.7	731,010.1
1994–95	13,753.90	4,438.6	10,349.8	0	0	28,542.3	899,707.0
1995–96	14,831.90	5,021.1	11,997	0	0	3,1850	122,6781.0
1996–97	10,198.70	4,232.6	12,725.1	0	0	27,156.4	1,389,199.0
1997–98	10,790.74	4,654.26	15,187.27	0	0	30,632.27	1,541,763.0
1998–99	13,203.80	2,908.74	19,219.08	0	0	35,331.62	1,783,317.0
1999–2000	23,995.86	11,512.05	11,819.43	699.38	1,144.52	49,171.24	2,155,285.0
2000–01	23,393.95	12,555.66	14,530.50	978.3	1,910.46	53,368.87	2,283,066.0
2001–02	35,046.68	16,619.16	18,305.10	1,725.28	1,719.48	73,415.7	2,451,997.0
2002–03	2,905.26	2,286.57	2,466.44	115.93	191.26	7,965.46	297,205.9
2003–04	3,298.33	2,180.54	3,314.18	177.83	375.67	9,346.55	359,107.7
2004–05	2,784.74	2,526.62	4,451.85	149.55	269.4	10,182.16	501,064.5
2005–06[P]	2,617.61	2,790.73	6,034.29	244.43	263.92	11,950.97	630,526.8

Notes: (P) Provisional; 1 billion = 100 crore.
Source: Foreign Trade Statistics of India (Principal Commodities & Countries) DGCIS, Kolkata.

of growth, but it reached a high point in 2001–02 and has been decreasing since that date. However, the import of ready-made garments began only after 1998–99. The overall performance of imports in the textile industry shows an increasing trend between 1992 and 2001. After falling in 2002–03 it resumed its upward trend thereafter.

4.6.4.1 Imports of raw materials

The imports of raw materials to the Indian textiles industry include raw jute, raw silk, raw wool, woollen and cotton rags etc. and raw cotton and waste. The variation in the imports of the raw materials to the textiles industry from 1992 can be seen in Table 4.11. It can be observed that in 2001-02 India's textiles industry recorded its highest level of raw materials imports. However, between 1993 and 1995 the level of imports rose, before falling to INR 46.332 billion in 1996–97. After 1996 imports again resumed their upward trend to 1999–2000. Then the years 2000–01, 2002–03, 2004–05 and 2005–06 showed lower levels of imports than in previous years. However, between these periods the imports were noticed to have increased compared to their corresponding previous year.

4.6.4.2 Imports of semi-raw materials

Synthetic & regenerated and man-made filaments/spun yarn are the most important semi-raw materials for the Indian textiles industry. The imports of semi-raw materials between 1992–93 and 2005–06 are presented in Table 4.11. In 2001–02 India was largely dependent on the exports of semi-raw materials, which accounted for INR 166.1916 billion. This dependence began in 1999–2000 when India started importing huge amounts of semi-raw materials, achieving a figure of INR 115.1205 billion rupees. But after 2001–02, the import of the semi-raw material fell dramatically to INR 22.8657 billion in 2002–03 – a decrease of INR 143.326 billion compared to the previous year. According to the latest data available, in 2005–06 India imported semi-raw materials of INR 27.9073 billion for the textiles industry.

4.6.4.3 Import of yarns and fabrics

In terms of yarns and fabrics, the major items imported into India are: silk yarn and fabrics, woollen yarn and fabrics, other textile yarns, fabrics and cotton yarn, textile yarn, and fabrics & made-up articles. The relevant data for imports between 1992 and 2005 are given in Table 4.11.

In 1998–99 India was particularly dependent on the import of yarn and fabrics as the import of these items reached its highest-ever figure of INR 192.1908 billion. This was the culmination of an upward trend from 1992–93. After falling back to only INR 73.9965 billion in 1999–2000, this figure began to rise again in the following year.

Table 4.12 Compound growth rate of the imports of textiles

Imports	CGR
Raw materials	−8.73
Semi-raw materials	5.58
Yarn and fabrics	−4.51
Ready-made garments	−27.96
Made-ups	−29.63
Total textiles imports	−4.17
Overall imports	−3.92

Source: Foreign Trade Statistics of India (Principal Commodities & Countries) DGCIS, Kolkata.

4.6.4.4 Ready-made garments and made-ups

As per the data up to 1998–99 India was not importing ready-made garments alongside made-ups. The trend of the imports of such items to the Indian market began only in 1999–2000 (Table 4.11). In the case of ready-made garments the increase in imports can be observed from 1999–2000 to 2001–02. After this time the import of ready-made garments fell, recording a figure of INR 1.1593 billion of imports in the following year. This trend has continued up to the most recent figures for 2005–06. However, the growth rate of the imports of ready-made garments from 1992 to 2005–06 fell to 27.96 per cent. A similar performance in imports can be seen in the case of made-ups. The import of made-ups began in 1999–2000 and continued to increase until 2001–02; after falling in 2002–03, the upward trend resumed between 2003–04 and 2005–06.

In conclusion, let us now observe the performance of the imports of total textiles to India. It can be observed that between 1997 and 2000 India was particularly dependent on the foreign market for the textile articles. By contrast, from 2001 onwards the import of total textile articles fell sharply, before increasing more slowly. Here it may be noted that for the period from 1992 to 2005 the growth rate of imports to the Indian market decreased at an average annual rate of 4.17 per cent. The compound growth rate of import of textiles as well as the overall level of imports to India is given in Table 4.12.

4.7 Competitiveness of the T&C industry

In the post-MFA period, following the abolition of restrictions, the developing countries in general and India in particular are experiencing strong global competition. If we consider the performance of the Indian textiles industry, it has been quite satisfactory during this period. Both Indian domestic production and exports have been growing. Over the course of the last 10–15 years the exports of textiles and clothing from India have been growing strongly. Since 1992, Indian textiles and clothing exports have grown by an average annual rate of 7.7 per cent, reaching US$13.4 billion in 2002 and accounting for 4 per cent of global trade in this sector. In 2002, India was the fifth-largest global exporter and the second-largest net exporter of textiles and clothing. Cotton-based products account for the bulk of exports. The dominant markets for India's textiles and apparel exports are the USA and the EU, which together accounted for nearly 83 per cent of exports in 2003. With a consistent growth of nearly 5 per cent in the domestic market and the opening up of exports options post-MFA, India's textiles industry has to grow further and take up a more significant position in both the domestic and global markets.

China is the world's largest exporter of textiles and is ahead of India in textiles and cotton exports. In 1999 Hong Kong and China both accounted for $77 billion of exports. Studies point out that China is concentrating on high-value processed fabrics, with sizeable investments in value-added processes. In addition to China, other developing countries are likely to steal a lead on India. The global market share by value of the Indian primary textiles hovers around 2.8 per cent (1996) compared to China's 12.5 per cent. Countries such as Korea (with a market share of 5.6 per cent) and Taiwan (5 per cent) are ahead of India while Turkey (2.75 per cent) has caught up and others, such as Thailand (2.3 per cent) and Indonesia (2.0 per cent), are catching up rather quickly. On the one hand, technology, which has become a commodity, has changed drastically over the course of this century – with spinning speeds having increased 25 times and weaving speeds having increased 20 times (Hartmann 1997).

India is an important player in textiles and cotton imports to the United States, while China remains the dominant source of imports. Furthermore, while China increased its share in the US market of textiles and clothing to 20 per cent and 17 per cent, respectively, in 2003, India could only achieve a marginal increase in its share of the US textiles market and its share of the US clothing sector fell slightly. A study by the US International Trade Commission (2004) predicts that China is expected to become the 'supplier of choice' for most US importers because of its ability to make almost any type of textiles and apparel product at any quality level at a competitive price.

Exports to the EU show a weakening of India's relative market share. In the T&C sector, while China accounted for 14 per cent and 20 per cent, respectively, of the European T&C market share by 2003, India's share in this market declined to 5 per cent and 9 per cent. The market structure in Japan is indicative of a post-quota world as Japan did not impose quotas in the pre-2005 period. In 2003, China accounted for nearly half and 80 per cent, respectively, of Japan's T&C imports.

4.7.1   Challenges for the Indian textiles industry

Among the lacunae of the Indian textiles industry are the following:

- There are protections in various forms.
- The wage rates are quite low compared to other developed countries; furthermore, they are either partly or wholly untrained.
- The equipment used in textiles production are old and its maintenance needs to be improved.
- The product mix of Indian textiles has remained more or less the same and has not changed in a decade.
- The transaction costs of Indian exports are relatively high.

A survey by the Export–Import Bank of India (2005) intended to estimate the magnitude of transaction costs of Indian exports revealed that although transaction costs have declined between 1998 and 2003, they still continue to impose significant costs in certain sectors of Indian exports. Among the leading export sectors, the study finds that the incidence of transaction costs is highest in textiles, resulting mainly from delays in receiving refunds (Reserve Bank of India 2004). The delivery times from India are longer than from other comparator countries. The minimum delivery time (transportation alone) from India to the United States is 24 days, compared to 18 days from Thailand, 15 days from China, 12 days from Hong Kong SAR and three days from Mexico (Winters and Mehta, 2003). While geographical location might offer a partial explanation, a major factor for the delays can be attributed to lower efficiency and smaller tonnage of berthing capacity at Indian ports.

The structure of the T&C industry in India is also a limiting factor to some degree. India's T&C sector has been dominated by fragmented small producers, and there is little vertical integration in the apparel industry (USITC, 2004). Even with all the lacunae the Indian textiles sector is the second-largest employer of the nation and also the trade statistics and the balance of payments have been quite satisfactory in the last decade. To grow and to compete in the new post-MFA era the Indian textiles sector has to overcome such difficulties. Similarly, new strategies will be required to meet the competition from firms around the world in a post-MFA era.

4.8   Case studies of selected firms

The Indian textiles industry has a significant presence in the Indian economy as well as in the international textiles economy. Its contribution to the Indian economy is manifested in terms of its contribution to industrial production, employment generation and foreign exchange earnings. In the world textiles scenario, it is the largest producer of jute, the second-largest producer of

Table 4.13 Case study firms

Sl. No.	Name of the industry	Product profile	Incorporation year	Registered office	Listing
1	Ambattur Clothing Ltd	Garments	1995	Chennai, Tamil Nadu	Not Listed
2	Gokaldas Exports Ltd	Garments	2004	Bangalore, Karnataka	Mumbai, NSE
3	Arvind Mills	Textiles	1931	Ahmedabad, Gujarat	Ahmedabad, Kolkata, Luxembourg, Mumbai, NSE
4	Indo Rama Synthetics	Textiles	1986	Nagpur, Maharashtra	Luxembourg, Mumbai, NSE

Source: Capitaline Databases.

silk, the third-largest producer of cotton and cellulosic fibre/yarn and the fifth-largest producer of synthetic fibres/yarn. It provides direct employment for around 20 million people. Textiles and clothing exports account for one-third of the total value of exports from the country. The Indian textiles industry continues to be based predominantly on cotton, with about 65 per cent of raw materials consumed being cotton (Planning Commission, GOI). This section attempts to study the firm-level performance of the Indian textiles industry. Each case study begins with the historical background of the firm and also covers its achievements to date. There is an analysis of the financial performances of the firms from 2002 to 2006. The data for this analysis are collected from Capitaline Databases, and from the homepages of the respective firms. We were able to obtain data about 11 firms. The author held personal interaction with executives in two of these firms – Ambattur Clothing and Celebrity Fashions.

Table 4.13 shows the case studies at a glance, detailing the basic information about the firms, including the year of incorporation, the area of operation and whether or not the company is listed on the Stock Exchange.

4.8.1 Ambattur Clothing Ltd

Ambattur Clothing Ltd started in 1981, with a single production unit. Ambattur Clothing Limited has now evolved into a US$140 million group manufacturing apparel for some of the world's leading brands. This industry is one of its leading exporters, with nine production facilities in India and one at Bahrain. The industry is concentrated in Chennai and has an annual sales turnover of US$140 million. The company has an employee base of

Table 4.14   Financial performance of Ambattur Clothing Ltd

Sl No.	Indicators/year	2003	2002	2001
1	Net worth	173.09	138.99	114.29
2	Gross block	109.13	99.34	96.44
3	Sales turnover	279.8	292.87	348
4	Gross profit	46.81	37.54	54.9
5	Profit margin (%)	15.78	12.82	16.73
6	Capital productivity (ratio)	3.18	2.94	2.90

Note: Variables 1–4 are presented in rupees in crores.
Source: Capitaline Databases.

5,200 workers managed by 400 professionals. The financial performance of Ambattur Clothing Ltd is presented in Table 4.14.

The net worth of the firm is growing at an increasing rate. However, due to the unavailability of data we are showing the performance of the firm between 2001 and 2003. The gross block of the firm has also followed an increasing trend throughout the time frame. But it is quite surprising to observe that the sales performance of the firm is no longer increasing – rather it is following a decreasing trend, having reported its highest-ever figure in 2001. The firm recorded its lowest gross profit in 2002, having achieved its highest figure in the previous year. In 2001 the firm also calculated its highest-ever profit margin of 16.73 per cent. However, it should also be noted that the capital productivity of the firm was at its highest level in 2003. And the capital productivity of the firm has shown an increasing trend since 2001.

4.8.2   Gokaldas Exports Ltd

Gokaldas Exports Ltd (GEL) was incorporated in 1979. The company, which is an ISO 9001:2000 certified company, is one of the largest manufacturers and exporters of outerwear, blazers and pants (formal and casual), shorts, shirts, blouses, denim wear, swimwear and active and sports wear. The subsidiaries of the company are Madhin Trading Pvt Ltd, Magenta Trading Pvt Ltd, Rafter Trading Pvt Ltd, Reflexion Trading Pvt Ltd, Deejay Trading Pvt Ltd, Rishikesh Apparels Ltd, Vignesh Apparels Pvt Ltd, SNS Clothing Pvt Ltd, Seven Hills Clothing Pvt Ltd, Glamourwear Apparels Pvt Ltd, Rajdin Apparels and All Colour Garments Pvt Ltd. Gokaldas Exports Pvt Ltd and Unique Creations (Bangalore) Pvt Ltd were merged with the company with effect from 1 April 2004. Additionally, in the period 2004–05 the company established three new factories: at Bommasandra Industrial Area, Bangalore: at Yeshwanthpur, Bangalore; and one at Doddaballapur, Bangalore. The financial performance of Gokaldah Export Ltd is presented in Table 4.15.

Table 4.15 Financial performance of Gokaldas Exports Ltd

Sl No.	Indicators/year	2007	2006	2005	2004
1	Net worth	407.76	345.52	166.30	12.94
2	Gross block	288.71	203.56	129.09	58.09
3	Sales turnover	1,034.43	884.49	719.05	39.25
4	Gross profit	124.92	100.31	67.06	4.1
5	Profit margin (%)	12.08	11.34	9.33	10.45
6	Capital productivity (ratio)	3.58	4.35	5.57	0.68

Note: Variables 1–4 are presented in rupees in crores.
Source: Capitaline Databases.

From the table we can observe that the net worth of the firm was quite low in 2004 and that a major shift took place in the following year. Thereafter the firm has experienced an increasing trend in its net worth up to 2007. In case of the gross block of the company we can see a major shift between 2004 and 2005 – the figure for 2005 was more than twice the amount recorded in 2004. Even the gross block of the firm is increasing at a faster rate from 2005. The sales turnover of the firm was also accelerating between 2005 and 2007. There is a clear distinction in sales turnover from 2004 to 2005. Data from 2004 to 2007 show that the gross sales of the firm have been on an increasing trend during this period. However, the figures also show that the profit margin of the firm in 2004 was 10.45 per cent. After falling in 2005, the margin has recovered strongly in 2006 and 2007. However, in 2005 the figure for capital productivity was at the highest level recorded during this period.

4.8.3 Arvind Mills

Arvind Mills was set up by the Lalbhai brothers in 1931. Arvind Mills started with a share capital of Rs 2,525,000 ($55,000), with the aim of manufacturing the high-end superfine fabrics. With 52,560 ring spindles, 2,552 doubling spindles and 1,122 looms, it was one of the few companies to start along with spinning and weaving facilities in addition to full-fledged facilities for dyeing, bleaching, finishing and mercerizing. By 1991 Arvind had achieved the production of 1,600 million metres of denim per year and it was the third-largest producer of denim in the world.

Arvind Brands, a group company, manages various brands owned by Arvind. These include Flying Machine, Newport and Ruf & Tuf in jeans and Excalibur in shirts. This company services the entire domestic market in India – and also exports to the neighbouring countries. In addition to its

Table 4.16   Financial performance of Arvind Mills

Sl. No.	Indicators/Year	2007	2006	2005	2004	2003	2002	2001
1	Net worth	NA	1,475.85	1,215.13	1,111.83	995.37	836.83	NA
2	Gross block	NA	2,192.24	2,110.33	2,035.21	2,000.64	1,988.46	NA
3	Sales turnover	1,844.91	1,588.79	1,654.91	1,435.28	1,480.11	698.91	1,191.65
4	Gross profit	423.3	421.46	394.37	364.9	431.2	153.7	119.59
5	Profit margin (%)	22.94	26.52	23.83	25.42	29.13	21.99	10.03
6	Capital productivity (ratio)	NA	0.72	0.78	0.71	0.74	0.35	NA

Note: Variables 1–4 are presented in rupees in crores.
Source: Capitaline Databases.

owned brands, the company has a number of licenses from reputed international brands such as Arrow, Lee, Wrangler and Tommy Hilfiger for the Indian market. From their office at Bangalore, India the management controls the entire operation (including manufacturing, branding, logistics, marketing and sales). AML's recent tie-ups include its technical and marketing alliance with F M Hammerie Von-Ogensver Waltungs, Austria, the US-based Alamac Knit Fabrics & Spinners and Webexi Dict Turt, Switzerland. The financial performance of Arvind Mills is presented in Table 4.16.

Between 2001 and 2007 both the net worth and the gross block of the firm have been increasing. The gross sales of the firm were Rs 1,191.65 crores in 2001 – although this figure fell to Rs 698.91 crores in the following year. But hereafter the firm has performed well and the sales of the firm have been growing throughout the period between 2002 and 2007. In fact, in 2007 the firm recorded its highest ever sales – with a figure of 1,844.91 crores. However, it is interesting to see that with gross sales of Rs 1,191.65 crores in 2001 the firm has incurred a gross profit of only Rs 119.59 crores in the same year. As per the current data the firm has recorded a profit of Rs. 423.3 crores in the financial year 2007. The highest profit margin of the firm is calculated for 2003 (29.13 per cent), but it then declined until 2005. Thereafter, the gross profit showed an increasing trend. It has been estimated that in 2007 the profit margin of the firm will be 22.94 per cent. Due to the current non-availability of data we were unable to calculate the capital productivity ratio of the financial years 2001 and 2007. The firm recorded its highest capital productivity ratio in 2005. Between 2003 and 2006 the capital productivity ratio of the firm remained consistent – at around 0.07.

4.8.4   Indo Rama Synthetics

Indo Rama Synthetics (India) Limited, established in India, boasts of covering diverse fields of polyester (staple fibre, filament yarn, and FDY, DTY

Table 4.17 Financial performance of Indo Rama Synthetics

Sl. no.	Indicators/year	2007	2006	2005	2004	2003	2002	2001
1	Net worth	544.19	539.51	533.41	524.19	416.14	NA	NA
2	Gross block	2,691.09	1,945.42	1,931.94	1,903.36	1,912.23	NA	NA
3	Sales turnover	2,156.87	2,101.9	2,198.71	1,987.93	2,014.34	1,676.15	1,986.03
4	Gross profit	177.02	191.19	239.12	395.97	370.44	281.45	284.62
5	Profit margin (%)	8.21	9.10	10.88	19.92	18.39	16.79	14.33
6	Capital productivity (ratio)	0.80	1.08	1.14	1.04	1.05	NA	NA

Note: Variables 1–4 are presented in rupees in crores.
Source: Capitaline Databases.

and textile grade chips). Indo Rama Synthetics (India) Limited is the country's largest dedicated polyester manufacturer (at a single location), with an Integrated Manufacturing Complex at Butibori, near Nagpur in Maharashtra which produces Polyester Staple Fibre (PSF), Polyester Filament Yarn (PFY – POY/DTY), Draw Textured Yarn (DTY) and Textile Grade Chips. The Butibori plant produces 300,000 tonnes of PSF, POY, FDY, DTY and fibre grade chips. Indo Rama has a dynamic workforce of about 3,000 employees. IRSIL has technical collaborations with Chemtex International, US, and M/s Dupont, US, and Barmag, Germany, for the POY and polyester chip projects; and Toyobo, Japan, for the PSF project. IRSIL exports its products to the US, Germany, France, Belgium, etc. The financial performance of the Indo Rama Synthetics is presented in Table 4.17.

The net worth of the firm has grown steadily throughout this period, with the highest net worth being recorded in 2007. The gross block of the firm was also growing during this period, but in 2004 the gross block of the company was lower then the figure recorded in the previous year. With the exceptions of the financial years 2001 and 2004 the firm has shown consistently good results in gross sales. In every one of those years the firm has recorded an increasing trend in gross sales. However, it should be noted that even though in the financial year 2004 the firm recorded lower sales than in 2003, the gross profit was a higher figure. From 2001 to 2004 the firm was incurring an upward moving growth, but between 2004 and 2007 the gross profit of the firm exhibited a declining trend. From 2001 to 2004 the profit margin of the firm increased, but from 2004 to 2007 the profit margin of the firm fell. However, the capital productivity of the firm is quite satisfactory and stood higher than one for four consecutive years. In 2007 the capital productivity of the firm is calculated to be 0.80 – a lower figure than recorded in the previous year.

Table 4.18   Compound growth rates of selected indicators for the firms (%)

Sl no.	Name of the firm	Sales turn-over	Gross profit	Net worth	Gross block
1	Ambattur Clothing Ltd	−10.33	8.30	23.06	6.38
2	Gokaldas Exports Ltd	172.43	190.16	202.90	69.31
3	The Arvind Mills	11.57	22.67	14.27	2.52
5	Indo Rama Synthetics	2.85	−8.98	5.82	7.31

4.8.5   Comparison of the market share of the firms during the study period

This section offers a comparative study of the case studies. Here an attempt has been made to understand the performance of different firms through various indicators. The growth rates for each individual firms over a time period are calculated, taking into account the availability of data. The growth rates of the individual firm are presented in Table 4.18.

Table 4.18 gives a broad picture of the growth rate of 11 firms over a period of time. That also reflects the levels of competitiveness of the 11 firms. Four different indicators have been chosen to compare the firms. When we consider the gross sales of the firm, it is quite evident from the table that Gokaldas Exports Ltd has captured the majority of the market and that its growth rate is outstanding when compared to that of other firms. The growth rate is calculated to be 172.43 per cent.

However, only one of our sample firms, Ambattur Clothing Ltd, has reported negative growth rates during the period. If we now move on to consider the profits that the firms recorded during the period it is clear from the table that Gokaldas Exports Ltd has the highest growth rate (190.16 per cent), followed by Arvind Mills. In fact, Indo Rama Synthetics has experienced a negative growth rate. Our calculations show Gokaldas Exports Ltd to have the highest net worth. In terms of the growth rate in gross block Gokaldas Exports Ltd is ranked highest. With all of this information we can now report that Gokaldas Exports Ltd has the highest sales turnover, gross profit and net worth. Of the sample firms, Indo Rama Synthetics was the only firm that reported any significant R&D expenditure for few years (Capitaline Databases).

4.9   Summary and conclusion

This study has focused on the structure, policy framework and performance of the Indian textiles and clothing industry. It began by describing the policy measures undertaken by the government in various five-year plans and went on to examine the trends in production, exports and imports. The difficulties encountered by the industry and its competitiveness are also briefly narrated in the study. We have also discussed firm-level trends in various performance indicators of the Indian textiles sector. It is notable that the Indian textiles industry is currently one of the largest and most important sectors in the economy in terms of output growth, foreign exchange earnings and employment. From the results of the study it can be seen that the Indian textiles industry is strengthening and has been on a steady growth path during the last two decades. There has been an increase in terms of output, exports and employment and the industry has the potential to grow and compete at the global level.

Over the course of the past few decades the domestic textiles sector in India has been quite competitive and has witnessed many upheavals. Domestic and foreign firms should be encouraged to invest in export production in order to produce more output. There is also a need to bring about technological improvements, structural changes, a liberalization from controls and regulations, increased labour and machine productivity and reliable quality assurance systems for the improvement of the industry. The textiles sector has gone through significant changes in terms of the expectation of increased levels of international competition. For the overall development of the economy, the textiles sector should be treated more favourably than any other industry, within the overall framework of India's industrial policy. The limited success of the T&C industry could be attributed to technological upgradation initiatives taken at the firm level, some policy initiatives (technological, marketing and financial) taken by the government, and the provisions of international trade rules – that is, the abolition of the quota system in January 2005. India is still enjoying the benefits of cheap labour compared to many other developing countries.

Acknowledgements

I am grateful to Dr K. Lal for his comments and suggestions on an earlier version of this chapter. I would like to thank Mr Santosh Kumar Sahu for excellent Research Assistance. The error(s) that remain are my own.

Appendix Table 4.1 Overview of the textiles industry

Items	Units	1999–2000	2000–01	2001–02	2002–03	2003–04	2004–05(P)
Cotton/ Man-Made Fibre	No.	1850	1846	1860	1875	1787	
Textile mills							
Spinning mills (Non-SSI)	No.	1565	1565	1579	1599	1564	1566
Composite mills (Non-SSI)	No.	285	281	281	276	223	223
Spinning mills (SSI)	No.	921	996	1046	1146	1135	
Exclusive Weaving mills (Non = SSI)	No.	202	203	207	209	206	
Powerloom units	Lakh No.	3.67	3.74	3.75	3.8	4.13	
Capacity Installed							
Spindles (SSI + Non-SSI)	Million No.	37.08	37.91	38.33	39.03	37.03	
Rotors (SSI + Non-SSI)	Lakh No.	4.44	4.54	4.8	4.68	4.82	
Looms (Organised sector)	Lakh No.	1.4	1.4	1.41	1.37	1.05	
Powerloom	Lakh No.	16.3	16.62	16.66	16.93	18.37	
Handlooms	Lakh No.	38.91	38.91	38.91	38.91	38.91	
Man-Made Fibres	Million kg.	1066	1081	1090	1096	1101	
Man-Made Filaments	Million kg.	1078	1128	1135	1191	1228	
Worsted spindles (Woollen)	Thousand No.	585	598	598	504	504	
Non-Worsted spindles (Woollen)	Thousand No.	419	426	426	437	437	
Production of Fibres							
Raw cotton*	Lakh bales	156	140	158	136	177	
Man-Made Fibres	Million kg.	835	904	834	914	953	1018
Raw Wool	Million kg.	47.9	49.2	50.7	50.7	50.7	
Raw Silk	Million kg.	15.21	15.86	17.35	16.32	15.74	

Production of Yarn						
Cotton yarn	Million kg.	2204	2267	2212	2177	2121	2270
Other spun yarn	Million kg.	842	953	889	904	931	950
Man-made filament yarn	Million kg.	894	920	962	1100	1118	1106
Fabric Production						
Cotton	Million sq.mtr.	18989	19718	19769	19300	18040	20488
Blended	Million sq.mtr.	5913	6351	6287	5876	6068	6000
100% Non-cotton (including Khadi, Wool & Silk)	Million sq.mtr.	14306	14164	15978	16797	18275	18200
Total	Million sq.mtr.	39208	40233	42034	41973	42383	44688
Per capita availability of cloth	Sq.mtrs.	30.55	30.68	31.97	31.37	31.01	
Production of Textile Machinery	Million US$	256.7	286.9	255.64	243.43	297.17	
Textile Exports (including Jute, Coir & Handicraft)	Million US$	10521.28	12014.4	10801.04	12444.9	13194.35	13038.64
Textiles Imports	Million US$	1128.59	1172.4	1537.1	1645.48	2021.96	2167.23

P: Provisional *: Cotton year.

Note: Source of Export/Import data from DGCI&S, Kolkata, Compendium of Textile Statistics, 2004.

Appendix Table 4.2   Market share of case study firms

SL. No	Name of the firm	Avg. gross sell (%)
1	Ambattur Clothing Ltd	4.02
2	Gokaldas Exports Ltd	8.76
3	Arvind Mills	18.50
4	Indo Rama Synthetics	26.41

Note

1. 1 crore = 10 million.

References

Avisse, Richard and Michel Fouquin (2001) 'Textiles and Clothing: the End of Discriminatory Protection', La Lettre du CEPII, No. 198, February.

Birnbaum, David (2001) 'The Coming Garment Massacre', 15 October, http://www.just-style.com/article.aspx?id=92676&lk=s.

Birnbaum, David (2002) 'Marginal Countries and Marginal Factories', 18 November, http://www.just-style.com/article.aspx?id=93031&lk=s.

Diao, Xinshen and Agapi Somwaru (2001) 'Impact of the MFA Phase-Out on the World Economy: An Intertemporal Global General Equilibrium Analysis', TMD Discussion Paper No. 79, Trade and Macroeconomics Division, International Food Policy Research Institute, October.

Dowlah, C.A.F. (1999) 'The Future of the Readymade Clothing Industry of Bangladesh in the Post-Uruguay Round World', *World Economy*, 22(7): 933–53.

Export–Import Bank of India (2005) 'Textile Exports: Post MFA Scenario, Opportunities and Challenges', Working Paper Series No. 9, February, Mumbai.

Flanagan, R. J. (2003) 'Labour Standards and International Competitive Advantage', in R. J. Flagnan and W. B. Gould IV (eds), *International Labour Standards: Global Trade and Public Policy*, Stanford, CA: Stanford University Press.

Francois, Joseph and Dean Spinanger (2001) "With Rags to Riches but Then What? Hong Kong's T & C Industry vs. the ATC and China's WTO Accession," Paper prepared for The Fourth Annual Conference on Global Economic Analysis, Purdue University, West Lafayette, Indiana, 27–9 June.

Government of India (various years) *Economic Survey, 2002, 2003, 2004, 2005, 2006*, New Delhi: Ministry of Finance.

Government of India, *Union Budget 2005–06*, New Delhi: Ministry of Finance.

Government of India (various years) *Annual Report*, New Delhi: Ministry of Textiles.

Hartmann, U. (1997) 'Strategic Alliances', mimeo, Presentation at Texcon 97, IIM Ahmedabad, 14–16 December.

Hyvarinen, Antero (2001) 'Implications of the Introduction of the Agreement of Textiles and Clothing (ATC) on the African Textiles and Clothing Sector', Papers on The Introduction of The Agreement of Textiles And Clothing (ATC), International Trade Center, UNCTAD/WTO, January.

ICICI (1996) *Beyond MFA: Strategies for the Indian Apparel Industry*, Mumbai: Industrial Credit and Investment Corporation of India.

IMF/World Bank (2002) 'Market Access for Developing Country Exports — Selected Issues', Report prepared by the staffs of the IMF and the World Bank, 26 September. www.imf.org/external/np/pdr/ma/2002/eng/092602.pdf.

Kathuria, S. and A. Bhardwaj (1998) 'Export Quotas and Policy Constraints in the Indian Textile and Garment Industries', Development Research Group, The World Bank, Policy Research Working Paper 2012. http://econ.worldbank.org/external/default/main?pagePK=64165259&theSitePK=469382&piPK=64165421&menuPK=64166093&entityID=000094946_99031911105435.

Kheir-El-Din, Hanaa and M. Maamoun Abdel-Fattah (2000) 'Textiles and Clothing in the Mediterranean Region: Opportunities and Challenges of Returning Textiles and Clothing to GATT Disciplines', Economic Research Forum Working Paper Series No. 2008. Available online at http://www.erf.org.eg/cms.php?id=publication_details&publication_id=149.

Krishna, Kala Marathe and Ling Hui Tan (1999) *Rags and Riches*, Ann Arbor, MI: University of Michigan Press.

Lankes, Hans Peter (2002) 'Market Access for Developing Countries', *Finance and Development*, 39(3). Available online at http://www.imf.org/external/pubs/ft/fandd/2002/09/lankes.htm.

Mattoo, Aaditya, Devesh Roy, and Arvind Subramanian (2002) 'The Africa Growth and Opportunity Act and Its Rules of Origin: Generosity Undermined?', World Bank Policy Research Working Paper 2908, October.

Parikh, J. K., V. K. Sharma, U. Gosh and M. K. Panda (1995) *Trade and Environment Linkages: A Case Study of India*, Indira Gandhi Institute of Development Research, Report prepared for UNCTAD.

Prasad Ananthakrishnan and Sonali Jain-Chandra (2005) 'The Impact on India of Trade Liberalization in the Textiles and Clothing Sector', WP/05/214, IMF http://www.imf.org/external/pubs/cat/longres.cfm?sk=18594.0.

Reserve Bank of India (2004) *Report on Currency and Finance, 2002–03*, Mumbai, India.

Someya, Masakazu, Hazem Shunnar, and T.G. Srinivasan (2002) 'Textile and Clothing Exports in MENA: Past Performance, Prospects and Policy Issues in Post MFA Context', Middle East and North Africa Region Working Paper, World Bank, August. http://siteresources.worldbank.org/INTMNAREGTOPTRADE/Resources/Textile-Clothing-Exports-MENA.pdf.

Spinager, Dean (1999) 'Textiles Beyond the MFA Phase-Out', *World Economy*, 22(4): 455–76.

Tait, Beverly (2002) 'Towards 2005: the Survival of the Fittest', 15 April, http://www.just-style.com/article.aspx?id=92976&lk=s.

Terra, M.I. (2001) 'Trade Liberalization in Latin American Countries and the Agreement on Textiles and Clothing in the WTO', Paper Presented at the Conference on the Impact of Trade Liberalization Agreements in Latin America and the Caribbean, Inter-American Development Bank.

Trela, Irene (1998) 'Phasing Out the MFA in the Uruguay Round: Implications for Developing Countries', in Harmon Thomas and John Whalley (eds), *Uruguay Round Results and the Emerging Trade Agenda*, New York and Geneva: United Nations.

Uimonen, Peter and John Whalley (1997) *Environmental Issues in the New World Trading System*, London: Macmillan.

USITC (2002) 'The Economic Effects of Significant US Import Restraints', Third Update 2002, June.

USITC (2004) 'Textiles and Apparel: Assessment of the Competitiveness of Certain Foreign Suppliers to US Markets', USITC, January.

Vijayabhaskar, M. (2002) 'Dimensions of Children's Work in the Cotton Knitwear Industry in Tiruppur', *Indian Journal of Labour Economics*, 45(3): 561–76.

Whalley, John (1999) 'Notes On Textiles And Apparel In The Next Trade Round', Paper prepared for a conference on Developing Countries in the Next WTO Trade Round, Harvard University, 5–6 November.

Whalley, John (2006) The Post MFA Performance of Developing Asia, Working Paper 12178, National Bureau of Economic Research, Cambridge, MA 02138, http://www.nber.org/papers/w12178.

Winters, Alan and Pradeep S. Mehta (2003) *In Bridging the Differences – Analyses of Five Issues of the WTO Agenda*, Jaipur, India: CUTS.

5

The Textiles and Clothing Industry and Economic Development: A Case Study of Mauritius

Aveeraj S. Peedoly

5.1 Introduction

The export-oriented development strategy promoted by the Mauritian government from the 1970s onwards and which was centred mainly around the manufacturing of textiles and clothing (TC) has been a key element in the take-off and sustained growth of the economy (Burn, 1996; Durbarry, 2001) and earned itself the success which has in many ways distinguished Mauritius from the rest of Africa (Wignaraja and Lall, 1998; Wignaraja, 2002). Over the course of three decades, the Mauritian TC sector has established itself as the most developed TC industry in Sub-Saharan Africa (HPC Report, 2002) and has arguably 'compacted in this time period what the industry in Western Europe achieved over almost 200 years and the "tigers" in Asia in almost 50 years' (Gherzi Report, 2000: 2). At the turn of the twenty-first century, Mauritius was the world's second-largest fully fashioned knitwear producer, the third-largest exporter of new wool products and Europe's fourth-largest supplier of T-shirts (Tait, 2002).

This progress has been all the more remarkable given a number of inherent disadvantages which had the potential to sink the economy before it even took off. In addition to being a tiny island with no indigenous raw materials and relatively remote from major markets,[1] Mauritius was in fact being tipped as having all the ingredients for failure[2] at the time of its independence from British colonial rule (see Mukonoweshuro, 1991; Subramanian, 2001). A whole gamut of internal and external factors and opportunities has worked in conjunction to attract foreign direct investment in the Mauritian EPZ and eventually led to what several writers have called a 'miracle' (see Kearney, 1990; Anker et al., 2001; Bowman, 1991; Dommen and Dommen, 1999).

However, over the last two decades, success has created its own problems. Gradually, at both the national and the international levels the sector has been confronted by challenges which have had an adverse effect on its growth. On the domestic front, there have been several weaknesses contributing to its vulnerability.[3] Among the main factors having a negative impact on the competitiveness of TC enterprises are: increasing labour costs coupled with low productivity levels; a lack of skilled workers; a mismatch between demand and supply on the labour market; an excessive reliance on the four clothing items (T-shirts, shirts, pullovers and trousers); and, finally, a lack of linkages (Tait, 2002; HPC Report, 2003; NPCC, 2005). In addition, an investment policy review of Mauritius carried out by UNCTAD (2001) with a view to assessing the investment and policy environment identified a number of weaknesses within the investment framework, particularly regarding the lengthy and demanding administrative and bureaucratic processes involved, and made recommendations relating to the creation of a more open and friendly framework in particular for FDI.

At the international level, the Mauritian TC sector is facing formidable threats and challenges as a result of trade liberalization and the emergence of low-cost producing countries such as China, India, Indonesia, Bangladesh and Sri Lanka (see World Bank Aide-Mémoire for Mauritius, 2001; Common Country Assessment for Mauritius, 2000; Wignaraja and Lall, 1998). Most importantly, the dismantling of quotas under the Multi-Fibre Agreement in January 2005 has had major implications for the TC sector. With the dismantling of the MFA, prices have fallen by some 30 per cent on a dozen apparel items[4] in favour of China and other low-cost producers. In 2003 and 2004, there were 33 closures and about 17,000 workers lost their jobs in this sector. Most of the enterprises from Hong Kong and Taiwan have relocated to cheaper sites of production in Asia or Africa and exports to the US which were their principal markets have suffered a drastic blow. The Lamy Initiative (Everything But Arms) which grants duty-free access to apparel products from LDCs is yet another threat to the local producers by exposing Mauritian exports to intense competition from countries which have much lower costs of production. The AGOA and negotiations to trade regionally offer some opportunities which have as yet to be fully tapped.

Over the past few years the local TC sector has therefore been compelled to undergo a deep restructuring process with a need to almost reinvent itself on the global TC market. This study provides latest evidence on the ways in which the sector itself and the government have responded to the changes which have affected the sector.

This study has been conducted over the period March to October 2006. It uses secondary sources of data, including government reports, official statistics and academic publications supplemented with case studies of four of the most important textile and clothing enterprises in Mauritius as well as interviews with officials from support institutions to analyse the evolution and performance of the TC sector in Mauritius. Equally important objectives of the study are to assess the role of government in assisting the sector to face the challenges of global competition and to provide an up-to-date picture of the state of the local TC sector as well as the new challenges and prospects that it currently faces. The chapter is organized as follows: (i) The first part provides an overview of the development of the TC industry in Mauritius with a particular focus on the performance of the sector over the last two decades; (ii) The second part of the study provides a critical review of government initiatives in assisting and supporting this sector over the last two decades. More particularly, the important policy reforms which have been made in order to address the impact of liberalization and global competition and make the sector more efficient and productive are captured; (iii) The third part analyses the opportunities and constraints facing this sector in the light of trade opportunities, more particularly under the AGOA; (iv) The analysis of the findings of the case studies of key companies in the TC sector makes up the next part; (v) The final part presents a brief summary and discussion of the main issues raised.

PART I: BRIEF HISTORICAL OVERVIEW AND PERFORMANCE OF THE TC INDUSTRY

5.1.1 History

Over the course of three decades the Mauritian TC sector has become the most developed TC industry in Sub-Saharan Africa. Although the available literature on the TC sector in Mauritius tends to lump together both the textile and the clothing sub-sectors, it is nonetheless worthwhile to bear in mind some basic distinctions between them. Textile activities involve the manufacture of textile yarn and fabrics and mainly include processes such as spinning, weaving and knitting. These activities are inherently capital intensive and usually require skilled labour. The textiles industry in Mauritius exists principally as a provider of yarn and fabric to local producers. The exports of yarns and fabrics are yet to show significant development. Given that the country has no indigenous sources of raw materials, its success in this sector is all the more impressive.

On the other hand, the clothing sub-sector is, as in most EPZs across the world, more labour intensive than capital intensive, employing about 92 per cent of the total TC labour force in 2005. It has traditionally concentrated on four main products, namely T-shirts, pullovers, trousers and men's shirts, which account for more than 90 per cent of total garments exports and around 70 per cent of total EPZ exports. The large companies, particularly those involved in knitwear, are vertically integrated, although some of them also source their fabrics from certain countries in Asia and Africa as they tend to be more economical, flexible and have the additional benefit of providing a greater variety of products.

Moreover within the clothing sector, it is worthwhile distinguishing between two types of operators, namely the majority which operate in the EPZ sector which is the focus of this report and a minority of small enterprises – many of which operate in the informal sector and generally cater for the domestic market. The bulk of the requirements of the domestic market needs of clothing products is in fact met by imports. According to Joomun (2006), producers in the EPZ can sell a small proportion of their production on the local market subject to prior authorization from the Ministry of Industry and Commerce. These producers normally sell their products in their own factory shops, usually to tourists and to the Mauritian middle and upper classes.

The export-oriented companies themselves vary considerably in size, employment and financial turnover. According to MEPZA officials in June 2006, ten groups of companies accounted for 54 per cent of total TC employment and 75 per cent of TC exports. It is also worthwhile to note that with the departure of the majority of foreign investors in the sector in the wake of the dismantling of the MFA, the remaining companies are either wholly or mainly owned and run by local entrepreneurs.

This section presents an overview of the TC sector in the country before focusing more specifically on its performance over the past two decades. Some observers argue that the EPZ which has from the outset been spearheaded by textile and clothing manufacturing – in terms of employment, exports and imports and contribution to national income – have undergone distinct phases since it was set up (see Durbarry, 2001; Burn, 1996).

The period 1970–76 corresponded to the take-off of this sector. The period 1977–83 witnessed a stagnation of the EPZ following the onset of stabilization and structural adjustment measures in Mauritius. The phase 1983–88 has been labelled the 'clothing boom years'.

The next phase, spanning from the turn of the 1990s to the early 2000s, was characterized by a phase of slowdown and reorientation. To these phases, which have been described by Durbarry (2001) and Burn (1996), it is important to add a fifth phase which started in the early years of 2000 and which has as its precursor the dismantling of the MFA. The impact of the dismantling of the MFA, as is explained in more detail later, has arguably been a turning point in the Mauritian TC sector. The following explains these developments in more detail.

5.1.2 The take-off of the EPZ and the TC sector in the 1970s

The textiles and clothing sector in Mauritius has its origins in 1970 following the enactment of the EPZ Act which was followed by a number of policies to facilitate the expansion of exports, liberalize trade and prices and reduce exchange controls. The promotion of an export-oriented strategy was the logical response by the Mauritian government to the findings of the Meade Report (1961) which established that the sole dominant local industry of the time, the sugar industry, could not provide a sufficient number of jobs for a rapidly increasing population and that export-oriented development was the best option to address the problems of underdevelopment which characterized Mauritius at that stage of its history (see Lamusse, 1995; Kothari and Nababsing, 1996).

The first few years of the EPZ witnessed an encouraging start fuelled by domestic investment of the sugar industry's profits (see Lamusse, 1989) as well as FDI arrivals, mostly from Hong Kong (Durbarry, 2001; Burn, 1996). Lamusse (1989) estimates that sugar capital invested in the Export Processing Zone was about 42 per cent of total local equity capital over the period 1970–1983. Hong Kong investors provided 39.3 per cent of the equity and were concentrated mainly in the knitwear sub-sector of the clothing industry (Lamusse and Burn, 1990). As mentioned earlier, the availability of cheap labour locally, the entry to the EEC market under the Lomé Convention, a favourable political climate by African standards, as well as the existence of a Sino-Mauritian ethnic community attracted foreign investment mainly from Hong Kong in those early years.

Mauritius was in fact one of the first African ACP countries to use the market-access preferences under the Lomé Agreement (later the Cotonou Agreement) to develop its textiles and clothing sector (Jeetah and Coughlin, 2001). The Multi-Fibre Agreement further restricted the industry in other garment-exporting countries, especially in Asia. As Durbarry (2001) puts it, the MFA has been a blessing in disguise by further restricting the imports into developed countries markets of textile products from developing countries. These have motivated 'Asian Tigers' to seek refuge in countries enjoying unrestricted and preferential access to the European markets. This partly explains the influx of Hong Kong and Taiwanese investors in Mauritius in the past.

With the main export product in the 1970s being knitted pullovers, exports grew from $1 million in 1971 (with only eight firms) to $116 million in 1980 (with 112 firms) with Europe being the main export market. Between 1970 and 1980, employment in the textiles and clothing sector rose from around 500 to 21,113 (Durbarry, 2001).

5.1.3   EPZ stagnation (1978–82)

The late 1970s and early 1980s were marked by a deceleration in the expansion of EPZs. According to Durbarry (2001), a broad gamut of factors at both the national and international levels contributed to the stagnation of EPZs during the years 1978–82. A combination of the world recession of the late 1970s together with a host of domestic problems, including a rising real exchange rate and large wage hikes, and a deterioration of the political climate (nearing the 1982 general elections in the country), impacted unfavourably on the local EPZ. These factors caused employment to stagnate in this sector and, in fact, resulted in the decline of the whole economy.

5.1.4   The clothing boom (1983–88)

The implementation of Structural Adjustment Policies in the early 1980s led to an explosion of employment over the next few years, rising from 23,000 in 1982 to over 80,000 by 1990. The sector was in fact rejuvenated in the 1980s with the setting up of a broad range of incentives offered by the government to foreign investors (Hureeram and Little, 2002; Kothari and Nababsing, 1996). These included long-term tax holidays, tax exemptions on shareholders' dividends, exemption from the payment of duty, and a levy or sales tax on materials and equipment. Investment was mainly from Hong Kong-based companies who were interested in cheap labour and having access to quota-free and, subsequently, quota allocations targeting – mainly the US but also EU markets. From 1984 onwards, changes in US Rules of Origin legislation led to further FDI arrival from Hong Kong – and also, to a lesser extent, from Taiwan and Singapore. Within this period, the government's renewed efforts to promote industrialization and economic diversification led to phenomenal growth rate of textiles and clothing exports from Rs 1 billion in 1982 to Rs 9.5 billion in 1990 with the EU being the main market, together with a foothold in the US market from the locally-based Far-Eastern companies. In fact from the late 1980s onwards, the bulk of Mauritian exports for the US market were manufactured on the basis of 'cut, make and trim' by those plants.

The period 1983–88 has also been referred to as *the EPZ crusade* (see Durbarry, 2001) or the *clothing boom years* (Burn, 1996) for which Mauritius has been seen as a success story of export-oriented industrialization. Employment for the clothing industry alone first grew to a significant size within this period, increasing from less than 20,000 in 1982 to 77,000 in 1988.

Moreover the late 1980s were also characterized by a steady increase in the proportion of exports from locally owned enterprises, some of which started to integrate backwards into wool spinning, fabric knitting, dyeing, and so on, in order to take advantage of the Lomé Convention. This rapid expansion of local small-scale 'cut, make and trim' enterprises is alleged to have been accompanied by a decline in productivity. The productivity index fell from 97 in 1983 to 93 in 1989 as a result of the recruitment of unskilled labour and high levels of absenteeism.[5]

5.1.5   The TC sector from the 1990s to the present

In the 1990s, the TC sector becomes increasingly complex to analyse as more factors come into play in affecting its performance. As mentioned earlier, the 1990s have been referred as a period of slowdown and reorientation. Over this period, the competitiveness of the sector has gradually been eroded with increasing labour costs, low productivity levels, lack of skilled workers, a mismatch between demand and supply on the labour market and a lack of diversification in product and destination which exposed the country to direct competition and fluctuations in terms of trade. Further compounding these problems, this period has been marked by the gradual elimination of trade preferences and the liberalization of trade at the global level. The accession of China to the WTO and the formidable threat it single-handedly poses to other countries, including but not limited to textile and garment producers has been well documented.[6]

At the beginning of the millennium, the dismantling of the MFA in particular has been a major blow to the sector. In Mauritius, the most daunting effect of the dismantling of the MFA has been in terms of its impact on arbitrary dismissals on a massive scale as a result of closures or downsizing as firms run out of business or relocate to greener pastures where the costs of production are lower. Women workers in particular, since they account for about two-thirds of employees in this sector, have been facing the direct consequences of firm closures, restructuring and downsizing in terms of job losses, lack of job security and declining labour standards.

The survival of the sector itself has been put into jeopardy as most of the enterprises from Hong Kong and Taiwan have relocated to cheaper sites of production in Asia or Africa and exports to the US, which were their principal markets, have suffered a dramatic decline as will be shown later.

This section attempts to capture and illustrate some of the most important trends in the performance of the sector from the 1990s to the present, although it has to be borne in mind that no summary can do justice to nearly two decades of the operation of any industry. Table 5.1 captures some of the main trends which have characterized the EPZ sector as a whole and the TC sector in particular (where disaggregated data is available) in the 1990s and 2000s.

5.1.6 Contribution to GDP

The Mauritian TC sector was fairly strong and resilient throughout the 1990s and the first few years of the twenty-first century until the dismantling of the MFA had the unprecedented consequences which will be elaborated below. The EPZ share of GDP in that period hovered around 12 per cent in the period 1991–2001, as shown in Table 5.1. Since then the EPZ share of GDP has been falling. From 2001 onwards, the EPZ share of GDP fell from 11.6 per cent in 2001 to 7.4 per cent in 2005.

5.1.7 Growth rate of the EPZ

This trend is even better reflected in the growth rate of the EPZ, as shown in Figure 5.1. The growth rate of the EPZ sector averaged approximately +5.4 per cent in the period 1991–2001. Since this time, negative growth has been recorded in the EPZ sector, particularly as the result of the important downturn which the TC sector has faced following the dismantling of the MFA. In the years 2002 to 2005 it registered negative growth rates of 6 per cent, 6 per cent, 6.8 per cent and 13 per cent, respectively. Most recent estimates

Table 5.1 Main economic indicators for the EPZ sector (selected years)

	1991	1993	1995	1997	1999	2001	2003	2005
No. of enterprises	586	536	481	480	512	522	506	506
New	52	38	25	26	37	24	23	24
Closures	34	60	38	27	20	20	23	19
Of which total TC firms	–	–	–	–	–	*286*	*272*	*263*
Employment as at December	90,861	85,621	80,466	83,391	91,374	87,607	77,623	66,931
Of which total TC employment	*80,498*		*70,141*	*77,921*	*80,118*	*77,003*	*67,251*	*54,807*
Including expatriate labour	*1,150*					*15,688*	*15,392*	*14,419*
Exports (fob Rs mn)	12,136	15,821	18,267	23,049	29,131	33,695	32,059	29,187
Imports (cif Rs mn)	7,067	9,326	10,856	13,880	15,735	17,140		
Raw materials	6,348	8,221	9,869	12,442	13,891	15,637		
Machinery and spare parts	794	677	1,109	1,117	1,438	1,844		
Value added current prices (Rs Mn)	4,406	5,705	7,096	9,086	11,697	13,681	13,447	12,103
Share in GDP (%)	12.2	11.9	11.7	12.1	12.3	11.6	9.8	7.4
Investment (Rs mn)	648	900	815	1,245	1,755	1,694	1,614	2,355
Machinery	(610)	(875)	(805)	(1,200)	(1,635)	(1,80)	(1,506)	(1,680)
Employment as at December	90,861	85,621	80,466	83,391	91,374	87,607	77,623	66,931
Of which total TC employment	*80,498*		*70,141*	*77,921*	*80,118*	*77,003*	*67,251*	*54,807*
Including expatriate labour	*1,150*		*6,145*	*8,838*	*11,690*	*15,688*	*15,392*	*14,419*
No. of enterprises	586	536	481	480	512	522	506	506
New	52	38	25	26	37	24	23	24
Closures	34	60	38	27	20	20	23	19
Of which total TC firms	–	–	–	–	–	*286*	*272*	*263*

Source: Central Statistical Office.

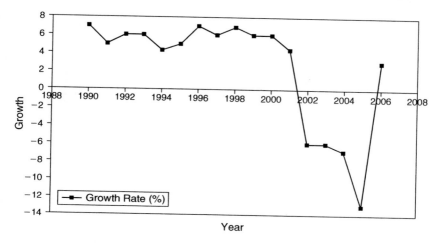

Figure 5.1   Growth rate of the EPZ (%)

in 2006 nevertheless indicate a slow improvement of these trends and the reasons behind this are elaborated later.

5.1.8   Foreign direct investment

FDI maintained an upward trend from 1986 to 1990 – at a time when the TC sector was registering significant growth rates. However, since this time, Mauritius has been much less successful in attracting FDI. According to the NPCC (2005), this could be linked to the lower performance of existing sectors facing increasing production costs as well as labour market rigidities. Figure 5.2 below shows FDI arrivals for the whole of the EPZ sector given the absence of disaggregated data for industrial sectors. The upsurge of FDI in 1999 was due to the acquisition of a tuna canning plant by British investors. According to the HPC (2002), the Mauritian TC sector is having difficulty in attracting FDI because of geopolitical changes that have taken place in the last decade.

A considerable amount of hope has been placed in the ability of the AGOA to attract FDI. In fact, the trends over the last couple of years have been more encouraging with reports of some cotton-spinning firms from China, India and Pakistan implanting (and announcing to implant) themselves on the local scene in order to benefit from the rules of origin of the AGOA.

Nevertheless, a lot of cynicism can be detected in interviews with key officials in the MCCI and the MEPZA about the opportunities which have been promised under the AGOA. Allegedly, FDI in TC from the US have been favouring the Caribbean and Latin American regions. Mauritius is too

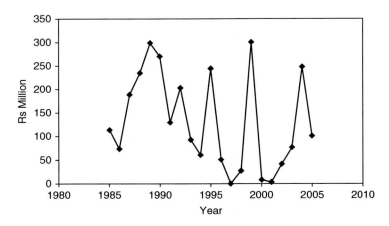

Figure 5.2   Foreign direct investment in EPZ

geographically remote to attract real US investment as sometimes overemphasized when evoking the AGOA prior to its enactment. The implications and the impact of the AGOA on Mauritian TC is discussed in more detail in a later section.

5.1.9   Relocation to cheaper sites of production

The rising costs of local labour have gradually led to a significant development in the TC sector. From the 1990s onwards many large groups have reacted to this situation by relocating to cheaper sites of production. Madagascar has been one of the most important sites of relocation from Mauritius-based TC companies and among other countries to have benefited from investment from Mauritius are Mozambique, Botswana and Lesotho.

Compared to the average wage in the TC sector, which is approximately US$130, the average wage in the industry in Madagascar is only about US$40 per month for a 40-hour week (Tait, 2002). As the case studies will later show, most of the most important TC firms have established subsidiary branches in Madagascar. The move offshore to Madagascar in particular has been mainly in terms of 'low-end' operations usually associated with the production of higher-volume runs of basic commodities which are generally labour intensive requiring basic skills.

It was estimated that in 2000 Floreal employed about 5,000 employees in Madagascar. The other major garment enterprise which has relocated part of its production in Madagascar is the Compagnie Mauricienne de Textiles (CMT). It has moved its 'low-end' operations to Madagascar and was reported to employ about 4,000 staff. Table 5.2 shows the extent of foreign direct investment (FDI) from Mauritius to Madagascar between 1990 and 2002.

Table 5.2 Investment in Madagascar from Mauritian TC companies

Year	1990	1991	1992	1993	1994	1995	1996	1997	1998	1999	2000	2001	2002
MUR million	5	5	–	20	4	5	–	13	19	57	2	2	–

Source: Bank of Mauritius.

FDI reached a peak of MUR 57 million (about US$2 million) in 1999. In 2002, however, an important political crisis and civil riots severely affected production in the Mauritian firms which were based there. According to Joomun (2006), firms like Floreal and CMT had to repatriate their machines to Mauritius in order to minimize losses. Most of the Mauritian firms are reported to have incurred important losses by failing to meet orders. Floreal lost a staggering US$14 million due to the crisis alone.

It is reported that the same groups have renewed interest in Madagascar in the aftermath of the riots. Together with its geographical proximity and the availability of plentiful and cheap labour, Madagascar has a 'Lesser Developed Beneficiary Country' (LDBC) status which it eventually obtained for preferential access under AGOA. LDBC countries in Sub-Saharan Africa benefit from a special apparel provision for duty-free and quota-free eligibility to US markets for garments made from fabrics and yarns produced anywhere in the world.

5.1.10 Textiles and clothing exports

An analysis of the exports figures over the last two decades (Table 5.1) reveals that EPZ exports rose roughly fourteenfold in the period 1984–2000. In particular, exports in the TC sector have shown an even steeper rise during that period, corresponding to nearly sixteenfold in 2000. However, over recent years, due mainly to the effects of the dismantling of the MFA, TC exports have faced a major set-back, as shown by the figures in Table 5.3. Its share of total EPZ exports has even reached an all-time low of 71 per cent in 2005. It is widely acknowledged that the majority of the foreign investors in this sector, mainly from Hong Kong, have left the country in anticipation of the dismantling of the MFA. Since the USA was their main market, the significant drop in exports to this country is reflected in their departure from Mauritius. A number of smaller and inefficient firms which were locally owned have also been driven out of business in the face of competition.

5.1.10.1 *Evolution of clothing exports by main destinations*

Table 5.4 shows the evolution of exports to the main destinations over the period (1997–2005). The most salient feature in this table is that it captures

Table 5.3 Textiles and clothing exports, 1984–2005 (MUR million)

	1984	1988	1992	1996	2000	2005
Total EPZ exports	2,151	8,176	13,081	21,001	30,961	29,187
Of which TC exports	1,663	6,626	10,944	17,634	26,504	20,745
Share of total EPZ exports (%)	77.3	81.0	83.7	84.0	85.6	71

Source: Central Statistical Office.

Table 5.4 Clothing exports by main destination, 1997–2005

	1997	1998	1999	2000	2001	2002	2003	2004	2005
Europe	16,304	17,960	19,214	19,545	20,660	20,253	20,507	21,760	21,487
UK	*5,341*	*5,488*	*6,289*	*6,622*	*7,169*	*7,635*	*7,848*	*8,895*	*9,237*
France	*5,669*	*6,259*	*6,911*	*7,510*	*7,872*	*7,637*	*7,253*	*6,995*	*6,082*
US	4,354	6,053	6,824	7,715	8,804	9,481	8,474	7,541	5,415
Other	2,391	2,062	3,093	3,701	4,231	2,949	2,463	2,745	2,285
Total	23,049	26,075	29,131	30,961	30,961	32,683	31,444	32,046	29,187

the significant drop in exports to the USA as a result of the departure of Hong Kong firms immediately prior to the dismantling of the MFA.

5.1.10.2 The US market

Since 1998 as far as garment exports are concerned, the USA has become the single largest market. The two items in which Mauritius had the greatest competitive advantage and had successfully penetrated the US markets were cotton trousers and cotton knitted shirts. However, from 2002 onwards after having made steady progress, there has been a significant drop in the share of exports to the USA. It is clear that the promises of the AGOA remain to be fulfilled and that this current situation is set to worsen given the depreciating US dollar with respect to the Mauritian Rupee.

5.1.10.3 The European market

Over the years the quota-free access to EU markets under the Lomé Convention (later the Cotonou Agreement) has given Mauritius a strong foothold in EU markets. The main exports destinations within Europe are France and the UK (along with Germany, Italy and Spain). At the turn of the millennium exports to Europe were hit by the strength of the Mauritian Rupee against the euro. Between January 1999 and June 2001, the Mauritian Rupee appreciated from Rs 28.89: euro 1.00 to Rs 24.50: euro 1.00. As Mauritian exporters

Table 5.5 Imports of yarn and fabrics (MUR million)

Year	1996	1997	1998	1999	2000	2001	2002	2003	2004
Yarn and fabrics	6,643	7,250	8,888	8,931	10,843	10,650	10,365	9,949	9,225
Total EPZ imports	12,077	13,880	16,179	15,735	16,399	17,140	16,977	15,579	17,195
Textile yarn and fabrics as a percentage of total EPZ imports	55	52	55	57	66	62	61	64	54

Source: Central Statistical Office.

price their exports to European markets in euros, their profit margins fell and their competitiveness suffered. Currently the situation has improved with the exchange rate being Rs 43.70: euro 1.00.

In interviews with key officials from support institutions to the TC sector, one issue which was raised consistently was that some niche markets within Europe have already been secured. These buyers are usually important brand names which tend to demand small volume runs of high value-added products requiring high standards of quality, reliability and working to tight schedules in markets which are marked by seasonality. Although the dismantling of the MFA did open up competition with China and other low-cost producers, some of the large TC groups in Mauritius were still taking orders from European companies which favour the trust and quality which Mauritian firms have successfully built up over years of experience in the sector. It is believed that the future of the sector is in terms of meeting the demands of these niche markets.

5.1.11 Imports of yarn and fabrics

The past success story of Mauritius in the TC sector is all the more impressive given that the country has no indigenous supply of fibres and, consequently, all of the textiles industry's raw materials requirements have traditionally had to be imported. The supply of locally made yarns and fabrics is limited. In order to improve supplies, in recent years a significant amount of investment has gone into the textiles industry. The Rule of Origin under the AGOA has encouraged the establishment of cotton spinning mills and a wide range of incentives to operators to invest in this sector.

Table 5.5 shows that from 2003 there has been a decline in the imports of yarn and fabrics, a development which can be explained by the setting up of the two cotton-spinning mills around this time. The two cotton-spinning mills began their operations in 2003 and 2004 respectively. Mauritius is now reported to produce almost one-third of the cotton yarn it consumes (Joomun 2006).

Table 5.6   Imports of knitted and non-knitted garments (MUR million CIF)

	1996	1997	1998	1999	2000	2001	2002	2003	2004
Knitted garments	58	85	85	115	116	134	167	171	186
Non-knitted garments	249	330	312	310	327	353	518	534	607
Total	307	415	397	425	443	487	685	705	793

Source: Central Statistical Office and MIDA.

Table 5.7   The distribution of TC sub-sectors in terms of number of firms and employment

	Spinning	Weaving & Knitting			Garment-Making				Total
		Weaving	Knitting	Pullover	T-shirts	Shirts	Trousers	Others	
No of Firms	5	2	3	9	74	62	47	61	263
Employment	1,300	1,800	1,500	4,879	22,500	9,700	6,450	6,678	54,807

Source: CSO.

5.1.11.1   *Imports of clothing*

Mauritius also imports a considerable amount of clothing items. According to the MIDA, the level of garments imports into Mauritius was approximately 3.8 kg per head of population (2001: 24). The direct imports for knitted and non-knitted garments are shown in Table 5.6. The table shows the constant progression of Mauritian imports of knitted and non-knitted products. The value of imports of garments has increased by almost 80 per cent between 2000 and 2004.

5.1.12   Overview of the current state of the TC industry

The significant number of closures experienced by the sector in recent years has caused a considerable change in its composition. Table 5.7 provides an illustration of the breakdown of the TC sector in its sub-sectors and the number of employees therein in 2006. The textiles sector accounts for about 8 per cent of total TC employment and consists of ten enterprises. Garments which involve the manufacturing of pullovers, shirts, trousers and T-shirts make up 73 per cent of total TC enterprises, 86 per cent of TC employment and 85 per cent of TC exports.

In itself the production of T-shirts represents nearly 30 per cent of total TC enterprises and more than 40 per cent of employment in the TC sector. In addition to those four main products, it is worthwhile noting that a wide range of other garments are also manufactured as part of the incentives (or pressure) to diversify production within the TC sector, albeit not to the same scale as the above. Among those figure lingerie, beachwear, dresses, skirts, children-wear, baby-wear, jackets, suits and vests produced mainly by SMEs.

Further it is also important to note that ten groups of companies are responsible for 75 per cent of total TC exports and generate about 54 per cent of total employment in this sector. The main disadvantage of this overreliance on these four products is the unfavourable terms of trade in terms of adverse currency fluctuations as well as increasing competition in lower-cost producers of similar products on the world market.

5.1.12.1 *Perceptions of the current situation by stakeholders*

As part of the empirical data collection for this study, interviews with key stakeholders of the sector have been conducted in order to assess their perceptions of the situation regarding the sector, particularly after the dismantling of the MFA. Apart from the interviews with employers as part of the case studies, the participants were officials from support institutions (MEPZA, MCCI and Enterprise Mauritius), a senior Labour Inspector from the Ministry of Labour, trade union officials from the FPU as well as employers of the sector.

There was a general consensus that the 'dust has finally settled' in the words of one participant who sums up the issue neatly. The relocation of important groups to cheaper sites of production was acknowledged and accepted as a rational response to the changing global context affecting trade in TC. The core group of firms within this sector is considered to have not only the expertise to be world-class competitors in their specific markets, but also the capabilities and resilience to do so. Furthermore, they are also benefiting from a whole array of support services from the government – as detailed below.

As elaborated in the case studies, there has been an important shift towards the production of higher value-added commodities in which Mauritius is more competitive. This represents a move away from the production of basic commodities in which Mauritius has been outperformed by low-cost producers who have emerged and flooded the market with such commodities. According to the officials interviewed from the MCCI and the MEPZA, the experience of supplying high-profile customers who value high standards of detail, quality and design as well as reliability have helped local firms to secure niche markets. However, there is also an acknowledgement that by going up the value chain Mauritius is only adapting to present competition. There is a constant pressure to keep innovating in order to stay one step above the ferocious competition which characterizes this sector.

Trade union officials were particularly critical of the authorities for failing to monitor and address the problem of massive retrenchment of labour which has affected the sector as a result of the closures of a considerable number of companies. Accordingly, the emphasis on addressing the problems facing the sector has been reactive rather than proactive. An important number of retrenched workers are now struggling to find new employment given their relatively high age and low educational profiles and the lack of avenues for their re-employment. The FPU criticizes the government for having failed to take the necessary measures given that there was ample time to prepare for such eventualities as a period of ten years was given for the phasing out of the MFA.

PART II: GOVERNMENT POLICIES TO SUPPORT THE TC INDUSTRY IN THE PAST TWO DECADES

As briefly shown earlier, from the outset, the government has been closely involved in the setting-up of the policy, infrastructural and economic environment necessary to kick-start this sector. At various stages of its development, the government has, through a combination of policy interventions and the provision of institutional and technical support, been attempting to promote and improve the performance of the TC sector.

However, the profound changes which have affected this sector prior to and following the dismantling of the MFA have catalysed the need for the Mauritian government to conduct a holistic review of its assistance to this sector. Over the course of recent years, undoubtedly prompted by the rocketing unemployment rate and the implications of the gradual demise of a key pillar of the economy, the government has been more involved than ever in attempting to face the challenges facing this sector. Government assistance to the TC sector has therefore mainly been in terms of policies and measures to attempt to redress a number of important weaknesses in the sector particularly concerning the need to restructure their operations, upgrade technology, upgrade quality and design, innovate, produce high value-added products for niche markets and reduce response time if they are to remain competitive in the face of global integration and trade liberalization. A number of initiatives taken by the government have thus been taken in areas relating to the restructuring of enterprises, export promotion and market access, vertical integration, quality and design, access to finance, provision of industrial space and institutional reforms.

This section outlines the main state policies and initiatives to assist this sector and improve its performance over the past two decades with a particular focus on the last five years which, as explained above, has witnessed an unprecedented need to support this sector.

5.2.1   Export promotion policies in the past two decades

At this point it is worth noting that the export-led industrialization strategy, and the export promotion policies which accompanied it, was the result of the failure of an earlier attempt in the 1960s to industrialize by following an import substitution strategy. The relatively small size of the domestic market in a phase of history marked by underdevelopment, poverty, high unemployment and acute economic difficulties further compounded, as

Maujean (1996) or Bheenick and Schapiro (1989) argue, by inadequate planning and the absence of support schemes or incentives to enterprises meant that this programme never actually progressed. The application of high tariff rates to stimulate local production and discourage imports and the high protection of domestic companies, were therefore unsuccessful and their levels of competitiveness and productivity remained low.

As early as the 1970s a whole array of incentives, advantages and facilities were already operation to attract investment in the export-oriented manufacturing sector, including tax holidays, exemptions from import duties and also preferential credit were provided to foreign and domestic investors who would specialize wholly in exporting. In addition, in line with EPZs worldwide, important concessions in terms of labour legislations have been offered to investors in the sector – much to the detriment of workers. The harsh conditions of work in this sector, particularly in terms of compulsory overtime, barriers to unionization and collective bargaining, low wages relative to other sectors of the economy and lack of family friendliness at the workplace, have been well documented.[7] The prerequisite of meeting deadlines for orders make of the EPZ a harsh and uncaring environment where family and social obligations are of secondary concern to employers. In fact, in terms of the conditions of work in that sector, there is a general consent in the mass media, among opinion leaders and the public alike that the little if any improvement in legislations and conditions of work in that sector, has been seriously lagging behind as opposed to all other employment sectors.

In general, many of the incentives to promote export-led industrialization have remained largely unchanged. By 1983, within its structural adjustment phase Mauritius began to take further measures towards an export-led policy. These measures typically involved trade liberalization, wage restraints, exchange rate management and export incentives, and export-oriented manufacturing thus began to emerge as the most dynamic sector. Mauritius increasingly pursued an aggressive export strategy which required intensive promotional efforts from the government through investment promotion institutions. A Government of Mauritius (1983) publication, 'A Guide for Foreign Investors' edited by the Joint Committee for the Promotion of Industry, provides a summary of revised incentives for export industries in the MEPZ which had as their main objective the promotion of export-oriented industries and which had been beneficial in securing investment in the TC sector. The main features are as follows:

- Ten-year income tax relief on corporate income.
- Five-year tax holiday on dividends.
- Duty-free inputs covering capital goods, raw materials, components and semi-finished products used by export industries are admitted into Mauritius free of customs and other duties.

- Partial tax exemption on re-invested profits.
- Tax rebates for foreign technicians.
- Guarantee given by government against nationalization.
- Free repatriation of profits, dividends and capital.
- Access to investment capital. Priority, whenever possible, is granted to export industries in the allocation of investment capital by the Development Bank of Mauritius.
- Loans at preferential rates from commercial banks.
- Protection against double taxation.
- Favourable freight terms.
- Government contribution to trade missions and trade fairs to facilitate the marketing of the products to be exported.

Other schemes added thereafter concerned the Industrial Building scheme in 1986. Under these schemes companies benefited from a lower corporate tax and a tax holiday for 10 and 20 years. In 1993, with a view to modernizing the existing schemes, amendments were made to the legislation leading to the 'Industrial Expansion Act 1993'. Under that legislation, the main advantage (for existing schemes) was that there was no corporate tax for export-oriented enterprises, whereas a 15 per cent corporate tax scheme was given for those local enterprises with the possibility of exports in specific sectors: those concerned include the Pioneer Status Enterprise, the Strategic local enterprise and the Small and Medium-Sized Enterprises. (See Appendix Table 5.2 for a list of existing incentive schemes to support or further encourage investment in this sector.)

In respect of trade policies, since the mid-1980s Mauritius has gradually adopted a number of trade liberalization measures. A major tariff reduction programme was implemented in 1994 when the tariff structure, which had consisted of as many as 60 different tariff rates, was reduced to just eight rates. The maximum MFN customs tariff was reduced from 600 per cent to 80 per cent and an eight-band customs tariff structure was therefore established with different rates ranging from 0 per cent to 80 per cent (0–5–15–20–30–40–55–80). At the time of writing Mauritius has a nine-band tariff structure with a new 10 per cent rate which has been added to the existing eight bands. Mauritius is still considered to be a high-tariff country, particularly when compared to other COMESA member states. Relatively high rates in the tariff structure in Mauritius are broadly acknowledged to be maintained for the protection of certain industries and also because customs revenue represents a significant share of government revenue (17 per cent in 2004).

The tariff regime for cotton and textiles from the region – that is, from the SADC and COMESA – is zero as these items are used as raw materials or inputs in the TC sector. On the side of non-tariff barriers, with the liberalization of trade, no permit is required for the imports of raw materials (with the exception of health permits for wool). In addition, in order to further promote exports, the government has also set up a whole range of policies and institutions. For instance, the MEDIA (later MIDA and more recently subsumed under Enterprise Mauritius) was initially set up in 1984 and the EPZDA in 1992 with the mission to help EPZ firms to penetrate markets, face international competition and improve productivity at technological and management levels. The following sections elaborate these points further.

Similarly, in addition to the provision of institutional support, several measures have also been announced by the government in an effort to reposition Mauritius in the global market for textiles and clothing and promote exports. The High Powered Committee (HPC) on Textile and Clothing published 'The Strategic Plan for the TC Sector' (2002) which lists a number of measures that promote even more aggressive marketing in existing and potential markets and encourage and assist SMEs to export. The HPC was established in 2001 under the chairmanship of the Minister of Industry, Commerce and International Trade precisely in the context of the challenges facing the sector in a context of ever-increasing global integration and competition. It comprised all of the key players in the industry and its main objective was to critically examine the problems and issues affecting the sector and to propose measures to come to the rescue of this waning sector and to establish Mauritius as a hub for textile and clothing. Regional cooperation has been found to be a viable avenue to overcome the constraints of size and lack of resources and for sustained economic growth. While acknowledging the intense competition in the US and EU markets, it also identifies new export opportunities which exist on the SADC and COMESA markets but also under the AGOA which provides duty- and quota-free access to the US market and opens up new avenues for enhanced trade, investment and transfer of technologies. The following lists measures which the HPC claims will boost TC exports. However, according to a number of officials from the authorities concerned, some of these measures have yet to be implemented.

- Organize trade exhibitions, trade fairs and personalized meetings in overseas targeted markets.
- Conduct surveys in markets not yet explored.
- Encourage establishment of strategic alliances between local suppliers and clients particularly in the EU or the USA.
- Setting up of distribution points or networks abroad in collaboration with foreign firms.
- Setting up of permanent display centres in targeted markets.
- Implementaion of SME export business support schemes.
- Provide market intelligence – market research.
- Reinforce the Mauritius Industrial Development Authority's presence abroad.

- In-store promotion in targeted markets.
- Protection of Industrial Property Rights.
- In-plant training and re-engineering programme of SMEs.
- Enhancing SMEs competitiveness in areas like training, access to finance and technology upgrading.
- Setting up of a local exhibition centre.
- Increase utilization of MRC Research Grant Scheme.
- Promotion of joint ventures with overseas partners.
- Sensitization of Export Credit Guarantee Scheme.

Source: Report of the High Powered Committee (2002): 'Strategic Plan for the TC sector'.

5.2.2 Technological policies

In order to assist the TC sector, from the outset the government has offered complete exemption from the payment of import duty on capital goods (that is, machinery, equipment and spare parts). One of the functions of the EPZDA since 1992 was precisely to improve the productivity of EPZ firms in general at technological and management levels.

Tait (2002) argues that many factories have invested in modern technology coming from a number of well-known suppliers from all over the world, including systems for grading and marker making from Gerber in the US and Lectra in France. Some factories are reported to have automatic cutting, although it is broadly acknowledged that band knife and straight knife cutting are used more often. The predominant brand of sewing machinery is Juki from Japan, although supplies have also come from Pfaff and Durkopp Adler in Germany, and Brother, Pegasus and Rimoldi in Japan. The most common make of embroidery machinery is reported to be from Tajima in Japan. In the case of pressing, equipment from Veit in Germany is reported to be predominant. Material handling systems include those manufactured by Eton of Sweden, INA of the USA and Schonenberger of Germany. However, according to Tait (2002) there is still some scope to enhance productivity further by improving factory layouts and introducing workplace engineering. Tait (2002) argues that many factories are still lagging behind in terms of efficiency and cost effectiveness. According to officials from the MEPZA, keeping up with technology has been the prerogative of only the larger firms which were still operating at a reasonable profit margin. In fact the latter argued that in contrast to the agricultural sector as a whole, and to sugar production and processing in particular, there is yet to be a formal industrial research and development service in Mauritius for the manufacturing sector, although this seems to be a concern which the government has been considering recently.

In a similar vein, the HPC (2002) reports that the textiles and clothing sector has not been adequately upgraded to keep pace with the changing competitive global environment. Accordingly, the technology and skill base is weak and manufacturing allegedly tends to concentrate in low value-added activity. In similar findings, Wignaraja and Lall (1998) found that enterprises identified inadequate technological support to be a major constraint in competitiveness. A study by Ramasawmy and Soyjaudah (2002) reveals that in the apparel sector, most material handling systems are still being carried out manually as most of the available automated systems are too expensive for firms to afford. Furthermore, they argue that in the event that a company succeeds in purchasing an automated system, the latter is underutilized and difficult and costly for them to maintain.

From the interviews with the informants in the case studies of large firms in the TC sector, as examined later, the evidence indicates that there is a technology gap between the largest enterprises and the other operators in the sector, which makes it harder for them to be efficient and competitive. The range of measures and policies which the government and competitive firms have been pursuing recently seem to indicate that there is an acknowledgement that the ability of the sector to effectively harness technology is an essential element of meeting the challenges facing this sector.

The Mauritian government is thus encouraging the greater use of CAD/CAM in design, pattern construction, auto spreading and cutting as well as an overall ICT-driven industry to promote supply chain management. It is also promoting technology diffusion, acquisition and transfer as well as product development through the application of state-of-the-art technology in fashion design to promote it as a regional centre of excellence for the apparel industry. (Refer to the range of incentives under the 'Modernisation and Expansion Scheme' in Appendix Table 5.2.) According to the HPC (2002), the priorities established to reinforce the technology base have included: (i) to upgrade existing testing facilities in accordance with international standards; (ii) to secure international accreditation; and (iii) to provide enhanced incentives for industry-specific training and specialized training on capital equipment.

From interviews with stakeholders, it is known that as part of the intention to develop local brand names and local design capabilities in order to further add value and sustain competitiveness, some firms have been developing their design capabilities, either in-house or through contacts with local designers. The vast majority are still receiving their designs from their overseas (mostly European customers). In 2003, with the assistance of the EU, the government established technology development schemes so as to facilitate the competitiveness and the integration of Mauritian enterprises in the global economy. Enterprises, including SMEs in the export-oriented manufacturing sector, have been encouraged through the provision of grants on a cost-sharing basis to invest in technology and skill development programmes. Among others, the upgrading of technology and practices involved the improvement in productivity and product quality, website development, management information systems, enterprise resource planning and quality system.

5.2.3   Financial policies

The financial incentives and fiscal measures available to EPZ companies as a whole since the 1970s have been outlined earlier (refer also to Appendix Table 5.2 for further schemes from which enterprises in TC can benefit). Since 1994, a floating exchange rate policy has been adopted. The role of the central bank has changed from market maker to market player. Intervention in the currency market is limited to dollar transactions with the objective of stabilizing the rupee.

Over the past few years a number of further measures have been introduced by the government during their yearly budgetary exercise in order to further enhance the capacity of supporting institutions, as well as to facilitate access to finance and provide fiscal incentives to firms in the TC sector. These measures have been implemented following the recommendations of prior reports which, in as much as financial aspects are concerned, have shed light on difficulties which TC companies have regarding their access to credit. High interest rates; heavy bureaucratic procedures resulting in delays to obtain foreign investment approvals, loan approvals from the Development Bank of Mauritius, refunds on import duties, and a general lack of access to finance (the need for collateral is still predominant for small enterprises) have been reported to be among the major constraints to firms.

Among the main and most recent measures that are applicable to the TC sector are a special line of credit to the EPZ sector, the availability of specific funds, concessionary registration duties, and the provision of special incentives to spinning, weaving and dyeing companies.

5.2.3.1   *Credit to the EPZ sector*

The special line of credit to the EPZ sector to a tune of Rs 500 million in November 2000 was increased to Rs 800 million by July 2001 and was geared to promoting modernization and the restructuring of textile and clothing enterprises with soft lending conditions.

5.2.3.2   *Debt restructuring*

In view of the high level of indebtedness and the difficult cash flow positions of enterprises in this sector a Corporate Debt Restructuring Committee (CRDC) was established to facilitate their financial restructuring. By 2005, of 16 applications to the CRDC for assistance, eight had been resolved and the others were at different stages of processing.

5.2.3.3   *Specific funds*

A range of specific funds were also made available as financial incentives and facilities to firms in this sector. The National Equity Fund was established in April 2003 to the tune of Rs 1 billion in order to encourage ventures in strategic areas, including cotton spinning, as well as to participate in equity of existing enterprises, including in the textiles and clothing sectors. The Textile Sub Fund was set up in 2004 with capital of Rs 200 million. The Textile Modernisation Fund was set up in 2003 with a loan ceiling increased twofold to Rs 20 million by 2004 and a favourable interest rate of 8 per cent. A Working Capital Scheme was introduced in 2003 to finance up to 80 per cent of the value of the export order with a ceiling of Rs 5 million and an interest rate of 10 per cent for textiles and clothing companies.

5.2.3.4 Incentives to spinning, weaving and dyeing companies

The special package of incentives for the promotion of investment in spinning, weaving and dyeing companies with the aim of promoting the vertical integration of the textiles sector involved a ten-year tax holiday and a special tax credit of 60 per cent of equity investments introduced for the promotion of spinning activities and spread over a maximum period of six years. Land is also being provided for lease at highly concessionary rates. This has already led to the creation of two new spinning mills and two more projects are imminent. The intention of this measure is to enable Mauritian producers to meet the AGOA rules of origin.

5.2.3.5 Concessionary registration duties

Concessionary registration duties involved the reduction by 2.5 per cent of the registration duty for the acquisition by manufacturing companies of land or buildings for modernization and/or expansion purposes until the end of 2007; the reduction of custom duties on a number of industrial inputs that are not produced locally; and the elimination of custom duties on work trucks, trailers and special purpose vehicles. In addition to or to channel these incentives to TC enterprises, a number of support institutions have been set up to meet the demands of a changing context. The following provides more details of such institutions and their role in the promotion of the TC sector.

5.2.4 Institutions and their role in the promotion of the TC sector

Institutions to assist the development of the sector in Mauritius have evolved in line with the needs of the sector. Institutional assistance to the TC sector from the government has principally been in terms of providing the support to attempt to redress a number of important weaknesses in the sector, particularly concerning financial issues, the need to secure markets, to upgrade technology, quality and design, to innovate and diversify, to produce high value-added products for niche markets and to reduce response times in order to remain competitive in the face of global integration and trade liberalization. To the existing institutions, the last couple of years have seen the emergence of additional facilities or reforms in order to provide more efficient support to the sector. This section outlines the main institutions which directly support the TC sector in Mauritius.

5.2.4.1   Enterprise Mauritius

Enterprise Mauritius is now regarded as being the main institution supporting industry in Mauritius. In July 2002, the Government of Mauritius commissioned a study with technical assistance from the Commonwealth Secretariat to advise on the setting up of an integrated institutional support framework for the industrial sector. An evaluation of the existing institutions supporting the industry highlighted a number of weaknesses such as duplication and the absence of a strategic focus. The main recommendations were that the activities of the various support institutions be more effectively organized and provided under one roof and/or integrated within a pragmatic matrix organization structure. In March 2004, the government set up a steering committee to draw up an implementation plan for the integration of the existing industrial support institutions – MIDA, EPZDA and TEST as described below – into Enterprise Mauritius.

5.2.4.2   MIDA (Mauritius Industrial Development Authority)

Before being subsumed under Enterprise Mauritius, MIDA was the focal point for the promotion of exports from Mauritius, but it was also responsible for the construction and management of industrial estates for lease to investors. The core objectives of MIDA over the period 2001–05 have been to position Mauritius as a reliable sourcing destination in overseas markets and to develop the export capabilities of SMEs. Pertaining more specifically to the Textile and Clothing sector, the MIDA has been actively involved in export promotion activities:

5.2.4.2.1   The EU market.   In relation to the EU market, the strategy has been to consolidate exports through niche marketing. Marketing surveys were conducted in several European markets, including Italy, Spain, Germany, the Netherlands and Scandinavia, in order to identify niches with high potential for Mauritius. The Mauritius International Apparel and Textile Exhibition (MIATEX), which is the showcase of the textiles industry, was organized in France and the UK. A marketing specialist was appointed in France to advise exporters and provide market intelligence.

5.2.4.2.2   The US market.   The strategy in the US market was to create awareness among buyers about the advantages of AGOA and to build up the capacity of exporters in the ways of doing business in the USA. Thus promotional activities were undertaken in Los Angeles, New York, Las Vegas and Hong Kong, which is a base for major US buying offices. A marketing office was opened in New York and workshops were organized on the US market.

5.2.4.2.3 Regional markets. Activities in the SADC and COMESA region were intensified with a view to promoting regional exports both within and also outside the clothing and textiles sector. Liaison offices were set up in Kenya and South Africa to enable the use of these countries as gateways to East Africa and Southern Africa respectively.

5.2.4.2.4 Other markets. With the commencement of direct flights to Dubai, MIDA updated the market survey conducted in the Middle East and participated in the Autumn Trade Fair in Dubai in line with the strategy of using Dubai as a gateway to the markets of the Middle East and Africa. The Australian market was also explored for the apparel sector.

5.2.4.3 The Export Processing Zone Development Authority (EPZDA)

The EPZDA was a parastatal institution set up in 1992 to 'ensure a smooth and successful transition at a time when Mauritius was embarking on a new phase of its industrial development'[8] which involved a shift from a labour-abundant to a skills-intensive economy requiring specialization, quality products, improved delivery times and creativity in product design amongst other things. The EPZDA has therefore been backing all export development activities to sharpen their competitive edge in order to face international competition.

In the early 2000s the EPZDA was involved in a number of activities to improve productivity, quality and competitiveness and to develop the creativity and design capabilities of enterprises. Some of the most pertinent ones are outlined below:

5.2.4.3.1 Launching of the industry portal of Mauritius. In May 2001 a web portal was established to work as a one-stop shop for entrepreneurs and business people in search of information in each sector and the economy as a whole. Easy and reliable, it enables research on various fields and generates a comprehensive Mauritius online directory; it also facilitates access to the whole list of services provided by EPZDA such as Textiles Services, User Schemes and E-Marketplace.

The E-Marketplace was introduced in February 2004 to provide easy access to information on suppliers of raw materials and automate the procurement process such as placing orders for raw materials accessories and equipment. Through the E-Marketplace, Mauritius-based traders can establish themselves in international markets by showcasing their local manufacturers to the rest of the business world. At the time of writing, around 50 enterprises are connected to this facility.

5.2.4.3.2 The Clothing Services Centre (CSC). The Clothing Services Centre was inaugurated in January 2002 and has invested heavily in machines and equipment in order to provide the industry with professional services and the know-how to better respond to market demands while meeting buyers' needs. The CSC is a centre of excellence where the latest technology related to CAD/CAM/CIM services is provided to the clothing sector. The CSC is staffed by experts who have experience in the TC industry, both internationally and locally. Its staff visits international exhibitions, fairs and forums on a regular basis in order to bring back knowledge which they can pass on to the industry in Mauritius. The centre runs a wide range of training courses and trend presentations. It has also a CAD bureau, provides consultancy and design services and arranges regular machine exhibitions. It has helped member companies by assisting with pattern creation, material sourcing, manufacturing techniques and technical specifications.

5.2.4.3.3   Training courses and workshops.   The EPZDA has also been behind a number of customized training courses. For instance, the Basic Customised Training for Sewing Machinists was launched in July 2002 to meet the current market demands for trained machinists. Under the scheme hands-on customized training is conducted with a view to imparting industrial sewing skills to trainees in order to enhance the competitiveness of the clothing manufacturing sector. Workshops have also been carried out successfully all year round in various fields ranging from quality management to exchange rate management and industrial engineering.

5.2.4.3.4   Textile Emergency Support Team (TEST).   The TEST was set up in July 2003 as a joint public–private sector initiative to facilitate the restructuring of individual enterprises with a view to enhancing their competitiveness. The services of institutions, namely the NPCC, EPZDA, MIDA, BOM and IVTB/HRDC, were secured under the TEST initiative for interventions at two levels. Level One involved the diagnosis of the performance of some 53 enterprises. Level Two focused on the production process and the financial restructuring and marketing of these enterprises.

A number of measures were adopted to assist enterprises to restructure their production processes and their debts. For production process restructuring, the EPZDA enlisted the services of Kurt Salmon Associates which carried out audits in 15 enterprises and undertook the restructuring of five of these enterprises. Productivity gains of around 30 per cent were recorded in a number of operations. A scheme was also set up to provide grants to meet 50 per cent of the cost of private consultancy services enlisted by enterprises to improve production processes. Five projects were approved under this scheme. In addition, 12 Gemba Kaizen workshops were organized by NPCC in nine enterprises to reduce wastage and improve processes.

As regards marketing, a subcontracting exchange platform was established under MIDA to encourage subcontracting activities among enterprises while the E-Market platform of the EPZDA was used to facilitate this activity and some 20 enterprises have registered themselves under this programme.

TEST has successfully enabled a number of enterprises to restructure their operations and to achieve appreciable gains in productivity.

The fusion of these three entities and the entry into operation of Enterprise Mauritius since late 2005 as the umbrella organization to carry out the above activities seeks to provide a more efficient and coordinated help to the sector through the merger of the above institutions. Enterprise Mauritius has been set up with the intention of promoting the interests of the exporting community and assisting them to become world-class players through value-added services as well as providing all relevant information to potential investors on any matter relating to investment. Its main objectives are as follows:

- the provision of advice and consultancy
- the provision of market and competitor intelligence
- supporting export expansion initiatives and
- facilitating networks, clusters and strategic partnerships
- assisting in developing new strategies and initiatives aimed at the manufacturing sector.

In an interview with an official of Enterprise Mauritius, the concept of clustering and the development of strategic partnership which can bring a competitive edge to local enterprises has yet to be translated into practice to the extent which is required. The case study of Floreal Knitwear, examined later, is an example of how this has the potential to enable firms to stay competitive. Much effort is being channelled into putting this idea across.

5.2.4.4 *Mauritius Export Processing Zone Association (MEPZA)*

Another important organization which provides support to the TC sector is the MEPZA, which is the earliest support institution for the EPZ sector. It was established in Ordinance in 1976 and since then it has been representing and promoting the interests of EPZ firms, both nationally and internationally. It acts as a consultative and advisory body on different issues of interest to its members such as budget proposals, industrial relations and long-term industrial strategy. In addition to acting as a liaison between EPZ companies and the government, it also organizes and facilitates training programmes in various fields aimed at building the capacity of the sector. It is generally considered to be the trend-setter of quality in the sector in Mauritius. The MEPZA has also played an important role in initiating and promoting the AGOA campaign since 1995.

The MEPZA runs a portal providing business information relating to economic and trade issues; labour and industrial laws; environmental legislation; updates on regional trade; international trade information; assistance with respect to members' request; education and training information and links with international organizations.

5.2.4.5   The Board of Investment (BOI)

As part of its strategy to promote investment and attract FDI in Mauritius, in March 2001 the government set up a BOI under the Investment Promotion Act of 2001. The primary objectives of the BOI, which operate under the aegis of the Ministry of Finance, are to act as the focal point for the promotion of Mauritius worldwide and for the local facilitation of business procedures.

The BOI's main functions as defined under the Act are:

- To initiate, undertake, encourage, facilitate, support, participate in, rationalize and coordinate activities in relation to investments having regard to the national, regional and international interests and needs of Mauritius.
- To prepare, fund, implement and monitor programmes relating to strategies for promotion investments in Mauritius.
- To improve the investment and business environment and to promote Mauritius as an attractive base for investments.
- To ensure coordination and cooperation between the public sector and the private sector in matters of investment.
- To maximize opportunities and arrangements for the development of all forms of investments and business activities in Mauritius.
- To coordinate multisectoral promotional activities.
- To consider investment proposals and issue investment certificates.
- To act as a one-stop shop service with a view to ensuring that any relevant permit is obtained expeditiously.

5.2.4.6   Human resource development institutions

Both the IVTB School of Design and the University of Mauritius are now running a number of courses in order to produce skilled professionals in a range of occupations within the sector, including fashion and textile design as well as textile engineering with a view of building the capacity of staff at a stage when the industry is moving up the value chain and requiring more skilled staff.

5.2.5   Government response to international trade rules

As the above sections of this report have shown, in response to the difficulties facing the sector in the face of trade liberalization and growing exposure to severe competition from low-cost producers, a number of measures, policies and institutional arrangements have been set up in the past few years in order to promote the TC sector and reposition it as a strong TC exporter on the world market. To sum up, against the difficult prospects lying ahead following the dismantling of the MFA and the ongoing liberalization of trade, the government's attempt to revitalize the TC sector has been in terms of creating the necessary conditions to assist enterprises to sharpen their competitive edge. In that context, the government has targeted its activities, amongst others, on industrial restructuring, industrial linkages, integration and clustering, business process re-engineering, multi-skilling and higher technological upgrading to promote the sustainability of the sector. Regular consultations with the main stakeholders are being held with a view to being constantly apprised of the problems faced by the various sectors and to act to alleviate them.

At this stage, however, there has been no evaluation of the contribution of the above measures to strengthening the sector and it is beyond the scope of this work to carry out such an exercise. It is perhaps also too early to undertake such an exercise given the relatively short timespan for which these different forms of support have been available. However, it is worth noting that key stakeholders who have regular insights into the functioning of the industry and who have been interviewed in the context of this study generally laud the initiatives taken by the government. Accordingly, this has helped to boost the morale in this sector after the departure of the foreign investors from Hong Kong and the resulting substantial job losses. There is now confidence that the core locally owned enterprises in this sector are making good use of the facilities at their disposal in order to have a strong foothold on the world market for clothing and textiles. For instance, the leading business magazine in the country, *Business Magazine*,[9] recently had for headlines a statement made by Amédée Darga, president of the Administration Council of Enterprise Mauritius, affirming his belief in the 'regain de croissance de l'economie Mauricienne'[10] with a particular emphasis on a new-found vitality in this sector.[11] The latest trends also indicate that after the negative growth which has been recorded in the EPZ sector over the last few years, 2006 showed a slight amelioration. (See the analysis of the case studies and the trends in Figure 5.1.).

Their main complaint, however, is that there is too long a delay between the formulation of recommendations to rescue the sector and the implementation of those measures. For instance, according to a top official of the MCCI, the time it takes for the government to address some of the difficulties of enterprises – mainly in terms of financial support – has been the difference between survival and closure. The interest rates provided to EPZ companies who take loans are still regarded as too high to truly benefit them.

PART III: EXISTING TRADE OPPORTUNITIES FOR TC IN THE POST-ATC ENVIRONMENT AND THE ROLE OF GOVERNMENT

In order to meet the challenges of trade liberalization and global competition, Mauritius has been actively seeking regional cooperation and integration. According to the officials interviewed from the MEPZA and the MCCI, economic diplomacy has been high on the government agenda over the past few years. Its intense lobbying efforts for preferential arrangements and special derogations are often based on its SIDS status[12] or on its special links with certain countries. For instance, the privileged historical and cultural links which Mauritius has with India is expected to give rise in the near future to the Comprehensive Economic Cooperation and Partnership Agreement (CECPA) which will lead to the setting up of a Preferential Trade Zone. Accordingly, Mauritius would then benefit from a quota for exports of 1 million pieces on a duty-free basis and an additional 2 million pieces on a margin of preference basis.

Mauritius is currently involved in a number of multilateral agreements through its membership of the WTO, the Abuja Treaty on African Economic Community, the Cotonou Agreement, the Common Market for Eastern and Southern Africa (COMESA), the Southern African Development Community (SADC), the Indian Ocean Commission (IOC), the Indian Ocean Rim Association for Regional Cooperation, the Generalised System of Preferences and the African Growth and Opportunity Act.

While according to some of the officials interviewed, administrative bottlenecks often hamper the implementation of many cooperation projects, particularly in the region, there is an acknowledgement of the many potential benefits of pursuing these efforts. Regional integration and cooperation has the potential of promoting cross-border investment, joint ventures, strategic alliances and the development of supply chains. Both as an end in itself – COMESA and SADC together provide a regional market of about 200 million people and a rich source of raw material and cheap labour – and perhaps more importantly as a means to an end, considering preferential access to the US market through the AGOA, the regional strategy has become a priority as part of a plan to make Mauritius a regional hub for TC (see HPC Report, 2002) as well as for industrial diversification (NPCC, 2005). Madagascar illustrates a fine example of such benefits through regional economic cooperation and it has become an important regional market for Mauritian exports of intermediate products for delocalized companies (see case studies of Floreal Knitwear Ltd and Compagnie Mauricienne de Textile in following section).

5.3.1 The AGOA and the Mauritian textiles and clothing industry

The Mauritian government lobbied for the enactment of the AGOA and was among the first group of countries to obtain political eligibility. The AGOA came into force on 2 October 2000 and provides for the enhancement of the economic partnership between the USA and Sub-Saharan Africa. It opens new avenues for enhanced trade, investment and transfer of technology. The AGOA provides for duty-free and quota-free access for textile and other products to a market of around 290 million consumers. The AGOA has been hailed by many as one of the most important opportunities for market access for its textiles and clothing. For instance referring to the opportunity presented by the AGOA, Jeetah and Coughlin (2001: 25) argue:

> As if balm for an ailment, in October 2000, the Africa Growth and Opportunity Act smashed the quota and tariff barriers to Mauritian exports to the US, a market already with a significant Mauritian presence. AGOA suddenly gave them a 16 per cent to 33 per cent advantage over Asian competitors if both the fabric and the yarn therein were produced in AGOA eligible countries...

On 19 January 2001 Mauritius obtained eligibility from the US authorities for the export of textiles and apparel on a duty- and quota-free basis. With intense lobbying, Mauritius succeeded in obtaining derogation for one year from October 2004, for the use of third country fabrics, thus enabling the export of clothing duty free to the US market. This derogation expired in September 2005. Mauritius seeks to play a leading role in the regional development under the AGOA, mainly by developing vertical integration at home (through the setting up of spinning plants in the country) or relocating and securing partnerships with other less developed African countries covered by the Act. However, according to stakeholders interviewed in the context of this study, there is a lot of uncertainty about any benefits stemming from the AGOA. The future of Mauritius, and of the textile industries of other African countries, as far as access to the US market is concerned is partly dependent on the good intentions of the US authorities.

Table 5.4 shows the decreasing trend in exports to the US in the period 2002–05. While exports to the USA, which consisted predominantly of garments, rose significantly from Rs 7.7 billion to nearly Rs 9.5 billion in the period 2000–02, since that time it has experienced a significant decline to Rs 5.4 billion in 2005. The main reasons for theis trend have been the departure of the main suppliers to the US market as a result of competition from lower-cost producers in the form of China and India who have flooded the market following the abolition of quotas.

The main problem which the Mauritian TC sector faces in the context of the AGOA is that by being in the category of African countries above the $1,500 threshold and therefore not classified as an LDC, Mauritius – together with South Africa, Seychelles and Gabon – does not reap the full benefits of preferential access appropriated by the first category. Mauritian apparel exports under the AGOA therefore do not enjoy 'unrestricted access' which refers to an absence of quota and tariff barriers and to a rule of origin that requires only assembly in the beneficiary countries – as under the MFA. According to Mattoo et al. (2002), AGOA has led to some trade diversion away from Mauritius to the LDCs by orienting the incentives of sourcing supply in their favour.

5.3.2   Relocation in the region to benefit from the LDC status of low-wage countries

The main responses which the TC sector in Mauritius has pursued in order to benefit from the AGOA has been in terms of relocating to cheaper sites of production with LDC status – Madagascar, Mozambique and Lesotho and to consider further investment in Senegal, Namibia and Uganda – and in encouraging the setting up of spinning mills within the country in order to meet the rules of origin (see Ng Ping Cheung, 2003).

As explained earlier, Madagascar has been the main site of relocation for Mauritian TC manufacturers. Madagascar provides the advantage of cheap and abundant labour (in contrast to Mauritius' own expensive and inadequate supply) as well as the benefits accruing from its status as a Less Developed Country under the AGOA. However, in the recent past some Mauritian manufacturers have been disillusioned with Madagascar. The benefit of the cost of labour in Madagascar has been offset by political instability and civil riots, the high cost of working in a country with a less developed society, where the infrastructure is less good and where the administration is less efficient and undermined by corruption. Other complaints are the lack of skilled and literate local labour.

Nonetheless, according to most observers, despite a number of bad experiences, the relocation of the Mauritian garments industry will continue in future years as a result of the shortage of labour in Mauritius and consequently its increasing cost. Under the AGOA Mauritius will be able to choose from 30 eligible countries. According to Jeetah and Coughlin (2001), Malawi has the lowest wage levels in the region and perhaps anywhere in Africa, but on the downside it has a poor infrastructure, a lack of professionals and is affected by political instability. Mozambique and Senegal can offer low wages coupled with political stability, but neither country has any experience of producing clothes for exportation, which means investors would have to do some real pioneering work.

5.3.3   Incentives to spinning mills

Another solution proposed to meet the rules of origin requirements under the AGOA is the introduction of incentives for spinning activities and the active promotion of vertical integration. The intention of these policies is to reduce lead times, and to have better control over the supply chain while meeting the rules of origin under AGOA. Officials interviewed in the context of this study, including the informants from the leading TC companies, argue that Mauritius can eventually emerge as a regional centre for the production of yarn and fabrics.

5.3.4   AGOA and employment

There has been no study to isolate the impact of the AGOA on the TC sector and employment creation or retention. To Ng Ping Cheung, 'The Mauritian economy badly needs much higher investment rate to be able to compete against the Asian emerging markets and to achieve sustainable growth and long-term reduction in unemployment in our country. It has perhaps saved jobs in the clothing industries, but not sufficiently to prevent a net loss of 6,329 in employment between March 2001 and June 2002 (2003: 4).

5.3.5   AGOA and the potential benefits to Mauritius

Mauritius has yet to see any benefits from the AGOA. Interviews with the officials of the MEPZA and the MCCI have revealed a sense of pessimism about the extent to which the Mauritian TC sector can truly benefit from the AGOA. However, as Ng Ping Cheung (2003) notes, although Mauritius is in itself too small and geographically too distant to attract real US interest, it can prove to be an attractive hub as a springboard to the region. According to Ng, the key issue for penetrating the American market boils down to capacity. Mauritius has no choice other than to seek regional strategic partnerships with African countries for spinning, knitting, sewing and finishing.

Mauritius, as a capitalist-oriented economy with a strong democratic tradition and politically stable as well as having good physical and telecommunications infrastructures (at least in comparison with other African countries), has been tipped to benefit from the AGOA in terms of investment, but in reality this has yet to happen.

PART IV: ANALYSIS OF CASE STUDIES OF TOP TC FIRMS

5.4.1   Methodological issues

This section presents case studies of four of the most important firms in the TC sector in Mauritius, providing an outline of their trajectory and performance, and focusing in particular on how they have adapted positively to the difficult situation on the market for TC commodities as a result of trade liberalization and global competition. The firms were selected according to a purposive sampling method, the main criteria being that they should be among the most important firms in their respective sectors in line with the criteria of the Terms of Reference of the study. Although there is no official baseline data identifying which are the most important firms in terms of financial turnover and profit margin, details of the ten most important firms by size of their labour force were obtained from officials of the CSO, MEPZA and MCCI. As explained earlier, the largest share of the TC sector Mauritius in terms of employment, production capacity and exports are concentrated in ten large groups of companies which are vertically integrated and are involved in the manufacture of both textiles and clothing. The four firms which have been selected for the case studies (Compagnie Mauricienne de Textile (CMT), Floreal Knitwear Ltd – which is a subsidiary of Ciel Textiles, Shibani Knitting Company Limited and Socota Textile Mills) can therefore be considered to be highly representative of the largest and most important enterprises in the TC sector and, by extension, about 75 per cent of the TC sector itself.

It is notoriously difficult to obtain access to and carry out research in private enterprises in Mauritius – particularly in busy EPZ enterprises. The initial intention was to obtain the data from the managing directors of the selected companies. However, this has been possible only in the case of CMT. For the remaining firms, human resource managers were delegated the role of performing the interviews. While accurate data on the evolution of the financial and labour aspects of the enterprises over the years of the firms' existence were not obtained (either because the data were patchy or unavailable or because the informant was unwilling to disclose them), the case studies were indicative of the distinctive profiles and strategies employed by the respective firms in order to firmly establish themselves as key players in the market for TC commodities. The case studies also locate the position of the firms in the global production network and illustrate the challenges and prospects which they face as a result of their participation in global production networks, particularly in the context of trade liberalization and increasing global competition from low-cost producers. They illustrate the learning process and strategies employed by the firms in order to face the changes at both the domestic and international levels over their years of existence.

The next part, as illustrated in Appendix Table 5.4, provides a basic profile of the case studies in terms of the number of years in the business, ownership, location, product profile and targeted markets as well as their financial turnover, output level and labour force. This is followed by a section on the general technology trajectories followed by the firms. The following part then locates the perceived positions of the companies in the global value chain/global production network, the merits and demerits of such networks in the opinion of the company and the learning process adopted. The final section considers the role of government policies and international trade rules as viewed by the company.

5.4.2 Technology trajectories followed by case study firms

In certain respects, many of the patterns which were uncovered in the company studies served as a corroboration of the data from the earlier part of the study which was based mainly on secondary sources of information. One of the main similarities noted has been the acknowledgement of the importance of keeping pace with and adopting new technologies in all aspects of the production process. In fact, the adoption of new technologies was considered to be one of the most important elements in securing the competitiveness of a firm. With the removal of quotas and the distance of Mauritius from the major markets in Europe and the United States, the competitive edge of the country in the production of basic commodities has suffered a considerable blow. With the aim to move away from the lower end of the apparel market, over the past few years there has been a clear effort in favour of new and innovative technology which enables the production of higher value-added products.

All four firms claim to use state-of-the-art equipment, including CAD/CAM, in performing the various operations in the processing process in order to be competitive. In the words of Francois Woo, the Managing Director of CMT, 'the best of the best' technology is required in order to compete as a world-class leader in T-shirt manufacturing. The production of T-shirts at CMT has achieved a high level of efficiency as a result of investment in automated assembly lines and workstations. Employees sit in ergonomically designed chairs – Francois Woo insists that the sweatshop mentality does not figure at CMT – plucking garments from automated assembly lines, which move the product from a motorized track suspended from the ceiling. According to the company's managing director, although the automated workstations are costly — $6,000 to $7,500 a piece — they can increase productivity by around 30 per cent. However, manual machines are also used extensively in the manufacture of T-shirts by highly skilled machine operators. CMTs' cotton-spinning mills, which have necessitated investment of the order of US$50 million, also contain the latest technology with rotational speeds of around 32,000 rpm. Similarly, in its weaving and finishing mill STM uses cutting-edge technology for its operations. Since beginning its activities in 1989 with weaving machinery doing 400 picks per minute, it has constantly upgraded its weaving equipment at fairly regular intervals in 1995, 2000 and 2004. Its weaving equipment now performs up to 1,000 picks per minute. FKL and SKL have also constantly upgraded their technology moving away from manually operated equipment to semi-automatic and fully automated production equipment. SKL has invested in Stoll Knit and Wear technology and seamless knitting machines to boost its productivity.

In addition, all firms have kept up to date with ICTs, including fax, tele-phone, e-mail, and customized IT systems, to ensure fast and reliable contact within the firms as well as with their customers. The companies also have their own websites and are registered with Enterprise Mauritius, which also provides a virtual gateway for the products manufactured by registered com-panies for potential customers. ICT tools have become increasingly important to management as they enable or greatly facilitate data storage as well as the fast and accurate circulation of information pertaining to accounting, stock control, and marketing and supply chain management, among others.

According to the informants, in addition to increasing productivity, an important reason which has prompted the adoption of new technologies in production has been to cut down on lead time without compromising quality, in meeting the demand of customers who are becoming more and more exi-gent. The distance from the main markets makes Mauritius quite vulnerable when it comes to products which are highly dependent on season and fashion trends. Reducing the lead time is one way of remaining competitive.

Furthermore, a considerable amount of effort has been – and is being – directed in design in order to be competitive. As mentioned earlier, one of the main strategies used by firms to match the increasing competition is to go up the value chain involving product differentiation and better quality commodities. According to the informant from SKL, the investment in computer design systems, and the movement of design professionals into product differentiation and value addition and the marketability of their products has improved substantially. All of the other firms studied also had state-of-the-art computer-aided design and their own in-house design departments.

5.4.3   Global Value Chain/Global Production Network and learning processes

The position of the companies in the Global Production Network offers corroboration to secondary information on the position of Mauritius in the Global Commodity Chain for TC outsourcing. The initial position of all the companies in the Global Commodity Chain was to provide (under the existing preferential market access arrangements – Lomé (Cotonou) and MFA and to a certain extent the AGOA from 2000 onwards) markets in the EU and in the USA high volume runs of generally basic products in which Mauritius was competitive as a result of the availability of cheap labour. The products and markets targeted by the selected firms are given in Table 5.1.

According to the key informants in the case studies, the main merits of participation in the Global Production Network has been the sector's enormous contribution to the socioeconomic development of the country and, in particular, the employment which it has provided to a significant part of the workforce. On the negative side, the informants have stressed the high level of competition which exists in this sector, particularly in a liberalized trade environment. The footloose capital which has characterized this sector and the 'easy come, easy go' of multinational enterprises in this sector has now led to an unprecedented social impact with a significant number of employees of this sector, predominantly women having lost their jobs. The relatively high age and the low educational profiles of the retrenched workers have made it difficult for them to be redeployed in other sectors of the economy.

It is interesting to note that when asked about the extent to which they have benefited from any form of technology transfer, particularly from the larger Far-Eastern companies, the informants answered that this has been minimal. CMT began mainly as a subcontractor to locally based Hong Kong companies, but acquired on-the-job experience in the sector. CMT's phenomenal success in this sector is all the more impressive given the anecdote that the two founders of the company had no prior experience of the sector – one working in human resources while the other was a chartered accountant. In fact, it was noted that there was competition within the country from the large Hong Kong firms, especially in respect of access to the US market.

According to one informant, this competition was allegedly so intense that competing firms were very secretive of their details (for example, raw materials used, the sources of the raw materials, the products, their customers, and so on) and this offers a partial explanation of why the concept of clustering in order to benefit from economies of scale has yet to be used widely in the country. The Hong Kong firms were in fact meeting the lion's share of the quotas available for the local TC to enter the US market. Europe was therefore the main market which the four companies targeted, although with time they managed to secure segments of the US markets (FKL in particular).

According to the informants, competition on the world market for textiles requires rapid adaptation to any changes, whether domestic or international, in order to remain competitive. There has been a consensus among the informants that they have adapted constantly to the changing environment. One of the informants argues that in this context of cut-throat competition, it is a case of 'adapt or perish' in which only the fittest will survive. In fact, the selected firms have been compelled to react to challenges throughout their existence, as the economy grew and the labour market tended at the turn of the millennium towards a situation of full employment and wages faced upwards pressures and the local TC sector was gradually losing its competitive advantage.

The main learning outcomes of these challenges were relocation towards cheaper sources of labour, principally in Madagascar (Floreal was the pioneer of this move, followed by CMT), the recruitment of more skilled and productive labour from China mainly and later followed by workers from Sri Lanka and India and also the adoption of new technologies in the production process and the recruitment or training of staff for the operation of the new machinery. Relocation to Madagascar, despite its many promises, proved to be a particularly costly move as the informants from FKL and CMT revealed, offering a stark reminder that low labour costs can sometimes be offset by a lack of political stability. These companies in fact incurred significant losses as a result of the political instability which affected the country in 2002, with temporary closures, repatriation or loss of fixed capital and assets. Business has nevertheless restarted from late 2003 onwards.

According to Francois Woo, one of the main factors behind the success of CMT is the reinvestment of a large proportion of its profits, sometimes without sharing the dividends among its shareholders, combined with the strategic need to secure the company's future at least three years into the future. By doing so, the company has until now been successful at gauging the challenges of an evolving context and adapt to it. As such, in the past few years CMT has made massive investment in backward vertical integration in spinning mills in order to produce its own raw materials as well as further increasing its capacity of production by setting up additional branches both locally and abroad (in Madagascar and, more recently, China).

However, all of the informants note that competition in the sector has been becoming increasingly intense since the accession of China to the WTO and the gradual dismantling of the preferential trade agreements for locally produced TC. These have further exposed local TC enterprises to emerging low-cost producers and have forced them to review and restructure their companies in order to meet the challenges. There are important similarities in the main lessons which the companies claim to have learnt in order to face this fierce competition. The outcomes of these lessons can be summed up as follows and they are indicative of the new direction in which the industry is now moving.

5.4.3.1   *Shift towards higher value-added products for niche markets*

All four of the firms in our case study have claimed that they have made a shift from high-volume runs of basic commodities to lower-volume runs of more value-added commodities for niche markets – particularly from the late 1990s and becoming much more accentuated in the post-MFA environment. There is a consensus that the local TC sector has lost its competitive advantage in the low-end segments of the market as low-cost producers have emerged and eroded the world market with similar products. There is clear evidence of recognition among the firms that there is room for innovative niche producers in the fashion market and in the medium- to high-technology parts of the textiles industry and they have therefore been trying to position themselves to remain important suppliers of quality products.

5.4.3.2   *Customer-centred approach*

As part of this shift, one related issue which has been considered important by the informants has been the need to develop a customer-centred approach. For example, according to the informant from FKL, in the cases of most high-profile customers targeted by local TC companies, the price of the product is only one of the aspects under consideration. The emphasis on other factors including the service provided, the social standards of the firm, its flexibility, the security, the innovation, and also the communication all these factors are very important in the global textiles trade business.

Rather similarly, as argued by the official from STM, the company has made great efforts to anticipate and meet the specific needs of their customers. To date Socota has successfully rebuffed the Chinese threat by providing customized production and reliable delivery dates while establishing an end-to-end relationship. In fact, Socota uses a marketing office in Paris in order to provide effective communication with its Northern customers. In addition, according to the informants much emphasis is also laid on innovative designs and materials in line with market trends. All of the companies have their own in-house design offices and engage in continuous technology development and the regular addition of new products.

All of the firms included in the study have acquired high standards of quality in their respective domains and argue that a large number of their customers continue to source from them precisely because they consistently maintain such high standards and are reliable suppliers. For instance, STM has received the 'National Quality Award' in 1992, 1998 and 1999 and has been certified ISO 9001–2000 since December 2002. Similarly, SKL is an ISO9002 certified company. Furthermore all of the firms state that they are constantly striving to cut lead times to a minimum by the use of efficient supply-chain management. The lead time is unanimously considered to be one factor in which Mauritius is struggling to stay competitive in terms of its relative remoteness from the markets in the North.[13] Cutting time in terms of the sourcing of raw materials has been partially addressed by the companies being vertically integrated with spinning mills locally (CMT and FKL).

5.4.3.3 *Maintaining high labour standards*

According to our survey, another important issue for the participants is the quality of their manpower. All of the firms studied have training programmes for a number of graduate (administrative, management, design and engineering) and technical positions at the University of Mauritius and the IVTB respectively. Many training sessions are also organized in-house while much of the training is also on the job. The different companies stress their employee-friendly environments which value the input of their employees and reward them accordingly. The different companies provide employees with a sense of belonging and organize regular social activities.

But in addition to the importance of these factors in improving the productivity of labour, the companies are also aware that a positive image is crucial to achieve business with some important customers. The ending of quotas has given more possibilities to buyers to operate strategic choices among their suppliers, retaining those who will not tarnish the good social image they want to present to their customers. SKL, for instance, is a company certified under WRAP (the Worldwide Response for Apparel Production), a scheme that lays emphasis on the respect for core labour standards which have become a key strategic element of buyers' policy and that it cannot be ignored in a business world in which outsourcing strategies are extremely volatile. Mauritius intends to make the most of its positive social image in order to retain the trust of big western buyers. Whilst things are far from perfect, working conditions and wages are less exploitative than is the case in China.

5.4.3.4 *Product diversification*

As discussed in an earlier section, the most significantly affected market segment has been in the export of pullovers. One of the lessons which firms in this sector have learned is product diversification. While SKL has diversified by establishing Shibani In-wear which specializes in the production of underwear and sportswear, FKL's merger with Ciel in 2002 illustrates both vertical and horizontal integration in a textile cluster which is involved in different activities within the TC industry.

5.4.4   The role of government policies and international trade rules as viewed by the companies

5.4.4.1   *Companies' perceptions of government policies*

In general, the companies in our case studies have found great benefits in the government policies that have been introduced in order to assist the development and survival of the sector, particularly at the turn of the millennium. However, the policies have been viewed as being particularly beneficial to the smaller and less competitive firms with fewer capabilities which were had not been well prepared to face the increases in competition following the liberalization of trade.

Among those government policies which the firms have found particularly helpful have been the incentives provided to investment in spinning mills, and the institutional support provided by Enterprise Mauritius, particularly in terms of promoting the 'Made in Mauritius' label in international trade fairs and exhibitions as well as the establishment of formal educational and vocational training courses in design and textile engineering at the IVTB and the University of Mauritius. FKL and CMT have made use of the incentives provided by the government in order to make further investment in spinning mills in order to increase local yarn production so as to cut down on time and also on the costs of sourcing their main raw materials.

However, they have argued that more effort will be required at the level of economic diplomacy and lobbying efforts in order to obtain further derogations for the sector and also to secure further preferential arrangements with friendly countries. For instance, the privileged historical and cultural links which Mauritius has with India have led to the signature of a Comprehensive Economic Cooperation and Partnership Agreement (CECPA) followed by the establishment of a Preferential Trade Zone. According to this, Mauritius would then benefit from a quota for exports of one million pieces on a duty-free basis and an additional two million pieces on a margin of preference basis. Although this was announced some time ago, it is still to be implemented. The status of Mauritius as a SIDS is considered to be the main card which could be used to protect the country from exposure to competition in a level playing-field. One of the participants argued that there is a pressing need to review the cost of air transport which, if favourable, could lead to a considerable improvement in the local competitiveness of TC exports.

5.4.4.2 *Perceptions of the international trade rules by the companies*

The case studies in this chapter have identified both challenges and opportunities in the international trade rules which have affected the TC market. As explained earlier, trade liberalization and, more particularly, the dismantling of the MFA has exposed them to intense competition and made them lose their competitive edge in the production of low-end basic products. In spite of the exposure to competition, there was nonetheless a firm intention to meet these challenges.

While there is a clear acknowledgement that they cannot rival the likes of China, India and other low-cost producers in terms of price, they can still compete in terms of other factors which are important to the customers. As explained earlier, these factors include excellence in the provision of the product to the customer from end-to-end. As such, they have reacted by adding value to their products and securing niche markets. However, they are equally aware that in order to remain competitive they will need to innovate constantly in terms of quality and design, and to cut down constantly on lead time.

According to the cases studied, as a result of the international reputation which they have built up over the years in terms of both reliability and high standards of quality (as well as labour standards), they are currently able to compete in world markets, but there is an awareness that, to quote Francois Woo, the 'going will get even tougher and only the fittest will survive'. However, the informants have also identified a number of opportunities which have presented themselves. Although they argue that they were expecting more from the AGOA, particularly in terms of FDI arrivals in the country or in the region, the preferential access to US markets (provided the criteria for rules of origin are observed) is beneficial to local TC manufacturers. The incentives to set up spinning mills in Mauritius as well as regional partnership with Sub-Saharan Africa, particularly in terms of backward vertical integration with Madagascar and other LDCs, can help to fulfil the rules of origin and to enhance TC exports to the USA.

Another opportunity which informants have found to be particularly useful while they last are the EU/US safeguards against China in the post-MFA environment. These safeguards were expected to end in 2007 for the EU and in 2008 for the USA. Until then these safeguards act as a breathing space for the companies. When asked to share their views on how they find the future of their respective firms in particular and the TC sector in general in the country, the response received was unanimous. On the one hand, there was an acceptance that the worst scenario, in terms of closures and job losses, is over, and that the remaining firms have now made the transition reasonably well. Nevertheless there is a strong awareness that competition will get tougher and tougher matched by the firm intention to meet the challenges ahead.

5.5 Conclusions

This study has shown that after having been one of the main engines of growth of the Mauritian economy, over the past few years the local TC sector has suffered a significant downturn. Inherent weaknesses such as the rising costs of labour, unfavourable terms of trade and declining productivity notwithstanding, the liberalization of trade and the dismantling of the MFA have forced the industry to restructure itself.

Until very recently, in a context where thousands of workers were being laid off as long-standing companies relocated to greener pastures, many observers had nearly written off the sector and the predominant mood was downbeat. There is now some evidence, as shown in the cases studied, that the sector has been making a successful transition to the manufacture of upper-range commodities where they can compete more successfully with emerging low-cost producers. What remains of the sector is predominantly a core group of large enterprises which account for the lion's share of the stakes as well as in terms of exports and employment. However, the experience and high standards of quality and reliability which Mauritian TC producers have acquired, allied to their constant endeavour to innovate and focus on the needs of the customers, have enabled them to secure niche markets.

Moreover, together with the challenges of globalization, there have also been some important opportunities presented to the sector, particularly in the form of the AGOA. The considerable investment in new spinning mills and the setting up of strategic partnerships and production sites in India (in the case of FKL) and China (in the case of CMT) reveal the attempts of the sector to attempt to make the most of preferential access to the US market.

Nonetheless there is a need for further research to find out to what extent the smaller firms will be able to cope with a context which is growing increasingly difficult. As Hurreeram and Little (2002) note, many companies have almost deliberately ignored the implications of competing against low-cost producers on level ground (without any protectionist policies including duty- and quota-free access to the markets) given the pressures of increasing demand from the market. These firms have been worst hit when exposed to compete on a level playing-field. A series of policies and measures taken by the government to redress a number of important weaknesses in the sector, particularly in respect of the need to restructure their operations, to upgrade technology, quality and design, to innovate, and to produce high value-added products for niche markets are expected to assist the sector and provide positive signals to the operators in the sector.

Time will tell if the government can achieve its objective of positioning the local TC sector as a 'textile hub'. Certainly, the employment of more than 50,000 workers and the future of the Mauritian economy itself will depend on how matters develop in future.

Appendix Table 5.1 Macroeconomic indicators for Mauritius, 2000–2004

	Unit	2000	2001	2002	2003	2004
Population	Thousand	1,186.9	1,199.9	1,210.2	1,222.8	1,233.7
GDP at market prices	Rs Million	119,494	132,092	141,903	156,906	174,485
Per capita GDP at market prices	Rs Million	100,677	110,086	117,256	128,317	140,155
Real GDP growth rate	%	9.3	5.8	2.5	4.4	4.7
Inflation rate	%	4.2	5.4	6.4	3.9	4.8
Budget deficit to GDP at market prices	%	3.8	6.7	6	6.2	5.6
Internal debt (central govt) to GDP at market prices	%	27.7	30.6	38.5	49.5	48.7
External debt (central govt) to GDP at market prices	%	5.8	4.1	5	5.2	4.8
Debt service to exports	%	7.9	9.8	8.4	8.2	
Gross Domestic Fixed Capital Formation to GDP at market prices	%	26.9	25.4	25.1	25.9	25.7
Foreign Direct Investment inflows	Rs Million	7,265	292	1423	1,966	1,308
Unemployment rate	%	8.8	9.1	9.8	10.2	
Trade						
Total exports	Rs Million	40,882	43,628	43,022	54,164	
of which						
Sugar exports	Rs Million	5,544	8,557	8,529	8,430	
EPZ exports	Rs Million	30,961	33,695	33,502	32,052	
Total imports	Rs Million	54,928	57,940	64,608	66,384	
Tourist earnings	Rs Million	14,234	18,166	18,328	19,397	
Ratio of imports to exports		1.34	1.33	1.5	1.23	

Appendix Table 5.2 Existing investment schemes and their objectives

Schemes	Objectives and Qualifying Activities	Incentives
Export Processing Zone Scheme	To encourage the establishment of export-oriented manufacturing enterprises	• No customs duty of VAT on raw materials and equipment • Corporate Tax of 15% • No tax on dividends and capital gains • 60 % remission of customs duties on buses of 15–15 seats • 50% exemption on the normal registration fee for the purchase of land and buildings • 50% relief on personal income tax for 2 expatriate staff
Export service zone scheme	To promote the establishment of export oriented service enterprises	• 15% Corporate tax, exemption from payment of income tax on dividends • No customs duty on office equipment
Industrial Buildings Enterprise Scheme	To invest in industrial buildings to be used by a manufacturing enterprise. Construction for rental purposes of industrial buildings or levels thereof, provided floor space is at least 1,000 square metres	• 15% corporate tax • no tax on dividends • 50% exemption on the normal registration dues for land purchase
Small and Medium Enterprises	To provide for the promotion and development of small scale industries which engage in manufacturing and which use production equipment, the aggregate value of which does not exceed approximately US $170,000	• No customs duty on production equipment and raw materials as per schedule list Corporate tax of 15%
Modernisation and Expansion Scheme	To provide a new legal framework for industrial modernization, transfer of technology, upgrading of SMEs, integration of non-EPZ into EPZ and for the protection of the environment. Investment in productive machinery and equipment, such as Automation equipment and processes and computer applications to industrial design,	• No customs duty on production equipment • Income Tax credit of 10% (spread over 3 years) of investment in new plant and machinery, provided at least Rs 10 million are spent within 2 years of date of issue of certificate. This is in addition to existing capital allowances, which amount to 125% of capital expenditures. An additional allowance of 30% over the

	manufacture and maintenance (CAD/CAM) Investment in antipollution and Environment protection technology to be made within 2 years of date of issue of certificate	normal initial allowance of 50% on investment made on anti-pollution machinery or plant
Spinning Incentives Schemes	An attractive tailor-made package of incentives is in fact offered to spinning units in Mauritius	• A ten-year tax holiday for spinning companies starting operation before 30 June 2006. Any unrelieved loss (after deduction of profits) incurred by a spinning company during the period of exemption shall be available for carry forward under section 59 of the Income Tax Act Investors subscribing at least 20% to the share capital of a spinning company, or over Rs. 60 million (whichever is the higher), will be granted a special investment tax credit. They may opt to deduct from their tax payable, 15% of the amount so invested per annum over 4 years or 10% over 6 years. The tax credit will be made available to the investing company right from the year the investment is made and not in the subsequent year as is usually the case. Any unrelieved special tax credit may be carried forward for a period of five consecutive income years following the year the investment is made. The deduction allowed in respect of the special tax credit shall be withdrawn if the spinning company has not started operations by 30 June 2006. • Land at very concessionary rates • 5% registration duty on purchase of land and buildings for industrial purposes • Possibility of equity participation up to a maximum of Rs 100 mn in the share capital of spinning units by the National Equity Fund
Strategic local Enterprise Scheme	Companies manufacturing for the domestic market and engaged in such activity likely to promote and enhance the economic, industrial and technological development of Mauritius	• 15% corporate tax • No tax on dividends

Appendix Table 5.3 SWOT analysis of the TC industry

STRENGTHS	WEAKNESSES
• Acquired know-how and experience of the industry • Current preferential regimes in terms of quota and duty-fee access • Appropriate and enabling environment for promotion of private sector development • Liberal and flexible industrial policies • Goodwill at international level – market image/reputation • Economic and political stability • Installed capacities • Products of good quality • Business culture – entrepreneurship • Capacity to make optimal use of external assistance • Good infrastructure and logistics support • Services from support institutions • Enterprising private sector and adaptable literate workforce • Incentive schemes • Industrial Relations Framework	• Rising costs of inputs and services • Lack of inter-industry linkages • Poor local image of factory work • Poor organizational structure • Human resource development and low skill base • Lack of motivation • Shortage of skilled middle-management/shop-floor supervision/skilled workers • Geographical remoteness • High costs of investment limiting technological applications in industry • Negative attitude of employers towards training • High absenteeism • High dependence on imported raw materials • High costs of finance • High concentration on few products • Lack of R&D on new techniques • Lack of FDI

OPPORTUNITIES	THREATS
• Regional markets with COMESA, SADC, IOR-ARC • AGOA • Business Process Re-engineering for productivity gains • Market-driven supplier of upgraded products • Product diversification • ICT application using E-Commerce • Spinning and Weaving activities • Clustering • Testing and Quality Assurance facilities	• Sourcing difficulties under the AGOA – e.g good-quality raw materials from Africa • Unwillingness of locals to join the textile sector • Trade liberalization and polarization of Trade • Emergence of low-cost, high-volume East Asian and Latin American competitors • Phasing out of preferential treatments • Dependency on Foreign Labour

Source: Report of the High Powered Committee (2002), 'Strategic Plan for the TC sector 2002–2005'. 'Adapting to the Changing Environment' (p. 20).

Appendix Table 3.4 Profile of case studies

	Compagnie Mauricienne De Textile (CMT)	Socota Textile Mills (STM)	Floreal Knitwear Limited (FKL)	Shibani Knitting Limited (SKL)
Year started operation	1986	1989	1972	1986
Ownership	Locally owned	Partnership Malagasy (Societe Commeriale de Tananarive) and Mauritian investors (Currimjee Ltd)	Set up by Oriental Pacific Export (OPE) a group of Chinese and Hong Kongese investors. Acquired in 1974, by the then Deep River Beau Champ sugar estate and became locally owned. Merged with Ciel Group in 2001.	Locally owned
Brief Description of Activities and Product Profile of the Firm	CMT is a modern and vertically integrated set-up which has become one of the world's largest manufacturers and exporters of **T-shirts**. It has successfully climbed up the value chain by producing medium to upper range products for product differentiation and meet competition from low-cost producers of basic products.	STM is a high-tech **weaving and finishing** mill. Involved in the manufacture of cotton shirting. The textile activities of the group in Mauritius and Madagascar represent a vertical integration, with the spinning, weaving and **garment-making** operations. It supplies the Mauritius EPZ garment manufacturers with fabrics having a high added value.	FKL is the world's second-largest producer of **Woolmark sweaters** after Benneton. It is also a world-class supplier of cotton sweaters and cardigans. It is vertically integrated with Ferney Spinning Mill in Mauritius and 3 production sites in Madagascar. Its merger with Ciel Group in 2002 makes it part of the largest integrated	SKL has traditionally been involved mainly in operations such as **knitting, sewing, dyeing, and finishing** and is one of the leaders in the manufacture of **knitwear** in Mauritius. Its product profile includes **fully fashion and cut and sew for men, ladies and children** on electronic flat knitting machines in carded wool and blends, worsted wool

(Continued)

Appendix Table 5.4 (Continued)

	Compagnie Mauricienne De Textile (CMT)	Socota Textile Mills (STM)	Floreal Knitwear Limited (FKL)	Shibani Knitting Limited (SKL)
		In addition it has diversified into the manufacture of products including **classic men's shirts and fashion shirts; men's casual chic and sports chic; women casual blouse, formal blouse, women nightwear sleepwear, women casual trousers as well as a collection for juniors.** And targets a wide range of markets in the EU principally and also in the US. PROFILE OF CASES STUDIED	textile cluster in Mauritius which is involved in into 8 business operations including knitwear, fine knits, shirts, spinning, dyeing and weaving mainly for exports but it is also involved in the commercialization of its own brand. The other main subsidiaries of Ciel are Aquarelle (**shirt manufacturer**) and Tropic knits (**T-shirt maker**). (CONTD)	and blends, synthetic fibres and cashmere. Since 2002, the group has diversified into the manufacture of **intimate wear** with the setting up of Shibani Inwear. Shibani Inwear proposes highly comfortable and high value added garments knitted on seamless machines using a blend of cotton, lycra or microfibre, combining antibacterial with anti-perspiring properties.
No. of Plants and Location	5 Production Sites in Mauritius including 2 spinning plants. 2 further Production sites in Madagascar and in China	1 Production Site in Mauritius 2 Production Sites in Madagascar 1 Office in France	In Mauritius FKL now has 3 branches after closing 7 production sites in 2004. FKL also operates 3 branches in Madagascar.	2 Production Sites in Phoenix Industrial Estate (SKL and Shibani In-Wear) 3 Shops for tourists and local customers (Floreal, Grand Baie and Port-Louis)

Employment	From 20 employees in 1986 to about 8,000 in 2006 of which 1,800 foreign workers	STM has a workforce of 475 employees.	FKL has a workforce of 3,000 in Mauritius after shedding 900 in 2004. It has a workforce estimated at 8,000 in Madagascar.	In total it has a workforce of 1,366 (of which 475 at Shibani In-wear) employees as at August 2006 of which 225 expatriate workers from India and 62 from China. SKL has grown today to produce 3 million sweaters annually in different gauges to meet the trends and demands of the knitwear market Shibani In-Wear has a monthly production capacity of nearly 600,000 pieces per month undisclosed
Output	It has attained a production capacity of more than 60 million pieces in 2006	In Mauritius, STM annual production is nearly 8 million metres of yarn dyed & Fancy piece dyed fabrics	FKL has an annual output of 4.1 million knitwear products. The other subsidiaries of Ciel Group have attained an annual capacity of 16 million knits products 5 million woven products	
Financial Turnover	Annual financial turnover for the last year was to the tune of Rs 5 billion. Its financial turnover is reported to have been averaging above 25% over the last 20 years. More particularly from a profit margin of Rs 700 million in 2003, the company has now reached the Rs 1billion profit margin by 2006.	Financial turnover of US $20 million Ciel Group in 2005	Attained above Rs 4.7 billion for the whole of	

(Continued)

Appendix Table 5.4 (Continued)

	Compagnie Mauricienne De Textile (CMT)	Socota Textile Mills (STM)	Floreal Knitwear Limited (FKL)	Shibani Knitting Limited (SKL)
Main Markets	The bulk of its exports, estimated at about 88% are to European countries, mainly UK, France, Germany and Spain. Nonetheless, CMT has some US customers, including the likes of Eddie Bauer Inc., Gap and Foot Locker Inc.	100% of products are exported towards Europe and the United States	Bulk of exports to EU (France, UK, etc) and estimates of 30–40% of its exports were to big retailers like the GAP, like Eddie Bauer, The Limited, Abercrombie & Fitch and J Crew.	Bulk of exports are to the EU and to the USA. Most of its customers are well-known brand names including La Redoute or 3 Suisse in France, Intersport in Germany, John Lewis in the UK, Levi Strauss in Belgium, Armani Jeans in Italy, or Eddie Bauer and Ralph Lauren in the USA, among others...

Appendix Table 5.5 List of abbreviations

ACP	AFRICAN CARRIBEAN PACIFIC
AGOA	AFRICA GROWTH AND OPPORTUNITY ACT
ATC	AGREEMENT ON TEXTILES AND CLOTHING
BOM	BANK OF MAURITIUS
BOI	BOARD OF INVESTMENT
CASR	CENTRE FOR APPLIED SOCIAL RESEARCH
COMESA	COMMON MARKET FOR EASTERN AND SOUTHERN AFRICA
EBA	EVERYTHING BUT ARMS
EPZ	EXPORT-PROCESSING ZONE
EPZDA	EXPORT PROCESSING ZONE DEVELOPMENT AUTHORITY
FPU	FEDERATION OF PROGRESSIVE UNIONS
HPC	HIGH POWERED COMMITTEE
HRDC	HUMAN RESOURCE DEVELOPMENT COUNCIL
IOC	INDIAN OCEAN COMMISSION
IVTB	INDUSTRIAL AND VOCATIONAL TRAINING BOARD
LDC	LEAST DEVELOPED COUNTRIES
MCCI	MAURITIUS CHAMBER OF COMMERCE AND INDUSTRY
MEF	MAURITIUS EMPLOYERS FEDERATION
MEPZA	MAURITIUS EXPORT PROCESSING ZONE ASSOCIATION
MFA	MULTI-FIBRE AGREEMENT
MIDA	MAURITIUS INDUSTRIAL DEVELOPMENT AUTHORITY
MRC	MAURITIUS RESEARCH COUNCIL
NPCC	NATIONAL PRODUCTIVITY AND COMPETITIVENESS COUNCIL
SADC	SOUTHERN AFRICA DEVELOPMENT COMMUNITY
SIDS	SMALL ISLAND DEVELOPING STATE
SME	SMALL AND MEDIUM ENTERPRISE
UNCTAD	UNITED NATIONS CONFERENCE ON TRADE AND DEVELOPMENT

Appendix Table 5.6 Composition of exports by main products (percentages)

Textile, yarn, fabrics, made-up articles	5
Articles of apparel and clothing	67
Fish and fish preparations	11
Crude materials, inedible except fruits	0
Chemicals and elated products	0
Machinery and transport equipment	1
Pearls, precious and semi-precious stones	5
Jewellery, goldsmith and silversmithware	3
Optical goods	1
Watches and clocks	1
Toys, games and sporting goods	0
Others	6
Total	100

Notes

1. Subramanian (2001) estimates that Mauritius is at least 25–30 per cent more distant from world markets than the average African country.
2. In the early 1970s, Mauritius displayed all the characteristics of underdevelopment and one of the findings of the Meade Report (1961) was that the country was heading straight into a classic Malthusian Trap. At the time, it was a monocrop economy with all the risks this entails (adverse climatic conditions, currency fluctuations, market access among others); poverty was widespread and was being further fuelled by a soaring populations and rocketing unemployment levels and a latent ethnic tension was prevailing.
3. See Appendix Table 5.3 for a SWOT analysis of the sector.
4. Speech by Hon. R. Jeetah, Minister of Industry, Small and Medium Enterprises, Commerce and Cooperatives at the Workshop on Textile and Apparel Industry: Meeting the challenges of a changing industry, University of Mauritius.
5. See 'Study on absenteeism among production workers in the MEPZ', University of Mauritius (1990).
6. See, for instance, 'The China Threat to World Textile and Apparel Trade' American Textile Manufacturers Institute (ATMI 2003).
7. See, for instance, UOM (1990) 'Report of the study on absenteeism among productivity workers in the Mauritian EPZ, Stage II'; CASR (2001) 'Survey of Attitudes of the unemployed towards taking up jobs in the EPZ'; CASR (2003) 'Work/Family Study'; CASR (2005) 'Study on Working Time'.
8. See www.mauritius-industry.com.
9. See *Business Magazine*, issue no. 716, 29 March–4 April 2006.
10. The Mauritian economy has started to grow again.
11. See Interview with Francois de Grivel, president of the MEPZA, 'Le textile et l'habillement: vers un regain de vitalité?', *Business Magazine*, no. 716: 29 March–4 April 2006 (p. 8).
12. See, for instance, WTO document, 'Initial Submission on Post-ATC Adjustment-related Issues from Bangladesh, Dominican Republic, Fiji, Madagascar, Mauritius, Sri Lanka, and Uganda', G/C/W/496, 30 September 2004. See also 'WTO Members Deadlocked on Impact of Jan. 1 Elimination of Textile Quotas', *International Trade Daily*, 27 October 2004.
13. It is estimated that shipping to Europe takes 24 days and to the USA 45 days.

References

Anker, R., Paratian, R. and Torres, R. (2001) *Mauritius*, Geneva: International Labour Office.

Bheenick, R. and Schapiro, M. (1989) 'Mauritius: A Case Study of the Export Processing Zone', in *Successful Development in Africa: Case Studies of Projects, Programs and Policies*, Washington, DC: World Bank Economic Development Institute, Analytical Case Studies No. 1, 97127.

Bowman, L. (1991) *Mauritius: Democracy and Development in the Indian Ocean*, Boulder, CO: Westview Press.

Burn, N. (1996) 'Gender and Export-oriented Industrialization: Case Study of Mauritius', in U. Kothari and V. Nababsing (eds), *Gender and Industrialisation*, Stanley: Editions de L'Ocean Indien, pp. 33–79.

Aveeraj S. Peedoly 193

CASR (2002) *Survey of Attitudes of Unemployed Regarding Taking Up Jobs in the EPZ*, University of Mauritius Reduit UOM Press.

Common Country Assessment: Mauritius (2000), Office of the United Nations Country Representative, Mauritius, May.

CSO (2003) *2002 Collection of Statistics of Economic Activities*, Port-Louis, Government of Mauritius: Central Statistics Office.

Dommen, E. and Dommen, B. (1999) *Mauritius: An Island of Success. A Retrospective Study 1960–1993*, New Zealand/UK: James Currey Publishers.

Durbarry, R. (2001) 'The Export Pocessing Zone' in: R. Dabee and D. Greenaway (eds), *The Mauritian Economy: A Reader*, Basingstoke: Palgrave – now Palgrave Macmillan, pp. 105–29.

EPZDA (2002) *Report of the High-Powered Committee: Adapting to the Changing Environment*, Government of Mauritius Port-Louis, Mauritius: EPZDA.

Gherzi Report (2000) 'Sectoral Study of The Textile and Garment Industry in Mauritius and Designing of a Blue-Print to Boost Exports'. Unpublished report prepared for the Government of Mauritius/UNDP/UNIDO.

Gibbon, P. (2000) 'Back to the Basics through Delocalization: The Mauritian Garment Industry at the End of the 20th Century', Centre for Development Research Working Paper sub-series on Globalization and Economic Restructuring in Africa no. 00.7, Copenhagen.

HPC (High Powered Committee) Report (2002) *Strategic Plan for the TC Sector*, Government of Mauritius, Port-Louis: Ministry of Industry and International Trade.

HPC (High Powered Committee) Report (2003) *Strategic Plan for the TC Sector*, Port-Louis: Ministry of Industry and International Trade, Government of Mauritius.

Hureeram, D. and Little, D. (2002) 'Apparel Trade: The Challenge Facing Developing Economies and Mauritius', *Science and Technology Research Journal*, University of Mauritius Reduit Mauritius, 19: 43–62.

Jeetah, R. and Coughlin, P. (2001) 'SADC Study of the Textile and Garment Industries: Mauritius'. Unpublished document, Ministry of Industry and International Trade Port-Louis Mauritius.

Joomun, G. (2006) 'The Textile and Clothing Industry in Mauritius', in H. Jauch and R. Traub-Merz (eds), *The Future of the Textile and Clothing Industry in Sub-Saharan Africa*, Bonn: Friedrich-Ebert-Stiftung, pp. 193–211.
   http://library.fes.de/pdf-files/iez/03796/14mauritius.pdf last accessed January 2007.

Kearney, R. (1990) 'Mauritius and the NIC Model Redux: or How Many Cases Make a Model?', *Journal of Developing Areas*, 24: 195–216.

Kothari, U. and Nababsing, V. (eds) (1996) *Gender and Industrialisation*, Stanley: Editions de L'Ocean Indien.

Lamusse, R. (1989) 'Adjustment to Structural Change in Manufacturing in a North–South Perspective: the Case of the Clothing Export in Mauritius', Working Paper No. 27, World Employment Programme Research, ILO.

Lamusse, R. (1995) 'Mauritius Country Study', in S. M. Wangwe (ed.), *Exporting Africa: Technology, Trade and Industrialisation in Sub-Saharan Africa*, London and New York: Routledge (in association with UNU Press).

Lamusse, R and Burn, N. (1990) 'Structural Adjustment, Employment and Poverty in Sub-Saharan', paper written for ILO/JASPA unpublished.

Lim Fat, E. (1985) 'The Mauritian EPZ', in PROSI May 1985 Issue, Port-Louis: Public Relations Office of the Sugar Industry.

Mattoo, Aditya, Roy, Devesh, and Subramanian, Arvind (2002) *The African Growth and Opportunity Act and its Rules of Origin: Generosity Undermined?*, Development Research Group World Bank, Policy Research Working Paper # 2908.

Maujean, R (1996) 'The Role of the Small Scale Sector in the Socio-economic Development of Mauritius', in SMIDO (1996), *A New Vision for SME Development*, Coromandel, Mauritius: SMIDO, pp. 14–27.

Meade, J. (1961) *The Economic and Social Structure of Mauritius*, London: Methuen.

MEPZA (2003, 2004, 2005) *Annual Reports and Directories*, Port-Louis, Mauritius: MEPZA.

Milner C (2001) 'International Trade and Trade Policy', in R. Dabee and D. Greenaway (eds), *The Mauritian Economy: A Reader*, Basingstoke: Palgrave – Palgrave Macmillan, pp. 79–104.

Mukonoweshuro, E. (1991) 'Containing Political Instability in a Poly-Ethnic Society: The Case of Mauritius', *Ethnic and Racial Studies*, 14(2): 199–224.

Ng Ping Cheung (2003) 'To What Extent is AGOA Pertinent?', *Business Magazine*, 8 January.

NPCC (2003) *Laying the Foundations for a Competitive Future*, Port-Louis, Mauritius: National Productivity and Competitiveness Council.

NPCC (2005) *Competitiveness Foresight: What Orientations for Mauritius? A Discussion Paper*, Port-Louis, Mauritius: National Productivity and Competitiveness Council.

Ramasawmy, H. and Soyjaudah, K. (2002) 'Scope for the Application of an Automated Overhead Material Handling System in the Mauritian Apparel Industry', *Science and Technology Research Journal*, 9: 79–87.

Subramanian, A. (2001) 'Mauritius: A Case Study', *Finance and Development: A Quarterly Magazine of the IMF*, 38(4). Available online at www.imf.org.

Tait, N. (2002) 'Prospects for the Textile and Clothing Industry in Mauritius' in *Textile Outlook International*, Wilmslow: Textile Intelligence Limited.

UNCTAD/WTO Discussion Paper for the session 'Building Business Competitiveness', at UNCTAD XI, Sao Paolo, Brazil, 17 June 2004, International Trade Centre.

UNCTAD (2001) *Investment Policy Review: Mauritius*, Geneva: United Nations.

Wignaraja, G. (2002) 'Firm Size, Technological Capabilities and Market-oriented Policies in Mauritius', *Oxford Development Studies*, 30(1): 87–104.

Wignaraja, G. and Lall, S. (1998) *Dynamiting Export Competitiveness in Mauritius*, London: Commonwealth Secretariat.

World Bank (2001) 'Mission to Mauritius: Aide-Mémoire and Policy Note', Washington, DC.

6
Technological Capacity-Building Initiatives in the Ghanaian Apparel Industry

Donatus Kosi Ayitey

6.1 Introduction

The textiles and apparel industries in Ghana have been central to the development of the country's economy given the fact that not only do they play a very important role in meeting the basic needs of the people, but they have also created large numbers of job opportunities. Skills in local textile production have been passed on from one generation to the next and, despite the advent of modern more efficient and effective technologies, archaic local technologies for spinning and weaving are still extant. Whilst cotton production is confined to northern Ghana, textile and apparel production is common in the Ashanti, Greater Accra and Volta regions of southern Ghana. The production of textiles comprises principally of a few large companies and many small and medium-sized enterprises. The apparel industry is mainly made up of small and medium-sized enterprises located in different parts of the country.

Currently, the textiles industry alone comprise of about 50 formerly registered small, medium and large-scale enterprises.[1] This is in addition to numerous informal textiles firms located in various parts of the country. Of the 80,267 people employed in the manufacturing sector in 1980, 19,637 were in the textile, wearing apparel and leather goods sub-sector, accounting for 24.9 per cent of the share of manufacturing employment. This share of employment dropped successively to 23.4 per cent in 1981 and then still further to 16.5 per cent in 1987 and 13.5 per cent in 1994. This decline has been attributed partly to the overliberalization of the economy and cheap imported products, especially from Asia.[2] The employment figures refer only to the formal sector. The size of Ghana's informal sector is estimated to be around 80 per cent of the total labour force (Hormeku, 1998). The national estimates confirm that the apparel industry alone employs between 600,000 and one million people, including the members and employees of the Ghana National Tailors and Dressmakers' Association and the Ghana Association of Fashion Designers, as well as the many independent tailors and seamstresses operating throughout the country (AGI, 2003).[3]

The international trade rules affecting Ghana's textiles and apparel industry have mainly been defined by Ghana's relations with international partners. Over the years Ghana's main trade partners have been the European Union (EU), the USA, and the Economic Community of West African States (ECOWAS), followed by the rest of the world. Essentially, over the course of the past five decades the international trade in textiles and apparel has been governed by various multilateral and bilateral agreements among and between nations. Many of these agreements on textiles and apparel exports and imports have been such that producers and government must come out with innovation policies that promote and make the industry competitive in the international market in order to survive.

The purpose of this chapter is to establish how 'international trade rules' on textiles and apparel have shaped the performance of the industry in Ghana. In recent decades there has been no comprehensive innovation policy in Ghana, with the exception of 1983 when the Structural Adjustment Programme (SAP) was launched. However, this was focused more on macro changes than on more sector-specific policies. Since whatever happens at the macro level has some influence on the micro sectors, there is no doubt the textiles and clothing sectors might have been shaped by those policies. This chapter is divided into two sections. The first section starts with an overview of international trade regimes and developments in the pre-trade liberalization period (1957–1983), analysing the textiles and apparel industries in relation to the international trade rules governing their performance and then moving on to discuss the performance within the trade liberalization era (1984–1995). Finally, it touches on the era dubbed the 'Golden Age of Business' in Ghana (2001–date). The second section of the chapter discusses some company-specific information in relation to their performance in terms of trade competitiveness.

The remainder of the chapter is organized as follows. An overview of the international trade regimes is presented in section 6.2 while section 6.3 presents the trajectory of development of T&C sectors in Ghana. Section 6.4 presents the capacity-building initiatives and the performance of the T&C industry. The case studies of a few selected firms are presented in section 6.5 and, finally, the findings are summarized in section 6.6.

6.2   Overview of international trade regimes

A look at the external trade regimes over the pre-reform period and their implications for textile-clothing production in Ghana indicated that the pre-reform period coincided with the second phase of the General Agreement on Tariffs and Trade (GATT) which lasted from 1959 to 1979. Its first phase began in 1947 and ended in 1959. With the good intention of taking advantage of the eighteenth-century economists Smith and Ricardo's proposed benefits from Free Trade through the elimination of restrictions and the promotion of international trade, GATT was seen as a better option when measured against full protection. The Generalized System of Preferences (GSP), which was formed in 1968 under the auspices of UNCTAD, sought to extend preferences that developed countries offer to developing countries with respect to tariffs imposed on imports. Whilst agreement on textiles and clothing was left out of GATT in 1947 due to its sensitive nature, it was not until 1974 that the Multi-Fibre Arrangement (MFA), which was basically an agreement governing developing countries' textile and apparel exports to developed countries with quota arrangement, was signed. Before this, France and her colonies signed the Yaoundé Convention in 1963 before renewing it in 1969 to actually establish formal trade relations between EU and ACP countries.

At the same time the USA had developed a Short-term Arrangement to govern international trade in Cotton and Textiles (STA). This agreement, involving 19 countries, began in October 1961 and lasted until September of the following year. The STA sought to eliminate disruptions in the textiles trade by allowing non-restricting countries to impose restrictions on textiles importation in order to prevent their markets being flooded by products from other countries to their disadvantage, but it thus went contrary to the principle of GATT which is based on the sprit of free trade. The goal of restraining textiles exports of other countries was further supported by the Long-term Arrangement on international trade in Textiles (LTA) which was signed in October 1962 following the ending of the STA. The LTA could also employ a bilateral approach in protecting their textiles markets and could even result in unilateral measures such as quotas when it was deemed necessary. The MFA agreements between the EU and other developing countries tended to discriminate more in favour of the African countries than countries from Asia. Most African countries were allowed to export with less restriction or no restrictions at all, while quotas were imposed on their Asian counterparts so as to give opportunity for other developing countries to compete effectively without necessarily shutting out big exporters such as China, India, Pakistan and Indonesia. Although MFA provided opportunity for bilateral deals, the US employed to her advantage by protecting the domestic market from been inundated with products from developing countries. The MFA was more welcome by the developing countries in particular compared with the LTA but even then trade was still restricted.

The first Lomé Convention, which came into effect in 1975, was a direct deal between the EU on one hand and the Africa, Caribbean and Pacific (ACP) countries, numbering 71 in total, on the other. The textiles and clothing sector in Ghana could not operate in isolation of other sectors as a good performance in other industries would have had some spillover effects, albeit indirectly through the increase in demand resulting from rising wages and employment in those sectors. Pomeranz (2001) noted that some of the

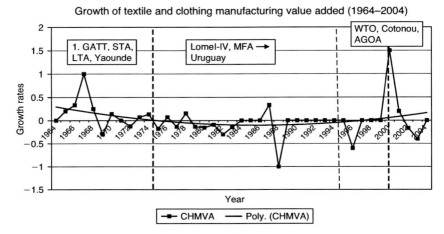

Figure 6.1   International trade rules and innovation within the T&C industry
Source: Constructed from WDI data 2007.

reasons why exports from most African countries were so skewed to the EU market emanated from the more favourable conditions of the Lomé Convention compared to the more restrictive GSP adopted by the USA. With regards to textiles and clothing products, the market in the USA exceeded that of the EU, mainly due to the presence of nearly 40 million African-Americans. Their demand for products from Africa by far topped that of niches of markets in the EU. Ghana could not be counted to have taken full advantage of the Lomé Convention as only Mauritius had been known to have benefited from the concessions on textile and clothing. This may be due to the fact that Mauritius is a larger exporter compared to Ghana.

Figure 6.1 depicts the performance of the textiles and clothing industries for the past four decades using the growth rates of value addition to the industry as a measure. In a nutshell, various international trade agreements are also captured and none of them appears to have correlated with any visible change in the sector.

6.3   The textiles and apparel industry in Ghana

The textiles industry in Ghana is made up of spinning, weaving and finishing companies producing yarn, grey cloth, dye/fabric, wax prints and quality 'kente'[4] made from woven yarn by traditional weavers, among others. The major textiles companies in Ghana were generally established in the 1950s, 1960s and 1970s. Such companies have gone through periods of ups and downs but the general trend explained in the first section reflected what is happening at the individual company level. Even if there might have been

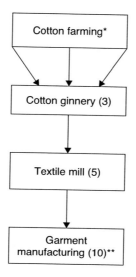

* Two large cotton plantations and many small-scale producers
** Garment Manufacturers excluding 179 small-scale exporters
NB: Number of textile mills and garment manufactures based on export promotion

Figure 6.2 Structure of Ghana's textiles and garment industry, 1997
Source: Ghana Export Bulletin (1997) and cited in Hoefter (2001).

some isolated success cases, the broader picture is not good. In 1997, the cotton producers were made up of two large plantation farms and several small farmers based in the Northern Region of Ghana (Figure 6.2).

As at early 1999 (Hoefter, 2001), only five textiles mills were still in business processing yarn from an equally small number of three ginneries that were in operation at the time. About ten major garments manufacturing firms were in operation at the time.

6.3.1 Developments in the pre-trade liberalization era: prior to 1984

6.3.1.1 *Historical context of the textiles and apparel industry*

After Independence in 1957, the focus of state policy was on how to build the industrial base of the country. This included the adoption of an Import Substitution Policy (ISP) which was completely new to Ghanaians at the time. This policy led to the establishment of the Ghana Business Bureau, a branch of the Management Development and Productivity Institute (MPDI) built in 1964 and entrusted with the task of overseeing the promotion of high-level management in industry and service sectors so as to promote productivity growth in those areas. It was not surprising therefore that, between 1957 and 1967, textiles and clothing manufacturing value added more than doubled

Figure 6.3   Textiles and clothing value added in manufacturing (percentages)

(see Figure 6.3). With the aim of reducing imports and promoting exports of manufacturing products in order to be more independent economically, the early 1960s saw the proliferation of state-owned industries – a more socially oriented development agenda that worked up to a point and began to fizzle out in the late 1960s.

However, despite the efforts made to satisfy local demand for manufacturing products with goods made in the domestic industry, raw materials and other manufacturing equipment would have to be imported – this made local price changes subject to other exogenous factors such as exchange rate and foreign prices. Coupled with a regime of price controls in the period, the initiative made a mockery of the entire exercise desired to spur the nation's industrial growth. Increasing attention was focused on traditional sectors such as cocoa cultivation and exports to the extent that non-traditional sectors such as textiles and clothing were not given due consideration. Producing goods such as textiles and clothing domestically would not only have eased dependence on foreign-made goods, but might have impacted positively on the foreign exchange stance of the country. It was no surprise that it became a secondary focus of the import substitution strategy in 1963. Understandably, however and, as later acknowledged by the policy makers in particular, the textiles and clothing industry did receive a boost between 1958 and 1968.

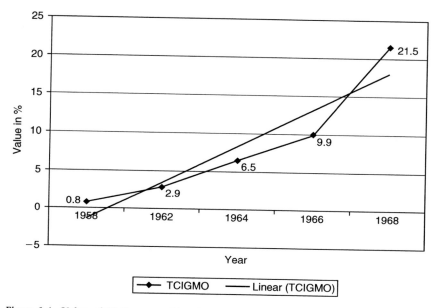

Figure 6.4 Value of T&C composition in gross manufacturing output in percentage
Source: Constructed from data in Steel (1972).

Over this ten-year period, the value in gross manufacturing output appeared to have increased by more than 26 times (Figure 6.4), an indication of serious efforts not only on the part of the manufacturers uniting to invest resources into productive activities but as a nationalistic holistic spirit demonstrated by policy makers as a whole. This period of rapid growth of the textiles and clothing sub-sector coincided with the period that Nkrumah's Seven Year Plan for National Reconstruction and Development (1962–1969) was in place. The plan, which was founded on the slogan 'Work and Happiness', actually galvanized the populace behind their newly found idol, Nkrumah, the chief strategist supported by then renowned scholars – Arthur Lewis, Nicholas Kaldor and Albert Hirchman among others.

6.3.1.2 *Mixed outcomes*

A closer examination of the textiles and clothing sub-sector revealed another scenario. Whereas there was a clear upward trend with respect to its contribution to manufacturing GDP (Figure 6.4), the evidence was mixed with respect to its growth over the period and, as the trend in Figure 6.5 accurately captured, the downward turn of events might have sent some signals that the situation could, after all, be imperfect. Figure 6.5 shows that in 1958 an improvement of more than 262 per cent in growth contribution to

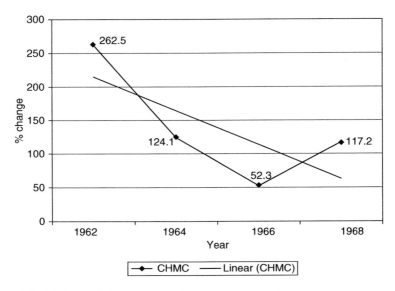

Figure 6.5   T&C growth in gross manufacturing output in percentages
Source: Constructed from data in Steel (1972).

manufacturing GDP was recorded, four years later in 1962 that had dropped to a little over 124 per cent over the next two years. However, the situation reversed over the course of the following two years and by 1968 had improved to 117.2 per cent. As Inikori (1989) pointed out, the import substitution strategy applied by Chenery (1960) and Hirchman two years earlier was meant to establish lead sectors that could be made to grow and contribute significantly to the economic development process of a nation than other sectors. In Ghana, the growth of the textiles and clothing sector remained positive throughout the 1960s and its contribution to industrial output over the period showed clearly that there was the potential for further growth and development.

In contrast to other sectors, textiles and clothing manufacturing activities are respectively capital and labour intensive and whilst textiles production chimed in with the development agenda at the time, clothing manufacturing did not fit properly within the policy push for capital-intensive industrialization process pursued immediately after independence. Even the reduction in government spending in the early 1960s, partly as a result of a fall in cocoa prices which, of course, formed the major source of foreign exchange earning, could not prevent the country from being plunged into a budget deficit. Investment in the clothing sub-sector, which was more labour-intensive,may perhaps have eased reliance on the unbridled importation of capital inputs

Table 6.1 Share of textiles and apparel employment in manufacturing

Industry	Male		Female		Increase (1960–70) No. of	
	1960	1970	1960	1970	Male	Female
Apparel	38.3	35.5	61.7	64.5	N/A	13,715
Textiles	89.6	85.4	10.4	14.6	N/A	2,519

Source: Constructed from Steel (1981: Table 6.5).

whilst promoting more labour-intensive activities such as clothing production. For example,[5] the gross national expenditure in constant local currency was in excess of 4 billion cedis in 1960, compared with a lower gross national income of about 4 billion — about 280 million cedis being the difference measured in constant local currency. It must be said that since 1960, a budget surplus has been a rare occurrence in the country's balance sheet.

6.3.1.3 Trade policy impact on employment in textiles and apparel manufacturing

Studying small-scale employment with a focus on firms with at least ten people[6] and sometimes 30 employees representing large-scale firms, Steel (1981) referred to the textiles and apparel industry in the 1960s and 1970s in Ghana as a high-growth modern industry. This sought to confirm the state of the industrial process and policy pursued at the time. Table 6.1 seeks to support the common knowledge that whilst the apparel industry is dominated by female employment, the textile sub-sector is male centred. Between 1960 and 1970, the share of female employment in the apparel sector varied from about 61 per cent to 64 per cent with the share of male employment in the textiles sector, dropping from around 89 per cent to 85 per cent. Women again increased their share from 10.4 per cent to 14.6 per cent over the period. Small-scale firms, however, played a major role in both industries with their share of industry employment in the apparel sector between 1962 and 1970 approaching 99.2 and 96.3 per cent respectively and that of the textiles sector not far off these figures – at 99 and 58 per cent over the period from 1962 to 1970.

6.3.1.4 Trade policy and value added in textiles and clothing manufacturing

The impact of trade policy on textiles and apparel firms has been given little attention except to identify the exact effects of trade policy, among other factors, on firm performance in Ghana, Pearson, Nelson and Stryker (1976) conducted a study on a sample of seven firms in Ghana, which included two textile manufacturing firms. They established that incentives in the form of tax concessions, credit subsidies and trade protection in general actually had a positive impact on their profits and that the situation could had been very different without the policy. The clear identification of which of the factors played the greatest role in facilitating the competitiveness of the firm remains rather unclear because of the difficulty of isolating the individual effects of each factor. Their study was limited by the very number of firms (only seven), including only two from the textiles sub-sector and none from apparel production. In a related study by Pearson and Ingram (1980), the country trade policy, in particular the high incidence of protection was revealed when Ghana was compared to Ivory Coast with respect to seven industries, including textiles manufacturing. The c.i.f. import price per square yard of textiles in 1972 was 0.48 cedis which was the same for Ivory Coast. However, the domestic price for the same square yard of textiles in the same year was 0.78 cedis with a difference of about 0.30 representing a huge deviation of about 63 per cent. At a relatively acceptable level, the social cost per square yard of textiles could have been much lower and not exceeding 0.68 cedis.[7] Tight policy control and inward-looking trade strategy, together with government incentives for industrial promotion even thought done in good faith yielded mix outcomes that might be more favourable with the process of economic integration as suggested in extant literature.

Figure 6.6 shows that textiles and clothing manufacturing value added followed an upward trend between 1964 and 1968, but then experienced a free fall and hit rock bottom in 1969 – a year that saw the worst annual performance throughout the course of the pre-reform period. The recovery was a slow one, however, as periods of continuous upwards and downwards turns characterized the manufacturing value added until the early 1980s. Even though the value of textile and apparel production rose, as illustrated in Figure 6.4, the growth in value added revealed a rather poor performance.

6.3.1.5 *Technology adoption and policy initiatives*

Since the pre-trade liberalization era in Ghana lasted a little over two decades (1957–83), it was clear that the policy measures designed to facilitate innovation at the level of the industry have had ample time to have materialized. Thus, assessing the performance of firms in relation to their choice of techniques and production technology became a task for some scholars, including Ahiakpor (1989), who investigated the level of choice of appropriate technology in a number of industries including that of textiles – which in 1970 comprised 57 firms employing at least 30 persons. Ahiakpor's measure of the choice of appropriate technology was based on characteristics such as the degree of capital intensity of the production technique, the degree of skill mix in the production process and the share of imported inputs in total inputs employed in production process. The measures were designed to reflect the unique features of a particular economy such that a developing country like Ghana should be able to ensure that its industrial performance meets its national agenda in the form of promotion of employment, boosting exports

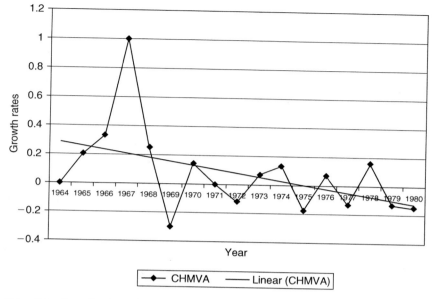

Figure 6.6 Growth of textiles and clothing manufacturing value added
Source: Constructed from World Development Indicators, 2006.

and be competitive not only at the local level but also on the international front. The appropriate technology and techniques of production in such circumstances should therefore be more labour- rather than capital-intensive, use more local skills and be more dependent on home-grown raw materials.

Whilst it can be argued that the policy measures at the time in seeking to foster the national agenda of industrial growth, among others, sought to undermine in some aspects their own progress, it did not come as a surprise that Ahiakpor's investigation into the technological choice stance could not produce any definite answers based on the measures employed. Even though his study sought to establish no significant differences across industries, the main sector of relevance in this study, textiles, did not yield any differences in capital intensity measured simply as the value of fixed assets per production worker in thousands of cedis[8] across firms within the 57 firms sampled. A measure of skill mix compiled as the ratio of professional worker wages to the total wage bill was also found not to be statistically significant across firms in the industry. Along with the variable on the share of imported inputs in total raw material used which did not also prove significantly different across firms and all three measures of the choice of appropriate technology together could neither be confirmed nor disconfirmed. One thing was clear for sure, which is that state-owned firms in 1970 were more capital intensive than a mix of private and publicly owned ones.

6.3.1.6 Technology transfer institutions for innovative textiles and apparel sectors

Numerous R&D institutions were established long before the liberalization period to help shape not only the textiles and apparel manufacturing but also production in other industrial sectors. Science and technology research has often been considered to be the foundation block for any meaningful industrial process. There was therefore the formation of the National Research Council (NRC) in Ghana in 1959. The aim of promoting science and technology transfer and development also led to the establishment of the Council for Scientific and Industrial Research (CSIR) in 1968 with the aim of developing and applying innovative technologies for industrial and other uses. However, it was not until 1981 that the Technology Transfer Center (TTC) was established under the direct control of CSIR but with the support of UNDP. TTC is to oversee the transfer of appropriate technology to Ghana by performing two tasks. The first is to oversee the building of local capacity for the adoption of these technologies by providing the necessary information to the local people. The second is to help in the process of identification of these foreign technologies, arrangement to acquire and delivery of these technologies to their respective users.

As a result, the government managed to help in acquiring various technologies such as the production of natural dyes[9] for use in the textile industry. The Ghana Standards Board, created in 1967, was responsible for overseeing issues on meteorology, standards, testing, quality management, and conformity assessment. These institutions have been constrained by many factors such as a reliance on funding from the government to carry out their mandate; furthermore, with more than half of the country's budget coming from unreliable foreign sources, their capacity to perform has been greatly compromised. Underfunded and understaffed, they are affected by mediocre performance in the delivery of their duties which affects both producers and consumers.

6.3.2 Post-trade liberalization era, 1983–1999

Trade liberalization has generally been considered to be inimical to the growth of the textiles and apparel industry in Ghana for a number of reasons. The industry hitherto not used to intense competition, both internal and external, all of a sudden has to gird against external rivals, especially the extremely competitive Asian products flooding onto the local market. The protection offered them before the liberalization did little or nothing to help them grow. The analysis of the performance of the sector with respect to manufacturing production, however, indicated that the 'must survive behaviour and managerial measures' taken during the early stages of the liberalization period saw an increase in the manufacturing production of the two industries. Plant capacity utilization also increased correspondingly and reflected the underlying growth rates.

Table 6.2 Rate of capacity utilization in the T&C industry for medium-sized and large firms (percentages)

Year → Sector	1977	1984	1987	1989	1991	1993	2005
Textiles	60	17.3	24.0	45.0	45.0	41.3	49.4
Garments	n.a.	20.2	25.0	22.0	30.0	53.0	n.a
All Manufacturing	n.a.	18.0	35.0	40.6	40.5	45.7	n.a

Source: Lall and Pietrobelli (2002) and Quartey (2006).

Presented in Table 6.2, capacity utilization rates computed for only medium-sized and large firms rose steadily in both the textiles and garments industry, with only 17.3 per cent in 1984 for textiles to 41.3 per cent in 1993. However, by 2005 the rate of capacity utilization in the textiles industry appeared to have recovered and risen to 49.4 per cent, but it was still well below the 60 per cent mark attained by the industry in 1977. The situation in the garment industry, even though similar, rose from 20.2 per cent in 1984 to more than 50 per cent – it reached 53.3 per cent by 1993. Excess capacity for the entire manufacturing production was 82.0 per cent in 1984 lower than in the garments industry but higher than in the textile firms. The situation was same in 1993. It is obvious that the problem of capacity under utilization applied to the entire manufacturing production with grave economic consequences in term of the rate of employment in a country where unemployment and underemployment are prevalent. Although sometimes good for a firm to carry excess capacity for both economic and non-economic reasons, it is quite unaccepted for firms to operate less than a quarter of its capacity as appeared to be the case for the textile and garment sectors during the early stages of liberalization.

In line with the recovery in capacity utilization, the growth in textiles and garment manufacturing production showed an improvement, as depicted in Figure 6.7. From 22.9 percentage growth rates in 1986, about two years after liberalization, there was a marked improvement to 28.7 per cent in 1988 – a figure that dropped a little in the following year to 24 per cent and increased again to 39.1 per cent in 1991. The subsequent years displayed no consistent pattern of growth even the rates were very unpredictable hitting 60.2 per cent in 1993, the highest registered over the 13-year period.

Primary surveys (including Hoefter 2001) have identified several factors as posing problems to the textiles and garments industry. Among them are the lack of access to adequate raw materials within the domestic market which prompts these inputs to be imported. Those available are priced higher than they would normally sell at the international market. The situation results in a large share of raw material costs in the total costs of production, averaging around 70 per cent. Small-scale cotton producers are unable to satisfy local

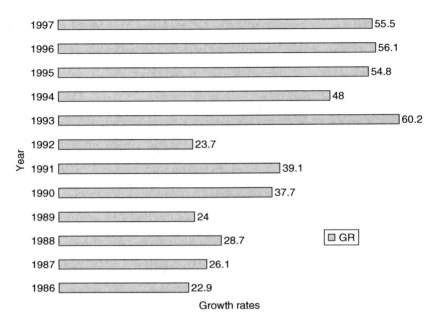

Figure 6.7   T&C manufacturing production growth rates (1977 = 100)

demand and sometimes their products are not of high quality. The lack of access to credit by both cotton growers and textiles and apparel manufacturers as a result of high bank lending rates, which reached 47 per cent the end of 2000, also compounded the situation. Even though this situation now appears to be improving as the lending rates have dropped considerably – to around 24 per cent by 2007 – a lack of collateral security is often cited as a problem. Furthermore, except in the cases of some large textiles and apparel manufacturing companies that are using the latest technologies and equipment in order to survive, over the years, the use of obsolete technologies and equipment has actually had a negative impact on production performance. The influx of foreign products has also caused all sorts of problems – even to those companies employing the latest technology.

6.3.2.1   Tariffs and trade in textiles and apparel

The tariff structure in Ghana is as follows: 0 per cent for basic and social goods, 5 per cent for raw materials, 10 per cent for intermediate goods and 20 per cent for finished products. Textiles and apparel imports are either in the raw material inputs or finished products and so they are affected mainly by the three upper bands (5 per cent upwards). The lowest import duty rate, as shown in Table 6.3, is 10 per cent. In addition, VAT is 12.5 per cent, there is also a 2.5 per cent National Health Insurance Levy (NHIL) on imports,

Table 6.3 Taxes on imports of some selected textiles and apparel products

Hs Heads Desc DES	2004–2008					2001–2003			
	Import duty (%)	Import VAT (%)	Import NHIL (%)	ECOWAS LEVY (%)	EDIF LEVY (%)	Import duty (%)	Import VAT (%)	ECOWAS LEVY (%)	EDIF LEVY (%)
1. Silk-worm cocoons suitable for reeling	10	12.50	2.50	0.50	0.50	10	12.50	0.50	0.50
2. Greasy shorn wool, not carded or combed	10	12.50	2.50	0.50	0.50	25	12.50	0.50	0.50
3. Cotton, not carded or combed: not ginned	10	12.50	2.50	0.50	0.50	10	12.50	0.50	0.50
4. Flax, raw or retted	10	12.50	2.50	0.50	0.50	10	12.50	0.50	0.50
5. Sewing thread of synthetic filament	10	12.50	2.50	0.50	0.50	10	12.50	0.50	0.50
6. Synthetic filament tow of nylon or other polyamides	10	12.50	2.50	0.50	0.50	10	12.50	0.50	0.50
7. Sanitary towels and tampons, napkins, etc,	20	12.50	2.50	0.50	0.50	25	12.50	0.50	0.50
8. Carpets and other textile floor coverings, etc	20	12.50	2.50	0.50	0.50	25	12.50	0.50	0.50
9. Woven pile fabrics and chenille fabrics of wool etc	20	12.50	2.50	0.50	0.50	25	12.50	0.50	0.50
10. Textile fabrics coated with gum	20	12.50	2.50	0.50	0.50	25	12.50	0.50	0.50
11. Long pile fabrics, knitted/ crocheted	20	12.50	2.50	0.50	0.50	25	12.50	0.50	0.50
12. Mens or boys coats, of wool knitted/crocheted	20	12.50	2.50	0.50	0.50	25	12.50	0.50	0.50
13. Mens or boys overcoats, etc, of wool or fine animal hair	20	12.50	2.50	0.50	0.50	25	12.50	0.50	0.50
14. Electric blankets	20	12.50	2.50	0.50	0.50	25	12.50	0.50	0.50

Source: Customs, Excise and Preventive Service Ghana (CEPS, April 2008).

an Economic Community of West African States (ECOWAS) Levy of 0.5 per cent and an Export Development and Investment Fund (EDIF) levy of 0.5 per cent. The NHIL was only added in 2004 by an act of parliament (Act 650, 2003), thereby contributing to the already high rates on imported textiles and apparel products. Ironically, the high rates have not helped in curbing these imports (see Tables 6.9 and 6.10).

6.3.3 'The Golden Age of Business' and the Ghana Export Promotion Action Plan

6.3.3.1   Ghana–US trade relations

The African Growth and Opportunity Act, which was signed into law in 2000, has presented a market opening to Ghanaian exporters as well as many other countries in Sub-Saharan Africa to do business with the USA in some selected products, including textiles and apparel products. In March 2002 Ghana become eligible for the textiles and apparel shipments to the US market after it was passed by the United States Trade Representative announcement (USTR). Thus Ghana became the 16th out of 36 eligible Sub-Saharan African countries who can access the facility. This is because the USTR has the duty to pass any country eligible for the facility as and when it is believed that all the conditions and rules to be fulfilled by the country are in place. The prevention of the transshipment of textiles and apparel products to the US is central to the qualification process which recognizes the adoption of the US visa system and abiding by the rules.

The other status that Ghana also achieved in 2002 under AGOA was the Lesser Developed Country standing which means that a member state under AGOA can export textiles and apparel products duty-free to the US utilizing fabric from any part of the world to manufacture products in Ghana. This is to circumvent the so-called originality convention rule where inputs might have to come from US or from Ghana. One thing is clear though that AGOA is mutually beneficial to both the US and sub-Saharan African countries and cannot be seen only as an opportunity provided for African exporters. One thing is certain: the US market is a very competitive one where products are marketed based on quality, price and capacity to deliver on time. This tends to challenge Ghanaian exporters to look out for those factors that would not only improve the quality and price competitiveness but delivery time as well.

Given duty-free and quota-free access for garments and textiles products and the fact that Ghana was relatively well positioned geographically to access the US market compared to other countries in the sub-region (given its sailing times of 21 to 25 days) and also its relatively competitive labour costs, positive outcomes from AGOA were not in doubt. The Ashanti and Ewe people have cultivated the reputation of producing uniquely woven, traditional cotton fabrics to take advantage of niche markets with less competition from other products in the international market. Textile and garments products of

Table 6.4 Value of US T&C imports from Ghana ('000 US dollars)

	2002	2003	2004	2005	2006
Cotton, wool & other natural fibre	30	17	6	14	5
Cotton cloth, fibre thread and cordage	14	32	14	34	20
Wool, silk, veg. cloth & fabric, thread	5	0	0	0	2
Synthetic cloth & fabric, thread & cordage	0	0	1	4	2
Finished textiles industrial suppliers	11	7	14	2	1
Apparel & household goods – cotton	407	4,395	6,846	4,707	4,929
Apparel & household goods – wool	0	0	0	0	1
Apparel & household goods – other textiles	55	47	547	439	4,606
Natural apparel & household goods	6	23	8	11	32
Total	**528**	**4,521**	**7,436**	**5,211**	**9,598**

Source: Computed from US Census Bureau Foreign Trade Statistics.

Table 6.5 T&C trade relationships between Ghana and the United States under AGOA ('000 US dollars)

	2004	2005	2006	2007
Ghana's exports to US	7,432	5,208	9,568	5,393*
Ghana's imports from US	11,467	9,110	7,123	3,532*
Exports-Imports (in '000 US $)	−4,035	−3,902	2,445	1,861

* The values were measured from January to June of 2007.
Source: US Department of Commerce.

Afro-centric origin were destined to be patronized by large African-Americans on the US market, thus presenting a rare opportunity for the Ghanaian exporters to break through.

Table 6.4 shows the composition of the products Ghana exports to the USA. Between 2002 and 2006, the bulk of the products have been in the form of household and apparel goods made of cotton.

The market value for these products appears to be falling – from $6.8 million to $4.9 million in 2006. Apparel and textile goods made of other textiles have been the next largest component of the exports followed by cotton cloth, fibre thread and cordage. The less significant components include finished textiles, synthetic cloths and fabrics, wool, silk and other natural apparel. Overall, more than $9.6 million worth of exports in 2007 reflects an encouraging sign and is a huge leap from the 2002 low figure of $528,000.

A consideration of the trade performance between the USA and Ghana in textiles and apparel shows some mixed performance (Table 6.5). Whereas Ghana's net exports were negative, an indication of imports in excess of exports up to the tune of $4 million in 2004, there was a marginal reduction by 2005 down to $3.9 million. The figures for 2006 and 2007 show some improvements, but in actual fact, if AGOA is to be of benefit to Ghana, foreign exchange from textiles and apparel exports should not only be able to meet textiles and apparel imports from the same country but also to meet other demands beyond the textiles and apparel sectors.

6.3.3.2   Ghana–EU trade relations

The European market has been one of the main destinations for textiles and apparel products from Ghana as one of the ACP countries since Independence in 1957. For over two and a half decades the textiles and apparel industry in Ghana (1975–2000) has been influenced by the multilateral agreement between the EU and ACP countries. The first Lomé Convention, which came into effect in 1975, was essentially an EU initiative based on unilateral free access designed to open the market of the EU for commodities from ACP countries to easily get to Europe. It was a one-sided agreement which permitted tariffs on European imports whilst at the same time giving free passage of ACP products into their market. At first glance, the rule seems to favour ACP; however, with deteriorating commodity terms of trade and fluctuations in prices for products with basically little or no value added a different picture emerges. Furthermore, the textiles and apparel industry in Ghana was not particularly favoured as the ACP agreement was skewed towards exports of primary products and did little to promote the manufacturing exports. Manufacturing products were imported from EU and other developed countries. It is noteworthy that the Multi-Fibre Arrangement (MFA) which was established in 1974 did not directly apply to Ghana because as part of the ACP countries, the country was exempted (McDonald and Dearden, 1992). This was supposed to put the country's textile and apparel exports in a better position to promote growth and development.

Focusing on Ghana's current trade relations, measured in terms of tons of textiles and apparel products imports and exports, it is apparent from Table 6.6 that over the period from 2004 to 2005, the country actually

Table 6.6   Export performance of Ghana to the European Union and vice versa

Sector	Ghana's exports to EU		Ghana's imports from EU		Balance (in tons)	
	2004(A)	2005(B)	2004(C)	2005(D)	A–C 2004	B–D 2005
Textile (tons)	2,966	1,746	1,324	1,719	1,642	27
Clothing (tons)	13	33	41,945	46,339	−41,932	−46,306
Total	2,979	1,779	43,269	48,057	−40,290	−46,279

Source: European Commission, external trade statistics.

imported more textiles and clothing products from EU than it actually exported. Ghana is a net importer – just like the situation with the USA. The Ghana textiles and clothing exports to the EU in 2004 was 2,979 tons compared to 43,269 tons of imports from the EU – a difference of 40,290 tons that rose to 46,279 tons in 2005.

As a member of ECOWAS Ghana continues to push for a new trade agreement with the EU known as the Economic Partnership Agreement (EPA) which officially started in 2003 and has been followed by a series of negotiations before it finally comes into effect in 2008. This is in addition to the Cotonou Agreement negotiated between the EU and ACP countries in 2000.

6.3.3.3 *Presidential Special Initiative on Textile and Garments (PSI, 2001–)*

In 2001, the government of Ghana launched an initiative known as the 'Presidential Special Initiative (PSI)' with the intention of revamping and promoting some selected sectors, including textiles and garments, within the export-led mass production industrialization for growth and development policy framework. The central idea is to help grow and transform the Ghanaian economy in general and the industrial sector in particular – with the private sector as the engine of growth. And to attract foreign direct investment in the form of large textiles and garment manufacturing firms to take advantage of the opportunities provided by the Export Processing Zone (EPZ) by relocating, producing and exporting from Ghana. It is expected that an accelerated export development strategy through export action programme for textiles and garments involving the mass mobilization of rural labour and vulnerable groups could help curb poverty.

However, the success of PSI on textiles and garments depends upon the pool of relevant skills available in the country. To this end, the training and development of skills necessary for the application of state-of-the-art industrial sewing machines has been facilitated over the years by the Clothing Technology Training Center (CTTC) in Accra which, since its inception in 2003, has had the capacity to train an average of 400 industrial sewing machine operators each month. It also undertakes R&D on how to enhance the existing techniques and make them work at various stages of the production process. Other CTTCs have been designated for Kumasi and Takoradi in an effort to develop the critical mass of human resources to feed more than100 medium-sized textiles and garment enterprises located within the Export Processing Zone and industrial hub of Ghana and beyond. The CTTCs are equipped with cutting-edge technologies including computer-aided design technology – an example of a broader information and communication technology (ICT) for accelerated development policy introduced in 2004.

Even though the attention is to encourage exports and value addition to exports, the core process is to develop the capacity for the increasing application of new technologies such as modern textiles and garment manufacturing technologies including ICT.

By 2007 the government, together with support from some financial institutions such as the National Investment Bank, the United Bank of Africa and the Eco-Bank via the Export Development and Investment Fund (EDIF), has invested about US$15 million to acquire new technologies in the form of new textiles and apparel manufacturing machines and to provide working capital for the initiative. EDIF was established in 2000 (Act 582) with the primary aim of facilitating the export of primary, manufacturing and service sector products. However, despite this laudable scheme of PSI, numerous challenges such as serious price competition from smuggled and pirated textiles and garments that find their way unto the local market, frequent power outages and lack of access to adequate and cheaper source of finance are threatening to undermine the efforts of the scheme. The PSI must first work in order to be able to realize its fundamental objectives of not only being totally export oriented but also seeking to keep its focus on the local market. An inability to compete at home might have even more serious consequences on the foreign market because the firms would be crowded out before they had the opportunity to grow and sustain themselves. Employment generation, especially for the medium-skilled workers, is considered to be an integral part of PSI and in that respect, since the beginning of the scheme, the evidence is there as presented in Table 6.7. The table displays a list of companies that have responded to the PSI on textiles and garments and indeed, by 2005, many companies, including those listed in the table, have generated thousands of jobs.

6.4   Technological capacity building and performance

6.4.1   Technology content of textiles and apparel exports from Ghana

Lall (2000) attempted to classify manufacturing exports according to their technology content and established that the varying degrees of technology content of exports has effects on the growth and development of a nation. Low-technology content exports have a lower level of influence than medium-technology content or high-technology content exports. According to Lall's classification, it is obvious that the bulk of Ghana's textiles and apparel exports fall into the low-technology content category, but the country also exports medium-technology textiles and apparel products. Synthetic filaments fall into the medium-tech category. The implication is that the country has no competitive edge in the manufacturing and export of these products.

6.4.2   Worsening textiles and apparel trade conditions in the world market

In both the textiles and clothing trade with the world, there are some disturbing trends that even the current PSI on textiles and garments has failed to address. The nation is a net importer of the textiles and clothing (Tables 6.9

Table 6.7   PSI on textiles and garments

Company	Location	Size of workforce as at 2005
Global Garments Ltd	Accra	300
Gold Coast Collection Ltd	Accra	200
Belin Textiles Ltd	Accra	200
1647 Ltd	Accra	100
Textile Pro	Tema	500
California Link EPZ	Tema	400
Network Knitwear fabrics Ltd	Tema	1,000
Oak Brook Ltd	Tema	100
Premier Quality Ltd	Tema	200
Total		3,000

Source: Ministry for Private Sector Development and PSI, 2005.

Table 6.8   Medium-technology content T&C products exports from Ghana

Year → Products	2004	2005	2006
HS CODES\Indicators	Custom Value (cedis)	Custom Value (cedis)	Custom Value (cedis)
5401100000: Sewing thread of synthetic filaments	182,151	0	194,553,791
5401200000: Sewing thread of artificial filaments	0	273,374	432,971,692
5404900000: Strip and the like of synthetic textile materials	0	160,642,503	937,028
5406100000: Synthetic filament yarn (excl. sewing thread),	0	0	186,255,200
5407300000: Fabrics of synthetic filament yarn	0	0	166,194,000
5407690000: Other	2,233,488	0	52,984,845
5407740000: Printed woven fabrics, >=85% synthetic filaments	0	911,345	0
5408100000: Woven fabrics of high tenacity synthetic filament yarn	0	1,822,690	0
5408330000: Coloured woven fabrics of artificial filament yarn	0	0	924,318
5501900000: Synthetic filament tow,	0	0	223,604,510
5503900000: Synthetic staple fibres	0	0	235,038,506
Total	2,415,639	163,649,912	1,493,463,890

Source: Ghana Statistical Service.

Table 6.9   Ghana's trade performance in textiles with the world in US million dollars at current prices

Year	Textile exports (X)	Textile imports (Im)	X-Im	% change in X	% change in Im
1992	0.538	33.6	−33.0	–	–
1998	2.0	32.2	−30.2	271.7	−4.1
1999	5.1	51.2	−46.1	156.2	59.1
2000	14.2	65.3	−51.0	177.8	27.4
2001	8.5	75.4	−66.9	−40.4	15.5
2002	8.8	61.1	−52.4	3.2	−18.9
2003	9.0	56.8	−47.8	3.2	−7.1
2004	3.7	76.5	−72.8	−59.1	34.7
2005	2.7	111.9	−109.3	−27.0	46.4
2006	2.3	103.1	−100.8	−14.6	−7.9

Source: Computed from the WTO trade statistics.

Table 6.10   Ghana's trade performance in clothing with the world in US million dollars at current prices

Year	Clothing exports (X)	Clothing imports (Im)	X-Im	% change in X	% change in Im
1992	0.05	10.9	−10.9	–	–
1998	2.0	10.7	−8.7	3673.6	−1.6
1999	3.0	12.5	−9.4	52.2	16.0
2000	0.7	11.4	−10.7	−75.4	−8.2
2001	0.6	9.7	−9.1	−18.3	−14.9
2002	1.2	12.4	−11.2	97.9	27.7
2003	2.4	24.2	−21.8	97.9	94.5
2004	1.4	21.3	−19.9	−43.5	−11.7
2005	1.1	24.2	−23.1	−21.3	13.2
2006	4.7	30.6	−25.9	344.1	26.7

Source: Computed from the WTO trade statistics.

and 6.10) products that comparative advantage should make the nation export more than it actually imports.

Over the period from 1998 to 2006, not a single year in both textiles and clothing trade with the world did the nation export more than its imports as the difference for textiles rose from $33 million in 1992 to more than $100 million in 2006. The same also applied to the performance in clothing, which rose from US$10.9 million to US$25 million.

6.5   Case studies

This section focuses on the information from interviews the author has conducted in some major textiles and apparel companies in Ghana. The intention is to assess the performance of three top textiles companies and three top apparel manufacturing companies in the country. Even though the focus was on these six companies, it is not limited to them alone as some information on other large companies in Ghana is also presented in the Appendix Tables 6.1 and 6.2. The assessment of the textiles industry centres around both indigenous manufacturers of textiles – specifically 'Kente' for niche markets in Ghana, Europe, the USA and other parts of the world on the one hand and those companies producing standard textiles products for domestic and foreign markets on the other. The top three apparel manufacturing companies are also analyzed with respect to products for niche markets and those standard products for common markets in Ghana and abroad.

6.5.1 Methodology

The interviews sought to find answers to how new technologies in general – and ICT in particular – as well as other strategies are contributing to the survival, growth and general performance of Ghanaian textiles companies. To do this, companies were taken on a case-by-case basis and discussions conducted with managers or their representatives on the path the companies have adopted since their inception in responding to the changing international trade rules and domestic policies. Some semi-structured questionnaires and interviews were employed. The questions and interviews centred around the history of the firm or company, product profile, growth in employment, cost of production and types of technology being used. Other questions were on the role of ICT and government policy in company performance. The extent of linkages to downstream main markets and networks among others also form part of the questioning. Other secondary information was also obtained during the interviews to support the discussions and follow-ups were carried out later in order to secure more information. Discussions were also held and information obtained from some stakeholders such as Ghana Export Promotion Council and some members of the Association of Ghana Industries (AGI).

6.5.2 Profile of sampled companies

The randomly selected textiles and apparel companies are the Printex Limited Company (formerly known as the Millet Textiles Corporation), Akosombo Textile Limited (ATL), Ghana Textile Printing (GTP) and a Pagbo Kente Weaving Village to represent indigenous Kente weavers producing for domestic and foreign markets. The apparel companies comprise of The Global Garments and Textile Limited, Sleek Garments Exports and Premier Quality Limited.

6.5.2.1 *Printex Limited Company (formerly Millet Textiles Corporation)*

Printex Limited Company is a 100 per cent Ghanaian-owned private limited company. It began in the late 1950s as the Millet Textiles Corporation and its name was changed to Spintex Limited in 1980. It is concentrated on textiles production, having engaged in vertically integrated activities such as spinning, weaving and finishing departments until 2000, when the spinning department was completely closed down and the weaving department was closed down partially. These developments were a deliberate strategy to remain in business and in operation as a result of intense competition from large manufacturing countries such as China which has unlimited access to the Ghanaian markets due to the unrestrictive trade liberalization climate prevailing in Ghana. The company produces a range of textiles products, including furnishing materials, suiting, shirting, school uniforms, traditional dress materials and factory work clothing materials.

These decisions saw a fall in the number of company employees – from record levels of 1,100 (including management staff) in 1985 to an undesirably low level of 300 in 2005. However, since then the sector has showed some signs of improvement with some marginal increase by 100 people in 2007, suggesting that it is perhaps recovering from the downward trend that has characterized the company since 1985.

6.5.2.2   Akosombo Textile Limited

Established in 1967 as a Ghanaian venture, Akosombo Textile Limited (ATL) is located at Akosombo in the Eastern Region of Ghana. The plant, which operates 24 hours a day, has a dyeing and finishing capacity of 30 million yards a month. ATL's main lines of business activities are in weaving, spinning and finishing. Operating from a site with a land area of 47 acres provides more opportunity to modernize and expand. It was in response to the competitive business environment being presented by products from China and other parts of the world that about 950 billion old Ghana cedis' (more than US$94 million) worth of wax print machinery was installed in 2005. This was a partnership arrangement with the UK-based company A. Brunnschweiler and Company (ABC) to boost production and exports and also to improve the quality of their products.

From spinning and weaving through quality inspection, cotton stores, water treatment tanks, wax printing and rotary screens printing, to dyeing and finishing plants, chemical stores and apartments, ATL has maintained its reputation as a giant textiles company in Ghana and it is by far the largest employer in the textiles industry with a workforce of 1,400 in 2007 – a slight fall from the 2003 figure of 1,450. Unlike other companies which have either introduced massive layoffs or closed down completely in the face of dumping from other countries, ATL is still performing relatively better amid intense competition. Apart from Real Wax and African Fancy Prints, which have been patronized by consumers over the years, ATL is also known for its high-quality designs and materials targeting at this stage the local market which comprise up to 80 per cent of the demand. The demand for ATL products is, however, not limited to Ghana as they sell well beyond the national borders.

However, ATL, in common with many other textiles companies, has its own grievances emanating from the unfair competition and market environment prevailing in Ghana where some textiles products find their way into the market through illegal routes, evading all the taxes and thereby being able to set lower prices for their items. Considering the relatively poor average Ghanaian consumer, who is more likely to be influenced more by price than quality, the choice is obvious. To address this concern, the government is charged to curb the smuggling of such items into Ghana as goods intended for other neighbouring countries such as Togo somehow find their way into the Ghanaian market.

6.5.2.3 Ghana Textiles Printing (GTP)

Ghana Textiles Printing is a subsidiary manufacturing company of Vlisco which was established in Holland in 1846. As a joint venture, known as GTP, between Vlisco, the Government of Ghana and some firms from the United Kingdom, started the production of Real Wax in 1966 and has maintained a good image among other apparel manufacturers – in Ghana in particular and West Africa in general. Located in the city of Tema, some 25 km from Accra, the capital of Ghana, in 2007 GTP maintained a workforce of around 500, having threatened to close down in 2005 and to lay off about 700 workers due to difficult market conditions. The difficulties of GTP was also compounded by the problems with the sister company, Juapong Textile Limited (JTL), which supply yarns to GTP. Since 2005 JTL has laid off its workforce of 1,000 people and announced its closure, before struggling unavailingly to resume its operations.

6.5.2.4 Pagbo Kente Village

Pagbo Kente Village is made up of a group of weavers pooling resources together to form a cooperative business with the aim of imparting and training young people in the art of weaving. It is located at Ho in the Volta Region of Ghana. The objective is to establish Kente weaving as a tradition that should attract young people since its trade has been – and still is – lucrative in both the domestic and international markets. In contrast to the standard textiles and apparel manufactured across the globe, Kente is unique in the sense that it is only produced in Ghana and mostly by the Ewe and Ashanti tribes. Registered in 1995 as a sole proprietor business, the village has earned an enviable reputation among the Kente weavers in the region whose products are patronized by buyers from USA and Europe. This is as a result of good customer relations developed by honouring quality specifications and contract agreements as well as securing on-time delivery. The village is managed and directed by Mr Gbortsyo, under whose initiative it was set up. The textiles village also serves as a training centre for foreigners who seek to learn new skills in Kente weaving or to develop and upgrade their skills. The village has networks with the Kente Weavers' Association of Ho.

The company, which began with one person operating two looms, currently employs 13 people and operates 15 international looms, producing quality Kente cloth for both men and women and batakari made of yarn and sewing thread. The technology is relatively simple and comprises international looms. The raw material inputs, which are obtained from Kpetoe, Agbosome, Ho and Accra townships, normally constitute about 33 per cent of the production cost. The raw material inputs are obtained in line with customer specifications to satisfy the demand for the products, not only on special occasions and royal use, but also for weddings. The operating capacity is currently 50 per cent and it is expected to approach 65 per cent by 2009 and to increase still further in the following year. With an initial capital of about US$50 in 1992 (not registered then), the company has grown and developed to about US$20,000 in value by 2008. To date, the demand for the products has far exceeded the capacity of production and has only been able to satisfy 30 per cent of the domestic market, whilst the demand from the USA and Europe are still not being met. This means that more expansion needs to take place and even though international looms have been installed progressing from the traditional ones, more sophisticated faster industrial looms would need to be developed so as to enhance both loom and labour productivity. The local price for a piece of male Kente cloth varies from US$250–400.

6.5.2.5 *Sleek Garments Export*

Sleek Garments Export is located in the Garment Village, a Free Export Processing Zone in Accra. Registered in 2002, it is a private limited company. It is also a sister company of Sleek Fashion Ltd. Sleek Garments is one of the companies that was set up in response to Export Promotion Action Plan being implemented by the Ministry of Trade under the Presidential Special Initiative (PSI) on Textile and Garments since 2001. The company is purely export oriented and exports to the European and US markets – and also some other African countries. The products range from trousers to uniforms, shirts, skirts, shorts, ladies pants and blouses among others. Among the buyers are the Superior Uniform Group, Wal-Mart and Rortex. Seeking to be competitive in both domestic and international markets, the company emphasizes the production of quality products that are price competitive and cutting cost through that use of latest technologies.

Sleek Garments therefore employs an array of technologies – including Double Needle Chain Stitch, Single Needle Lock Stitch, Double Needle Lock Stitch, Kansa machine b2000sc and Pocket creasing machines. Others include electric snap fixing machines, Eastman cutting machines, end cutters, zig zag machines, thread safety stitch machines, blind stitch machines and 'feed of the arm' chain stitch machines with three needles. In 2007, the company was operating eight production lines of 40 machines each and employing 470 people. The company has established a reputation for producing good-quality products and often cited as one of the few success stories in garment exports. Sleek Garments has also established networks with companies in the USA such as Ross Stores that provide for the direct market by placing huge orders. An example is the 75,000 pieces order of shirts that was shipped to Rose Stores in 2007. Supported by benefits in locating at the export processing zone, Sleek Garments targets the huge and largely unexploited US and African markets.

6.5.3 Assessment of sampled top textiles and apparel companies

6.5.3.1 *Technology transfer and skills acquisition*

Responding to questions relating to the technological position of the companies, the author gathered that the latest technologies, including ICT, are being employed in both textiles and apparel manufacturing. The companies have made continuous investment in new technologies and the training of staff. ATL, for example, is competing favourably with other manufacturers with their real wax and African fancy prints. With their current six plants, including a dyeing and finishing plant, new investments from the sister company ABC up to the tune of US$94 million, and the movement of the production of standard wax to Ghana in order to satisfy the local demand have led to the transfer of the latest machinery and equipment to Ghana. In order to maintain the quality standards associated with ABC, the workforce has been retrained to a high level. The movement of production from developed countries to Ghana in labour-intensive textile production could help in the transfer of technological skills to local people. New designs of wax prints help to introduce innovative products to markets and currently ABC develops about 200 of these designs every year. With 1,144 weaving looms and 30,240 spindles, ATL is striking a balance among techniques that would safeguard its competitiveness.

Companies such as GTP are employing the best technologies in responding to their customers' tastes. These technologies might not necessarily be cost saving because they are a blend of rapid automated processes together with more traditional manual operation in the creation of their block prints demanded by West African markets. With around 800 designs already in stock, new ones are being created continually. The GTP Company is a joint venture between the Government of Ghana, a Dutch company, Vlisco, and Lever Brothers and some other firms in United Kingdom such that, when required, the latest technologies are transferred by their parent companies. Because the Chinese have used automated processing in producing the entire print, it is of low quality and cheaper to produce when compared to GTP's technique of using manual techniques to produce the block print.

6.5.3.2 *Product profile*

There are two broad categories of textiles and apparel products manufactured in Ghana by the sampled firms – the Afro-centric and standard products. The Afro-centric products are basically from different varieties of Kente products. These include cloth and shirts for men and women, along with tablecloths, handbags, place mats, Kente neck and bow ties and smocks. These products

Table 6.11 Change in production capacity of four major textiles firms (in million yards)

Company	1970 output (mil. yards)	2005 output (mil. yards)	% change
GTMC	15	2.24	−85.1
ATL	13	18	38.5
GTP	30.7	9	−72.3
Printex	6	9.84	64

Source: Computed from data cited in Quartey (2006).

are mainly for niche markets sold locally and abroad. The other category includes the standard products that are meant for the mass market. They include uniforms, shirting, yarn, grey cloth and print fabric, male and female tops, and professional clothing, including lab coats, scrubs, and surgical gowns. The standard products are produced by the large textiles and apparel companies such as ATL, GTP, Printex and GTMC, Global Textile and Garments, Sleek Garments and Premier Quality Ltd.

6.5.3.3 *Declining production capacity*

As noted previously, the output performance of the textiles industry supported by the 'big four', namely GTMC, ATL, GTP and Printex, has been declining since 1970 and Table 6.11 gives an idea of the state of some of these companies in 2005 compared to 1970. Interviews with the management of these companies provided some understanding as to the poor showing in the capacity to produce. The 'big four' produce what can be classified as 'standard products' where the competition for market share is very high both at home and abroad. Even a company such as GTMC, which does not export, finds it difficult to compete at home. The problem with these import-competing industries arises from the domestic policies governing textiles and apparel manufacturing. In Ghana, there is currently a 12.5 per cent value added tax (VAT) and 2.5 per cent national health insurance levy (NHIL), making it a total of 15 per cent tax on finished products. By contrast, Nigerian companies enjoy 0 per cent VAT, a duty incentive grant of 10 per cent, and an export expansion grant of 30 per cent. In addition to these incentives the Nigerian textiles industry also benefits from extensive protectionist measures – with a ban on all finished textiles products. ATL is one of the few Ghanaian companies to have risen to the challenge of competing within the highly liberalized market, even though it has also been affected.

6.5.3.4 *Price competitiveness in the domestic market*

The Chinese and other Asian products are crowding out the 'made in Ghana' products due partly to huge differences in prices. Figure 6.8 depicts the market

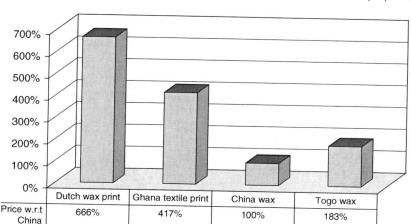

Price w.r.t China	Dutch wax print	Ghana textile print	China wax	Togo wax
	666%	417%	100%	183%

Figure 6.8 Price differences of textile prints in percentage with respect to China

prices situation for some selected textiles products. The price of Ghanaian textiles products is more than four times higher than the Chinese wax print and buyers naturally go for the cheaper products for economic reasons. This is because the Chinese use fully automated production processes. With the exception of the Dutch wax, Ghana textiles prints are relatively less competitive than even Togo Wax. Pirated logos and the designs of companies are believed to be contributing to the flooding of the markets by fake products that are sold at prices several times lower than the originals. The managers of textiles companies are rethinking their strategies and debating whether to continue producing quality products or to compete on the grounds of low-quality, low-cost products. The apparel companies appear to be facing a different set of challenges from those experienced by textiles companies. The apparel companies are seeking to attract contracts in the foreign markets and to be able to deliver on time and according to a given specification.

The evidence points to the fact that the woes of textiles companies emanate from the domestic market for which their products are designed. Currently the local consumers have several options to go for used clothing and textiles products, for relatively cheap products that have been smuggled into the local markets, or even for pirated goods unknowingly because of low income and a shift in the taste for western products. Efforts are being made to reintroduce local consumers to 'made in Ghana' products by promoting a nationwide cheap and affordable National Friday Wear.

6.5.3.5   Increased delays in delivery times

Based on our primary study and other secondary sources (see, for example, Biggs, 1994) delivery schedules continue to create headaches for Ghanaian

Table 6.12   Changes in the delivery times of exports to the United States

Origin	Destination	Total time (in days)	Year
Tema Port Ghana	East coast of the United States	21–25 days	2002
Tema Port Ghana	East coast of the United States	38–46 days	2008

Sources: Interviews in 2008.

exporters. In the first quarter of 2008, exporters from Tema Port to the United States were taking a longer time to reach the USA than had been the case five or six years previously (Table 6.12). Compared to other countries, especially from Asia, Ghana is at a disadvantage when it comes to the shipment of textiles and apparel products to the USA because shipping lines tend to charge fees well above those faced by Asian countries such as India.

With high ocean freighting costs and delays at the ports due mainly to bureaucratic administrative procedures at local ports, AGOA is likely not to be of optimal benefits to the exporters in particular and the nation as a whole. Even though the US market is there for exporters to exploit, the achievement of success does not come easily. For example, an exporter cannot just wake up and start exporting to the USA without having first built the networks and the reputation to encourage bulk purchases.

6.6   Conclusions

This chapter has conducted an analysis of the development of Ghana's textiles and apparel industry with respect to three time periods – the pre-liberalization era (1957–83), the liberalization period (1984–2000) and the period dubbed the 'Golden Age of Business' (2001–date). The general conclusion is that the sector is currently experiencing many difficult challenges. The sector-wide performance with respect to the growth in manufacturing value added can normally be described to have been relatively good in the pre-liberalization period only to be affected badly in the post-liberalization era – and not to have recovered since that time. The level of textiles and clothing value added in manufacturing continue to fall. The level of employment continues to fall. The continual application of old technologies over the period has not helped to turn around the fortunes of the sector and technology transfer centres will have to do more in this respect. The technology transfer centres also appear to be facing their own difficulties, such as inadequate funds. Tariffs on imported textiles and apparel products have understandably not been entirely effective in rectifying the problems.

The study found that the pre-liberalization gains could be attributed to a few factors, such as the protection that these firms enjoyed before the 1980s.

Textiles firms such as GTP were able to establish themselves as main companies producing to satisfy the taste of the local customers. Focusing on the local market meant that the international trade agreements such as MFA and first Lomé Convention to open overseas markets were little exploited. Thus, the capacity utilization in the textiles industry therefore reached its peak in 1977 recording 60 per cent. By 1970, the import substitution agenda initiated in the late 1950s and the greater degree of government involvement in the production of essential items enabled the big four textiles companies – GTMC, ATL, GTP and Printex – to produce one of their biggest outputs yet. In total, the four companies produce a total of 64.7 million yards of textiles, of which GTP accounted for 30.7 million yards, followed by GTMC's 15 million yards, ATL's 13 million and Printex's 6 million yards. It could be said that there was a departure from the free trade philosophy advocated by the GATT in 1947 as many countries sought to protect their domestic markets against textiles and apparel products from international markets flooding their markets. For Ghana, the big textiles companies expanded and employed up to 25,000 people in the 1970s – compared to only 7,000 by 1995.

The liberalization period actually ushered in a level of serious competition from international producers that the Ghanaian textile and apparel industry was not used to. It was thought that about two decades of protection would have given them ample time to build up capacities and become competitive, but unfortunately that was not the case. It must be said that the protection even led to a shortage of basic textiles and clothing products in the domestic market as local demand could not be satisfied by the local producers; this went beyond the textiles and apparel industry to nationwide shortages of basic products such as soap and meat items. The capacity utilization rate of the textiles industry fell from around 60 per cent in 1977 to a low of 17.3 per cent by 1984. The situation was mixed for the garment industry as it experienced mixed fortunes in the liberalization era with the capacity utilization for large and medium-sized companies rising slightly from 20.2 per cent in 1984 to 25 per cent in 1987; it then decreased to 22 in 1991 before rising dramatically to 53 per cent by 1993. Both textiles and garment companies appeared to have responded to the external competition by increasing their combined capacity utilization from only 18 per cent in 1984 to 45.7 per cent by 1993. In line with the recovery in capacity utilization, the growth in textile and garment manufacturing production also showed an improvement. From a growth rate of 22.9 per cent in 1986, two years after liberalization, there was a marked improvement to 28.7 per cent in 1988, which dropped a little in the following year to 24 per cent before increasing again to 39.1 per cent in 1991. The subsequent years displayed no consistent pattern of growth, hitting 60.2 per cent in 1993, the highest figure registered over the thirteen-year period.

In the so-called 'Golden Age of Business' in which Ghana developed better relationships with the USA, the EU and the rest of the world, both textiles and clothing trade with the world displayed some disturbing trends that even the current PSI on textiles and garments has failed to address. The nation is still a net importer of textiles and clothing products; however, given its comparative advantage with respect to labour costs (comparable to those of Asian countries) and the abundance of mid-level textiles and garment skills should mean that the nation exports more than it actually imports. In the period from 1998 to 2006, Ghana's textiles and clothing trade with the world showed a persistent deficit – rising from $33 million in 1992 to over $100 million in 2006. The same also applied to the performance in clothing – which rose from $10.9 million to $25 million.

The PSI on textiles and garments and also AGOA have essentially been supportive of the garments companies located within the Free Zone area, but these developments have not impacted on the textiles industries, which have survived several decades of policy shocks. The diffusion of old innovations such as electricity to help in the production process has actually not reached a critical mass and frequent power outages have been identified as having a negative impact on the sector. The sampled companies have continued to lose their competitive position with each passing day. The declining productive capacity, coupled with relatively higher prices compared to competitors' products, has contributed to this situation. The delays in delivery times being experienced by the Ghanaian exporters compared to their Asian competitors are proving to be a serious challenge, especially for the garments industry. However, the industry can be expressed as having great potential and those can fully be realized when effort is made to address not only domestic problems but also to get bilateral and multilateral negotiations right. The textiles industry, in particular, is suffering from unique problems such as the pirating of designs that can only be affected by a well laid-down policy to curb this from within.

The findings of our study suggest that although international trade rules such as AGOA and the Lomé Convention have contributed to the improvement in the performance of the garments sector to some extent, governance has been a major problem for the expected growth of both the textiles and the garments sectors. In the case of the garments sector the government needs to assist exporters by providing better and more efficient shipments facilities. One of the possible ways could be to provide single window services to exporters for shipment and delivery in international markets. For the textiles sector, which is predominantly domestic oriented, government can help local producers by enforcing existing piracy laws and, if needed, it might enact suitable new legislation to curb the menace of smuggling and other illegal trading activities. Firms in the textiles sector need to encourage the adoption of automated production technologies. We conclude that good governance, coupled with international trade rules, could change the present levels of performance of the textiles and clothing industry in Ghana.

Table A6.1 Profile of some textiles manufacturing companies in Ghana

Company	Year Established	Types of products	No. of Machines	Employees
Pagbo Kente Village	1995	Quality Kente made from woven yarns	13 international looms	13
TV Kente Weaving Enterprise	1992	Quality Kente products	24 international looms	24
Printex Limited	late 1950	Furnishing materials suiting, shirting, School uniforms, Traditional dress, Factory work clothing	N/A	400
Akosombo Textile Limited	1967	Yarn, Grey Cloth Dye/Print Fabric	1,144 weaving looms, 30,240 spindles	1,400

Source: Author's own visits to the companies.

Table A6.2 Profile of some apparel manufacturing companies in Ghana

Company	Types of products	Production Capacity	No. of Machines	Employees
AfricStyle	Casual & formal made from wool, Polywool, linen etc.	na	73 machines	120
Global Garments	Casual wear – shirts, trousers, Skirts; police & military Uniforms, hospital & home Fabrics	40,000 pieces/ month	1,115 and 19 head embroidery machines	570
MaaGrace Garments	Men, Women & Children woven & Knitted garments	na	6 production lines of 50 machines	250
Network Knitwear Fabrics	Socks finishing including stitching bleaching, scouring & packaging	75,000 dozen/ week	60 seaming machines, 6 bleaching tubs 2 extractors 80 dryers' boiler	250
Oak Brook Ghana Ltd	Men and women slacks & shorts, men's Shirts and uniforms	na	6 production lines of 40 machines each	460

(Continued)

Table A6.2   (Continued)

Company	Types of products	Production Capacity	No. of Machines	Employees
Premier Quality	Woven & knit garments men & women slacks, Fleece jackets, polo shirts, Bib overalls, workers Uniforms	33,000 woven pieces/month; 26,000 pieces knit products	210 machines	360
Decent Touch	Men & women slacks & shirts uniforms and scrubs	na	250 machines	185
California Link	Woven garments including lab coats, jeans; ladies & men's Wear including slacks & casual shirts. Also produces knit- t-shirts	na	358 machines	547
Sleek Garments	Men & women slacks & casual shirts, school uniforms, medical Scrubs and lab coats	na	8 production lines of 40 machines each	470

Source: Textile Sector Brochure, 2007, by West African Trade Hub and a visit to some of the companies by the author.

Notes

1. Association of Ghana Industries (AGI).
2. Yaw Asante (2002).
3. Ghana Investment Promotion Centre (GIPC).
4. Kente is a traditional textile cloth produced in Ghana.
5. The figures quoted here are derived from World Development Indicators reported by the World Bank.
6. Information on firms with at least ten people was cited to have come from Labour Statistics in Ghana and those with at least 30 employees came from Industrial Statistics, see Steel (1981: 154).
7. Refer to table 1 of Pearson S. R.; William D. Ingram (1980) for detailed analysis.
8. At the time of Ahiakpor's study using the data in the 1970s, 1 cedi was equivalent to US$0.98.
9. Natural dyes are basically made from natural sources such as roots, flowers, rinds, lichen and wood among others.

References

AGI (2007) 'Textile and Garments, Food Processing and Wood Processing: The Country Case of Ghana. A Draft Report' (unpublished).

Ahiakpor, J.C.W. (1989) 'Do Firms Choose Inappropriate Technology in LDCs?', *Economic Development and Cultural Change*, 37(3): 557–71.

Amor-Wilks, D.A. (2007) *Peasants, Settlers and Weavers in Africa: Structural and Institutional Change in a 'Peasant' and 'Settler' Economy of Africa. Ghana and Zimbabwe, 1890–2000*. London: Department of Economic History, London School of Economics and Political Science.

Ampofu-Tuffuor, E., DeLorme, C. D. and David R Kamerschen (1991) 'The Nature, Significance, and Cost of Rent Seeking in Ghana', *Kyklos*, 44(4): 537–59.

Asante, Y. (2002) 'African Imperative in the New World Order: A Case Study of the Manufacturing Sector in Ghana', AERC Collaborative Research Project presented in Kampala Uganda, Accessed on September 17, 2008. Available at http://www.cepa.org.gh/archives/research-working-papers/African%20 Imperatives%20Revised%20%20Report%20for%20Cepa.doc.

Biggs, Tyler (1994) 'Africa Can Compete! Export Opportunities and Challenges for Garments and Home Products in the US Market', World Bank Discussion Papers, Africa Technical Department Series, No. 300. Washington: IBRD.

Biggs, T., Miller, M., Otto C. and Tyler, G. (1996) 'Africa Can Compete! Export Opportunities and Challenges for Garments and Home Products in the European Market', World Bank Discussion Papers, Africa Technical Department Series, No. 300. Washington: IBRD.

Busy Internet (2003) 'ICT-enabled Development Case Studies Series: Busy Internet (Accra)' *An Initiative of IICD and bridges.org*. Accessed at http://www.bridges.org/ case_studies/127.

Chenery, Hollis (1960) 'Patterns of Industrial Growth', *American Economic Review*, 50.

Cohen, D.L. and M.A. Tribe (1972) 'Suppliers' Credits in Ghana and Uganda – An Aspect of the Imperialist System', *The Journal of Modern African Studies*, 10(4): 525–41.

Desai, M., S. Fukuda-Parr, C. Johansson and F. Sagasti (2002) 'Measuring the Technology Achievement of Nations and the Capacity to Participate in the Network Age', *Journal of Human Development*, 3(1): 95–122.

Dzisah, J. (2006) 'Information and Communication Technologies and Development in Ghana', *Science, Technology and Society*, 11(2): 379–96.

Enos, J. L. (1995) *In Pursuit of Science and Technology in Sub-Saharan Africa: The Impact of Structural Adjustment Programmes*, UNU/INTECH Studies in New Technology and Development. London: Routledge.

Fosu, A. K. (2001) Emerging Africa: The Case of Ghana in the African Economic Outlook a joint African Development Bank – OECD Development Centre project.

Hoefter, Anton Fidelis (2001) 'The Competitiveness of Ghana's Industry', Universität St Gallen, Bamberg. http://www.unisg.ch/www/edis.nsf/wwwDisplayId... Accessed 16 September 2008.

Hormeku, Tetteh (1998) 'The Transformation and Development of the Informal Sector and the Role of the Trade Unions', Paper Prepared for OATUU/ILO/ETUF Seminar on Trade Unions and the Informal Sector. Cairo, Egypt, 4–6 May.

Ingram, D.W. and Scott R. Pearson (1981) 'The Impact of Investment Concessions on the Profitability of Selected Firms in Ghana', *Economic Development and Cultural Change*, 29(4): 831–9.

Inikori, J.E. (1989) 'Slavery and the Revolution in Cotton Textile Production in England', *Social Science History*, 13(4): 343–79.

Intsiful, J.P.F. Okere and Shiloh Osae (2003) 'Use of ICT for Education, Research and Development in Ghana: Challenges, Opportunities and Potentials'. 2003 Round

Table on Developing Countries Access to Scientific Knowledge, the Abdus Salam ICTP, Trieste, Italy.

JICA (2007) *Research Report on Good Practices and Experiences of Sampled Successful SMEs in the Manufacturing Sector in Ghana*. Accra: Pentax Management Consultancy Services.

Lall, S. (2000) *The Technological Structure and Performance of Developing Country Manufacturing Exports, 1985–1998*. QEH Working Paper Series-QEHWPS44. Oxford.

Lall, Sanjaya, and Carlo Pietrobelli (2002) *Failing to Compete: Technology Development and Technology Systems in Africa*, Cheltenham: Edward Elgar.

Leith, Clark J. (1974) *Foreign Trade Regimes and Economic Development: Ghana*, New York: National Bureau of Economic Research.

Mainsah, E. (2003) 'Is Ghana an Attractive Proposition for IT Services and Business Processes Outsourcing', The Trustees of Columbia University in the City of New York.

McDonald, F. and S. Dearden (1992) *European Economic Integration*, 4th edn, Glasgow: Bell and Bain.

Pearson S.R. and William D. Ingram (1980) 'Economies of Scale, Domestic Divergences, and Potential Gains from Economic Integration in Ghana and the Ivory Coast', *The Journal of Political Economy*, 88(5): 994–1008.

Pearson, S.R., G.C. Nelson and J.D. Stryker (1976) *Incentives and Comparative Advantages in Ghanaian Industry and Agriculture*, prepared for World Bank (Stanford University and Food Research Institute).

Pomeranz, D. (2001) 'Africa and the Uruguay Round: Did Sub-Saharan Africa Lose as a Result of the Trade Agreement?', Discussion Paper Presented for the Seminar on International Trade Policy: Theory and Practice of Prof. R. Blackhurst.

PSI (Presidential Special Initiative) (2005), p. 13. http://ghana.gov.gh/files/bartels.pdf. Accessed on 17 September 2008.

Quartey, Peter (2006) 'The Textiles and Clothing Industry in Ghana', in Herbert Jauch and Rudolf Traub-Merz (eds), *The Future of the Textile and Clothing Industry in Sub-Saharan Africa*, Bonn: Friedrich-Ebert-Stiftung, pp. 134–46. Also available online at http://library.fes.de/pdf-files/iez/03796/10ghana.pdf.

Republic of Ghana (2003) 'The Ghana ICT for Accelerated Development (ICT4AD) Policy: A Policy Statement for the Realization of the Vision to Transform Ghana into an Information-Rich Knowledge-based Society and Economy through the Development, Deployment and Exploitation of ICTs within the Economy and Society'. Available at http://www.ict.gov.gh/pdf/Ghana%20ICT4AD%20Policy.pdf.

Steel, W.F. (1981) 'Female and Small-Scale Employment under Modernization in Ghana', *Economic Development and Cultural Change*, 30(1): 153–67.

UNDP (2001) *Human Development Report 2001: Making New Technologies Work for Human Development*, New York: Oxford University Press.

Wangle, S. M. (1995) *Exporting Africa: Technology, Trade and Industrialization in Sub-Saharan Africa*, London: Routledge.

7
International Trade Rules and the Textiles and Clothing Industry in Uruguay

Adriana Peluffo

7.1 Introduction

In Uruguay, the textiles industry is a traditional production and export sector. Wool industrialization processes were in operation as long ago as the end of the nineteenth century. From its earliest days the industry has been characterized by family enterprises that focus primarily on the processing of wool, and has been oriented to the domestic market. The clothing sector developed at a later stage, during the import substitution period, and at first it was also geared to the domestic market. The sector is made up of firms that vary in terms of market orientation and type of product. The clothing sector is an example of a global chain led by the customers.

Since the 1940s the proportion of manufactured wool exported has increased, and during the 1970s the exports of textiles and clothing products experienced considerable growth. This was fostered by export promotion policies for the textiles sector. Firms manufacturing other fibres (cotton and synthetics) appeared in the domestic market, and in the 1970s they oriented their exports to regional markets in the framework of the preferential trade agreements prevailing at that time.

The textiles sector is made up principally of two sub-sectors which account for the majority of production and exports: one produces wool tops and the other produces knitted wool fabrics. Other activities in this sector have become less competitive and less important, although a few firms have done relatively well. The textiles sector is mainly built around wool supply which, over the course of the past twenty years, has managed to survive the challenges of new international and domestic conditions. In this relative success the strategies developed by wool weaving and spinning firms and other textiles enterprises have been a major factor. The main sub-sectors are the washing and manufacturing of wool-tops, and spinning and weaving.

The clothing sector employs a variety of inputs, and in Uruguay the two that are used most often are wool and leather. In the past, there were a number of firms producing synthetic and artificial threads for the manufacture of fabrics, but these have now closed down. The level of cotton production in the country is insignificant. The clothing sector is made up of the following sub-sectors: (i) leather apparel; (ii) knitted apparel; (iii) garments based on wool and based on cotton. These sub-sectors differ in terms of both their productive processes and their target markets. Wool-based clothing is mainly formal apparel, while production based on cotton is more for informal wear. The textiles and clothing sector grew until the 1990s, and then experienced a reduction in production, value added, employment and exports as we will show in the following sections.

In 1981, the textiles industry accounted for 7.6 per cent of gross product, 8.4 per cent of value added and 12 per cent of total employment in manufacturing. These shares increased from 1981 to 1991, but by 2001 they had fallen by 5.2 per cent, 4.4 per cent and 4.5 per cent respectively. During this period the clothing sector also experienced a decline in its performance. In 1981 the gross product of the clothing sector was $233,179,000; in 1991 it increased to $351,613,000 and then in 2001 it fell to $113,729,000. Value added and employment followed a similar pattern. In 2001 the clothing sector accounted for 1.5 per cent of Uruguay's GDP and 4 per cent of its manufacturing products. In 2001 the sector accounted for 5 per cent of total manufacturing exports, which is an indication of how it is geared to exports. In 1981, clothing production amounted to 3.85 per cent of total manufacturing products, in 1991 it increased to 5.47 per cent but then decreased, and in 2001 the figure was 2.35 per cent.

The objective of this work is to conduct a qualitative and quantitative analysis of the evolution of the textiles and clothing sector in the 1981–2001 period, by means of semi-structured interviews with six T&C firms which have survived the challenges of the new competition.

The chapter is organized as follows: First, we present the evolution of the both sectors, separately, in terms of production, value added, import competition and export performance. We also present some productivity indicators as labour and total factor productivity. Secondly, we examine the main institutions related to these sectors and describe their goals and functions. Then, we describe the industrial policies implemented in the country. Finally, we present the results of the interviews and finally we conclude.

7.2   Textiles sector

7.2.1   General features

In Uruguay the textiles industry is a traditional production and export sector. Wool industrialization processes were in operation as early as the end of the nineteenth century, and they became more dynamic during the import substitution period. Since its early days the industry has been characterized by family enterprises that concentrate on the processing of wool, and has been oriented to the domestic market.

Since the 1940s there has been an increase in the proportion of manufactured wool that is exported, and during the 1970s the exports of both textiles and clothing products grew considerably. This was fostered by export promotion policies for the textiles sector. Firms manufacturing other fibres (cotton and synthetics) appeared in the domestic market, and in the 1970s they oriented their exports to regional markets in the framework of the preferential trade agreements prevailing at that time.

The textiles sector is comprised principally of two sub-sectors which account for most of its production and exports: one that produces wool tops and one that produces knitted wool fabrics. Other activities in this sector have become less competitive and less important, although a few firms have done relatively well.

The textiles sector is built principally around wool supply which, over the course of the past twenty years, has managed to survive the challenges of new international and domestic conditions. The strategies developed by wool weaving and spinning firms and other textiles enterprises have been a major factor in this relative success. The main sub-sectors are washing and manufacturing of wool-tops, and spinning and weaving.

It can be seen from Table 7.1 that between the early 1980s and the 1990s the sector grew, and then production, value added, total wages and employment all fell. In 2001 exports were higher than in 1981, but they were still below the 1991 figure. On the other hand labour productivity, defined as value added in relation to the number of workers, increased continuously over the period.

In 2001, the gross product of the textiles sector was US$257.5 million, the value added was US$77.7 million, total employment was 4,373 workers, and exports amounted to US$200 million.

Table 7.1 Main features of the Uruguayan textiles sector

	1981	1991	2001
Gross product (US$ 000s)	461,553.00	606,252.00	257,521.00
Value added (US$ 000s)	218,946.00	277,302.00	77,617.00
VA/gross product	0.47	0.46	0.30
Wage bills (US$ 000s)	82,624.80	75,871.60	36,562.00
Employment (number of workers)	19,400.00	18,280.00	4,373.00
VA/employment (US$ 000s)	11.29	15.17	17.75
Wage bills/employment (US$ 000s)	4.26	4.15	8.36
Exports (US$ 000s)	120,573.50	291,053.10	202,082.00

Source: Author's preparation based on data from Nicita and Olarreaga (2007).

Table 7.2   Share of the textiles sector in the total manufacturing sector

	1981	1991	2001
% Gross product	7.60	9.20	5.20
% Value added	8.4	9.2	4.4
% Employment	12.6	11.1	4.5
% Exports	13.34	21.79	10

Source: Author's preparation based on data from Nicita and Olarreaga (2007).

Table 7.2 shows the share of the textiles sector in gross product, value added, total employment, and exports of manufacturing industries as a whole. It can be seen that in the 1981–91 period the textiles sector's share in total manufacturing increased in terms of gross product, value added and exports, and that it decreased in the period 1991–2001. Note that its share in employment decreased throughout the entire period. The larger increase in exports between 1981 and 1991 was due to the contribution of exports of wool-tops, which have a lower value added than the other sub-sectors that make up the textile sector (Terra et al., 2004). The decrease in value added is due to the higher decrease in spinning and weaving and knitted products compared to the washing and manufacturing of wool-tops.

The washing and manufacturing of the wool-tops sub-sector is in the first stage of the wool textile chain. It receives the wool from the agricultural sector and carries out every process – from washing the wool to manufacturing the tops. It mainly uses wool that is produced in Uruguay, but in recent years the supply of this domestic wool has fallen and it has been necessary to import raw wool. This sub-sector is very important because of its contribution to textiles sector production and exports, but it is less important in terms of value added and employment. Most production and exports are in the hands of seven enterprises that are able to produce on a scale adequate for international standards (Terra et al., 2004). The spinning, weaving and finishing sector is made up of firms that manufacture wool thread and fabrics, and four big enterprises dominate production and exports in this area.[1]

In 1981, the textiles industry accounted for 7.6 per cent of gross product, 8.4 per cent of value added and 12 per cent of the employment in manufacturing as a whole. These shares increased between 1981 and 1991, but by 2001 they had fallen back to 5.2 per cent, 4.4 per cent and 4.5 per cent respectively.

7.2.2   Evolution of production, value added and employment

During the 1990s, the manufacturing sector in Uruguay performed very poorly. The share of the gross product of manufacturing in GDP fell from 27 per cent in 1988 to 16 per cent in 2001, as can be seen in Table 7.3.

Table 7.3 Share of manufacturing product in gross domestic product

	GDP	Manufacturing gross product	% Manufacturing product in GDP
(current Uruguayan pesos)			
1988	2,944,611.00	802,784.00	27.26
1989	5,242,091.00	1,406,280.00	26.83
1990	10,874,807.00	3,041,182.00	27.97
1991	22,610,288.00	6,401,089.00	28.31
1992	38,953,979.00	9,654,682.00	24.78
1993	59,124,802.00	12,475,923.00	21.10
1994	88,140,376.00	16,639,451.00	18.88
1995	122,520,863.00	24,130,056.00	19.69
1996	163,545,806.00	31,305,523.00	19.14
1997	204,925,566.00	38,688,474.00	18.88
1998	234,266,812.00	43,124,704.00	18.41
1999	237,143,036.00	39,545,625.00	16.68
2000	243,027,071.00	41,036,410.00	16.89
2001	247,211,395.00	40,284,040.00	16.30

Source: Banco Central del Uruguay.

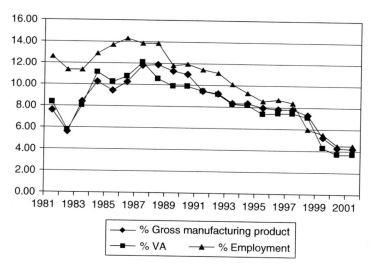

Figure 7.1 Share of the textiles sector in total manufacturing
Source: Author's preparation, data from Nicita and Olarreaga (2007).

The performance of the textiles industry was even worse and its share in manufacturing as a whole decreased, as can be seen in Figure 7.1. There were far-reaching adjustments in the textiles sector which resulted in a reduction in the number of firms and a change in the profile of the sector.

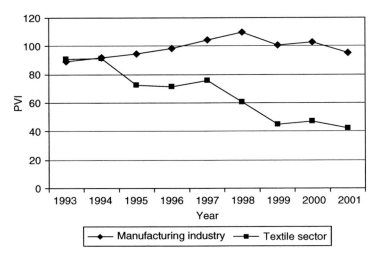

Figure 7.2   Physical volume index (base year 1988)
Source: Author's preparation, data from Instituto Nacional de Estadistica.

Figure 7.2 shows the index of physical volume for manufacturing as a whole and for the textiles sector in the period 1993–2001. It can be seen from Figure 7.2 that the fall in physical volume is greater in the textiles sector than in the overall total for manufacturing.

The index of employment gives a similar picture (Figure 7.3). Nevertheless, this process did not have the same impact on every one of the sub-sectors that make up this industry. The washing of wool and manufacture of tops sub-sector, which has lower value added, a closer relationship with its source of inputs (raw wool) and greater export propensity, performed better than the spinning and weaving sub-sector.

As mentioned above, this performance profile was the result of a fall in the spinning and weaving sub-sector and a less serious decline in the washing and manufacture of tops sub-sector. In spinning and weaving there was a decrease in knitted wool products (which fell by half between 1993 and 2003), and a large decrease in production based on fibres other than wool.

Table 7.4 shows the performance of the various sub-sectors that make up the textiles sector. In terms of gross product and value added, the most important sub-sector in 1990 was spinning, weaving and finishing, and this was followed by the washing and manufacturing of wool tops sub-sector and then other textiles products. In spinning and weaving the main raw material was wool, and this was followed on the list by synthetic fibres and cotton. During the 1990s there was a large fall in production in all of the sub-sectors, except for those involving the washing of wool and the manufacture of wool tops. Spinning and weaving showed the greatest decline, which was due mainly

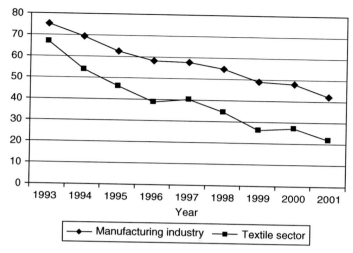

Figure 7.3 Employment index (base year 1988)
Source: Own preparation, data from Instituto Nacional de Estadistica.

to the loss of domestic and regional markets, while exports to the rest of the world also decreased but to a lesser extent. The manufacture of knitted fabrics made with cotton and synthetic and artificial fibres also decreased during this period.

In the period 1990–2000, in the Uruguayan domestic market the textiles sector was exposed to increased competition from imports. Textiles manufactured with cotton and synthetic and artificial fibres (which were not competitive in third markets) were oriented mainly to domestic and regional markets, which was not the case for the spinning and weaving of wool. This increased competition in the domestic market and the loss of competitiveness in regional markets explain the fall in the production of spinning and weaving based on fibres other than wool.

At the beginning of the 1990s Uruguay implemented a policy of trade liberalization, but the impact of this on the textiles sector was delayed since this sector was considered to be 'sensitive'. The main protection instruments were tariffs, reference prices (RPs) and minimum export prices (MEPs). The government was permitted to apply RPs or MEPs when import prices were not in line with world prices, which were considered to be 'normal' prices. These measures were aimed at preventing unfair trade practices. In 1993 RPs were eliminated and new criteria in line with multilateral regulations and aimed at establishing clearer trade rules were used to set MEPs. In fact, MEPs became less important as a protection mechanism in the 1990s, and since 1995 they have only been applied to goods produced outside the Mercosur (Spanish: *Mercado Común del Sur*, English: *Southern Common Market*).

Table 7.4 Share of the various sub-sectors of the textiles industry in gross product, value added, exports and employment

Year	Spinning, weaving and finishing of textiles products	Preparation and spinning of wool	Manufacture of other textile fibres	Total textiles sector
Gross product (%)				
1990	62.7	27.2	10.1	100
1991	57.5	34.1	8.4	100
1992	50.5	40.7	8.8	100
1993	49.5	40.6	9.9	100
1994	44.1	47.3	8.6	100
1995	37.8	53.7	8.5	100
1996	37.5	53.8	8.7	100
1997	30.8	62.1	7.1	100
1998	33.9	61.1	5.0	100
1999	33.8	60.2	6.0	100
2000	35.5	59.4	5.1	100
2001	29.8	65.8	4.5	100.1
Value added (%)				
1990	67.2	24.3	8.5	100
1991	65.8	25.4	8.8	100
1992	54.1	35.8	10.1	100
1993	57.6	31.6	10.8	100
1994	49.8	41.5	8.7	100
1995	38.5	53.6	7.9	100
1996	45.1	44.5	10.4	100
1997	35.4	56.6	8.0	100
1998	47.4	46.2	6.4	100
1999	48.3	43.8	7.9	100
2000	50.8	42.4	6.8	100
2001	45.7	48.1	6.2	100
Exports (%)				
1990	47.6	48.3	4.1	100
1991	48.0	49.6	2.4	100
1992	48.5	49.8	1.7	100
1993	48.9	49.2	1.9	100
1994	50.0	47.7	2.3	100
1995	45.8	51.7	2.5	100
1996	31.6	66.2	2.2	100
1997	37.9	60.0	2.1	100
1998	39.9	57.0	3.1	100
1999	37.9	58.7	3.4	100
2000	38.4	57.4	4.2	100
2001	34.2	62.5	3.3	100

(*Continued*)

Table 7.4   (Continued)

Year	Spinning, weaving and finishing of textiles products	Preparation and spinning of wool	Manufacture of other textile fibres	Total textiles sector
Employment (%)				
1990	74.8	15.6	9.6	100
1991	72.6	16.7	10.7	100
1992	73.0	17.2	9.8	100
1993	68.9	20.1	11.0	100
1994	68.0	19.9	12.1	100
1995	66.4	21.8	11.8	100
1996	66.4	21.2	12.4	100
1997	65.4	20.8	13.8	100
1998	63.3	20.5	16.2	100
1999	69.0	21.5	9.5	100
2000	66.7	21.5	11.8	100
2001	68.0	20.6	11.4	100

Source: Department of Economics, University of the Republic (2004).

In 1994, when the Common External Tariff (CET) was set, the prevailing tariffs on many textiles sector products were higher than the CET. Of the 963 products that Uruguay listed under the Mercosur customs union adjustment regime, 170 were from the textiles sector. Customs union trade liberalization for these products was postponed. In addition, 150 products from the textiles and clothing sectors were put on the list of exceptions to the CET, that is to say products on the adjustment regime list for which intra-Mercosur tariffs were higher than the CET. For these reasons trade liberalisation only made an impact in this sector after 1997.

7.2.3   The evolution of imports

Figure 7.4 presents the evolution of textiles imports in relation to the gross product for the textiles sector for the period 1981–2001. It can be seen that imports increased in the 1990s, and were even higher after 1997.

A clearer picture can be obtained for the period 1990–2001. It can be seen from Table 7.5 that there was a large increase in import penetration, defined as the ratio of imports to apparent consumption. Import penetration varied in different sub-sectors and it was not so marked in the washing and manufacturing of wool tops sub-sector. In 1999 the situation worsened following the devaluation of the real in Brazil. Import penetration in the textiles sector increased from 10 per cent in 1990 to 33 per cent in 1996 and 60 per cent in 2000.

The spinning and weaving of cotton and synthetic and artificial fibres was the sub-sector that was most significantly affected, with falls in production

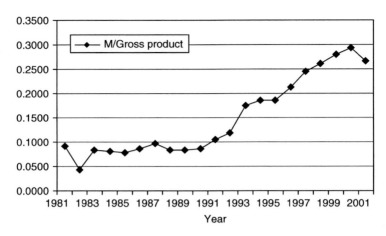

Figure 7.4   Textiles imports in relation to textiles sector gross product
Source: Author's preparation with data from Nicita and Olarreaga (2007).

Table 7.5   Import penetration during the period 1990–2001

Year	Spinning, weaving and finishing of textiles products	Preparation and spinning of wool	Manufacture of other textile fibres	Total Textile Sector
1990	9.3	n/d	31.6	9.9
1991	17.3	10.2	21.9	18.4
1992	24.6	6.8	34.5	31.2
1993	30.3	0.0	54.3	31.0
1994	56.9	0.9	46.2	34.5
1995	51.8	0.0	36.6	47.1
1996	39.6	0.3	34.0	32.8
1997	71.9	0.7	57.5	41.6
1998	77.8	0.2	75.4	49.6
1999	79.9	0.4	76.0	52.4
2000	83.2	1.0	80.6	59.5
2001	93.7	1.5	89.8	69.4

Source: Department of Economics, School of Social Sciences, University of the Republic (2004).

and employment. This sub-sector had developed when it was protected by import substitution policies. Its exports were protected in the framework of ALADI trade agreements by trade preferences that usually involved quantitative restrictions, so there was no security as regards long-term access to these markets and consequently no long-term conditions to promote sector development. Trade liberalization in regional markets reduced protection and promoted exports to these markets, but at the same time it increased competition from lower-cost imports in the domestic market. Traditionally, the spinning and weaving of cotton and synthetic and artificial fibres sub-sector was made up of a few big firms and some medium-sized ones. In the 1990s a number of these firms closed down. The cotton and synthetics industry contracted so much in that decade that it practically disappeared.

One factor that probably has a considerable effect on the evolution of this sub-sector was that it was in the position of being a producer of intermediate goods and depended upon imported inputs. This weak relationship with respect to the sources of fibres for production and with respect to the final consumer made for difficulties in this sub-sector. Cotton weaving takes place on a larger scale than wool weaving which means that when firms in this sub-sector are faced with increasing competition they have to make bigger investments in order to increase their scale and keep in line with international standards. There were no clear long-term rules in the country to give firms incentives to undertake investment on this scale in order to be competitive. Imports grew and exports decreased. Most exports went to Uruguay's immediate neighbours in the region. Faced with increased competition, these exporting firms chose to rationalize production and gear themselves to the big Mercosur markets.

7.2.4   The evolution of exports

The wool textiles sector has an export tradition and historically it has made a large contribution to Uruguay's total exports – as an exporting sector it is second only to meat products. Table 7.6 shows the evolution of exports, export propensity,[2] and the share of this sector's exports in total exports of manufactures.

In Uruguay, this sector has comparative advantages in that wool is widely available in the country, and exports go to all parts of the world. These comparative advantages have made it possible to export to extra-regional markets. Even though export propensity in this sector increased over the period as a whole, in the last decade it became less dynamic and its share in total exports decreased. In 1981, exports amounted to US$121 million; they rose to US$291 million in 1991 and US$365 million in 1996, before falling to US$175 million in 1999. In 1981, exports accounted for 26 per cent of production, and over the period this share rose, reaching 75 per cent in 2001. The share of exports from this sector in total exports increased from 13 per cent in 1981 to 23 per cent in 1992 but then declined – the 2001 figure was 11 per cent.

Table 7.7 shows the coverage rate and the regional orientation index for the textiles sector. At the beginning of the 1990s the coverage rate[3] of the textiles sector was 5.8, but following a rise to 6.37 it decreased in subsequent years and in 2003 had a value of 1.0. This indicates that export specialization in this sector fell due to the decrease in exports and the increase in imports.

Table 7.6 Exports and export propensity of the textiles sector

Year	Exports (US$000s)	X/gross product (%)	X/total manufacturing exports (%)
1981	120,573.5	26.12	13.34
1982	90,312.3	34.01	14.17
1983	145,360.5	55.54	16.08
1984	154,729.5	45.58	19.05
1985	164,382.2	54.71	21.68
1986	206,288.0	56.00	21.44
1987	244,740.5	53.56	22.42
1988	305,451.1	63.90	25.89
1989	285,160.2	51.42	21.25
1990	300,887.3	52.51	20.59
1991	291,052.1	48.01	21.79
1992	339,734.0	56.31	22.93
1993	284,676.3	53.61	19.83
1994	293,931.8	52.98	17.07
1995	324,233.1	53.76	17.89
1996	364,592.7	62.45	17.25
1997	362,042.3	59.32	15.34
1998	238,400.8	57.38	10.29
1999	175,224.0	60.05	10.18
2000	186,159.3	66.02	9.36
2001	192,438.4	74.73	11.06

Source: Author's preparation with data from Nicita and Olarreaga (2007).

Table 7.7 Coverage ratio and regional orientation index

Year	Coverage rate	Regional orientation index
1990	5.78	0.39
1991	5.07	0.39
1992	6.37	0.37
1993	5.14	0.32
1994	4.13	0.31
1995	3.27	0.40
1996	5.06	0.36
1997	3.61	0.42
1998	3.33	0.43
1999	3.05	0.46
2000	4.56	0.46
2001	3.22	0.29

Source: Terra et al. (2004).

These figures conceal the fact that the wool complex as a whole has been strongly oriented to exports after an increase in the imports of textiles made of cotton and synthetic and artificial fibres. On the other hand, the regional orientation index, defined as the ratio between the share of Mercosur in the sector's exports and the share of Mercosur in the country's total exports, shows that regional orientation is lower for this sector than for total exports from Uruguay. Even during the period when Uruguay oriented its exports to the Mercosur, the index for the sector was 0.4, which means that the sector's share in the Mercosur market was 40 per cent lower than its share in the country's total exports. This index rating decreased in 2001, when exports from this sector were reoriented to extra-regional markets.

The main export markets are the EU, China and Southeast Asia. In the aftermath of the crisis in Asia there was a fall in exports to that market and an increase in exports to the Mercosur. However, when the crisis hit, the Mercosur region exports to customs union partners decreased, those to the EU increased, and exports to the Chinese market recovered to a certain extent. In 2003, 64 per cent of total exports went to the EU, China, and Southeast Asia (Terra et al., 2004).

Table 7.8 shows the composition of exports by type of fibre. More than 90 per cent of textiles exports are wool products. The main export product is combed wool tops followed by wool and fine hair fabrics, which together account for approximately 80 per cent total wool product exports.

Table 7.9 shows the heterogeneity in trade specialization and in the regional orientation of trade for different types of fibre. Only wool and silk manufactured products show coverage ratios greater than one, which indicates that these goods have comparative advantages. They tend more often to be exported to markets outside the region, while textiles products in which Uruguay does not have comparative advantage go to more local markets. Regional trade orientation is very low in wool products, in which Uruguay is a net exporter, while in the case of other fibres the degree of regional orientation is very high.

7.2.5 The evolution of labour productivity

Figure 7.5 shows the evolution of labour productivity, defined as value added per worker, and measured in terms of US dollars. In the 1981–2001 period value added per worker increased, and there was some variation between different years. There was a steady rise until 1997 and then a fall, but the figures for the period 1997–2001 are higher than for the beginning of the 1980s.

Figure 7.6 shows the evolution of total factor productivity (TFP) for the period 1988–95 with 1988 as the base year, estimated using Petrin and Levinshon methodology (Casacuberta et al., 2004). It can be seen that TFP is lower for the textiles sector than for manufacturing as a whole.

Table 7.8 Composition of exports by type of fibre

	1993–1995			1996–1998			1999–2001		
	Volume, thousands	Value, thousands	% Value	Volume, thousands	Value, thousands	% Value	Volume, thousands	Value, thousands	% Value
Cotton	846	3,466	1.1	707	4,128	1.2	188	855	0.4
Wool	70,698	292,049	90.5	62,499	296,246	88.1	51,846	178,101	89.5
Synthetic	4,611	19,871	6.2	6,680	26,251	7.8	3,925	11,498	5.8
Silk	10	346	0.1	65	2,121	0.6	42	1,357	0.7
Other fibres	62	417	0.1	17	36	0	43	80	0
Textile products except clothing	1,098	6,690	2.1	893	7,662	2.3	725	7	3.5
Total textiles sector	77,326	322,839	100	70,862	336,444	100	56,770	198,929	100

Source: Department of Economics, University of the Republic (2004).

Table 7.9 Coverage ratio and regional orientation index of textile products

	1993–1995		1996–1998		1999–2001	
	Coverage	ROI	Coverage	ROI	Coverage	ROI
Cotton	0.37	1.84	0.35	1.77	0.13	1.41
Wool and hairs	13.96	0.16	12.94	0.19	16.26	0.20
Synthetic and artificials	0.87	2.16	0.80	1.82	0.60	1.90
Silk	1.44	0.58	3.59	0.38	2.59	0.21
Other fibres	0.15	1.65	0.03	1.73	0.15	1.91
Knitted fabrics	0.30	1.58	0.48	1.30	0.57	1.33
Textile products except clothing	0.40	2.01	0.27	1.75	0.35	1.67
Total textiles sector	4.16	0.35	3.29	0.38	3.26	0.37

Note: ROI: Regional Orientation Index.
Source: Terra et al. (2004)

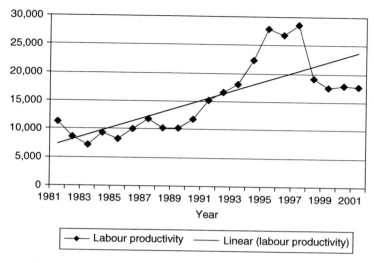

Figure 7.5   Evolution of labour productivity
Source: Author's preparation with data from Nicita and Olarreaga (2007).

Figure 7.6   Total factor productivity, textiles and total manufacturing, 1988–1995
Source: Author's preparation based on data from Casacuberta et al. (2003).

In conclusion, the reasons behind the poor performance of the textiles sector could be difficulties stemming from increasing trade openness, domestic currency appreciation and the fall in wool prices. Although trade preferences in regional markets increased, there was no long-term guarantee that access to these markets would be maintained so there was no solid incentive to invest in modernizing the sector. This led to a migration of MNEs, which tended to be concentrated in the larger regional markets. As a consequence, most of the textiles activity oriented to domestic and regional markets disappeared, and this led to an increase in import penetration and increased export propensity in the sector.

Trade openness and domestic currency appreciation facilitated increased competition from imports, and industries oriented to the domestic market became less competitive. The domestic market was supplied by imported goods, and the domestic industry that has survived is strongly oriented towards exports. Other factors that help to explain the difficulties the sector underwent included: the elimination of the General System of Preference in the European Union; the economic crisis in the region; devaluation in China and other Asiatic countries (which led to a reduction in foreign demand); and the fact that domestic industries became less competitive in relation to their main foreign competitors.

7.2.6   Cost structure

Table 7.10 shows the cost structure of the textiles sector estimated from the input–output matrix for 1997 drawn up by the Central Bank of Uruguay. The intermediate inputs with the highest share were from agriculture – mainly raw wool – and from the textiles sector itself, which reflects the fact that this sector is vertically integrated. Wool tops are inputs for manufacturing

Table 7.10   Cost structure of the textiles sector, input–output matrix, 1997

Cost Structure	%
Agriculture	0.56
Cattle	23.56
Forestry and fishing	0.15
Mining and quarrying	0.02
Food, beverages and tobacco	0.01
Textiles	15.89
Wearing apparel, tanneries and leather products	0.06
Wood, paper and printing	0.03
Chemical products	3.89
Electricity, gas and water	1.50
Other services	0.48
Other expenditures	12.22
Total intermediate consumption	58.90
Total value added	41.10
Total gross product	100

Source: Terra et al. (2004).

fabric and thread, and thread is an input for knitted fabrics. Intermediate consumption accounted for 59 per cent of costs in this sector, and value added accounted for 41 per cent.

7.2.7 Factors that affect competitiveness in the textiles sector

The factors that affect the competitiveness of the textiles and clothing sectors include the following:

7.2.7.1 *The availability of raw materials and other inputs*

The availability of good-quality, cheap wool has contributed to the competitiveness of the sector, particularly in the manufacture of tops. The Uruguayan Wool Secretariat (SUL – Secretariado Uruguayo de la Lana) has played a major role in promoting the production of high-quality wool. However, although the country produces high-quality wool this is mainly of medium thickness so it is not the most suitable kind for producing smooth fabrics. This type of wool is more suitable for heavy fabrics, sweaters and wool for knitting, so it competes in a market segment characterized by a high rate of substitution between wool and other fibres. To produce smooth fabrics, producers have to import finer wool.

7.2.7.2 *Productivity, labour costs, and the availability of a skilled labour force*

Uruguay is a middle-level country as regards the costs of labour and productivity, but this is dependent to a large extent on the exchange rate. In the 1990s Uruguay's currency rose against the dollar, making the cost of labour higher and the country less competitive on foreign markets. 2002 saw financial crises and devaluation, and there was a fall in the price of exportable goods and the cost of labour.

The sub-sector that produces wool tops is relatively intensive in capital, and wages have less weight in production. In the spinning and weaving sub-sector, the availability of qualified workers is an important factor in competitiveness, although it is not considered vital. Entrepreneurs who were interviewed consider that the availability of a skilled workforce it is not a problem for the development of the sector since firms have been conducting in-company training programmes.

7.2.7.3 *Technology*

By international standards, the sector is in a relatively good position in respect of technology. The technology in the wool-tops manufacturing sub-sector was updated in the 1980s and 1990s, and in any case there has been no major technological change in terms of the necessary machinery and equipment.

In the spinning and weaving sub-sector, some firms are using state-of-the-art technology. This sector has made an effort to keep up to date, and the machinery and equipment is considered to be of a relatively good standard. The main problem is in the weaving sub-sector, where some firms have a low level of investment in technology and no access to credit, and have been unable to upgrade their equipment. In the washing and tops sub-sector the problem of limited access to credit is not so serious, and firms have been able to keep pace with technological progress. This may be due to the fact the firms in question are bigger and some of them have foreign capital participation.

On the other hand, scale became a problem for firms that manufacture cotton fibres since they did not reach the minimum production scale. Wool processing firms can operate on a smaller scale so they did not encounter this problem.

7.2.7.4   Design and product differentiation

Design and product differentiation is not an issue in the manufacturing of tops, but it is very important in the weaving sub-sector. The firms interviewed have their own designs and also work with customer designs. Some of the producers in this area have agreements with Italian firms, which have made it possible to access high-quality segments of the market.

7.2.7.5   Proximity to big markets, and problems in telecommunications

The manufacturing of wool tops sub-sector has a problem because Uruguay is not close to the largest and most important markets, but this is not a problem for weaving. In addition, telecommunications are expensive, and this has led to some problems.

7.2.7.6   Relationship with clients and quality of services

This is an important factor for the competitiveness of the sector. The firms that have survived have a portfolio of clients that know them and trust them. Two factors that seem to have been important in enabling these firms to stay in production are the fact that their products are of good quality, and the fact that the have met their delivery deadlines.

7.2.7.7   Exchange rate policy, wages and prices in dollars

The exchange rate policy implemented in Uruguay in and after 1991 led to a big rise in the cost of the local currency against the US dollar, and this had a negative impact on the competitiveness of firms in this sector. These firms sold in foreign markets so their income was linked to the level of export prices in the world, but their cost structure was heavy in non-tradable goods so the price of their products in dollars increased.

Labour costs were an important factor in the performance of weaving, but were less important in the manufacture of tops. In the 1990–2002 period wages in the private sector, measured in dollars, rose by more than

65 per cent. Furthermore, in the 1990s there was an increase in the cost of public services, measured in dollars. The cost of electricity, water, and telephone services increased steadily until 1998, and fuel costs also rose, albeit to a lesser extent.

7.2.7.8 Domestic trade policies

By the end of the 1990s the sector was being affected by trade openness, and the impact was felt mainly in the production of textiles that did not use wool as an input. At the beginning of the 1990s the textiles sector was protected by high tariffs, reference prices (RPs) and minimum export prices (MEPs), protection instruments that applied to regional as well for extra-regional imports and affected textiles produced with fibres other than wool. In 1993 RPs were removed, and in 1995 the MEP system began to be dismantled. By the end of 2000 MEPs were replaced by specific duties for countries that were not members of the Mercosur. These specific duties ceased to operate in 2002.

7.2.7.9 Access to foreign markets

The textiles sector no longer enjoys preferential access mechanisms in important markets, and it has been unable to avoid the impact of non-tariff protective measures inside the Mercosur.

The final implementation of the Agreement on Textiles and Clothing (ATC) would lead to a slight improvement in Uruguay's access to the large markets in developed countries, but it would also improve access for Asian countries which would increase competition in those markets.

On the other hand, the main importers of textiles, the EU and the United States, have made preferential trade agreements which discriminate against imports from countries not included in those agreements, principally by imposing high tariffs and insisting on rules of origin. The Mercosur has been negotiating these matters with the developed countries, but so far it has been unable to reach any final agreement.

Another problem is that although the Mercosur has succeeded in liberalizing trade among its members there are no long-term rules for the development of an industry oriented to regional markets. Non-tariff restrictions on trade, such as the mechanism of custom valuation, are still in place, and this has generated uncertainty about long-term access to these markets.

Finally, there is still uncertainty about whether the Southern Customs Union will eventually come into full operation, and this was worked against reconstruction in an industry oriented to the region. In Ouro Preto (1994), the Mercosur reached agreement on mechanisms to extend the customs union and establish the free circulation of goods. However, in the transitory phase some protective measures have remained in place, such as the double payment of tariffs, the regime of origin system, and temporary admission. These measures were due for elimination, but this has now been postponed, so at the time of writing the Uruguayan textiles industry has received no clear indication as to what will happen in the long term. Industries that depend upon imported inputs can use the temporary admission regime to export to the region if they satisfy the rules of origin. However, this is a transitional instrument so there are no clear rules to underpin investment in areas like technological modernization or increases in scale. This could explain why the textile wool-processing sub-sectors that have a small minimum scale and do not depend on the region have been able to maintain their technology renewal efforts, while the processing of cotton and synthetic and artificial fibres has almost disappeared. Firms in the latter sector came into being to supply the domestic market. In order to be competitive in the world market they would have had to increase in scale, but restrictions on access to the regional and world markets have discouraged this kind of investment.

7.2.7.10 Export promotion policies

The textiles sector has made use of the general export promotion regime, which consists mainly of reimbursement for indirect taxes, the pre-financing of exports and temporary admission. The temporary admission regime is used in the import of wool, but it has been more significant in the import of other fibres. Another specific measure in the sector was the Pineda Law, which involved tax advantages for goods produced with domestic wool. At the beginning of 1990 this rebate amounted to 18 per cent, but it was reduced to 9 per cent in 1992 and was then eliminated in 2003.

7.2.7.11 Quality and cost of public services

When it comes to public services, the main hindrances to the development of the textiles sector are that port costs are high and communications and energy are expensive.

7.2.7.12 Access to credit

Another restriction on the development of the sector is that it is difficult for the spinning and weaving sub-sector to access credits for long-term investment. This is not a problem for firms manufacturing tops because they tend to be larger and can therefore obtain credit at low financial cost. Spinning and weaving firms are smaller and do not have this option, so they have had to finance their investments with their own capital.

7.2.7.13 Promotion of investments

The general mechanism for promoting investment, which allows machinery and equipment to be imported without paying tariffs, has been widely used by firms in this sector.

7.3 The clothing sector

7.3.1 General features

Like the textiles sector, the clothing sector developed during the import substitution period, and at first it was geared to the domestic market. Since the 1970s it has been oriented to the foreign market, taking advantage of export promotion policies. The sector is made up of firms that vary as regards, market orientation and type of product. The clothing sector is an example of a global chain led by the customers. This sector was bigger than it is today from the 1970s through to the 1990s, when it was negatively affected by a series of factors such as the creation of the Mercosur, the reduction in trade protection to third countries, changes in the currency exchange rate, and the economic recession since 1999. As in the textiles industry, the activity that suffered most was the manufacture of cotton and synthetic apparel.

The clothing sector employs a variety of inputs, and in Uruguay the two that are used most often are wool and leather. In the past, there were firms producing synthetic and artificial threads for the manufacture of fabrics, but these have now closed down. The production of cotton in the country is insignificant. The clothing sector is made up of the following sub-sectors: (i) leather apparel; (ii) knitted apparel; and (iii) garments based on wool and based on cotton. These sub-sectors differ in terms of their productive processes and in their target markets. Wool-based clothing is mainly formal apparel, while production based on cotton is more for informal wear.

In 1981 the gross product of the sector was $233,179,000, and by 1991 it had increased to $351,613,000; however, by 2001 it had fallen to $113,729,000. Value added and employment also followed a similar pattern. In 2001 the clothing sector accounted for 1.5 per cent of Uruguay's GDP and 4 per cent of its manufacturing product. In 2001 the sector accounted for 5 per cent of total manufacturing exports, which is an indication of the extent to which it is geared to exports. A snapshot of the sector is presented in Table 7.11.

Table 7.11 Main features of the clothing sector

	1981	1991	2001
Gross product (thousands of USD)	233,179.00	351,613.00	113,729.00
Value added (thousands of USD)	99,681.30	144,231.00	46,437.30
VA/gross product	0.43	0.41	0.41
Wage bills (thousands of USD)	45,748.60	42,486.30	26,079.30
Employment (number of workers)	12,000	16,610	5,122
VA/employment (thousands of USD)	8.31	8.68	17.75
Wage bills/employment (thousands of USD)	3.81	2.56	8.36
Exports (thousands of USD)	108,298.60	141,915.90	91,260.90

Source: Author's preparation using data from Nicita and Olarreaga (2007).

Table 7.12   Importance of the clothing sector in total manufacturing

	1981	1991	2001
% Gross product	3.85	5.47	3.95
% VA	2.7	4.89	2.63
% Employment	7.81	10.4	5.27
% Exports	3.67	2.31	4

Source: Author's preparation using data from Nicita and Olarreaga (2007).

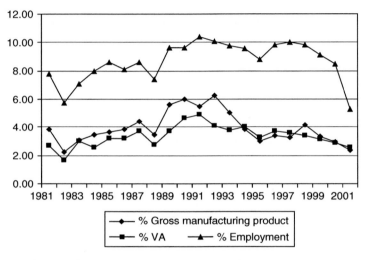

Figure 7.7   Share of the clothing sector in total manufacturing
Source: Author's preparation based on data from Nicita and Olarreaga (2007).

As can be seen from Table 7.11, production, value added, employment and exports all increased in the 1981–1991 period, before falling between 1991 and 2001. The evolution of the sector is shown in Table 7.12.

7.3.2   Evolution of production, value added and employment

Figure 7.7 shows the share of the clothing sector in total manufacturing between 1981 and 2001 in terms of gross product, value added and employment. The sector grew in terms of all of these variables until the start of the 1990s and declined thereafter. In 1981, clothing production amounted to 3.85 per cent of total manufacturing product, in 1992 it increased to 6.23 per cent but then decreased, and in 2001 the figure was 2.35 per cent.

The index of physical volume for the period 1993–2001 (base year 1988) also shows a decrease (Figure 7.8) which is greater than that of the manufacturing sector as a whole.

Figure 7.8 Physical volume index
Source: Own preparation, data from Instituto Nacional de Estadistica.

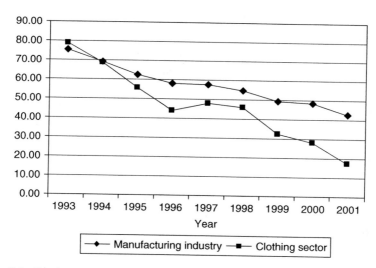

Figure 7.9 Employment index
Source: Own preparation, data from Instituto Nacional de Estadistica.

The index of employment exhibits the same trend (Figure 7.9). The index of physical volume and of workers employed show a decrease in the period 1993–2001. This fall was greater than the decline in manufacturing as a whole.

There are a number of reasons for the poor performance of the sector. First, trade protection lessened in the 1990s, and it was reduced still further in 1997 with the lowering of tariffs included in the Mercosur adjustment regime. In this period the cotton products sub-sector practically disappeared. In addition, Brazil devalued its currency in 1999, making Uruguay even less competitive, and the economy went into a period of recession. The evolution of the price of clothing products in the domestic market was very stable from 1993 until 1999. In fact, in 1999 clothing prices increased less than the Consumer Price Index, and they actually fell in 2000 and 2001.

7.3.2.1 *Employment and informality*

The clothing sector is characterized by low investment requirements, relatively skilled workers and small-scale production, and these features permit a high degree of informality in the sector. The Ministry of Industry and Energy's (MIEM – Ministerio de Industria y Energia) estimations of informality, measured as industrial production and consumption, found that 60 per cent of the manufacturing sector was operating informally.

Uruguay's clothing sector is characterized by a high level of informality, and garments produced informally are usually sold in street markets and 'expo fairs'. The clothing sold at these 'expo fairs' is usually made either by the stall owners themselves or by other informal producers. These outlets compete with formal shops, and usually they do not have registered accountants or pay VAT or other taxes. Most of the apparel they sell is casual clothing made of cotton or synthetic fibres.

There are other informal groups in the clothing sector, including dressmakers and people who work at home making hand- or machine-knitted products and supplying formal and informal shops. Yet another element in this panorama is that clothing is smuggled in from abroad. With informality so widespread, it is hard to estimate the real extent of work or employment in this sector.

7.3.3 The evolution of imports

In the 1990s the sector was affected by trade liberalization and the creation of the Mercosur, and it was exposed to increased competition in the domestic market from imports. Figure 7.10 shows the evolution of imports in relation to manufacturing product in the sector.

7.3.4 The evolution of exports

Table 7.13 shows the evolution of exports and export propensity in the clothing sector. Exports increased between 1981 and 1992 and then fell thereafter. The sector is strongly oriented to exports, as measured by the proportion of exports in gross clothing sector product. However, the weight of clothing sector exports in total exports decreased after 1992. The overall export fall in the 1990s was due to a decrease in exports to the other members of the

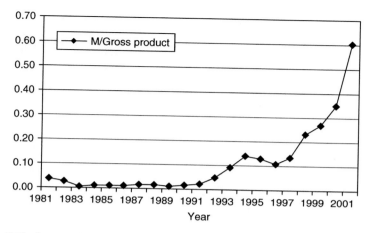

Figure 7.10 Imports in the clothing sector in relation to gross product
Source: Own preparation with data from Nicita and Olarreaga (2007).

Table 7.13 Exports and export propensity of the sector

Year	Exports (thousands of dollars)	X/gross product (%)	X/total manufacturing exports (%)
1981	108,298.60	46.44	11.98
1982	79,076.36	74.77	12.41
1983	89,024.53	93.33	9.85
1984	103,341.80	90.03	12.72
1985	75,297.70	65.39	9.93
1986	92,264.38	66.97	9.59
1987	134,706.00	78.60	12.34
1988	127,220.90	91.61	10.78
1989	141,746.60	51.38	10.56
1990	130,084.90	41.76	8.90
1991	141,915.90	40.36	10.63
1992	155,904.70	38.11	10.52
1993	119,544.30	37.21	8.33
1994	116,987.80	46.03	6.79
1995	113,061.30	49.24	6.24
1996	122,404.40	48.63	5.79
1997	130,452.70	51.58	5.53
1998	125,839.70	55.32	5.17
1999	92,091.59	54.45	4.96
2000	88,562.34	70.33	4.45
2001	70,335.50	84.78	4.04

Source: Author's preparation based on data from Nicita and Olarreaga (2007).

Table 7.14   Coverage rate and regional orientation index for the clothing sector

Year	Coverage rate			Regional orientation index		
	Leather and hides	Textiles	Total	Leather and hides	Textiles	Total
1990	184.5	9.9	17.4	0.1	1.1	0.6
1991	122.8	7.3	12.5	0.1	1.3	0.8
1992	74.2	4.9	8.1	0.1	1.4	0.8
1993	111.5	2.5	4.2	0.1	1.3	0.8
1994	91	2.1	3.7	0.1	1.5	0.9
1995	77.9	2.4	4	0.2	1.7	1.1
1996	69.2	2.7	4.3	0.2	1.7	1.1
1997	85.6	2.7	3.7	0.2	1.8	1.3
1998	58.8	2.5	3.4	0.1	1.6	1.2
1999	49	2.1	3	0.1	1.8	1.2
2000	47.8	1.9	2.8	0.1	1.5	1.0
2001	52.3	1.2	1.9	0.1	1.5	0.9

Source: Terra et al. (2004).

Mercosur, although exports to other countries such as Mexico did increase. Between 1993 and 2001 the item that was exported most, by type of fibre, was clothing produced with wool, and apparel produced with synthetic materials was the biggest single item in exports to Mercosur members. The export of clothing produced from cotton has almost disappeared in the last years under consideration (Terra et al., 2004).

A more detailed picture can be obtained using data from the National Customs Department (Division Nacional de Aduanas) for the period 1990–2001. This allows a distinction to be made between two types of export products, clothing made of leather and clothing produced from textiles. Between 1990 and 2001 the export performance of these two main types differed in that textiles clothing followed the behaviour of the clothing sector as a whole while the export of leather products decreased. It can be seen from Table 7.14 that both of these sub-sectors have a clear export orientation. The sub-sector with the greatest weight in total sector exports is clothing made from textiles. A comparison of the two sub-sectors shows that clothing made from leather and hides is more oriented to exports and that extra-regional markets for these goods are more important than regional ones.

Table 7.15 shows the main markets for the two sub-sectors. In recent years, the Mercosur became less important as an export destination while there was a growth in sales to Mexico, Canada and the United States. The main destination for leather clothing is the United States, which takes 66.4 per cent of the total volume exported by this sub-sector. In 2000 and 2001 the export destination profile of the textiles clothing sub-sector changed considerably.

Table 7.15 Main export markets for clothing sector products

	EU 15	Southeast Asia	Mercosur	Other Aladi	US and Canada	Rest of the World
Value of clothing of leather as % of total clothing of leather						
1990	50.1	4.3	4.9	2.5	33.1	5.0
1991	52.9	2.9	3.6	4.0	30.3	6.4
1992	50.5	3.2	2.5	7.6	30.2	6.1
1993	43.3	1.6	4.5	7.9	33.9	8.7
1994	44.5	2.6	5.8	6.4	33.7	6.9
1995	45.8	1.7	8.0	8.8	30.0	5.6
1996	39.6	3.1	9.7	14.3	22.8	10.5
1997	54.3	10.0	10.0	13.6	12.4	8.5
1998	59.6	7.3	7.3	15.3	10.3	6.6
1999	63.1	5.2	5.2	16.9	11.5	2.6
2000	56.6	6.1	6.1	11.5	17.1	6.9
2001	48.1	3.7	3.7	14.9	28.9	2.6
Value of clothing of textiles as % of total clothing of textiles						
1990	4.1	0.7	31.4	3.3	54.3	6.2
1991	6.1	1.0	41.3	3.8	38.3	9.6
1992	5.8	0.9	37.9	4.8	35.8	14.8
1993	4.4	0.9	50.9	7.9	27.7	8.3
1994	4.5	1.1	68.4	9.2	15.3	1.5
1995	0.8	1.2	83.5	2.9	10.6	1.0
1996	0.8	0.8	79.4	5.0	12.5	1.5
1997	1.5	0.2	87.8	3.3	6.6	0.5
1998	3.3	0.0	80.4	5.5	10.0	0.8
1999	5.2	0.2	75.6	9.7	9.1	0.2
2000	5.0	0.2	64.9	18.0	11.6	0.3
2001	5.0	0.2	62.0	21.0	11.2	0.5

Source: Department of Economics (2004).

In 1998 the main destination was the Mercosur, which took 87.9 per cent of the total value exported, however, by 2001 the share had fallen to 62 per cent.

The sector's main export products in terms of the value of exports are leather and hide apparel and accessories, and knitted wool sweaters.

7.3.5 The evolution of labour productivity

Labour productivity, defined as value added per worker in United States dollars, increased between 1981 and 1995 and then fell somewhat, but remained at a higher level than in the 1980s (Figure 7.11).

Figure 7.12 shows total factor productivity (TFP). It can be seen that TFP in the clothing sector was similar to that of manufacturing as a whole.

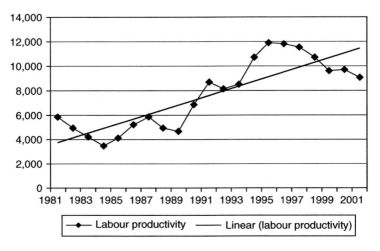

Figure 7.11   Evolution of labour productivity
Source: Author's preparation with data from Nicita and Olarreaga (2007).

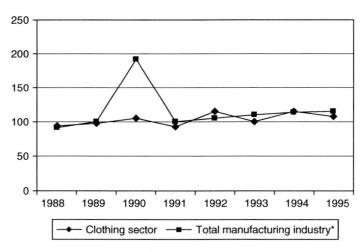

Figure 7.12   Total factor productivity, clothing and total manufacturing, 1988–1995
*Includes the clothing sector
Source: Own preparation, data from Casacuberta et al. (2003).

7.3.6   Cost structure

Table 7.16 shows the cost structure of the sector according to the input–output matrix for 1997 drawn up by the Central Bank of Uruguay. It shows the share of the various inputs used in the production of clothing. It can be

Table 7.16 Cost structure of the clothing sector

Cost Structure	%
Agriculture	0.80
Food, beverages and tobacco	0.30
Textiles	29.00
Wearing apparel	0.10
Tanneries and leather products	5.85
Wood, paper and printing	0.10
Chemical products	0.60
Other manufacturing industries	1.90
Electricity, gas and water	1.20
Other services	0.70
Other expenditures	22.55
Total intermediate consumption	63.10
Total value added	36.90
Total gross product	100.00

Source: Banco Central del Uruguay.

seen that textile goods are important as they accounted for 46 per cent of sector inputs in that year.

7.3.7 Factors that affect the competitiveness of the clothing sector

The factors that affect the competitiveness of the Uruguayan clothing sector are similar to those that affect textiles. In the 1990s the value of the currency rose and this led to unfavourable exchange rates, which was an important factor in making the sector less competitive. Another factor was trade policy, and the sub-sector manufacturing apparel from cotton did not survive the liberalization of trade in the 1990s. In addition, there were negative impacts due to informality in the sector and a fall in domestic demand.

In interviews, some actors in the sector indicated that international demand for Uruguayan clothing is based largely on the reliability of export firms, a reasonable cost/quality ratio, the maintenance of standards in production, the fact that small quantities are involved, a good record for meeting delivery deadlines, flexibility and communication. Domestic demand was not very dynamic in the 1990s, and it decreased when recession came in 1999.

Management training in this sector started in the 1980s. The beginning of the 1990s witnessed another development – with the emergence of industrial design firms. In 1992 the first five designers to specialize in textile design and fashion graduated from the new Industrial Design Centre. At the time of writing, there are a number of schools and institutes that give training in design and fashion: the Industrial Design Centre, the ORT, the Enterprise

University (Universidad de la Empresa), the Strasser School, and the Peter Hamers Fashion Academy.

7.3.7.1 *Trade mechanisms specific for the sector*

At the beginning of the 1990s the sector was protected by the Minimum Export Prices regime that provided extraordinary tariff protection for extra-regional and regional exports. This mechanism began to be dismantled in 1995, there was a reduction in the number of protected items, and it was no longer applied to exports to the region. The MEP continued to operate until the end of 2000 and was then replaced by specific import duties for countries that were not members of the Mercosur. Specific import duties were eliminated in 2002.

7.3.7.2 *Other policies*

The clothing sector has taken advantage of the general regime to promote exports. This is based on rebates for indirect taxes paid and pre-financing for exports, which is important for firms that export. The general mechanism to promote investment, which allows capital goods to be imported free of taxes, has been of benefit to firms in this sector, particularly in the knitwear sub-sector. The temporary admission regime allows fabrics (and synthetic cloth, sewing thread, linings, buttons and yarn) to be imported without paying taxes if they are inputs to produce final goods that are exported.

The textiles and clothing sectors have also benefited from Pineda's Law, which is a specific measure for the two sectors whereby export goods made with home-produced wool are subsidized. These policies have been important in helping to create and develop the sector, and in the 1980s trade protection and export promotion policies were a major factor in its growth.

7.3.7.3 *Evolution and main features of exporting firms*

At the beginning of the 1990s the larger firms exported to the world market, principally to the United States. Following this, the US market went into recession and the dollar gained in value against European currencies, making it difficult for the textiles and clothing sector to export to the United States.

These difficulties in selling to the United States and extra-regional markets caused Uruguayan firms to reorient their exports to Brazil and Argentina between 1992 and 1998. In 1999 there was a devaluation in Brazil and recessions in Argentina and Uruguay, and many firms were forced to close down. Even some of the bigger export firms had to quit the market or adapt to decreased sales, although some did manage to reorient their exports to other destinations. Firms in the knitted apparel and leather clothing sub-sectors were able to continue selling to the United States throughout the period.

7.3.7.4 Other factors that affect the competitiveness of the sector

The interviews with entrepreneurs have shed light on some of the factors that affect the competitiveness of the sector. There is excessive bureaucracy, the response time is slow and there is a lack of flexibility. The evolution of the exchange rate also gives cause for concern. These actors also feel that the level of competitiveness is poor because public service charges are high and telecommunications are expensive. Another point to note is that the sector has not used subsidies available from the National Science, Technology and Innovation Board (DINACYT) to develop innovation projects.

The entrepreneurs interviewed do not consider that the Agreement on Textiles and Clothing (ATC) has brought about an improvement in market access. The general opinion is that access to foreign markets would be improved by bilateral preferential trade agreements, especially with the United States. A few years ago an agreement was made with Mexico, and this is seen as a great success for the sector. Another aspect of the situation is that in the Mercosur there are still some non-tariff barriers such as domestic taxes on imported products and other regulations that work against free trade in the bloc.

7.4 Institutions

7.4.1 The Uruguayan Chamber of Industries

The Uruguayan Chamber of Industries (CIU – Camara de Industrias del Uruguay) is a private organization which represents the country's industrial sector. It was set up on 12 November 1898 to promote the interests of Uruguayan industries, to defend their rights and to encourage industrial development in the country. In order to accomplish these objectives it seeks constructive dialogue with the government and with workers. The CIU represents not only the bigger industries and small enterprises with manufacturing activity, but also industrial associations representing more than 50 sectors. Inside the country, the CIU plays an active role in different business organizations and institutions, and it is one of the members of the Higher Entrepreneurial Council.

Internationally, it represents employers before the International Labour Organization (ILO) and at the International Employers Organization (IEO). In addition, it is a member of the Mercosur Industrial Board, which is made up of the Argentine Industrial Union, the Brazilian National Confederation of Industries, the Paraguayan Industrial Union and the CIU. The CIU Board of Directors, which is elected every two years in a secret ballot by chamber members, is responsible for running the institution. In order to make CIU activities more efficient different advisory committees have been set up. These are made up of entrepreneurs and experts specialized in each subject, and presided over by members of the Board of Directors. In November 2000, the CIU quality management system received ISO 9001 certification. The CIU provides entrepreneurs with a range of technical services. It offers advice on the industrialists' needs and runs 'tailor-made' services such as technical assistance, business cooperation, training, technology, information, origin certification, advisory services and publications.

The link between enterprises and the CIU is the Member's Attention Unit. Here firms receive assistance and information on the scope of each of the services offered, and this facilitates the relationship with the technicians responsible for each service. In the CIU there are employers' organizations that represent the interests of the various industrial activities involved. For the textiles and clothing sector these are the Chamber of Clothing, the Association of Manufacturers of Knitted Fabric Clothes, and the Chamber of Textile Industries. These organizations have played an important role in coordinating negotiations for these sectors, such as in foreign trade agreements, wage agreements and anti-dumping measures (reference prices and minimum export prices). They have also promoted access to markets, marketing mechanisms, and consultancy and sector studies.

7.4.2   Uruguayan Technological Laboratory (LATU – Laboratorio Tecnologico del Uruguay)

The LATU was set up in April 1965 as a mixed (public and private) organization. It is a non-state public law entity administered by a directorate made up of representatives from the current presidential administration, members of the Chamber of Industry and representatives from the Bank of the Republic. The LATU's mission is to analyse, optimize, find solutions, and develop different aspects of technological processes or products. The services it offers include technological development, consultancy in technology, applied research, training, the management of technological projects, and the organization of trade fairs, exhibitions and meetings. The LATU started implementing a quality management system in 1993, and today it runs an ISO 9000 Quality Certification Programme.

The LATU has a textiles department that carries out research in areas like comparing different clothes production processes with a view to meeting the needs of the market. This involves fabric design analysis, finishing, and improving process and products performance. It also offers different kinds of training with courses, conferences, organized visits in the industry and courses designed specifically to meet customer needs.

7.4.3   Uruguayan Wool Secretariat (SUL – Secretariado Uruguayo de la Lana)

This organization's mission is to promote all activities to do with the production and manufacture of wool. It has played an important role in helping wool producers to improve both the production and the quality of their wool.

It also contributes to quality control on exports of raw and processed wool, for which it has a cooperation agreement with the LATU. The wool industry in Uruguay is mainly oriented to export markets. Eighty per cent of the wool produced is exported as wool tops, and another 10 per cent is processed by the local textile manufacturing industry to produce fabrics and garments for export and also for home consumption.

The Uruguayan Wool Secretariat (SUL), which was set up in 1968, is a reflection of the importance of the country's wool industry. It is a private organization founded by wool producers and its aims are to support and promote the production, processing and consumption of wool. SUL has a technical staff of thirty, and in line with its mission it engages in a wide range of activities, including applied research in aspects of sheep farming, the transfer of new technological techniques, sheep breeding programmes, shearer training courses, wool market analysis and information, the promotion of Uruguayan wool, and cooperation with the government, manufacturers and the wool trade. It also operates its own experimental station and a wool laboratory that is recognized by Interwoollabs and services wool producers, exporters, top-makers, research programmes, and Uruguayan Woolmark licensees.

There is a particular emphasis on farmers adopting production technology geared to improving the quantity and quality of wool produced, and the development of stricter wool harvesting and handling procedures in order to eliminate contamination and improve the quality of Uruguayan tops. These programmes are run jointly in cooperation with local processors and exporters. Since SUL came into being in 1968, Uruguay has been a member of the International Wool Secretariat (IWS), whose objectives were research, innovation and the promotion of wool in the world. The IWS changed into the Woolmark Company and New Zealand and South Africa withdrew, but Uruguay decided to remain as an affiliate member of the new company, supporting its activities, maintaining control and running the administration of Woolmark in Uruguay.

7.5 Public industrial policies

In this section we present the main public policies in Uruguay that are geared to promoting industry in general, and specific policies for the textiles and clothing sector. Public policies to promote the industrial sector include investment promotion policies, export promotion policies and specific sector policies for the textiles and clothing sector. Investment promotion policies include the Investment Promotion Law of 1974, the Investment Law of 1998, the free trade zone regime and the capital goods import regime. General measures to promote exports include the tax rebate regime, the export-financing regime, the temporary admission regime, and export insurance. The textiles and clothing sector has benefited from Pineda's Law, which involves a regime of tax rebates for exports with domestic wool content.

7.5.1 Investment promotion policies

7.5.1.1 *Industrial Promotion Law*

The aim of this law (Decree Law 14.178 of March 1974) is to promote industrial activities that the Presidency has declared to be 'in the national interest'.

The declaration of national interest and the concession of promotion measures have to be oriented to some of the following objectives:

a. greater efficiency in production and commercialization,
b. the increase and diversification of export goods with higher value added,
c. the generation of new industries and the widening or reform of existing ones, if this involves a greater use of domestic inputs and employment,
d. support for technological research programmes oriented to the use of domestic raw materials and to promoting human resources and quality control,
e. the development of services (excluding financing) so long as this translates into growth in industrial or tourist fishing.

The investment promotion measures in question include credit assistance, taxes exemptions and the channelling of savings.

7.5.1.1.1 Credit assistance. Credit assistance measures include (partially or totally) the following:

a. Credits for periods not exceeding twenty years, of up to 75 per cent of the value of the buildings and works to be constructed for the installation of a new industry or to expand an existing one.
b. Credits to buy home-produced or imported equipment and machinery, for a period not exceeding eight years, and of up to 80 per cent of the cost.
c. Credits to buy domestic inputs to manufacture and export goods, for a period not exceeding one year, and of up to 80 per cent of the cost.
d. Credits to carry out projects to analyze technological and economic feasibility.
e. Credits for expenditure and the installations of a project, for a period not exceeding two year after the plant has started production.
f. Credits in foreign currency to buy equipment and special materials overseas.
g. Credits in foreign currency to buy inputs abroad to be processed in Uruguay and exported.

7.5.1.1.2 Tax exemption. Tax exemption includes total or partial exemption from taxes, and reduction in the prices or charges for services that are supported by the state.

7.5.1.1.3 Channelling savings. The benefit of channelling savings is that physical persons or legal entities can deduct the amount invested when paying IRIC (the tax on income for industrial and commercial firms).

The Executive Power ran this scheme with assistance from an Industrial Promotion Unit at the Ministry of Industry. This unit was in charge of analysing whether a particular activity was in the national interest, and calculating amounts, repayment periods and other benefits. Table 7.17 shows textiles and clothing projects that were declared to be in the national interest in the period 1992–98. Under this scheme, over the period from 1992 to 1997 investment in physical assets for the textiles and clothing sector amounted to US$9.5 million per year. The benefits granted were mainly fiscal exemption

Table 7.17   Projects of national interest, 1992–1997

Firm	Res.	Loc.	Investment (millions of US dollars)						
			1992 AF	1993 AF	1994 IT	1995 IT	1996 IT	1997 AF	1997 CT
Atersa SA	1	M						0.74	0.23
Cedetex SA	2	I					3.62		
Comex SA	1	M						0.4	0.17
Dancotex SA	1	M		1.63					
Encatex SA	2	M	0.49				1.06		
Fabril Exportadora SA	2	I	0.96						
Generacion 2001 SA	1	M	0.94						
Hipertex SA	2	M						0.25	0.5
Hisud SA	1	I					5.3		
Lanas Trinidad	1	I		4.12					
Lordix SA	1	M		3.15					
Medea SA	2	M						1.15	0.01
Others	4	M	0.33					0.11	0.01
Paylana SA	2	I	0.02					2.63	0.98
Polimeros Uruguayos SA	1	I					4.74		
Prili SA	2	M	0.53						
Fafael Facciolo	1	M	0.39						
Rajchman y Hnos. SA	2	I				1.88		1.1	
Rualer SA	1	I							
Sudamtex SA	4	I		3.76	24				
Tagle SA	1	M	0.23						
Textil Uruguaya SA	1	M	0.24						
Twins SA	1	M							
Total			4.13	12.66		25.88	14.72	6.38	1.9

Re: number of resolutions, Loc: location, M: Montevideo, I: outside Montevideo.
Source: Department of Economics, School of Social Sciences, University of the Republic, 2004.

since credit assistance was not in operation at that time. In 1998 the Investment Law (Law 16.906 of January 1998) came into force. This allowed the Executive Power to concede the fiscal benefits established in the Industrial Promotion Law for investments declared to be in the national interest.

7.5.1.2   *Investment Law (Law 16.906 of January 1998)*

This law makes it possible to declare the promotion and protection of certain investments in the country to be in the national interest. It involves fiscal benefits and it allows to the Executive Power to grant other benefits to manufacturing and agricultural activities. These benefits apply in particular to investments that involve technical progress, increased value added and employment, the diversification of exports, fostering small enterprises and contributing to geographical de-centralization. The Executive Power acts in consultation with the Application Commission, which is made up of representatives from ministries and the Budget and Planning Office.

The production of textiles with domestic wool has been declared to be in the national interest. This benefit came into operation at the same time that Pineda's Law, which involved rebates for exports from the textile and clothing sector, was overturned. Table 7.18 shows the textile and clothing sector industrial projects declared to be in the national interest in the period 1998–2001. Appendix Table 7.1 gives the objectives of these projects.

7.5.1.3   *Free Trade Zone Regime (Law 15.921 of December 1987)*

Law 15.921, which comes under Decree 454/988, stipulates that the promotion and development of free trade zones is in the national interest. The aim of this law is to promote investment, increase exports, increase employment and promote integration into the world economy. Free trade zones are specific areas in the country – under public or private ownership – where industrial, commercial and service activities are carried out. These activities are exempt from all domestic taxes.

7.5.1.4   *Capital, information technology and telecommunication goods import regime*

It is laid down in Decree 479/982 of 1982 that capital goods liable to tariffs of over 10 per cent and which are not produced in the country shall pay a tariff of 6 per cent. In 1986, Decree 317/986 stipulated a set of activities, including the manufacture of textiles and clothing, to be in the national interest. This decree exempts firms in these sectors that export from having to pay tariffs and VAT when they import machinery and equipment, so long as these resources are not produced in the country. Decree 548/988 of 1988 exempts firms that export from having to pay the 6 per cent tariff when they

Table 7.18   Projects of national interest, 1998–2001

Firm	Res.	Loc.	1998 AF	1998 CT	1999 AF	1999 CT	2000 AF	2000 CT	2001 AF	2001 CT
Dancotex SA	2	M	4.8	0.47	1.13					
Darcy SA	3	I					0.48	0.47		
Filaner SA	1	M								
Hipertex SA	2		0.36				0.32			
Kabyr Confecciones SA	1	M	1.3	0.05						
Kamaris SA	1	I					0.77	0.3		
Lanera Piedra Alta SA	1	M								
Lavadero de Lanas Biengio	1	M	1.46							
Martex SA	1	I			1.42					
Medea SA	2	I	1.61	0.22	0.6		0.94	0.08		
Monbebe SA	1	M	2.58	0.87						
Paylana SA	2	M			1.55				1.51	0.05
Prili SA	2	M	0.31	0						
Rajchman y Hnos. SA	1	I			1.05					
Reston Uruguay SA	1	I			1.56					
Rualer SA	1	M			0.41					
Textil Montevideana SA	1	M								
Tops Fray Marcos SA	1	I							13.17	1.59
Twins SA	1	I	0.23							
Others	3	I			0.16	0.02				
Total			12.65	1.61	7.88	0.02	2.51	0.85	14.68	1.64

Re: number of resolutions, Loc: location, M: Montevideo, I: outside Montevideo.
Source: Department of Economics, School of Social Sciences, University of the Republic, 2004.

import spare parts or equipment components for up to 3 per cent of the value of their exports over the course of the previous six months.

In mid-1993 there was a Mercosur agreement about a number of products and sectors under the Common External Tariff (CET) regime. However, it was difficult to reach agreement about the CET for capital, information technology, and telecommunication goods. There were two positions: Brazil wanted a high CET for these goods, but Argentina and Uruguay wanted zero CET for them. In the end it was agreed that the CET should be 14 per cent for capital goods and 16 per cent for information technology and telecommunication goods, with lineal and automatic convergences to these levels. The implementation process started in 1991 with a tariff of 0 per cent for these goods and it was supposed to finish by 2010, but it was ended in 2001 because of the recession in Argentina and Uruguay.

7.5.2　Export promotion policies

Export promotion policies included general and specific measures for the textiles and clothing sectors. The general policies included the tax rebate regime, the export financing regime, the temporary admission regime and export insurance.

7.5.2.1　*Indirect tax, direct tax and VAT rebate regime*

There are two tax rebate regimes: the indirect tax rebate system instituted in the 1960s, and the tax rebate regime of the 1990s. In addition, there is also a VAT reimbursement system to promote exports. It was laid down in Law 13.269 of July 1964 that the indirect tax rebate regime should consist of rebates of up to 20 per cent of the fob value of exported goods paying domestic taxes, and reimbursement for tariffs paid on imported inputs for goods that would be exported. In 1967 these benefits were extended to exports of goods that used wool as inputs (textiles and clothing). In 1970 the rebate was raised to 40 and 50 per cent for products made of wool.

In 1990, as part of fiscal adjustment in the country, these measures were suspended. By mid-1991 the fiscal situation had improved, and the regime of rebates for indirect taxes on exports was reintroduced with Decree 393/991. The list of products covered by the regime is the same as before, but the amounts and percentages of rebates are lower. These measures were to be provisional until new and definitive criteria for rebates on indirect taxes were established. In Law 16.492 of 1994, a provisional direct tax rebate regime for all exported good was instituted. The rebate was to be 2.5 per cent of the fob value of the exported goods. Goods that benefited from rebates of indirect taxes for values higher than this retained their benefits, and those with benefits below this level received a supplementary payment. Exports of wool products received an additional benefit of 0.4 per cent and those of leather 1.15 per cent.

At the end of 1994 these provisional regulations were overturned by Decree 558/994, covering Law 16.492. Under the provisions of Decree 512/996 of 1996, the indirect and direct tax rebate regimes were adjusted to comply with common Mercosur nomenclature, and one system of regulations was brought in for the list of product and rebate amounts. Between 1977 and 2001 the tax rebate regime was prorogued several times, and it was suspended in 2002 because of the economic crisis in the country. Under the provisions of Decree 220/998, firms exporting goods and services are exempt from having to pay VAT on goods used to produce the exported good.

7.5.2.2　*Export financing regime*

This regime grants exporters access to credit at preferential interest rates for the production the goods in question or their sale on foreign markets.

Table 7.19   Imports under the temporary admission regime (US$ million)

Sector	1999	2000	2001
Textile	5.18	12.55	12.19
Clothing-Textile	8.1	7.6	5.2
Clothing-Leather	13.5	9.5	12

Source: Department of Economics, School of Social Sciences, University of the Republic (2004).

7.5.2.3   Temporary admission regime

The temporary admission regime grants benefits to industries that export goods produced in the country using foreign raw materials. In the Mercosur negotiations, entrepreneurs are concerned about this question and want to see the temporary admission regime maintained. This also applies to the capital, information technology and telecommunication goods import regime, and to the special agricultural input import regime. Table 7.19 shows the values imported under the regime by the main textile and clothing exporters.

7.5.2.4   Export insurance

Export credit insurance is a mechanism to protect exporters from the risk of not being paid in the credits given to firms importing from abroad. In Uruguay the Banco de Seguros del Estado is the only insurance institution that offers insurance for export credits.

7.5.2.5   The regime of reimbursements for textile and clothing exports containing home-produced wool

It is laid down in article 80 of Law 13.695 of 1968 that, as part of the move to promote wool industrialization, firms exporting fabrics or apparel would be eligible for a 22 per cent rebate of the fob value of such goods. Decree-Law 14.926 of 1979 made it possible for the Executive Power to reduce the rate of reimbursement or to eliminate it altogether. At the beginning of the 1990s, wool fabrics and apparel exports enjoyed an 18 per cent rebate. In March 1990, as part of a policy to reduce the effective protection rate, the Executive Power reduced the rebate by 2 per cent from June 1990, and by another two percentage points from January 1991.

In Decree 430/990 of September 1990 there was a further rebate reduction of 2 points to take effect as of July 1991, 3 per cent from January 1992, and another 3 per cent from July 1992. In July 1992, in Decree 315/992, this final reduction was postponed for a year. In mid-1993, under the provisions of Decree 287/993, the prevailing 9 per cent rebate rate was maintained and extended for a further year. It was also laid down that the rebate would be entirely eliminated as of 1 July 1994, when the general indirect tax regime would be applied to the sector. In Decree 204/994 of May 1994 the prevailing rebate rate was extended until 30 April 1995 – with the aim of eliminating it completely on 1 May of that year. In March 1995, the provisions of Decree 204/994 were prorogued until 30 June 1995 by Decree 127/995.

In June 1995, Decree 235/995 prorogued the prevailing rebate rate again, until 31 December of that year, and set a reduction of three percentage points for the period between 1 January 1996 and 30 June 1996. Yet again, this new decrease was not put into effect, and Decree 456/995 prorogued the rate prevailing on 31 December 1995 for a year. In December 1996, the rate was prorogued again (Decree 472/996) until 30 June 1998. After that the 9 per cent rate was prorogued for 12 months three more times by a new decree each year (135/998, 172/999, 189/000). In June 2001, the termination date that had been set in Decree 189/000 was postponed for six months (Decree 249/001), and in December of that year there was another six-month postponement (Decree 529/001). In June 2002 it was postponed again (Decree 246/002), but this time only for 90 days. There was one more postponement (Decree 330/002), but finally on 30 June 2003 the regime of rebates for wool-based textiles and clothing exports was finally eliminated.

There was an attempt to compensate for the negative impact of losing this benefit by increasing the aliquots of rebates on the taxes in question: generally, they were approximately doubled (Decree 525/001). This compensated products made from home-produced wool to about 50 per cent for the loss of the rebate. Table 7.20 shows the evolution of the rebates for textiles and clothing with home-produced wool content between 1995 and 2001. In 2001 the rebate was raised above the 2000 rate, but it was still considerably lower than the rate in preceding years. This reduced use of the regime coincided with the fall in exports.

Table 7.20   Evolution of the rebate for textiles and clothing exports

Year	Amount
1995	1,681
1996	1,485
1997	1,902
1998	1,712
1999	2,003
2000	995
2001	1,200

Source: Department of Economics, School of Social Sciences, University of the Republic, 2004.
Note: Amount is in thousands of US dollars.

7.5.3 Trade policy

In this section we outline some trade policy instruments, including the minimum export price and specific duties regime, the trade liberalization programme, and the customs union final adjustment regime.

7.5.3.1 Minimum export prices and specific duties

At the beginning of the 1990s, reference prices (RPs) and minimum export prices (MEPs) constituted an important and highly effective protection instrument applied in particular to products in the textiles and clothing sector. Reference prices (RPs) were promulgated at the end of 1979 (Decree 787/979) and came into use at the end of 1981. The RP establishes a fixed value per unit of physical volume for a given item, and taxes are calculated on this if it is higher than the import price. The declared aim of RPs is that they provide a defence against unfair trade practices. The anti-dumping law (Decree-Law 15.025), which incorporates multilateral regulations on dumping and subsidies, requires that evidence of unfair trade practices be submitted, evidence of damage or cause of damage and evidence that there is a causal relationship between the unfair practices and the damage. These requirements were such that the regulations were not applied and there was systematic recourse to RPs and MEPs.

At the beginning of 1983, the MEPs were instituted (Decree 5/983) as a mechanism for cases in which the use of RPs was insufficient to prevent damage to home production caused by unfair trade practices. In the MEP system, a fixed value is set per unit of physical volume of a given item, and if the import price is lower than the MEP the importer has to pay the difference between the two prices – the so-called adjustable surcharge (*recargo movil*) – and taxes on imports are calculated not on the real price but on the MEP. The aim of the decree was to provide an instrument that was easier to apply than the anti-dumping law because it allowed the fact that there were marked price differences for imported goods to stand as evidence of unfair trade practices, which obviated the need for proof.

In the first half of the 1990s, in response to the need for procedures for employing MEPs, a mechanism to fix MEP levels was introduced, and the rules governing applications for them were stiffened. The regime had to become more transparent in order to comply with multilateral regulations, and this made it increasingly difficult to obtain additional protection in line with GATT rules. In spite of this, MEPs were used intensively throughout the 1990s – albeit with decreasing intensity – in response to the greater exposure to foreign competition that resulted from generalized trade opening. From 1995 onwards MEPs were applied only to imported products that did not originate in the other member countries of the Mercosur. MEPs were abolished in November 2000 in line with Uruguay's commitments to the World Trade Organization (WTO) and the Mercosur.[4]

The MEP system was replaced by a system of specific import rights (SIR), which were applied for the first time at the end of 2000 for products in the textiles and clothing sector. This SIR mechanism (Decree 394/000) was used to fix a value per unit of physical volume of a given item, this was then compared to the value that resulted from applying the general customs tariff, and the importer had to pay the higher of the two. This system for textile and clothing imports from countries that were not members of the Mercosur was prorogued several times, the last of which ran until 30 June 2002.

7.5.3.2   Trade liberalization programme and customs union adjustment regime

The trade liberalization programme in the Treaty of Asunción sets a target of 100 per cent preference for intra-bloc trade in accordance with a schedule of linear, automatic customs duty reductions for the lowest import tariffs prevailing in each member country on 1 January 1991, for products from countries not belonging to the ALADI. This tariff reduction mechanism was to come into effect in June 1991, with a minimum preference margin of 47 per cent, and was to continue with twice-yearly reductions of 7 per cent until there was a zero tariff in December 1994. In the case of most favoured nation tariff reductions, the trade liberalization programme would apply to the new level automatically on the date it came into force.

Exceptions were made for certain items negotiated in the ALADI system by the member countries and for products in the sugar and automobile sectors. Each member country also drew up its own list of exceptions to intra-bloc tariff reduction, and these would be resolved through progressive agreements until they disappeared at the end of 1994 in Argentina and Brazil, and at the end of 1995 in Paraguay and Uruguay. There were 394 items on the Argentinean list, 324 on the Brazilian list, 439 for Paraguay and 960 for Uruguay. In Uruguay, the textiles and clothing sector was given ample coverage on the exceptions list. The Mercosur common external tariff (CET) was agreed at the Ouro Preto meeting in December 1994, and there was also agreement about the transition conditions for the move towards a customs union, which could come into force in January 1995. These included provisional exceptions to the common external tariff and intra-bloc free trade.

The CET ranged from 0 to 20 per cent, with an average of 12 per cent, and there were tariff increases of up to two percentage points depending upon the degree of processing involved in the chain of production. This gave the CET 11 levels. The aliquots for intermediate goods varied between 0 and 12 per cent, those for agricultural products between 10 and 12 per cent, those for capital goods between 12 and 16 per cent, and those for consumer goods ranged from 18 to 20 per cent. This tariff structure was quite similar to the system adopted in Brazil, and to make the CET viable, exceptions had to be allowed. One kind of exception was products included in the adjustment regime, and these had tariffs that were higher than the CET. When linear, automatic reductions were made for all items under the regime, there would be zero tariffs on intra-bloc trade in January 1999 in Argentina and Brazil, and January 2000 in Paraguay and Uruguay. Of Uruguay's 963 products on the list (common Mercosur nomenclature), 230 were in the textile and clothing sector.

7.5.4 Incentives for innovation and training

In Uruguay, a technological development programme is being put into operation. The aim is to make the country's production more competitive through granting non-repayable finance for innovation and training projects. In February 2001 science and technology in the country was given a new structure (Law 17.296) under the Ministry of Education and Culture. Article 308 of this law established a new executive unit, the National Science, Technology and Innovation Board (DINACYT – Dirección Nacional de Ciencia, Tecnología e Innovación), which comes under the Ministry of Education and Culture. The DINACYT's mission is to coordinate, administer, implement and evaluate policy instruments in the area of science, technology and innovation, to strengthen the National Innovation System (SNI – Sistema Nacional de Innovación) and to promote the development of Uruguay's science and technology system.

The main tasks of the DINACYT are to advise the Presidency on these matters through the Ministry of Education and Culture, to administer all funds from whatever source that are allocated, to coordinate, administer and carry out science, technology and innovation development projects resulting from loans from multinational cooperation and finance organizations, to do whatever is necessary in the state administration, and to handle all aspects of international cooperation in the areas of science, technology and innovation. The DINACYT is organized into different departments – international cooperation, information technology and communications, promotion and diffusion, projects and administration management, and programming and policies consultancy.

In addition to being currently responsible for implementing the Technological Development Programme, the DINACYT is in charge of the Clemente Estable Fund and the National Research Fund. The general aim of the Technological Development Programme is to help to mobilize innovation potential to make production more competitive, especially in small and medium-sized enterprises, and to improve the country's capability for scientific and technological development.

The Technological Development Programme will improve the capacity to innovate by generating, using and adapting new technologies in products and in production, management and distribution processes, and in communications and technology. It will also promote efficient management and financing for communications and technology activities, strengthen linkages between centres that generate knowledge and potential knowledge users, foster research into the main social and environmental problems the country is facing, and stimulate the private sector to participate more in the development of communications and technology. The Programme is run with support from the Inter-American Development Bank (IDB) in the form of a loan (contract No. 1293/OC-UR, of 17 March 2001) to the Uruguayan government. This involved setting up a programme coordination unit.

The Programme has funds amounting to US$50 million, made up of US$30 million from the IDB, US$10 million from the Uruguayan government and US$10 million from Uruguayan enterprises, which corresponds to projects in which they will participate. The Programme consists of three sub-programmes: sub-programme I is support for innovation and making enterprises more competitive; sub-programme II is for developing and applying science and technology in areas of opportunity; and sub-programme III is designed to strengthen institutions.

The funds for sub-programme I will go on making Uruguayan enterprises more efficient by promoting innovation in production, management and distribution processes. The aim of sub-programme II is to strengthen research capability and the generation of knowledge that is useful to society. It will finance projects that make a contribution to resolving specific problems in particular areas of opportunity identified by the DINACYT. Sub-programme III is geared to integrating activities in the various areas through three components: (1) strengthening institutions in the National Innovation System; (2) supporting regional and international activities; and (3) providing and disseminating information. As regards training, Decree 840/88 makes it possible to deduct one and a half times the costs of training from the IRIC (company tax) payments.

7.6   Case studies

7.6.1   General observations

The textiles and clothing sectors in Uruguay are going through a difficult period, as has been shown in sections 7.1 and 7.2. To make matters worse, in October–December 2007, when the interviews were carried out, the country failed to reach agreement on a prospective free trade agreement with the United States. This possible agreement would mainly have been of benefit to these sectors, as the entrepreneurs interviewed pointed out, and as has been documented in reports from the Chamber of Industry. The difficult situation and the loss of this chance of easing access to the US market made a number of entrepreneurs and managers unwilling to be interviewed.[5] Some said they were too busy to spare time for an interview, and others kept asking us to phone them back in a few days – a situation that went on for three months.

This is what happened with Dancotex, one of the bigger firms in the sector, which has had a series of problems with its trade union which finally led to an occupation by the workers in January 2007. The owners are being sued for wages that the firm owes to employees.

In another firm, Welcolan SA, the manager flatly refused to be interviewed and explained that he did not want to say 'bad' things about the government. It is worth noting that in 2006 the government, in the form of the Ministry of Industry and Labour and the Presidential Planning and Budget Office, had meetings and worked with entrepreneurs and managers from some firms to define promotion measures for both sectors. The large number of textiles firms that refused to be interviewed has given rise to a methodological problem in this study, and even more firms in the clothing sector declined interviews. The enterprises that agreed to be interviewed were open and receptive, but they are not always the biggest in their sector. Furthermore, in some cases the firms were not willing to give figures on its sales. The selection of firms was based on information in Chamber of Industry reports about their importance in sales and exports.

7.6.2 Textiles sector firms

The textiles sector is made up of firms involved in the washing and manufacture of wool tops and spinning, weaving and finishing. We selected firms belonging to the last sub-sectors on this list since they incorporate more value added. The washing and manufacture of wool tops has lower value added, and it is the sub-sector that, relatively speaking, has been able to cope best with increased competition from foreign markets. Among the biggest firms in this sub-sector are Otegui Hnos. SA, Lanera Santa Maria SA, Laneras Trinidad SA, Lanasur SA, Fabex SA, Central Lanera Uruguaya, and Tops Fray Marcos. Spinning and weaving is also dominated by a few large enterprises. The four biggest are Paylana,[6] Dancotex, Fibratex and Hisud, and they account for 30 per cent, 21 per cent 17 per cent and 10 per cent, respectively, of total exports from the sub-sector (Iroz et al., 2005).

Of the three firms that granted interviews, two were founded in the import substitution period in Uruguay and the other dates from the export promotion period. The economic situations of these firms vary considerably. While one of them can be considered a leader in the sector and, according to the representative interviewed, is doing very well, another (Fibratex) had to close down in January 2007 because of large debts to the state-run Banco República del Uruguay and to private banks.[7] The workers have been organized by the trade union to help to take care of the plant and keep the machinery in good order in the hope that the company will reopen if a solution can be found. The main stockholder has offered to give his shares to the employees, and foreign clients have offered to do the same, if this will help to put the firm back on its feet. The Association of Textiles is having talks with the

Ministry of Industry and Labour, the Ministry of Economics and the Banco Republica del Uruguay to try to reach a solution that will enable the plant to re-open.

7.6.2.1　Paylana

The company representative interviewed was Sonia Goldemberg, a young marketing manager with a degree in Marketing and a postgraduate qualification from the United States in textiles and fashion. The interview lasted approximately one hour, and Miss Goldemberg provided printed material on the firm.

7.6.2.1.1　Main features.

This is the biggest firm we interviewed. Today it is a public limited company, but it started out in 1944 as a family business run by immigrants from Italy. At that time Uruguay was seeking to industrialize and trying to attract foreign investment,[8] and a group of Uruguayan entrepreneurs went to Italy looking for new investors in order to set up a textile plant in Paysandu.[9] Conditions for the investment were agreed, and Italian entrepreneurs travelled to Uruguay and became established in the country. The equipment and machinery was bought in Italy and Italian technicians and workers were hired to work at the plant. In the beginning the enterprise only processed wool, it and was oriented to the domestic market and the fabrics it produced were mainly for men's clothes.

In the 1960s the firm realized that in order to grow they would have to change from just processing wool to production with mixtures of wool with cotton, thread and synthetics, and to reorient sales to developed foreign markets. The firm's strategy changed and it began to specialize in differentiated high-quality fabrics. It also developed a strategy focusing on working in close association with its customers and meeting client needs. This has meant not only having agents in foreign countries but making continuous trips abroad.

In the 1990s there was another strategic change, which was to increase installed capacity at the plant so as to expand production to a scale that would be competitive internationally. If this had not been done because of an aversion to taking risks, the firm would probably have had to close down. The key decision to expand was taken at a time when there was high dollar inflation, which was having a negative impact on profits. When the investment in new capacity was made the firm was deep in debt, but today that strategy is paying off.

Today the firm enjoys vertical integration. It produces fabrics and sells them abroad, usually to international chains or clothing brands. In most cases the client will design the clothing and then look for the fabric, but sometimes the client asks to the firm to imitate some existing design. Often the clothing is actually manufactured in Asia and then sold on to world markets. Paylana S.A. has a strong relationship with well-known brands, including the Armani Group in Italy, Zara and Mango in Spain, Donna Karan, Ann Taylor, Liz Claiborne and Oscar de la Renta in the United States.

The firm has cooperation agreements with the LATU, the SUL, and its suppliers – which in the domestic market are wool-tops firms. It is also well connected, with a network of sales agents in neighbouring countries, the United States, China, Japan, Russia and the European Union. In the EU the firm has a number of sales agents in countries such as the UK, Spain, Italy, France and Belgium. In addition, it is involved in a joint venture with the Italian company Bonotto, and has a line for women called *Amor Tessuto*, and a line of menswear called *Immagine Uomo*. The firm presents two collections each year – the Spring–Summer collection and the more important Autumn–Winter collection. The main markets are the United States – where the firm is a key supplier - and the Mercosur region, followed by the European Union. The current goal is to increase sales to the EU.

Paylana has a competitive advantage based on its know-how and its good management of production processes, and this has made for greater flexibility in that it is able to adapt to new trends in the fashion market and develop new high-quality products. Another advantage is that its vertical structure enables it to offer pre-sales and post-sales services to its customers.

7.6.2.1.2 *Production profile.*

Paylana began with a menswear line based on its wool manufacture and then switched over to new product lines based on mixtures of wool with other natural and synthetic fibres, and this made for more design possibilities and better quality. With this new differentiated range of products the firm tried to conquer new markets abroad.

Its main competitors are China, India, Turkey and other countries that have lower production costs, so Paylana adopted a strategy of high quality and design in an effort to differentiate its products from the competition, and close cooperation with clients to meet their specific needs. One aspect of the firm that is considered an asset is that Uruguay is culturally closer to the United States than it is to either the EU or Asia.

7.6.2.1.3 *Evolution of employment, sales, costs and exports.*

The firm has grown continually since the 1940s, although it has experienced some fluctuations along the way. When Paylana came into being it was protected by import substitution policies and it was geared to the domestic market, but today it is strongly oriented to exports, and more than 90 per cent of its total sales are in foreign markets. The main market is the United States, which accounts for 35 per cent of total sales, and it also sells in Brazil (19 per cent), Argentina (15 per cent), Mexico (11 per cent), Spain (5 per cent), Japan (3 per cent) and the UK (2 per cent). Some 10 per cent of sales go to other countries.

The domestic market is not significant and the fabrics sold in it are usually not of the highest quality. The firm's representative explained that

Uruguayan clothing manufacturers cannot afford the high-quality fabrics produced by Paylana. The firm's output is three million metres of fabric per year, its annual income is around US$25–30 million, and it employs 600 workers at the plant and 30 staff at its Montevideo offices. Paylana is at a cost disadvantage compared to Asian manufacturers, but this is offset by the fact that it has high-quality products that generate high income.

7.6.2.1.4   Technology.   Paylana has a tradition of investing in technology, training its workers and employees and using outside consultants, and this has paid off in terms of improvements to the quality of its products and the services offered to clients. This ongoing investment in technology and training means that they can address the needs of even the most demanding designers.

Employee training is very important in the enterprise. There is training inside the firm and foreign trips to visit other plants and learn from them. Management is sensitive to training proposals that come from workers and employees, and it tries to implement these ideas. The company's sales agents are trained. The firm imports its machinery from Italy, and this means that technicians come over to teach the workers how to use it. The last batch of looms were bought in 2004, and this in spite of the fact that Uruguay was going through a severe economic crisis. Also in 2004, the firm invested in improved plant layout, which was mainly aimed at making better use of space and having more natural light indoors. But the most important change has been the adoption of information technologies and the automation of all production processes.

The marketing manager is highly qualified, possessing a postgraduate degree from the United States, and the marketing network covers all of the main global markets. Paylana maintains close ties with its clients, not only through telecommunications but also with personal visits. From time to time the firm receives requests for specific designs, its response is always reliable, and one of the key aspects of this reliability is that it meets its delivery dates. As regards supply chain management, most of the wool is bought on the domestic market – except for finer wools which are not produced in the country – and some fibres and threads are bought abroad. The main supplier of synthetic fibres is China, and line flax comes from Italy and Brazil.

7.6.2.1.5   The learning process.   Paylana has learned a lot from its participation in the Global Value Chain and Global Production Network. The company managers feel that being in foreign markets makes growth essential, and developed markets create a culture of service, and this poses new challenges and makes new demands on the firm. In addition, close contact with customers yields an ongoing feedback of ideas and suggestions on how to improve services, and also makes clients more loyal to the firm.

7.6.2.1.6 Position of the company in the Global Value Chain and Global Production Network. Paylana is involved in all the activities that go to make up the production of fabrics, and these processes are all integrated. The firm operates at the basic level as a supplier of fabrics, and its product lines are planned and developed a year in advance. Its fabrics go mostly to international clothing chains, and most of the garments are actually made up in low-cost countries in Eastern Europe and East Asia.

The company has explored the possibility of joint ventures with firms in Colombia and other countries that have free trade agreements with the United States as a way to gain access to that clothing market, but to date none of these projects has reached fruition. The production of high quality apparel is not a feasible option in Uruguay itself since the clothing sector has high costs and low quality.

7.6.2.1.7 Role of government policies and international trade rules. At the present time there are no industrial policies geared to developing the textiles and clothing sector in Uruguay, although in 2006 the government did carry out studies to see what promotion measures might be employed. This effort involved meetings between government representatives and entrepreneurs and managers from the sector in order to define what kinds of promotion might be suitable.

In repect of trade policy, a free trade agreement with the United States would certainly be of benefit to the whole sector since Uruguayan textiles have to pay high tariffs of between 18 and 25 per cent in that market. To make matters worse, the United States does have bilateral trade agreements with a number of other countries, and this makes Uruguayan textiles relatively uncompetitive. A free trade agreement with the United States would be a boon to the entire textiles sector. Paylana has an advantage in this situation as it competes in high-quality products, and is a key supplier in the US market. As to the European Union, prospects are not good because competition in the market will probably become even more intense as more and more textiles-producing East European countries are joining the EU. What is more, an agreement on textiles and clothing (ATC) in that market is not likely to benefit Uruguayan textiles exports as it might well be of more benefit to goods from Asia. It follows that the way to help this sector would be to make bilateral trade agreements with the bigger (US and EU) markets.

7.6.2.1.8 Role of trade unions. The workers in the firm belong to a trade union, but there have been no serious problems between management and the union, and labour relations are said to be good. The union has not raised any objections to the adoption of new technology.

7.6.2.2   Hisud SA

The company representative interviewed was Moises Maman, a qualified accountant, who is the manager of the firm. The interview lasted approximately half an hour.

7.6.2.2.1   Main features.   Hisud was founded in 1972 and it is a public limited company. The plant is in Pando[10] in the department of Canelones, and the firm has offices in Montevideo. It produces plain weave suiting for both men's and women's clothing. The weaves are of wool and mixtures of wool with other fibres such as silk, cashmere, linen, lycra, nylon and polyester, and production is geared to middle-high market segments. The firm operates alone and is not involved in any alliances with other Uruguayan or international institutions. It exports fabrics to neighbouring countries and to the rest of the world.

7.6.2.2.2   Production profile.   Over the course of the the past twenty years Hisud has changed its production mix, and it now uses a variety of different fibres. In the beginning, the firm only manufactured wool to produce fabrics, but it later changed to mixtures of wool with synthetics and other fibres. Some 90 per cent of its production is exported to neighbouring countries and to the rest of the world and only 10 per cent is sold on the domestic market, where the main customers are clothing exporters.

The main foreign markets are Brazil, Argentina, Mexico and Canada. Exports to Mexico go ultimately to the United States since Mexico buys fabrics from Uruguay and produces apparel that is sold on the US market.

7.6.2.2.3   Evolution of employment, sales, costs and exports.   Over the course of the past two decades there has been a decrease in both employment and sales. In the 1980s, 370 workers were employed, but at the time of writing (2006) there are only 231. Over the same period, sales have fallen from US$14 million to US$8 million. Labour costs are a large factor in the company's cost structure, and there are high charges for both public services and energy. The weight of labour costs makes it difficult to compete with Asian producers. The evolution of exports mirrors the trend in total sales. Exports stood at approximately US$11 million in the 1980s, but fell to US$7.5 million in 2001.

7.6.2.2.4   Technology at the firm.   For a number of years now Hisud S.A. has been training its workers and adopting new technology. Over the course of the past two decades new machinery has been brought in to enable the firm to change its production mix from wool to mixtures. With regard tomarketing, the company has a sales department, and sales agents in Uruguay and abroad. In the past twenty years Hisud has adopted new technologies in management and to automate production.

7.6.2.2.5 The learning process. The company has been learning from its participation in Global Value Chains and Global Production Networks, and it has adapted to the needs of foreign customers.

7.6.2.2.6 Position of the company in the Global Value Chain and Global Production Networks. The firm is at the beginning of the value chain, which is the production of fabrics. It is not well-placed to be able to offer a full production package in Uruguay.

7.6.2.2.7 Role of government policies and international trade rules. There are no specific government policies to promote this sector, but there are general policies to promote exports, namely rebates on indirect taxes. However, reimbursement for these financial outlays takes more than 13 months to come through – this is a very long time for the firm to wait. In the interview the manager said that international trade agreements have had a positive effect on the performance of this sector in Uruguay. He felt that the country accomplishes much more than other countries do the field of the international agreements.[11] A trade agreement with the United States would have benefited, and would benefit, the firm itself and the whole sector.

7.6.2.2.8 Role of trade unions. In the 1980s Hisud S.A. encountered some opposition from the trade unions when the workers reacted against the introduction of new technologies. Then the two parties made an agreement to link pay to worker productivity and this translated into increases in real wages. However, it also meant that labour costs increased, and in fact wages rose more than the Consumer Price Index. In addition, the firm has had to cope with a dollar inflation rate of 77.8 per cent, mainly due to the burden of charges for public services.

7.6.2.3 Clothing sector firms

This sector is less concentrated than textiles. The biggest exporting firms are Welcolan,[12] Tom Mix and Everfit, and on the next level there are a number of companies, including Exlan, Reston, Hipertex, Pelsa and Sirfil. The big three, Welcolan, Tom Mix and Everfit, account for approximately 12, 11 and 10 per cent respectively, of total clothing exports, and each of the companies in the second group accounted for 4–5 per cent of total clothing exports. Representatives from three firms agreed to be interviewed – Pelsa Internacional SA, Sirfil SA, and Tom Mix SA.

7.6.2.4 Pelsa Internacional SA

The company representative we interviewed was Pablo Fuscaldo[13] who, together with his father, is responsible for management and marketing. The interview lasted approximately 25 minutes.

7.6.2.4.1 Main features. This is a family enterprise. It was founded in 1980 and later became a public limited company. The plant is vertically integrated and concentrates on the production of woven wool scarves, mufflers and accessories for men, women and children. The plant and offices are in Montevideo. The firm has no formal links to networks involving other public or private institutions, but it does have informal connections with some firms, mainly commercial links with other enterprises and suppliers. The company is geared to a diversity of markets, but its products are not diversified. Its strategy is to specialize in the production of accessories, and it seeks to grow by selling in a wide range of different markets. It is a relatively small firm, and because it is flexible it has succeeded in maintaining itself in the market. It has even managed to grow, in spite of the crises that this sector has been experiencing in Uruguay. Almost all of its production, more than 99 per cent, is exported.

7.6.2.4.2 Production profile. The production profile of the firm has changed; products have been modified in response to changes in demand and in an effort to meet new customer needs. The firm engages in market research, product development, product design, product process control, sales and customer services. As mentioned above, Pelsa is export-oriented and it does not feature in the domestic market. The firm exports to 18 countries, with the main markets being Mexico, the Mercosur, Chile and the EU (principally Spain, Germany, the Netherlands and Finland). The firm also sells to Russia. Uruguay has a trade agreement with Mexico that facilitates access to that market for the entire sector.

7.6.2.4.3 Evolution of employment, sales, costs and exports. At Pelsa, employment has increased over the past twenty years, and the company has invested in technology. It is a small enterprise with 15 permanent workers and also subcontracts third party firms to carry out some activities. Since the 1980s sales have tended to increase and have shown little fluctuation. In addition, the pattern of exports has followed that of sales since almost all of its production is sold abroad. The objective is to maintain a sales growth rate of 5 per cent per year. Competition in foreign markets has become stiffer in the last ten years, mainly because of increased exports from Asia.

It emerged in the interview that labour costs are not a weighty factor. The company representative expressed that costs should not be a crucial issue if the firm is really competitive, and so the emphasis should be on competitiveness. However, the company representative did make the point that Uruguay is a 'high-cost' country, and that this is mainly to the result of its overweight bureaucracy. In other countries some bureaucratic procedures can take ten minutes on a computer, but in Uruguay the same process may take more than a week. In addition, public service charges for electricity, water, and telephone communications are high, and oil tends to be more expensive in Uruguay than elsewhere.[14]

7.6.2.4.4 *Technology.*

In recent years, the firm has invested in technology and also in worker training. The training consists of courses and work practice outside the firm. New technology has been adopted, mainly through investment in the latest generation of weaving machinery. In addition to the weaving and finishing that Pelsa undertakes on its own account, it also subcontracts third party firms to weave and finish fabrics. There is a problem in the spinning area since Uruguayan wool is too thick for the products Pelsa wants in order to meet market needs. It is cheaper to import spun Merino wool[15] from Italy than to buy it on the domestic market.

Pelsa's marketing strategy used to be revised every two years, to analyse and evaluate current strategy and its results, but now it is reviewed twice a year.[16] Furthermore, 15 years ago the firm's sales agents used to travel with one small suitcase of samples to show potential clients the collection, but today they travel with three big suitcases. Information technology and computers have been brought into various activities including office administration, production processes, marketing, and communication with clients and suppliers. The automation of these activities is regarded as essential if Pelsa is to compete in foreign markets.

Human capital is highly prized, and the firm has an explicit policy of promoting human resources. When it comes to adopting new technology there are various different possibilities. Since Pelsa could not afford to contract a specialized firm to develop its management software it hired young information and computer technology graduates, and today all management activity is run through this software.

7.6.2.4.5 *The learning process.*

Pelsa has learned from its experience in foreign markets, and representatives of the firm who travel abroad frequently buy publications to keep up to date with the latest trends. This is another aspect of investment in the business.

7.6.2.4.6 *Government policies and international trade rules.*

The government has no specific policy to promote the clothing sector. Trade agreements are important because they ease access to foreign markets. For instance, the trade agreement with Mexico has yielded good results. However, the firm's representative stressed that it is still important to be competitive, and that a free trade agreement is of little practical value if the country is uncompetitive. There are several different types of agreements, and the prevailing type has an effect on the benefits that may accrue. The Chamber of Clothing[17] actually participated in the negotiations for the agreement with Mexico, and this paid off in that clothing was included in the agreement while otherwise it would have been excluded.

7.6.2.4.7   The role of trade unions.   This is a small enterprise and there is no trade union, so union reaction to the adoption of new technology is not a factor.

7.6.2.5   Sirfil SA

The company representative was the firm's manager, Mrs Michelle Levitin, the current manager of the firm. The interview took approximately 15 minutes.

7.6.2.5.1   Main features.   The firm went into operation in 1982, during the export promotion period, and it has since become a public limited company. It produces plain woven men's and women's clothing. The production plant and offices are in Montevideo. It does not belong to any network with other domestic firms or institutions. It is essentially export-oriented.

7.6.2.5.2   Productive profile of the firm.   Over the course of the past twenty years this firm has changed its productive mix in reaction to changes in market demand. Since the 1990s both production and sales have fallen. It is not competitive, and the firm's representative attributed this to the rise in Uruguay's currency on money markets, high public service charges, and the weight of contributions to the state. Most production is exported, and the home market share is insignificant.

7.6.2.5.3   The evolution of employment, sales, costs and exports.   In recent years the level of sales has decreased, the firm has a smaller workforce, the costs have risen and income has fallen. In 1995 the number of workers was 239; today it is around 100. Export performance reflects the evolution of production and sales, that is to say there has been a decline since the 1990s. Labour costs are now a bigger factor, and the level of profitability is fallen. This reduced profitability and a lack of credit have translated into problems in accessing resources for investment, which has made it hard to keep up with technological progress, and this in turn has harmed competitiveness.

7.6.2.5.4   Technology.   Sirfil S.A. is still using the same technology as ten years ago, and many of its processes are not automated. Because of low profitability and problems with obtaining credit, it has not been possible to invest in up-to-date technology or in training. In respect of the marketing system, one of the firm's agents will take samples of its product lines abroad, and in fact this is more like direct sales than marketing. The customers are big brands in Argentina, Brazil, Chile and Mexico, and it these organizations that take care of the marketing.

7.6.2.5.5   The learning process.   The firm is sensitive to the needs of foreign markets and it learns from its experience in exporting.

7.6.2.5.6   Position of the company in the Global Value Chain and Global Production Network.   The firm sells its production to well-known brands in neighbouring countries and the Mercosur, and in Mexico.

7.6.2.5.7   The role of government policies and international trade rules.   There are no policies to promote this sector, but trade agreements like the Mercosur do help by providing easier access to some foreign markets. The company representative said that a trade agreement with the United States would be of benefit to the whole clothing sector.

7.7   Conclusions

During the 1990s, the manufacturing sector in Uruguay performed very poorly. The performance of the T&C sectors was even worse and there was a decrease in their share of overall manufacturing. In the textiles industry, this process did not have the same effect on every one of the sub-sectors that make up this industry. The washing of wool and manufacture of tops sub-sectors, which has lower value added, a closer relationship with the source of inputs (raw wool) and greater export propensity performed better than the spinning and weaving sub-sector.

The spinning and weaving of cotton and synthetic and artificial fibres was the most badly affected sub-sector, with falls in both production and employment. This sub-sector had developed when it was protected by import substitution policies. Its exports were protected in the framework of ALADI trade agreements by trade preferences that usually involved quantitative restrictions, so there was no security as regards long-term access to these markets and, consequently, no long-term conditions to promote sector development. Trade liberalization in regional markets reduced protection and promoted exports to these markets, but at the same time it increased competition from lower-cost imports in the domestic market.

One factor that has probably affected the evolution of this sub-sector is that it was in the position of being a producer of intermediate goods and was therefore dependent upon imported inputs. This weak relationship with respect to the sources of fibres for production and with respect to the final consumer made for difficulties in this sub-sector. Cotton weaving takes place on a larger scale than wool weaving so when firms in this sub-sector are faced with increasing competition they have to make bigger investments in order to increase their scale and keep in line with international standards. There were no clear long-term rules in the country to give firms incentives to undertake investment on this scale in order to be competitive. Imports grew and exports decreased, with the majority of exports going to Uruguay's immediate neighbours in the region. In the clothing industry, as in the textiles industry, the activity that suffered most was the manufacture of cotton and synthetic apparel.

In the past the availability of good-quality, cheap wool has contributed to the competitiveness of these sectors However, although the country produces high-quality wool this is mainly of medium thickness so it is not the most suitable kind for producing smooth fabrics. This type of wool is more suitable for heavy fabrics, sweaters and wool for knitting, so it competes in a market segment characterized by a high rate of substitution between wool and other fibres. The poor performance of the textiles and clothing sector can be explained by a series of factors such as the creation of the Mercosur, the reduction in trade protection to third countries, changes in the currency exchange rate, and the economic recession since 1999.

In 1991 Uruguay signed the Asuncion Treaty which aimed to create the Southern Common Market (Mercosur), thereby deepening the trade liberalization process that has been carried out since the early 1980s. Nevertheless the impact on these sectors was delayed since they were considered to be 'sensitive'. At the beginning of the 1990s the textiles sector was protected by high tariffs, reference prices (RPs) and minimum export prices (MEPs), protection instruments that applied to both regional and extra-regional imports and affected textiles produced with fibres other than wool. In 1993 the RPs were removed, and in 1995 the MEP system began to be dismantled. By the end of 2000 MEPs were replaced by specific duties for countries that were not members of the Mercosur. These specific duties ceased to operate in 2002.

By the end of the 1990s the sector was being affected by trade openness, and the impact was felt mainly in the production of those textiles that did not use wool as an input. The exchange rate policy implemented in Uruguay in and after 1991 led to a large rise in the cost of the local currency against the US dollar, and this had a negative impact on the competitiveness of firms in the sector. These firms sold in foreign markets so their income was linked to the level of export prices in the world, but their cost structure was heavy in non-tradable goods so the price of their products in dollars increased. In the 1990–2001 period wages in the private sector, measured in dollars, rose by more than 65 per cent. Furthermore, in the 1990s there was an increase in the cost of public services, measured in dollars. The costs of electricity, water, and telephone services increased steadily until 1998, and the fuel also rose, albeit to a lesser extent.

Regarding the access to foreign markets, these sectors no longer enjoy a preferential access mechanism in important extra-regional markets, and they have not been able to avoid the impact of non-tariff protective measures inside the Mercosur. The final implementation of the Agreement on Textiles and Clothing (ATC) would lead to a slight improvement in Uruguay's access to the large markets in developed countries, but it would also improve access for Asian countries which could increase competition in those markets. On the other hand, the main importers of textiles, the EU and the United States, have made preferential trade agreements which discriminate against imports from countries not included in those agreements, mainly by imposing high tariffs and insisting on rules of origin. The Mercosur has been negotiating these matters with the developed countries, but has been unable to reach final agreements.

Another problem is that although the Mercosur has succeeded in liberalizing trade among its members there are no long-term rules for the development of an industry oriented to the regional markets. Non-tariff restrictions on trade, such as the mechanism of custom valuation, are still in place and this has generated uncertainty about long-term access to these markets. Finally, there is still uncertainty about whether the Southern Custom Union will eventually come into full operation, and this worked against the reconstruction in an industry oriented to the region. In Ouro Preto (1994), the Mercosur reached agreement on mechanisms to extend the custom union and to establish the free circulation of goods. However, in the transitory phase some protective measures have remained in place – including the double payment of tariffs, the regime of origin system, and temporary admission. These measures were due to be eliminated, but this has now been postponed, meaning that the industry has received no clear indication about what will happen in the long term. Industries that depend on imported inputs can use the temporary admission regime to export to the region if they satisfy the rules of origin. However, this is a transitional instrument so there are no clear rules underpin investment in areas like technological modernization or increases in scale.

In interviews, entrepreneurs highlighted some of the factors that make this sector less competitive. There is excessive bureaucracy, the response time is slow and there is a lack of flexibility. The evolution of the exchange rate also gives cause for concern. These actors also feel that the level of competitiveness is poor because public service charges are high and telecommunications are expensive; there is a lack of clear long-term rules and a need for bilateral trade agreements to ease access to foreign markets.

Finally, it seems that the main factors that enable firms to compete successfully in foreign markets are that there is continuous investment in training and technology, that sales are targeted to high-quality segments of the market, and that the firm has a clearly defined marketing strategy.

Appendix

Appendix Table 7.1 Objective of the projects promoted

Firm	Re	Objective	TI
Anzatex SA	1	To buy modern machinery to improve knitted apparel versatility and products	0.18
Dancotex SA	2	No information	6.4
Darcy SA	3	To buy modern machinery to increase production and differentiation and incorporate new products	1.27
Filaner SA	1	To increase production of knitted fabrics and apparel	0.25
Hipertex SA	2	No information	0.68
Kabyr Confecciones SA		No information	1.35
Karmaris SA	1	To incorporate latest generation technology to reduce waste and increase productivity in the production of clothing made from knitted fabrics	1.06
Lanera Piedra Alta SA	1	To increase wool tops production capacity	0.50
Lavadero de Lanas Blengio	1	No information	1.46
Martex SA	1	To buy latest generation technology equipment and to increase industrial and management capacity in the making and distribution of clothing in foreign markets	1.42
Medea SA	2	To increase installed capacity, reduce costs and improve the production, stock control and ordering management system	3.45
Monbebe SA	1	No information	3.46
Paylana SA	2	To buy new machinery to improve production, reduce direct costs and change the production mix in smooth fabric and yarn	3.12
Prince SCA	1	To buy new machinery to increase production and quality in the production of knitted fabric apparel	0.20
Prili SA	2	To increase production capacity and incorporate new products	0.63
Rajchman y Hnos. SA	1	To incorporate latest generation technology to improve competitiveness in the production of acetate fabrics	1.05
Reston Uruguay SA	2	To incorporate latest generation technology to increase the quantity and the quality of clothing	1.56
Rualer SA	1	No information	0.41
Textil Montevideana SA	1	To install a polyester fabric plant	14.75
Tops Fray Marcos SA	1	To increase the production and quality of wool tops	1.81
Twins SA	1	To buy textile mills	0.23
Total			45.23

Re: number of resolutions.
Source: Department of Economics, School of Social Sciences, University of the Republic (2004).

Notes

1. Paylana, Fibratex SA, Dancotex SA, HISUD SA.
2. Export propensity is proxied by the ratio of exports to gross production in the sector.
3. Coverage rate is defined as $(X_j/M_j)/(X_t/M_t)$, where X_j are exports of the product j, M_j imports of the product j, X_t total exports of the country, and M_t the total imports of the country. The regional orientation index is defined as $(X_j^R/X_j)/(X_t^R/X_t)$, where X_j^R is the value of exports to regional markets of the product j, X_t^R the total value of exports from the country to regional markets, and R is the Mercosur region.
4. In May 2000, the General Committee of the WTO authorized Uruguay to maintain the minimum values officially set for the customs valuation of certain products until January 2001.
5. After 110 telephone calls and 20 e-mails, only six interviews actually took place.
6. Paylana and a joint venture of Paylana with an Italian firm account for 50 per cent of exports from this sector.
7. The newspaper *Brecha*, 12 January 2007.
8. The firm was founded during the import substitution period in Uruguay.
9. Paysandu is in the north of the country, on the Uruguay River.
10. Pando is a small city about 30 kilometres from Montevideo.
11. Textiles exports from Argentina to neighbouring countries and to the rest of the world are subsidized.
12. As mentioned previously, Welcolan declined to be interviewed.
13. He is a graduate in marketing.
14. For instance, in Argentina oil costs half the price charged in Uruguay.
15. Merino sheep produce thinner wools (17 microns).
16. The firm's representative has a degree in Marketing, and he travels abroad to promote Pelsa product.
17. The Chamber of Clothing is a member of the Uruguayan Chamber of Industry.

References

ALADI (2004) ' "Identificación de potenciales alianzas estrategicas entre empresarios del Sector Textil-Confecciones de Bolivia y Uruguay', Departamento de Promocion Economica, No. 07/04, www.aladi.org.

Banco Central del Uruguay (BCU): www.bcu.gub.uy.

Banco de Datos, Faculty of Social Sciences, University of the Republic: www.fcs.edu.uy.

Camara de Industrias del Uruguay, Asociación de Industrias Textiles del Uruguay (2006) 'Impacto del Acuerdo de Libre Comercio con EE.UU. sobre la cadena textil lanera Uruguaya', mimeo, www.ciu.com.uy.

Comision Sectorial para el MERCOSUR (1994) 'Analisis del Sector Textil', Comisec/IDB-EU-UNDP Project, http://www.mercosur-comisec.gub.uy/Documentos/sectortextil.pdf.

Casacuberta, C., G. Fachola and N. Gandelman (2004) 'The Impact of Trade Liberalization on Employment, Capital and Productivity Dynamics: Evidence from the Uruguayan Manufacturing Sector', Departamento de Economia, FCS, Universidad de la Republica, http://ideas.repec.org/a/taf/jpolrf/v7y2004i4p225-248.html.

Instituto Nacional de Estadisticas (INE): www.ine.gub.uy.

Iroz, M. and T. Perez de Castillo (2005): 'Restricciones a las Exportaciones Textiles', University of Montevideo, http://www2.um.edu.uy/ieem/Revista/200412/Revista%20IEEM%20200412-10.pdf.

Nicita, A. and M. Olarreaga (2007) 'Trade, Production and Protection, 1976–2004', *The World Bank Economic Review*, 21(1): 165–71.

Terra, María Inés, Gustavo Bittencourt, Rosario Domingo, Carmen Estrades, Gabriel Katz, Alvaro Ons and Héctor Pastori (2004) 'Estudios de competitividad sectoriales. Industria manufacturera', Department of Economics, Faculty of Social Sciences, University of the Republic, http://ideas.repec.org/p/ude/wpaper/2305.html.

Index

Note: Entries under "textiles & clothing", "clothing sector" and "textile sector" have been kept to a minimum, and readers should refer to the different countries, companies and policies for a more detailed discussion.